European political cultures

European Political Cultures looks at a neglected area of European Studies – the political cultures of the various countries that make up Europe, both East and West. It is written by an international team of contributors who address a variety of crucial issues such as the factors that help make nations and states, the main characteristics of national cultures and sub-cultures, and whether major changes are taking place in national politics.

The world shows signs of increasing inter-dependence and uniformity, both political and cultural. In Poland, for example, democratic values undoubtedly helped bring about the downfall of communism. Advertising campaigns are increasingly designed to cross national boundaries; products are even named for their multi-lingual appeal.

However, it is important not to exaggerate the process of homogenisation. Europe is the cradle of modern nationalism, and there are ominous signs of a new nationalist wave; even in Western Europe ethnic tensions are increasing. *European Political Cultures* explores these issues, illustrating the dangers of a movement towards ever-closer union which does not take note of the growing populist resistance to 'Europe'.

Roger Eatwell is Reader in Politics at the University of Bath.

European political cultures

Conflict or convergence?

Edited by Roger Eatwell

London and New York

First published 1997
by Routledge
11 New Fetter Lane, London EC4P 4EE

Simultaneously published in the USA and Canada
by Routledge
29 West 35th Street, New York, NY 10001

Typeset in Times by Routledge
Printed and bound in Great Britain by Mackays of Chatham PLC,
Chatham, Kent

British Library Cataloguing in Publication Data
A catalogue record for this book is available from the British Library

Library of Congress Cataloguing in Publication Data
Eatwell, Roger.
    European political cultures: conflict or convergence? / Roger
    Eatwell.
    p. cm.
    1. Europe–Politics and government–1989–   2. Comparative
    government.   3. Political culture–Europe   I. Title.
    JN12.E22 1997
    306.2´094–dc21   97-3697
                                                                CIP

ISBN 0–415–13867–1 (hbk)
ISBN 0–415–13868–X (pbk)

Contents

Contributors

Hans-Georg Betz is Associate Professor of European Studies at the Paul H. Nitze School of Advanced International Studies in Washington, DC. He has published widely on aspects of parties, political culture and political economy in Western Europe. Among his publications are *Postmodern Politics in Germany* (1991) and *Radical Right-Wing Populism in Western Europe* (1994).

António Costa Pinto is Professor of Modern European History at the ISCTE, Lisbon. His main area of interest is Portuguese politics. Among his publications are *Os Camisas Azuis. Ideologia, elites e movimentos fascistas em Portugal, 1914-45* (1994), *Salazar's Dictatorship and European Fascism. Problems and Perspectives of Interpretation* (1995), and (ed.) *Modern Portugal* (1997).

Nicolas Demertzis is Associate Professor in the Department of Communication and Mass Media at the National Capodistrian University, Athens. His main interests are contemporary Greek studies and political culture approaches to politics. He has published widely on these themes, including *Cultural Theory and Political Culture* (1985) and (ed.) *Greek Political Culture Today* (1994).

Roger Eatwell is Reader in Politics at the University of Bath. His main interests are Western European politics, especially fascism and radical political movements. His main publications include (joint ed.) *The Nature of the Right* (1989), *Contemporary Political Ideologies* (1993), and *Fascism: A History* (1995), together with a large variety of articles/chapters.

Brian Girvin is Reader in Politics at the University of Glasgow. His main interests are Irish politics, comparative conservatism and nationalism, and parties and public opinion in Western Europe and the US. Among his many publications are *The Right in the Twentieth Century* (1994), and *The Green Pool and the Origins of the Common Agricultural Policy* (1995).

Roger Griffin is Principal Lecturer in History at Oxford Brookes University. His main areas of interests are political history and philosophy, comparative fascism, especially its ideology, German culture and Italian history and politics. Among his publications are *The Nature of Fascism* (1993), (ed.) *Fascism* (1995), and various articles and chapters relating to these themes.

Stein Ugelvik Larsen is Professor of Politics at Bergen University. His main research interests are comparative studies of fascism, European politics and the development of theory in social science. Among his publications are (joint ed.) *Who Were the Fascists?* (1980), *Modern Europe after Fascism* (1997), *Was There Fascism Outside Europe?* (1997) and numerous articles and chapters.

James F. McMillan is Professor of History at the University of Strathclyde. His main area of interest is nineteenth- and twentieth-century France. Among his publications are *Housewife or Harlot: The Place of Women in French Society 1870–1940* (1981), *Napoleon III* (1991) and the widely used text, *Twentieth Century France: Politics and Society 1889–1991* (1992).

Xosé M. Núñez is Professor of Modern History at the University of Santiago de Compostella. His main area of interest is modern Spanish political history, especially nationalism. Among his publications are *Historiographical Approaches to Nationalism in Spain* (1993) and (joint ed.) *Nationalism in Europe. Past and Present* (1994), and a variety of articles and chapters.

Martijn Roessingh was a research student at the University of Amsterdam working on the politics of the Low Countries; he is currently a journalist.

Bogdan Szajkowski is Professor of Pan-European Politics at the University of Exeter. He is especially interested in ethnic, political and religious conflict in the communist successor states. Among his many recent publications are *Encyclopaedia of Conflicts, Disputes and Flashpoints in Eastern Europe, Russia and Successor States* (1994) and *Political Parties of Eastern Europe, Russia and Successor States* (1995).

Ingrid Louise Ugelvik is a research student at the University of Bergen, specialising in Nordic culture and politics.

Stephen White is Professor of Politics and a member of the Institute of Russian and East European Studies at the University of Glasgow. His main area of interest is Russian politics. His extensive publications include *Political Culture and Soviet Politics* (1979), *The Origins of Détente* (1985), *The Bolshevik Poster* (1988), *After Gorbachev* (1993) and *Russia Goes Dry: Alcohol, Society and the State* (1996).

Herman van der Wusten is Professor of Social Geography at the University of Amsterdam. He has published extensively in journals and books on aspects of Dutch political culture. His latest books are (with John O'Loughlin) *The New Political Geography of Eastern Europe* (1993), and *The Urban University and its Identity: Roots, Locations, Roles* (1997), and he has a large variety of other publications.

Ekkart Zimmermann is Professor of Sociology at the University of Dresden. He has published widely in journals and books on aspects of national development, violence and related themes. Among his books are *Soziologie der politischen Gewalt. Darstellung und Kritik vergleichender Aggregatdatenanalysen aus den USA* (1977), *Political Violence, Crises and Revolutions: Theories and Research* (1983).

Preface

We live in a world of increasing inter-dependence and uniformity. Think-tank futurologists, like Francis Fukuyama, preach the 'end of history' – the world victory of democracy and capitalism. Marketing executives welcome a 'Coca-Cola culture', in which standardised products can be sold in all markets. Media gurus envision a 'global village', with a satellite dish on every mud hut.

Within Europe, it is easy to pick out specific examples of these trends. In East Germany, for example, the downfall of communism in 1989 was partly caused by the diffusion of democratic values and the desire for Western affluence. Advertising campaigns are now frequently designed to cross national boundaries; products are even named for their multilingual appeal (there will be no more French soft-drinks named '*Pschitt*'). And the media become more cosmopolitan with every year: even the English, the founding-fathers of football – and epitome of the nationalist soccer-hooligan – now watch live Italian matches, while quaffing German beer.

But it is important not to exaggerate the process of cultural homogenisa-tion, or to play down the forces of resistance. Europe is the cradle of the modern nation, and recent events in both its Western and Eastern heartlands have shown that nationalism and racism remain powerful forces. In some cases, the antagonism is aimed at 'immigrants', but in many areas old rival-ries and hatreds have lost little or none of their force. Indeed, they seem to be increasing. Whilst the political cultures of European countries are in some ways becoming more homogenous, major divisions undoubtedly remain.

These optimistic and pessimistic views can be related to two broad teleo-logical views about the nature of European development. The first holds that the exact geographical boundaries of Europe may be hazy, but the growing impetus towards integration is not. This process has both cultural and economic causes. The latter include the strong trade patterns which have existed for centuries, and which are now reinforced by corporate and formal institutional linkages, including the development of the European Union. The former include the Judaeo-Christian tradition, which has influenced social values generally. Cultural forces also include the classical Greek and

Roman legacy in a myriad of ways, including a tendency to define what is 'European' in terms of the barbarian 'Other'.

The second broad interpretation of European development is very different. It stresses the centrifugal rather than centripetal forces. Europe is portrayed as a group of states characterised by bloody wars and invasions, schisms which have been caused by recurring dynastic, religious, national and economic conflicts. Even in the twentieth century, two 'world' wars have left over forty million dead (and required the 'New World' to rescue the 'Old'). This second approach also underlines the very different political traditions which have flourished in Europe. It requires a highly selective reading of history to see Europe as the font of democracy stretching back to Ancient Greece, whilst ignoring its authoritarian trends (including powerful twentieth-century fascist and communist variants).

These opening points about the nature of Europe raise a series of major conceptual and theoretical perspectives, not least – given the title of this book – what is political culture? The term entered common academic usage in the 1960s, following the pioneering opinion-poll-based work of Almond and Verba, who sought to study the crucial values which underpinned political systems. A major political culture 'school' quickly developed, using a variety of techniques, both social scientific and historical. The term also entered more everyday usage, often becoming a synonym for national character. Predictably, an academic reaction set in, which pointed to the failings of the political culture approach, not least its eclecticism and vagueness. Fresh schools arose to take its place, including 'new institutionalism' and especially rational choice theory. But the introductory chapter of this book defends the importance of the broad cultural perspective, in particular by arguing that meso and macro factors are crucial to understanding micro (individual) behaviour.

The main focus of the twelve 'national' chapters which make up the bulk of the book is on concrete politics rather than methodology. The book looks at the way in which national identity and nationalism developed in these countries, and at the ideas and social structures which have influenced more recent developments. These broad issues are important subjects of study in their own right, as there is no comparable volume which sets out to delineate a dynamic map of the political cultures of individual European countries. However, the topic has a wider connotation. One of the great founding-fathers of the European Union, Jean Monnet, stated near the end of his life that if he could start again, he would have begun with culture. The comment raises sweeping questions, which cannot be answered fully in this volume. But the two concluding chapters return to more conceptual and theoretical themes, arguing that a more affective European identity is necessary, and that this should be based on the view that Europe constitutes a 'Third Way' – although it is important to stress that this is not a call for a revival of old highly statist forms. The emphasis is more on openness and the willingness to learn from others, without losing sight of the strengths of Europe's own culture – an openness which must encompass a rapid expansion of the EU to admit new democracies in order to help stabilise them. The central theoretical perspective developed in this book is that changes are taking place in the macro and meso cultures which underpin politics, and that these offer the opportunity to achieve greater European unity – although they also open the possibility of a major extreme or particularist nationalist revival. History is not predetermined by socio-economic forces; rather, we should accept the 'primacy of politics' (though not a narrowly defined institutional politics), which points to the possibility of different outcomes – to the power of human agency.

From the outset in planning this book, I decided that a primarily national chapter focus was necessary for the majority of chapters in order to base the overarching conclusion on a contextual analysis of past and current trends. However, it is impossible to cover all European countries adequately in a single volume, especially given the profusion of new Eastern European states since 1989.

Of those selected for coverage, some have been accorded a specific chapter, whilst others have been grouped together. The former includes the four largest countries in the EU: those with the most 'clout' in the main decision-making processes. But there would be dangers in according these four countries privileged status, given that the book is not about the history or workings of the EU. Ireland and Greece were therefore added to the list of countries which receive single chapters. The former raises a series of questions about small, peripheral and divided societies. The latter has similar aspects and is crucial to the conception of Europe – both in view of its historical role in shaping modern culture, and as a result of its geographical position on the boundary where Europe meets Asia (a situation made more poignant in view of Turkey's aspirations to enter the EU). Russia was also given a single chapter, as the major country in Eastern Europe, and one which is often seen as not suited by culture to inclusion in a common European home. Poland too is covered in this way, reflecting its crucial position in some ways between East and West – and as a country which is trying hard to re-enter the concert of Europe by distancing itself from its former communist neighbour. The multi-national chapters cover countries which are frequently – though with varying degrees of justice – seen as similar. This offers a particularly useful way within a single chapter of highlighting the extent to which there are major similarities within European political cultures. The countries covered in this way are: Austria and Switzerland; Belgium and the Netherlands; Portugal and Spain; and the main Scandinavian countries (Denmark, Finland, Norway, and Sweden).

When recruiting contributors, I did not impose my own general approach to 'political culture'. Indeed, I deliberately recruited contributors from both history and social science backgrounds, as part of the point of the book is to see how the elusive concept of political culture is currently being used by specific national experts. Predictably, some differences of approach have resulted, with the historians tending to dwell on the relatively long run and to write about national traditions, whereas the social scientists tended to relate more to 'grand theory' or to employ behaviourist techniques, especially opinion poll evidence relating to more recent developments. However, some variation is explained by the differing nature of the subject matter: for instance, it is understandable why a country which has undergone notable recent change requires a more contemporary focus than one in which deep-rooted images of its national tradition remain central. Moreover, all the chapters offer both historical and contemporary coverage, and in general they point to the same crucial themes which are highlighted in the conclusion.

I am most grateful to the international team which I recruited for accepting – on the whole – my suggestions to ensure as great a level of standardisation as possible (especially for accepting major cuts and editing of some chapters). I am also grateful to various people who contributed during the writing and production of this book. Academically, I was helped by Anna Bull, Jolyon Howorth, Mathew Humphrey, Tim Mobley, Cas Mudde, and especially Dennis Kavanagh, who refereed the first draft of the manuscript. At Routledge, Caroline Wintersgill expertly took my original idea for a book which linked case studies to much grander themes, and which could interest both the more advanced student and the specialist, through to contract; and Patrick Proctor efficiently saw the book through to publication. Last, but by no means least, my wife offered comments on argument and style, and my father proof-read the book – his fifth such effort for me: may there be many more.

Roger Eatwell
University of Bath
December 1996

1 Introduction

The importance of the political culture approach

Roger Eatwell

INTRODUCTION

Belief in the importance of studying the values which underpin politics can be traced back in time through a variety of major writers, including de Tocqueville in the nineteenth century (who clearly perceived the importance of individualism and the frontier spirit in American politics), and Aristotle and Plato in Ancient Greece (who wrote about a state of mind which encouraged stability or revolution, and the importance of socialisation in forming adults). It is also interesting to note that the Greeks attributed notably different characteristics to Athenians, Spartans, and Corinthians – as well as to the barbarian 'Other' (who encompassed peoples to the north and west, as well as the east).

However, the actual term 'political culture' was coined in the 1950s by Gabriel Almond, an American political scientist, who argued that 'Every political system is embedded in a particular pattern of orientations to political action'.[1] Together with fellow academic, Sidney Verba, Almond went on in the early 1960s to publish a pioneering five-state (Britain, Italy, Mexico, USA, West Germany) study of such political cultures entitled *The Civic Culture*, which was based on opinion polls of some 1,000 respondents in each country during 1959.[2] Behind Almond and Verba's resulting collections of percentages was the theory that a stable democracy required a specific set of attitudes, based on a complex balance of 'subject' and 'participant' cultures, and needed high levels of system support and social trust fostered by overlapping memberships of different groups. Their data indicated that Britain and the USA were the paradigmatic 'civic cultures'. Among the other social scientists who contributed notable early work in this area was Seymour Martin Lipset, who argued that long-enduring democracies were disproportionately found in the wealthier and more Protestant nations.[3]

The main impetus behind this work was fourfold. First, there was a growing academic reaction to the study of constitutions and institutions – a reflection of the belief that such approaches missed important aspects of political systems (there was a partly parallel reaction in history to 'high politics', resulting in a growth of social history). Second, there was the development of behaviourist social science techniques. Arguably the most important of these was 'scientific' opinion polling, which had grown up rapidly in the USA during the late 1930s and 1940s. Third, there was a reawakening of interest in the work of some of the classic figures in European sociology, notably Durkheim and Weber, with their emphasis on the crucial role of norms and traditions – for example, the family and religion – in political development. This was partly linked to a fourth factor, namely a widespread concern about why some democratic systems, like Weimar Germany, had collapsed. Linked to this was the fear that Soviet totalitarianism rather than the American liberal democratic-capitalist system was the force of the future (though some, especially in Europe, optimistically envisaged a 'Third Way', often epitomised by welfare-democratic Scandinavia).[4]

Almond and Verba were followed by a plethora of (mainly Anglo-American) students employing the term, though not always the same techniques. Some focused on elite interviews; others borrowed from the methodologies of psychology and anthropology, for example using less structured interviews or participant observation. The number of countries studied grew dramatically too. Communist systems witnessed a particularly notable flowering of political culture studies: although in part a result of the increasing academic professionalisation of Soviet studies, this trend reflected the belief that political culture gave important insights into why communist systems arose and especially into the success and failure of the attempt to create a new communist (wo)man. Political culture appeared to have become a major tool in the armoury of social science, probing beyond the façade of formal politics. More generally, the term was borrowed especially by historians, area studies specialists and journalists – though in the process it often became little, if anything, more than a synonym for stereotypes of 'national character' (at worst, a comedy in which Heaven was filled with British policemen, French cooks, German organisers and Italian lovers, whilst Hell was populated by British cooks, French policemen, German lovers and Italian organisers).[5]

THE ATTACK ON POLITICAL CULTURE

But it was not long before a major attack was mounted against the political culture 'school'. One common charge was that the approach had become increasingly debased and confused. Certainly it was a term that was often undefined, and even among those who sought to flesh out the concept there were notably different emphases: for instance, some saw political culture as essentially referring to the values of individuals, whereas others wanted to talk in more group-oriented or institutional terms, and yet others used the term to refer to almost everything (from summaries of national histories to highly specialised studies, such as specific aspects of cinematic culture).[6]

Other criticisms fell within three broad (though not necessarily inconsistent) approaches.[7]

The first line of attack pointed to hidden assumptions. It was argued, especially by critics on the left, that Almond and Verba were celebrating 'actually existing' Anglo-American democracy, in particular its relatively low levels of participation and deference towards authority. A related line of attack was the relationship between Almond and Verba's view of an 'advanced' political culture and ethnocentric modernisation theory: there seemed to be a clear assumption that all systems should develop along relatively homogenous paths towards some form of largely capitalist economic system and largely non-ideological liberal democratic polity.[8] Partly because of this, Almond and Verba and most of their followers tended not to be interested in sub-cultures, such as radical class-based or ethnic ones, implicitly seeing these as 'un-modern' – although there were a handful of notable studies of sub-cultures, such as Edward Banfield's work on 'amoral familism' in southern Italy.[9] They also missed the fact that other forms of stable democracy seemed possible, notably 'consociational' ones based on 'elite accommodation' in 'pillared' societies like Belgium or the Netherlands.[10]

The second broad form of attack related to more specific methodological issues. Some pointed to the problems of using opinion polls, especially for probing complex attitudes. Such problems were compounded, when transnational comparisons were being made, by difficulties in translating both words and concepts. Ask Germans whether they are 'racist' and few will say 'yes', as this has been a taboo word since the Nazi era; predictably, these connotations are much weaker in, say, France (though even here there may be some reluctance to admit to what could be seen as an 'illegitimate' view). Behaviourist approaches often have a 'scientific' air, but what are commonly seen as central aspects of the scientific method – namely verification and prediction – pose serious problems for political culture approaches. In spite of their frequently quantitative façade (only 3 per cent of Italians admired their political system, and so on), there is an important sense in which such studies are qualitative. Almond and Verba, for example, never made it clear exactly what balance of factors made up a 'civic culture'. And their work certainly did not anticipate the troubles which American and British cultures were to experience during and after the 1960s: for instance, the rise of Welsh and Scottish nationalism, and more general decline in system support. Part of the problem here was the difficulty of operationalising some of the central concepts: thus deference has typically been seen as central to British values. But exactly how is deference defined and measured? And what are its causal implications? For example, no matter how defined, some 'deferentials' seem to have voted Conservative whereas others have voted Labour.[11]

A third attack on political culture related more to the causality and primacy implied. Many on the left argued that it was vital to ask how attitudes were formed in the first place, or to stress how powerless individuals were – and not just in dictatorial states like Franco's Spain or Salazar's Portugal. The focus here was usually on the 'dominant' structure of capitalism (though some left-wing approaches, especially the Gramsciite emphasis on the socialising power of 'hegemonic' values, were not totally inconsistent with political culture approaches). More commonly, political culture approaches were accused of having problems explaining the causal process by which change took place: the emphasis on the power of socialisation and tradition seemed more suited to explain continuity. Others pointed to the relationship between the civic culture and stable democratic government. For Almond and Verba, the causality ran from the former to the latter. But it could be argued that it was more sensible to conclude that a civic culture was the product of an extended period of stable and good government and the specific nature of its structures. In Britain, for example, this would point to the need to bring back onto centre stage the state and elites, an argument put forcefully by the growing school of the 'new institutionalists' who sought to redress the 1950s and 1960s behaviourist fashion. This ability to reverse the causality plausibly was for many the ultimate proof of the flabbiness of the 'sociological' method, and played a part in the rise of the 'harder' 'economic' method encapsulated in rational choice theory, which during the 1970s increasingly came to dominate American political science.[12]

Unquestionably there are problems relating to political culture studies. Moreover, the 'new institutionalism' (somewhat misleadingly named as it never really went away, especially among European academics) and rational choice theory have brought many insights. The former, for example, has been used to offer an institutional (broadly defined to include 'less formal organisational networks') explanation of historical continuities and cross-national variations in policy.[13] The latter has taught us, for example, not to study bureaucracy simply in terms of values such as those epitomised by the French *Ecole Nationale d'Administration*, namely technocracy, efficiency and the public interest. It is also necessary to think in terms of bureaucracy's tendency to maximise budgets and empires. This questioning of the public interest function, and implicitly of collectivist ideologies which claim to be motivated by the public good, has unquestionably since the 1960s been a major factor in the intellectual underpinning of the New Right.[14] But the methodological pendulum has swung too far, especially towards the fashionable rational choice theory. Or it might be more accurate to say rational choice theories in the plural, for it is useful to distinguish between 'thick' and 'thin' theories.

'Thin' approaches are those most influenced by economic theory. They make few assumptions other than that individual actors calculate expected consequences, choose the best actions for their self-interest (subject to information and opportunity costs), and that their behaviour is essentially the same in both the economic and political worlds. Supporters of such approaches describe them as 'elegant' and 'parsimonious'. Critics see their rigid logic as making them of limited value – even of being downright wrong in most cases. Take, for example, the belief that voting behaviour is determined by an attempt to maximise individual economic gain. Certainly there has been a growth of such behaviour in Western democracies in recent years. But does this explain support for parties like the German Greens, whose radical wing seeks zero or negative economic growth? Or does it explain the longevity of many socialist parties, like the Austrian Social Democrats, whose support now seems to be determined partly by habit ('cognitive dissonance' in the terminology of psychologists) rather than old class-community norms? And what about Britain in the 1990s, where there is evidence that some voters who are economically optimistic for themselves still vote against government in regions which are economically troubled. It is possible to some extent to resolve these queries: for instance, Green voters have often been portrayed as archetypally non-productive middle-class professionals, who might think that they have little or nothing to lose economically by radical change. But in general, it seems more sensible to conclude that people's motives and influences are varied, and even in capitalist Western society many people still think in community as much as individual terms.[15]

The view that politics is essentially founded on groups has been a major target of rational choice theorists.[16] The role of groups was at the heart of classical sociology: for Marx class was central and based on the mode of production; Mosca held that there was almost a primordial desire to belong to 'herds'; in the 1940s and 1950s Talcott Parsons argued that new group formation and kinship were necessarily rooted in the process of modernisation, which destroyed old communities. Against this, rational choice theorists like Mancur Olson held that individuals require some separate and selective incentive to act in a group-oriented way. Here the approach seems on especially weak ground except where economic interests are most clear cut (for instance, an Olson-type approach could explain the relative strengths of consumer and producer groups and their role in different countries' protection policies). Whilst some group behaviour may exhibit such characteristics (note especially the 'free rider' problem), it seems more vital to ask how people come to adopt the different identities which underlie groups, and how norms and trust are developed. Rather than assume that behaviour is essentially individually rational, it seems more important in this context to look to the bases of trust, and here the role of the family, religion, class and nation seems more crucial than selective incentives – especially economic ones. Take the growth of Christian Democrat parties in Europe at the end of the Second World War; these clearly had a strong religious motivation. Religion too played a notable role in the mobilisation of dissent in communist Poland during the 1980s (the role of religion has consistently been underplayed in American political science), as did nationalism. Similarly, it is hard to understand why the British Conservative Party has remained important for so long without examining the power of nationalism to bond people with very different economic interests. Certainly individuals have been consistently willing to sacrifice themselves – to the point of death – for these wider social units.

It could be argued that an economist can be defined as someone who thinks that Demi Moore's husband married her simply for the money. However, whilst rational choice theory frequently uses the language of economics, it is important not to parody it as necessarily obsessed with material maximisation: the focus is more on 'utility', which as in economics theory proper is not a single object (compare a firm maximising its profits with a consumer maximising utility).[17] The variability of exactly what is meant by utility is recognised by 'thick' rational choice theory. Jon Elster, for example, accepts that individuals have multiple identities, whose importance varies according to cultural and situational contexts: in particular, he distinguishes between 'economic man' who strives for personal hedonistic satisfaction and 'social man', governed by moral and social norms.[18] More generally, there has been a realisation that institutions affect choice too. Thick rational choice theories are therefore less 'elegant', but are much more realistic than thin ones. However, they retain some of the same central flaws. For instance, what explains the existence and efficacy of institutions? What is the theory which explains the development of agent identities and values like trust? Some have sought to respond to these points by using rational choice explanations of the existence of institutions and structures, but this points to another central problem in the approach.

In the words of two leading critics, Green and Shapiro: 'Formidable analytical challenges have attracted a number of first-class minds; rational choice theories have grown in complexity and sophistication as a result. On the other hand, successful empirical applications of rational choice models have been few and far between.'[19] They argue in particular that empirical research has become theory rather than problem driven: and the theory is based on methodological individualism. But this is not a universal scientific truth; indeed, it can be a form of ethnocentrism which denies the label 'rational' to forms of action that affirm an individual's social identity and which are not based on self-interest.

We might also ponder whether in some ways rational choice theory is in part a cultural theory. Can its attraction in America be separated from this country's individualist, market-oriented culture and history? Rational choice theory has its exponents in Europe, but its relative lack of popularity on this side of the Atlantic may not simply reflect the lack of professionalism among its 'backward' academics. It also reflects the fact that in Europe group values, be they religious, class or national, have been central to political development. Take, for example, the issue of how to explain why parties were formed and supported in the nineteenth and early twentieth centuries. In frontier America, an individualist-based method may well provide the central insights, with parties being seen as reducing the transaction costs of electoral involvement by providing a low cost signal. But such a transaction cost approach seems totally misguided when used to explain the formation of the German Catholic Centre Party – or the Nazi Party.

Almond has noted that before the market metaphors of the rational choice theorists, a variety of others were common in the discussion of politics.[20] One common form of parlance was politics as religion, with conversion, disciples and worship. Another was politics as warfare, with paramilitary movements fighting for control of the streets and targeting the enemy. Other metaphors included politics as a game which people enjoyed playing, or as a drama in which 'acting' was the central activity. Indeed, in Clifford Geertz's classic study of the Balinese court, theatre and symbol were the highest form of political activity. '[M]ass ritual was not a device to shore up the state, but rather the state, even in its final gasp, was a device for the enactment of mass ritual'; legitimacy did not come through any conception of economic activity, but rather through a series of historical myths which were used to interpret contemporary experience.[21] It is also interesting to note Geertz's notion of 'thick description': behaviour must be described objectively, but its meaning too must be considered. Actions therefore need viewing in terms of systems of belief and structures, and symbolic action and myths are crucial to politics.

IN DEFENCE OF A POLITICAL CULTURE APPROACH

Britain's leading student of political culture, Dennis Kavanagh, has written that its study is concerned with

> *orientations* towards *political objects*. Orientations are predispositions to political action and are determined by such factors as traditions, historical memories, motives, norms, emotions and symbols. We can break these down into their component parts as follows: cognitions (knowledge and awareness of the political system); affect (emotional disposition to the system); and evaluation (judgement about the system).[22]

The leading contemporary American defender of the cultural approach to politics, Ronald Inglehart, has argued that the political culture approach argues (1) that people's responses to their situations are shaped by subjective orientations, which vary cross-culturally and within sub-cultures; and (2) that these variations in subjective orientations reflect differences in socialisation experience, with early learning conditioning later learning.[23] He adds that cultural theory implies that culture cannot be changed overnight, though the young are easier to influence. Indeed, observed cross-cultural differences reflect the experience of generations, even centuries, rather than relatively short-run factors.

Inglehart's main work has been based on large-scale opinion poll surveys, including the European Union's *Eurobarometer*, and surveys remain a central tool in the cultural approach. Kavanagh's distinction between affective and evaluative support also remains an important part of the political scientists' armoury. For example, studies of the attempt by the Western Allies after 1945 to remake Germany's authoritarian political culture were for a long time concerned with the fear that opinion poll evidence showing growing support for democracy was really picking up a feel-good factor which resulted from West Germany's economic miracle.[24] Recent studies of East German attitudes towards reunification have similarly been concerned that the basis of support lay more in instrumental economic expectations than in deep-rooted admiration for the (West) German political system and society. *Eurobarometer* studies of attitudes towards the European Union have produced similar worries that favourable opinions have been based on the belief that union brings economic benefits rather than on more affective attitudes, which could help the EU through hard times, or aid redistribution from rich to poor. Kavanagh's cognitive dimension also remains important. For instance, recent polls have shown widespread ignorance among people in EU states about its workings or even its main institutions: typically, a 1995 poll revealed that 40 per cent of Germans were unaware that Bonn had held the rotating Presidency for the previous six months, and almost 60 per cent had no idea what was the most important decision-making body in the EU.

However, it is vital not to equate the political culture approach simply with opinion polling – or other behaviourist techniques such as psychological studies of youth socialisation. Political culture should be seen as essentially a syncretic approach: it seeks to understand behaviour by considering a broad range of factors and using various methods. Hence the frequent use of the term by social scientists, historians and others – often in very different contexts. This tendency towards eclecticism has frequently been a source of criticism, especially from those who have sought a core methodology akin to economics, but such criticisms are essentially misguided: heuristic insights can often be gained from such approaches, but human behaviour cannot be modelled in a way more appropriate to the physical sciences.

Rather than dismiss political culture because of its eclecticism, it is more important to systematise it. In particular, I want to argue that it is helpful to adopt three perspectives on the understanding of behaviour: the micro, meso and macro. It is impossible in a book which primarily seeks to look at the concrete issue of the development of European national political cultures, including sweeping issues related to nationalism and the future of the EU, to set this argument out fully. But the outlines can be delineated and a case study used here to illustrate it (the argument is developed further in Chapter 15).

The micro is essentially concerned with the individual and his or her cognitions and basic motives for behaviour. Without accepting methodological individualism, there is an important sense in which the individual is the basis of politics and it is important to see individuals as having an element of free choice (unlike in structuralist approaches where they become virtually robots). The crucial question is what is the basic form of human nature and what influences individual action. Human nature is elusive, both in philosophical and behavioural terms.[25] But the argument that I am putting forward here is that in modern Western society, instead of using a single individualist-economic model, it is more sensible to add two further dimensions to individual motivations: a more affective group-oriented side and a more idealistic side, attracted by principles like equality or justice. In other words, human behaviour is seen in modern Western society as essentially three dimensional, and the crucial question is what determines which side predominates. A psychologist might try to answer this in individual terms, but the political culture method argues that it is helpful to look at two areas beyond the micro.

The meso is concerned with intermediate social organisations to which individuals belong, or through which they gain knowledge and norms, such as the family, local community groups, party and religious groups – groups which are not necessarily overtly political. It looks at their values (including changes) and the way in which they influence and constrain individual behaviour. It also looks at the local socio-economic situation in which the individual is involved, its prosperity, work structures, and so on. The macro is concerned with the widest level or organisation, with which the individual has least direct social contact. In modern society, this is normally the state level. It seeks to examine the way in which factors like the state, national identity or specific institutions such as electoral systems might influence behaviour. It also looks at the impact of the broader socio-economic situation and structure (for example, how might living in an economically depressed community within a wealthy nation affect an individual?).

It is important when considering macro and meso perspectives not to lose sight of the central truth of rational choice theory, namely that in order to offer a full explanation of any political phenomenon we have to be able to account for the behaviour of individuals. What this means is that instead of crude generalisations about, say, national traditions, we need to make clear exactly how these influence individual behaviour. It is also important to stress that the divisions are heuristic rather than ones which always offer clear-cut operational guidelines. For instance, a local political party is part of the community, but there are more diffuse long-term national party ideological traditions. Within categories, there can also be different levels of influence (compare the influence of a 'strong' family with that of a party to which a person somewhat apathetically belongs). However, this tripartite division poses the right questions: what are the key influences on individuals? From what levels of social organisation do these come? And in what way exactly is the influence exerted? Individual behaviour cannot be modelled by simple micro or micro–macro divisions; it is the relationships between three levels (including the macro–meso) which are crucial.

This threefold division has an important explanatory power beyond that of rational choice theory. It is particularly enlightening here to examine the rise of fascism, given the recurring focus on nationalism in this book, and the fact that it has recently begun to attract rational choice explanations, especially from the American sociologist William Brustein.[26] Brustein holds that in Italy fascism made its major breakthrough when it developed an agricultural programme promising benefits to the peasants, a programme effectively disseminated by the Fascist Party. In the German case, he similarly seeks to show the primacy of economic interest: for example, a disproportionate number of people who joined the Nazi Party worked in industries, such as construction or food production, which stood to gain from promised Nazi policies to protect the domestic market. The work offers useful insights, and it is important to take rational choice theory on board rather than reject it outright.

But it is more useful to see Nazi support in the following way. In terms of the micro perspective, there is no doubt that economic interest has been underplayed by some commentators. However, there was also an important affective side to fascist support, for example, those who were attracted by Hitler's charismatic powers; there was also, especially among activists, a more paranoid, psychopathic side.[27] It is also important not to reject fascist ideology as totally incoherent; it is now increasingly being treated as capable at times of serious argument.[28] In terms of the meso perspective, it is interesting to note that the Nazi vote could vary dramatically between neighbouring communities with no apparent economic differences (though a more diffuse sense of national economic crisis was undoubtedly important); the role of local opinion makers and community norms was clearly crucial. It is also interesting to note who did not vote Nazi: this included especially practising Catholics and union members, who were 'protected' by their intermediate group membership and norms.[29] Finally, it is important to look at macro factors. Fascism succeeded in part because it appeared to many as a legitimate extension of national traditions; certainly in Germany there had been a tradition of looking for strong leadership. It was also helped by institutional structures, for example the electoral system.[30]

It is important to stress that this threefold approach has not been imposed on the contributors of the following national chapters: each was allowed to write within their own understanding of the term 'political culture', as part of the point of the book is to take stock of how national political cultures are currently viewed by notable country specialists. However, the underlying picture which emerges from the following pages is that major changes are taking place in macro and meso cultures which are having a significant effect on the micro. Among the most important are the decline of traditional influences like class, religion and family. Society is becoming more atomised, people are less embedded in structured norms.[31] As a result, individuals are increasingly undergoing a complex process of political dealignment and realignment. Old mainstream parties and ideologies are losing their appeal, and the media are now increasingly helping to set the agenda.

The overall situation is one of considerable flux, and there are notable national variations as the following chapters show. However, it is possible to highlight two related, though divergent political trends that could emerge from this set of developments. On the one hand, there is a potential for the creation of a more affective 'European' political culture, but on the other there are mounting forces which could provide succour for radical nationalism. This is the dichotomy that forms the basis of the concluding section of this book, which highlights that the future is not determined by purely socio-economic developments – that politicians, and others who help set the agenda, have power to shape the future

NOTES

1 G. Almond, 'Comparing Political Systems', *The Journal of Politics*, 1956, 18, p. 396.
2 G. Almond and S. Verba, *The Civic Culture*, Princeton, Princeton University Press, 1963.
3 S. M. Lipset, *Political Man*, London, Heinemann, 1960.
4 On the intellectual background to the rise of 'political culture' see G. Almond, 'The Intellectual History of the Civic Culture Concept' in G. Almond and S. Verba (eds), *The Civic Culture Revisited*, Boston, Little, Brown, 1980.
5 The example is taken from A. Weale, 'From Little England to Democratic Europe?', *New Community*, 1995, 21, p. 216.
6 For an example of this last tendency see J. Gaffney and E. Kolinsky (eds), *Political Culture in France and Germany*, London, Routledge, 1991.
7 For critiques of the political culture approach see W. Rosenbaum, *Political Culture*, London, Nelson, 1975; S. Welch, *The Concept of Political Culture*, New York, St Martin's, 1993. For other criticisms, and a defence of the concept and up-dating of the original work, see also Almond and Verba, *The Civic Culture Revisited*.
8 Verba made a notable contribution to modernisation theory. See especially L. Binder *et al.*, *Crises and Sequences in Political Development*, Princeton, Princeton University Press, 1971.
9 E. Banfield, *The Moral Basis of a Backward Society*, New York, The Free Press, 1958.
10 A. Lijphart, *The Politics of Accommodation*, Berkeley, University of California Press, 1975.
11 R. Jessop, *Traditionalism, Conservatism and British Political Culture*, London, Allen and Unwin, 1974.
12 For a classic early critique see B. Barry, *Sociologists, Economists and Democracy*, London, Macmillan, 1970.
13 P. Hall, *Governing the Economy*, Cambridge, Polity Press, 1986.
14 On ideological trends, of both left and right, see R. Eatwell and A. W. Wright (eds), *Contemporary Political Ideologies*, London, Pinter, 1993.
15 On rational choice theory, especially criticisms of it, see D. P. Green and I. Shapiro, *Pathologies of Rational Choice Theory*, New Haven, Yale University Press, 1994; K. R. Monrow (ed.), *The Economic Approach to Politics*, New York, HarperCollins, 1991.
16 See especially M. Olson, *The Logic of Collective Action*, New York, Schocken Books, 1965.
17 For instance, G. Brennan and L. Lomasky, *Democracy and Decision: The Pure Theory of Electoral Preference*, Cambridge, Cambridge University Press, 1993.

12   *Roger Eatwell*

18 J. Elster (ed.), *The Multiple Self*, Cambridge, Cambridge University Press, 1986, esp. pp. 25–6.
19 Green and Shapiro, *op. cit.*, p. ix.
20 G. Almond, 'Rational Choice Theory and the Social Sciences' in Monrow, *op. cit.*, pp. 32ff.
21 C. Geertz, *Negara: The Theatre-State in Nineteenth Century Bali*, Princeton, Princeton University Press, 1980, pp. 23 and 14.
22 D. Kavanagh, *Political Culture*, London, Macmillan, 1972, pp. 10–11. The threefold division of cognitions, affect and evaluation follows the pioneering work T. Parsons and E. Shils (eds), *Toward a General Theory of Action*, Cambridge, Mass., Harvard University Press, 1951.
23 R. Inglehart, *Culture Shift*, Princeton, Princeton University Press, 1990, p. 19.
24 S. Verba, 'The Remaking of German Political Culture' in L. Pye and S. Verba (eds), *Political Culture and Political Development*, Princeton, Princeton University Press, 1965; see also Almond and Verba, *The Civic Culture* and Almond and Verba, *The Civic Culture Revisited*.
25 For an introduction to the issue of human nature in politics see C. Berry, *Human Nature*, Basingstoke, Macmillan, 1986; and R. Trigg (ed.), *Ideas of Human Nature*, Oxford, Blackwell, 1988.
26 W. Brustein, *The Logic of Evil*, New Haven, Yale University Press, 1996; see also W. Brustein, 'The "Red Menace" and the Rise of Italian Fascism', *American Sociological Review*, 1991, 56.
27 On these aspects see I. Kershaw, *The 'Hitler Myth'*, Oxford, Oxford University Press, 1987; and P. Merkl, *Political Violence under the Swastika*, Princeton, Princeton University Press, 1975.
28 See R. Eatwell, 'Towards a New Model of Generic Fascism', *Journal of Theoretical Politics*, 1992, 4; and R. Eatwell, 'On Defining the "Fascist Minimum": the Centrality of Ideology', *Journal of Political Ideologies*, 1996, 1.
29 See T. A. Tilton, *Nazism, Neo-Nazism and the Peasantry*, Bloomington, University of Indiana Press, 1975; and D. Mühlberger, *Hitler's Followers*, London, Routledge, 1991.
30 For the tripartite approach developed systematically see R. Eatwell, *The Rise of Fascism*, London, Edward Arnold, forthcoming.
31 On the general problems of recent social change see A. Giddens's voluminous works, e.g. *Beyond Left and Right*, Cambridge, Polity, 1994.

2 Austria and Switzerland

Hans-Georg Betz

INTRODUCTION

There are good reasons today to group Austria and Switzerland together under the same roof. But this was not always the case. Until 1918, Austria was both an empire and a great power, while Switzerland had been forced to abandon its great power pretensions centuries before. The Habsburg monarchy industrialised relatively late, developing its markets behind a wall of protective tariffs. By contrast, Switzerland industrialised relatively early, adopting a strategy of export-oriented growth and free trade.[1] Finally, full democracy did not come to Austria until after 1945, while Switzerland has been one of the oldest democracies in the world (though not in terms of female suffrage, which only came in the 1970s).

Despite their historical differences, Austria and Switzerland have come to share a number of important features. Both have been among the most stable and prosperous countries in post-war Western Europe. Both share in their domestic politics a highly complex system of interest intermediation designed to promote a culture of compromise and social consensus, which has made them highly competitive in the global economy. Both share in international affairs a status of permanent neutrality, which has allowed them to stay out of conflicts. Most important of all, both are small countries, which has been decisive in shaping how Austrians and Swiss think of themselves.

Despite these common traits, differences in historical experience have had a significant impact on the formation of national identity and political culture in the two countries. These differences go a long way to explain differences in the way the two countries have responded to some of the major social, cultural, and political challenges with which they have been confronted during the past few years.

14   *Hans-Georg Betz*

THE MAKING OF THE MODERN NATION

Switzerland

Swiss history starts in 1291. In that year, the small, German-speaking, mountain cantons of Uri, Schwytz, and Unterwalden formed an alliance against the Austrian Habsburgs who ruled Switzerland in the name of the Emperor. After the towns of Lucerne (1332), Zurich (1352), and Berne (1353) joined the alliance, the confederation soon demanded administrative autonomy. Although the Swiss remained part of the Holy Roman Empire, they gained some measure of autonomy. The fifteenth century saw a new wave of expansion in the west (with the important addition of Basle) and particularly in northern Italy. It was not until the Swiss were decisively defeated in 1515 by the French army at the battle of Marignano that they abandoned power politics.

In the sixteenth century, the Reformation had a major impact on internal developments in Switzerland. Confessional division led to a protracted struggle between the Catholic and Protestant cantons that paralysed the confederation in the face of the Thirty Years' War. The confederation could do little beyond declaring its neutrality. Without an army strong enough to defend its neutrality, it was constantly threatened by outside interference. It was not until the Peace of Westphalia in 1648 that Switzerland's sovereignty, neutrality, and complete independence were finally recognised.

In 1798, Switzerland was overrun by the armies of the French Revolution. Under French pressure the reigning oligarchies, the privileges of towns and guilds, and the remaining vestiges of feudal law were abolished and Switzerland was turned into a centralised state. French domination had two important consequences.[2] It introduced modern ideas, a written constitution, universal male suffrage, the separation of powers, and fundamental civil rights. And it expanded the Latin elements in the confederation with the addition of four French-speaking cantons and the Italian-speaking Ticino between 1803 and 1815. Otherwise, the French reorganisation of the Swiss polity was only of short duration. With Napoleon's defeat in 1814, power was returned to the old regime dominated by a small group of families. The 'Federal Pact' restored full sovereignty to the cantons and restricted the federal state's rights to foreign policy and national defence. This arrangement collapsed in the 1840s under the double strain of economic and political changes. Industrialisation led to the emergence of new elites whose status derived from entrepreneurial success rather than family standing. In the face of a rapid spread of industry it became increasingly evident that a system based on 22 separate currencies, militias, customs duties, and economic laws was an obstacle to economic growth.

As early as 1830, some of the most industrialised cantons had cautiously begun to implement liberal democratic reforms. Soon, a majority from the mainly Protestant, industrialised cantons called for a new federal constitution, which would give the country a central political authority and create a common economic market. A minority of mainly Catholic, rural cantons, clinging to particularism, vehemently opposed this plan, going so far as to form their own separatist league. The conflict escalated into a short civil war which ended with a decisive victory by the progressives. In 1848, a committee representing both victors and vanquished established a new constitution for a modern Swiss federation. The constitution created a Federal Assembly consisting of the popularly elected National Council and the Council of States, and a central government, the Federal Council, consisting of seven members elected by the Federal Assembly. The constitution also revived old democratic traditions in the form of the popular referendum as the cornerstone of the Swiss model of direct democracy. It thus assured the sharing of power among the diverse regional, religious, and social groups and laid the foundation for a system of political accommodation, cooperation, and negotiation.[3]

The establishment of the federation was an important step in the development of modern Switzerland. However, it was not an end to conflict. When, at the beginning of the First World War, the German-speaking elites opted for the German side while the French-speaking Swiss sided with France, their conflicting sympathies threatened to tear the Swiss nation apart. In response, Switzerland reaffirmed its position of strict neutrality while strengthening its commitment to humanitarian initiatives such as the Red Cross. The Second World War saw the emergence of reactionary groups which sought to use fascist methods to revise the outcome of 1848. Even if the small number of Swiss Nazi sympathisers was quickly repressed, the Third Reich posed a serious threat to the Swiss federation. In the face of overwhelming German power, the Swiss managed to maintain their independence only by making important concessions to the Axis powers which seriously compromised their neutrality.

After the war, Switzerland became active in a number of international cultural and economic organisations, including membership in the European Free Trade Association (EFTA). However, despite the fact that a number of international organisations took their seat in Geneva, Switzerland refused to join the United Nations. In domestic politics, one of the most important events was the decision in 1959 to include the Social Democrat Party (SPS) in government, which ever since 1919 had been dominated by a coalition of the three largest parties, the Christian Democrats (CVP), the Free Democrats (FDP), and the Swiss People's Party (SVP). Since 1959, Swiss governments have been put together according to the so-called 'magic formula' which accords two seats in the federal government each to the CVP, FDP, and SPS, and one seat to the SVP. Other major political events were the belated introduction of women's suffrage in 1972 and the lowering of the voting age from 21 to 18 in 1991.

Austria

If modern-day Switzerland is the result of a gradual process of the voluntary growing together of different linguistic and cultural groups, present-day Austria is largely the result of the collapse of a multi-ethnic experiment. At its beginning stood the dismemberment of an empire that included nationalities as diverse as Magyars and Poles, Rumanians and Germans, Italians and Croats. The Austro-Hungarian Monarchy of 1867 never managed to develop a pan-Austrian national consciousness nor was it prepared to concede autonomy to its diverse nationalities. 'Instead of a convincing national consciousness, a defensive government ideology was developed which was strengthened by the fact that the German Austrians saw themselves as the dominant group in the monarchy and endeavoured to retain this position.'[4] When the particularist tendencies among the national minorities exploded in 1914, Vienna proved too weak to contain the nationalist tide.

The end of the war left Austria reduced to its German-speaking territory. Few Austrians wanted or identified themselves with the new state. The First Republic defined itself as the nation-state 'of the "Germans" within the Austro-Hungarian Monarchy, or at least within its western half'. Appealing to the right of national self-determination, the new republic declared itself a part of the German Reich.[5] The Peace Treaty of St Germain, however, prohibited this terminology and with it the obvious connotations it implied. Economically, the country was confronted with severe problems. Whereas the Dual Monarchy had been virtually self-sufficient, the new republic lacked raw materials, food, and above all markets. The 1920s were years of mass unemployment and hyperinflation which nourished social unrest and political extremism. Lacking a sense of national consciousness or a fundamental democratic consensus, the republic soon succumbed to violence and dictatorship. Between 1932 and 1934, under Engelbert Dollfuss, democracy and democratic rule were gradually eliminated. After destroying the left-wing opposition in a bloody civil war in early 1934, the government set up an authoritarian, 'Christian corporate state'.[6] After Dollfuss was assassinated by Nazi putschists, his successor, Kurt Schuschnigg, came under increasing pressure from both Austrian Nazis and the Third Reich to legalise the Nazi Party and appoint some of its members to cabinet posts. Refusing to go along with Hitler's annexation plans, Schuschnigg was forced to resign. In March 1938, Hitler's troops occupied Austria and declared it part of the Third Reich.

Perhaps the most important legacy of the war years was the 'social consensus' which the experience of dictatorship, *Anschluss*, and war fostered among Austria's future leaders. Behind barbed wire, politicians from all social camps sought accommodation.[7] After liberation, a coalition between conservatives and socialists formed a provisional government and organised democratic elections. This created the basis for national reconciliation and unity and laid the foundation for a system of compromise decision making which became the hallmark of the post-war political system.

The demonstration of national unity was essential if Austria hoped to regain national sovereignty. In 1943, the Allied powers had declared Austria the first victim of Hitler's aggression and agreed to reconstitute Austria as an independent country. This, however, did not spare Austria from occupation by the four victorious powers. It was not until the government accepted a non-aligned status in the Austrian State Treaty of 1955 that the country regained full independence. Once the last occupation troops had left Austria, the national parliament declared the country's 'permanent neutrality'.

Over the next three decades, Austria developed into one of Western Europe's most stable and prosperous democracies. In foreign affairs, the country maintained its strict neutrality while at the same time joining the European Free Trade Association and the United Nations. In domestic politics, the gradual erosion of the polarisation of Austrian society into two distinct camps rendered the logic behind coalition governments increasingly obsolete. In 1966, the grand coalition fell apart, giving way to a short-lived ÖVP government which was followed by the long 'Kreisky era' (SPÖ) which lasted until 1983. In the following years, Austrian politics was increasingly characterised by turbulence and instability. The transformation of Austrian politics found its most visible expression in the growing support for the environmentalist Greens and particularly in the dramatic revival of the FPÖ. Under its charismatic new leader, Jörg Haider, the FPÖ launched a frontal attack on the established socio-political system which proved disastrous for the established parties. Although the FPÖ performed less well than expected in the 1995 legislative elections it recovered notably in the 1996 Euro elections, and Austria's future is more uncertain than ever before.

NATIONAL CONSCIOUSNESS AND IDENTITY

Switzerland

Switzerland is a multilingual and multicultural society. Three-quarters of its citizens belong to the German-speaking community, roughly 20 per cent speak French, another 4 per cent Italian, and less than 1 per cent Romansch. Despite its relative heterogeneity, Switzerland developed a common sense of national purpose. It centres around those characteristics that distinguish Switzerland from other European countries. Unlike its neighbours, Switzerland is above all a *Willensnation*. Rather than being built on ethnic, linguistic, or cultural unity, the Swiss nation is built on the historically grounded will of its people to maintain a common polity.[8] In this, the 'role of political institutions was fundamental in uniting a people with four languages, two religions and different regional cultures and in turning these disadvantages into advantages'.[9] Three institutions have been of particular importance: federalism, democracy, and armed neutrality. In 1991, three-quarters of the population expressed pride in direct democracy and about two-thirds in federalism.

A second important aspect of Swiss national identity has been the experience of economic achievement and material wealth. Closely linked to the pride in economic achievements is a distinct appreciation of the importance of work. Grounded in the teachings of Calvin and Zwingli and reinforced by an educational programme emphasising industriousness and discipline, the Swiss version of the work ethic was instrumental in transforming a country with scarce natural resources but an abundant labour force into one of the world's wealthiest countries.[10]

Compared to their American, British, or French counterparts, Swiss citizens have been rather subdued in expressing pride in being Swiss (in 1989, only 31 per cent said they were very proud to be Swiss). This reinforces the impression of a rather dispassionate and pragmatic approach to national identity. However, this does not necessarily mean that the Swiss are also secure in their identity.

In the early 1990s, the stability of Swiss national consciousness was severely shaken.[11] The occasion was the debate over European integration. It revealed that there existed deep fissures in Swiss society which threatened the country's cohesion. Shortly before his death, the dramatist and writer Friedrich Dürrenmatt even warned that Switzerland might eventually dissolve or break apart.[12] What created this profound sense of insecurity was the prospect that the Swiss might have to abandon some of their traditions. There were concerns about what future membership in the EU might do to Switzerland's neutrality as well as to the practice of direct democracy. Noted scholars warned that membership would invariably reduce the people's ability to influence parliamentary decisions via referenda and popular initiatives and that this would entail a considerable 'loss of direct democracy'.[13]

The referendum on the European Economic Area (EEA) in December 1992 polarised Swiss society along a distinct socio-cultural cleavage. The supporters saw in membership an opportunity to avoid isolation and argued that membership would bring economic advantages, especially for Swiss youth. The opponents generally distrusted the process of European integration. They not only feared that Switzerland would lose its independence, but also that membership would have a negative impact on the Swiss economy and lead to a further 'foreignization' of the country. Opposition was highest in traditional rural areas and lowest in the modern urban centres.[14] The referendum was thus as much about economic integration as about how to respond to the challenge of modernisation in a rapidly changing world.

The narrow defeat of the pro-EEA forces suggested that the traditional foundations of Swiss identity were no longer as stable as they had been in the past. It confirmed trends that had already emerged in 1989 with the popular initiative on the future of the Swiss army. Its sponsors demanded the abolition of the Swiss army and the pursuit of a comprehensive peace policy. This 'most radical demand since the foundation of the federation' represented a clear challenge to the country's policy of armed neutrality. Yet, more than a third of those participating in the initiative voted in its favour.[15] Opinion polls further dispelled the notion of the sacrosanct status of Swiss neutrality. In December 1993, a quarter of the population said it could imagine a non-neutral Switzerland, another 31 per cent a Switzerland abandoning its neutrality 'under certain conditions'.[16]

The result of the EEA referendum revealed the extent to which society was split both between supporters and opponents of modernisation and between the linguistic communities. Whereas in French-speaking Switzerland, almost 80 per cent of the participants voted for membership, in the German-speaking areas, almost 60 per cent voted against it. For Swiss observers this represented a reopening of the so-called 'Röschti-Graben', the linguistic gap separating *Suisse romande* from the German-speakers.

The EEA referendum has hardly ended the debate on European integration, mainly because the referendum had been about the EEA, not the EU. Furthermore, the Austrian decision to join the EU in 1995 revived serious concerns of growing economic and political isolation. It was feared that Swiss companies might move to western Austria to profit from European economic integration. As a result, by 1994, EU supporters clearly outnumbered opponents, with the French Swiss, young people, the highly educated, the self-employed, and Socialist Party supporters being most in favour of membership. By 1995, EU membership threatened to turn into a new enduring cleavage splitting Swiss society along several lines.

Has modernisation exacerbated the fragmentation of Swiss society? Will Switzerland disintegrate? There are good reasons to consider such an outcome rather unlikely. Even if the historical and cultural foundations of Swiss identity are in decline, there are still strong economic reasons holding the country together. Were Switzerland to disintegrate, the resulting linguistic communities would be faced with the unpleasant prospect of turning into peripheral and, at best, marginal regions of their respective large neighbours. This prospect, if nothing else, should be enough to counteract the impact of individualisation and fragmentation on Swiss society.

Austria

One of the central characteristics of Austrian post-war identity has been its fragility. This stems primarily from an acute awareness that the post-war state was largely a 'product of power politics and expedience and not the fruit of aspirations for national or social independence'. The establishment of an independent Austrian national consciousness was above all the result of a 'struggle for national identity' largely mandated from above.[17] This was made easier by the devastating effects of the experience of National Socialism, war, and German defeat on a majority of the Austrian population, which 'permanently weakened the German orientation of the

Austrians' and thus 'decisively contributed to the emergence of Austrian national consciousness'.[18]

The mobilisation of anti-German resentments was facilitated by the Moscow declaration of 1943. Its formulation created a first 'founding myth' of the Second Republic, allowing the Austrians to escape responsibility for their involvement in the Nazi crimes.[19] When the satirist Helmut Qualtinger, in his famous monologue 'Herr Karl', dared to expose petty opportunism and lack of principles as quintessential flaws in the Austrian character, he was derided by the public. Collective amnesia and denial allowed the Austrians to escape coming to terms with their immediate past. This process was greatly facilitated by official government policies on issues regarding the past. One of the most important examples was the denial that Austria had a legal responsibility for compensating Austrian Jewish victims of Nazi persecution. In fact, the first response of the Austrian government to Jewish claims for reparations (*Wiedergutmachung*) was to argue that as an occupied country Austria had no obligation to make reparations 'since the crimes against the Jews had been committed by Germans'. Even when international pressure finally forced the government to change its position, it still refused to accept the principle of responsibility.

Given the Austrian government's staunch resistance to recognising Austrian responsibility, the public's lack of willingness to confront the past was hardly surprising. Unlike the Germans, Austrians did not need 'to materially unburden their guilty consciousness, since politically they were not required to have one' – neither by their own government nor by the United States, which by the early 1950s had no interest in jeopardising Austrian internal stability in the face of the Soviet challenge.[20] It was not until 1961 that Jewish refugees were finally recognised as victims. The negation of historical responsibility has had a long-lasting effect on Austrian political culture. According to recent surveys, Austrian attitudes towards National Socialism are still considerably more positive than they are in Germany. Thus in 1989, only 16 per cent of the Austrian population thought that there were only negative aspects to National Socialism (in West Germany, 29 per cent); more than 40 per cent thought there were as many good as bad sides to it (35 per cent in West Germany).[21]

Despite massive mobilisation campaigns, an independent Austrian national consciousness developed only gradually. As late as 1956, less than half of the Austrian population thought that Austrians constituted a separate people; 46 per cent thought they were Germans. It was not until the late 1960s that a majority of Austrians believed they constituted a nation. By the early 1990s, a stable four-fifths majority agreed with that statement.[22]

Of central importance for the evolution of an independent national consciousness have been two features: on the one hand the experience of economic prosperity, material affluence, and political stability, which have been crucial achievements of the Second Republic;[23] on the other hand, Austria's status of permanent neutrality. In 1992, in a survey on objects of national pride, neutrality ranked second (41 per cent) behind landscape and natural beauty (68 per cent). Its fundamental importance for Austria's collective self-understanding is underlined by the decision to make the day the Neutrality Law was ratified in parliament the official national holiday.

Despite its significance, for Austrians neutrality has never had the same meaning as for the Swiss. For the majority of the Austrians, there was no commitment to armed neutrality. Rather, neutrality revived Austria's traditional self-perception as an intermediator and 'bridge' between East and West. By accepting neutrality, Austrians resigned themselves to their status as a small power but also expected that neutrality and small-state status would make them a zone of peace between the blocs immune to the turbulence and uncertainties of international affairs. In a poll conducted in the late 1980s, only a third of the population said it was prepared to defend the country.[24] The Austrians' pride in their neutrality was thus less a reflection of their 'heroic determination to defend themselves' than of 'the hope to be left alone'.[25]

By the late 1980s, the struggle for Austrian national identity appeared to have been decisively won. Not only did Austrians generally consider themselves a nation, they also showed considerably more pride in their nationality than the Germans or Swiss.[26] However, Austria's national identity was largely a product of the post-war settlement and the confrontation between East and West. With the end of the Cold War, the question of national identity thus almost automatically re-emerged.

The challenge to the established interpretation of Austrian national identity found its most vocal expression in the populist rhetoric of Jörg Haider.[27] Haider launched his first attack in 1988 with the remark that the Austrian nation was an 'ideological miscarriage', insisting that ethnicity, language and common culture should be separated from the question of citizenship. In response to imminent German unification two years later, Haider called for a revision of the State Treaty and a reconsideration of the policy of permanent neutrality. Although a clear breach of the post-war consensus, his challenge resonated among many Austrians. Between 1986 and 1996, electoral support for the FPÖ grew from 9.7 to 27.6 per cent.

In the early 1990s, the proposed Austrian membership in the European Union posed a new challenge to Austrian identity. Although EU supporters consistently outnumbered opponents, membership raised a series of concerns – not least with regard to Austrian neutrality. When asked how they would vote if Austria could only become an EU member if it renounced neutrality, more than two-thirds said that in this case Austria should renounce EU membership. Despite these reservations, however, a two-thirds majority voted for EU membership.[28]

The positive response to European integration should not conceal the fact that since the collapse of the post-war system, Austrian national identity has entered a new phase of uncertainty and instability. Although a large majority of Austrians has come to accept an identity separate and distinct from the Germans, Austrian national consciousness rests on shaky ground. In the post-war period, Austrians could escape confronting the past. The end of the Cold War and the growing appeal of radical right-wing populist positions has forced the Austrians to start reappraising their position. What is at stake is Austria's future as a stable and self-assured democracy.

XENOPHOBIA AND RACISM

Switzerland

With more than 1 million foreigners in a population of roughly 6.6 million, Switzerland has, after Luxembourg, the highest proportion of foreign residents in Western Europe. In the 1960s, most foreign residents were foreign workers with limited work permits, many of whom sought to stay in the country. The Swiss have been quite ambiguous with regard to the country's foreign residents. While the country has traditionally relied on a relatively large number of foreign workers (already in the first decade of this century, more than a quarter of the industrial labour force were foreign workers), the Swiss have hardly been immune to those proclaiming that 'the boat is full'. The most notorious instance occurred in the late 1930s when the Swiss insisted that the Germans stamp a 'J' into the passports of German Jews in order to allow the Swiss authorities to turn potential Jewish refugees back at the Swiss border. It took the Swiss government 50 years to officially recognise Swiss responsibility and guilt and to admit that 'the fear of foreignization (*Überfremdung*) associated with mass immigration and the concern that this might boost anti-semitism, which exists also in this country, have sometimes been stronger than our tradition of asylum and our humanitarian values'.[29]

After the war, xenophobic sentiments found their expression in the formation of various anti-foreigner movements and parties and a number of anti-foreigner initiatives. The first anti-foreigner movement, the Nationale Aktion für Volk und Heimat, emerged in 1961. Together with other movements it launched five 'anti-foreignization initiatives' intended to severely reduce the foreign presence in Switzerland. All of them failed, although at times by a rather slim margin. After spectacular successes at the polls in the early 1970s, the anti-foreigner movements' fortunes rapidly declined. This was largely due to the fact that in response to the referenda, the federal government enacted increasingly restrictive immigration legislation.[30]

It was not until the mid-1980s that rising public concern over the growing number of refugees provided new opportunities for xenophobic movements. In 1985 and 1986, National Action and its French counterpart, Vigilance, made spectacular gains in local elections in Berne, Lausanne, and Geneva. However, the most significant development was the rise of the Autopartei – Die Freiheitlichen – in the late 1980s. With its mixture of radical market liberalism and militant xenophobia, the party gained 8 parliamentary seats in the 1991 national election. At the same time, Switzerland witnessed the rise of fringe groups on the extreme right together with a growing number of violent attacks on foreigners.[31]

In the early 1990s, there was growing anxiety over the rising tide of refugees and growing resentment towards them. As in other West European countries, a growing number of Swiss associated immigration with insecurity and a threat to their culture. One indication of the change in political climate was a referendum in September 1994 on a new law outlawing racial discrimination. Despite broad backing from the media and politicians, the referendum passed by a narrow margin. A subsequent referendum on measures designed to further tighten Switzerland's immigration laws, passed by an overwhelming majority.

Despite their long tradition of anti-foreigner movements, the Swiss are not more xenophobic than other West Europeans. A 1993 survey even found the level of tolerance of the Swiss population to be 'relatively high'. Other surveys paint a similar picture: in 1994, 72 per cent disagreed that Jews had too much influence in Switzerland.[32] Although a relatively sizeable minority is strongly opposed to the foreign presence in the country, most Swiss have recognised that they need foreigners to do the work which Swiss citizens no longer want to do. Given this sense of pragmatism, militant forms of xenophobia have remained a fringe phenomenon.

Austria

Save for small Croatian and Slovenian minorities in Carinthia and Burgenland, Austria is a relatively homogeneous country. In the early 1990s, Austria's resident foreign population was less than 600,000. As in Switzerland, the great majority were foreign workers. During the Cold War period Austria served as an important temporary haven for East European refugees en route to the West and as a transit point for Soviet Jews on their way to Israel or the United States. Few of the estimated 2 million refugees from the East remained in Austria. Those who remained were quickly assimilated.[33]

In spite of the relatively minor foreign presence in Austria, hostility towards foreigners appears to be deeply entrenched in Austrian society. Perhaps its most significant manifestation has been the persistence of anti-semitic tendencies among substantial portions of the Austrian population.[34] Thus, in 1991, half of the population thought Jews had, at least partly, to blame themselves for so often being persecuted; 37 per cent thought Jews exerted too much influence on world affairs; 31 per cent preferred not to have Jews as neighbours; and 19 per cent thought it would be better for Austria if there were no Jews in the country. Even if other surveys suggest that, in the wake of the Waldheim affair, social tolerance of anti-semitic attitudes has been slowly declining, anti-semitism remains a serious challenge to Austrian civil society.[35]

If anti-semitism has been a persistent characteristic of post-war Austrian political culture, xenophobia came into the open only recently in the aftermath of the Eastern European revolution. The dramatic increase in the number of refugees seeking asylum in Austria led to growing anti-foreigner sentiments in the Austrian population. In 1990, two-thirds thought there were too many foreigners in Austria and associated them with insecurity, disorder, and crime. In 1992, 38 per cent saw 'being swamped by floods of refugees' as the biggest threat to the country. In 1993, 42 per cent of the population thought foreigners represented a threat to the Austrian way of life.[36]

This climate of anxiety provided new opportunities for Jörg Haider and the FPÖ to promote themselves as champions of the anti-foreigner cause. Haider argued that no people could allow itself to become 'foreigners in their own country'. Lashing out against 'the utopia of a multicultural society', the FPÖ initiated a nation-wide petition drive in support of 12 anti-foreigner measures designed to severely curtail the number and social rights of immigrants and foreign workers in Austria. Despite a relatively low turnout, the party's aggressive anti-immigrant position gained it new supporters and contributed to its dramatic rise in the 1990s.

In response to the rise of xenophobia and its exploitation by the radical right, the government enacted several legal and practical measures designed to severely limit access to Austria. This moved Austria 'from being one of the most liberal countries in Europe in its treatment of asylum seekers to being one of the least'. Thus in order to prevent illegal border crossings, the government has deployed military personnel along its eastern borders while Austrian authorities deport thousands of illegal immigrants.

Even Austria's harsh measures against foreigners and potential immigrants were not enough to satisfy those most opposed to the vision of a more tolerant society. In early 1995, a bomb killed four gypsies. This was the climax of a series of bomb attacks by a 'Bavarian Liberation Army' which previously had been primarily directed against prominent left-leaning politicians. These attacks were a powerful reminder that Austria was hardly immune to right-wing violence and thus contradicted the notion that by severely tightening its immigration laws, the Austrians would be able to prevent the wave of anti-foreign violence that had shaken Germany in the early 1990s from reaching their country. Instead, the massive mobilisation against foreigners only reinforced existing authoritarian tendencies while strengthening trends towards parochialism and provincialism.

ATTITUDES TOWARDS THE POLITICAL SYSTEM

Switzerland

Switzerland serves as one of the last consociational models in Europe. Although traditional religious and cultural cleavages no longer play a critical role in Swiss society, Swiss politics is still dominated by a 'non-competitive pattern of interest aggregation and conflict resolution'. One of the driving forces behind this system of compromise and accommodation has been the fact that in Switzerland, most parliamentary decisions are subject to a mandatory or facultative referendum. In addition, citizens can propose amendments to the constitution by a popular initiative. Referendum and initiative serve as cornerstones of the Swiss form of direct democracy. They enable citizens 'to intervene at the end of a legislative process'. In theory, referenda and initiatives allow citizens to veto parliamentary decisions and thus exert strong control over the making of public policy. In reality, laws have been challenged relatively rarely. In the 1980s, there were no more than 12 facultative referenda and 40 initiatives. Their impact on the decision-making process in Switzerland is of a more indirect nature. In order to minimise the risk that disenchanted minorities would bring down laws by means of a popular referendum, the major political actors have found themselves compelled to include key parties and interest groups in the decision-making process. The constant threat of a referendum or an initiative thus reinforces the consociational patterns of decision making and assures that 'compulsory pragmatism' remains a central characteristic of Swiss political culture.[37]

The fact that decisions are generally reached in pre-parliamentary negotiations has greatly diminished the importance of representative democracy. It is further reduced by the 'magic formula', which allocates the seats in the seven-member federal government among the four major parties. Given the low importance of electoral outcomes on the national level, there is little incentive for voters to go to the polls. In fact, conventional participation has dropped continuously since the end of the war, a trend which was reversed neither by the enfranchisement of women in the early 1970s nor by the lowering of the voting age in the early 1990s. In 1991, turnout was below 50 per cent, and even in the canton Schaffhausen, where penalties exist for non-voting, only about two-thirds of eligible voters bothered to vote. Unlike in other West European countries, however, low voter turnout is not necessarily a sign of general political disinterest, disenchantment, or alienation. In the late 1980s, almost two-thirds of the Swiss population thought their political system was good or very good. Between 1983 and 1993, the proportion of those expressing 'high' interest in politics increased from 43 to 67 per cent.[38]

Since the early 1970s, unconventional forms of participation have increased considerably. Switzerland witnessed a wave of social protest by environmental, anti-nuclear, and women's rights groups and other new social movements.[39] Opinion polls showed significant support for these activities. Thus in 1989, 60 per cent of the population said they would participate in some form of protest (initiatives, demonstrations, strikes) with a small minority even being prepared to use violent means to make themselves heard.[40]

This was as much a reflection of an intensified process of individualisation as it marked a profound change in social and cultural values. As in Austria and Germany, the post-materialist mobilisation led to the creation of several green and alternative parties. The most successful of them, the Green Party of Switzerland, gained 6.1 per cent of the vote in 1991. The party not only appealed to growing concern over environmental issues, it also appealed to a significant portion of voters who felt excluded from the decision-making process and, as a result, increasingly disenchanted from the political system. As Claude Longchamp has demonstrated, in the late 1980s, a growing number of citizens felt disaffected with respect to the established political parties and the government. Between 1988 and 1992 alone, the number of respondents distrustful of politics increased from 29 to 39 per cent of the population. Measures of internal and external efficacy produce similar results. Thus in 1991, 58 per cent thought parties were only interested in votes, and half of the population thought that people had no influence on the workings of government. At the same time, however, an overwhelming majority rejected the notion that parties should be abolished altogether. What the Swiss wanted instead were up-to-date parties.

Growing political disaffection, together with a worsening of the Swiss economy and an increase in social marginalisation in the late 1980s and early 1990s, proved fertile ground for radical populist forces. They found their home in the Automobile Party, which emerged in the late 1980s to challenge the government's efforts to restrict traffic in the interest of the environment. However, the party soon abandoned its exclusive advocacy of 'unrestricted driving for free citizens' in favour of a frontal assault on the state bureaucracy, the welfare state, and Switzerland's 'liberal' asylum laws. The party's success has brought movement into Switzerland's political landscape. In Ticino, a Populist League was founded and made spectacular gains in the 1991 election. Perhaps the most important new political force, however, was Christoph Blocher, the *enfant terrible* of the SPV in Zurich, whose vocal opposition to the EU had been decisive in defeating the EEA referendum. After the 1991 election, Blocher started thinking aloud about uniting the rival populist groups on the right into a new radically pro-market party modelled after the Austrian FPÖ. Although his overtures proved largely unsuccessful, radical right-wing populism has remained a significant challenge to the political establishment.

Austria

As in Switzerland, post-war political culture in Austria was profoundly shaped by consociationalism. Until well into the 1960s, Austrian society was deeply divided into two main sub-cultures (*Lager*), one Catholic, the other socialist. These *Lager* integrated their members into educational, cultural and occupational organisations, within which 'they could live their lives from womb to tomb' while offering them a sense of 'political belonging' in the two dominant parties, the ÖVP and SPÖ. Mutual distrust and hostility between the sub-cultures were compensated by close cooperation between the political elites in a series of subsequent grand coalition governments. Consocialism was supplemented by a neocorporatist system of 'social partnership' which incorporated the relevant economic interest groups in a number of chambers and associations with compulsory membership which participated in political decision making. As the Socialists dominated the labour chambers and the Conservatives the business chambers, the two sides had 'to agree on virtually every economic action, thereby assuring peace'.[41]

The Austrian system of conflict resolution increasingly turned into an extensive system of spoils and patronage which awarded jobs, housing, and public contracts according to party affiliation. At the same time, the system of social partnership was instrumental in imposing the sense of discipline necessary for Austria to compete successfully in the global market. The Austrian model proved its worth in the turbulent 1970s and 1980s when it managed to maintain both a relatively high degree of monetary stability and one of the lowest levels of unemployment in Western Europe.[42] It is thus perhaps not completely surprising that in 1993, almost half of the Austrian population agreed with the statement that cooperation between the social partners was more important than parliament.

These results are instructive in more than one way. Not only are they an indication of the extent to which neocorporatism still finds support among the population, they also serve as a reminder of the ambiguous attitudes harboured by a large portion of the Austrian public with respect to democratic decision-making processes. Although after the war the vast majority of the Austrian population accepted democracy as the best possible political system, Austrian attitudes towards the political system remained informed by traditional orientations. Until this day, desire for social subordination mixed with a large measure of trust in state authority are major aspects of Austrian political culture. As late as the mid-1980s, more than two-thirds of the Austrian population thought that obedience and respect for authorities were the most important virtues a child should learn. With respect to the state, Austrians continue to be heavily output-oriented. In 1989, 55 per cent associated their state with social security, but only 28 per cent with freedom. Concurrently, Austrians appear considerably less enthusiastic about institutions associated with political participation and political competition. Although in the 1980s, Austria witnessed growing environmental activism, anti-nuclear demonstrations, and growing demands for extended democratic rights for women and minorities, the level of willingness to participate in non-conventional forms of political protest and participation was considerably lower than in other West European countries.

The shortage of trust in representative political institutions results largely from a low sense of political efficacy and little confidence in governmental responsiveness. The result is a fundamental ambivalence with respect to the political system that was already noted in the well-known Political Action Study of 1974 as a typically Austrian trait. Whereas the study found

Austrians generally to see 'their government as having low responsiveness and their individual potential for influence as low in both an absolute and relative sense' this did not appear to lead to a serious feeling of 'dissatisfaction with the policy performance of the government'.[43] As in other West European countries, the most immediate consequence of socio-economic modernisation and social fragmentation has been growing disenchantment with politics. The party that has benefited the most from this has been the FPÖ. Particularly since the 1994 election, Haider has owed much of his success to his regular disclosure of bloated salaries being earned by old party hacks in sinecure positions within the chambers and nationalised companies. But polls indicate that the dramatic rise of radical right-wing populism is more than a mere protest vote. There is considerable evidence that FPÖ support is the expression of a new socio-cultural cleavage in Austrian society. Not only are FPÖ supporters more xenophobic, more disenchanted with the established political system, and more prepared to challenge the central pillars of Austria's post-war identity than the general public; surveys also show FPÖ supporters to be most strongly in favour of dismantling the post-war socio-economic system.

CONTINUITIES AND CHANGE

The growing success of non-conventional political formations is perhaps the most significant symptom of profound changes in the political culture of Austria and Switzerland. Confronted with the dual challenges of a global information economy, changing value systems, and processes of social fragmentation and individualisation, the consociational and neocorporatist arrangements which characterised both countries in the post-war period are under increasing pressure. Given the differences in the historical experiences, which gave rise to and shaped the political culture in the two countries, it is hardly surprising that the impact of these changes has been substantially more pronounced in Austria than in Switzerland. In Austria, the socio-economic and socio-cultural challenges of the past few years have put into question the continued viability of the Austrian model of conflict resolution which until very recently guaranteed social stability and economic prosperity. It is thus hardly a coincidence that Haider's Freedom Party has become the most successful radical right-wing populist party in Western Europe. In Switzerland, global change has put into question the continued viability of the country's exceptionalism. Again it is hardly a coincidence that it is the EU question that has emerged as the potentially most divisive new cleavage in Swiss society. Neither development is likely to be quickly resolved. However, the matter in which they will eventually be resolved is likely to have a significant impact on the future development of democracy and political culture in both countries.

NOTES

1 See P. Katzenstein, *Small States in World Markets*, Ithaca, Cornell University Press, 1985.

2 J.-F. Aubert, 'Introduction historique: La formation du régime politique suisse', *Pouvoirs*, 1987, 43, p. 7.

3 See V. Bogdanor, 'Federalism in Switzerland', *Government and Opposition*, 1988, 23; W. Linder, *Swiss Democracy: Possible Solutions to Conflict in Multicultural Societies*, New York, St Martin's Press, 1994.

4 P. Gerlach, 'National Consciousness and National Identity' in A. Pelinka and F. Plasser (eds), *The Austrian Party System*, Boulder, Westview, 1989, p. 23.

5 E. Bruckmüller, 'The National Identity of the Austrians' in M. Teich and R. Porter (eds), *The National Question in Europe in Historical Context*, Cambridge, Cambridge University Press, 1993, p. 198.

6 See A. Whiteside, 'Austria' in H. Rogger and E. Weber (eds), *The European Right*, Berkeley, University of California Press, 1965.

7 G. Wagner, 'Von der Staatsidee zum Nationalbewusstsein' in Georg Wagner (ed.), *Österreich: Von der Staatsidee zum Nationalbewusstsein*, Vienna, Verlag der Österreichischen Staatsdruckerei, 1982, p. 122.

8 J. Steinberg, 'Imitation of Switzerland: Historical Reflections', *Government and Opposition*, 1988, 23, p.17; G. Kreis, 'Die Frage der nationalen Identität' in P. Hugger (ed.), *Handbuch der Schweizer Volkskultur*, vol. II, Zurich, Offizin, 1990, p. 789.

9 Linder, *op. cit.*, p. 5; see also A. Melich, *Les valeurs des Suisses*, Berne, Peter Lang, 1991, p. 20; C. Longchamp, 'Politisch-Kultureller Wandel in der Schweiz' in F. Plasser and P. Ulram (eds), *Staatsbürger oder Untertanen?*, Frankfurt, Peter Lang, 1991, p. 88.

10 Steinberg, *op. cit.*, p. 30; see also U. Im Hof, 'Nationale Identität der Schweiz: Konstanten im Wandel', *Schweizer Monatshefte*, 1990, 70, pp. 932–4.

11 P. Stadeler, 'Eine Schweiz zwischen Mythenjagd, Identitätskrise und Verfremdung', *Schweizer Monatshefte*, 1991, 71; G. Kreis, *Die Schweiz unterwegs, Schlussbericht des NFP 21 Kulturelle Vielfalt und nationale Identität*, Basle, Helbing and Lichterhahn, 1993, pp. 1–16.

12 See E. Wiedemann, 'Eine dumpfe Verstimmung', *Der Spiegel*, 1991, 31; W. Linder, 'Die Schweiz zwischen Isolation und Integration', *Aus Politik und Zeitgeschichte*, B47–8/92, 13 November 1992.

13 H. Kriesi, 'Direkte Demokratie in der Schweiz', *Aus Politik und Zeitgeschichte*, B23, 1991, p. 54.

14 See C. Longchamp, 'Den Pelz waschen, ohne ihn nass zu machen' in H. Rust (ed.), *Europa-Kampagnen*, Vienna, Signum-Verlag, 1993.

15 C. Longchamp, 'Analyse der eidgenössischen Abstimmung vom 26 November 1989', *VOX-Publikation*, 1990, 23.

16 *GfS-Forschungsinstitut*, Schweizer Gesellschaft für Sozialforschung Adliswil, December 1993.

17 F. Fellner, 'The Problem of the Austrian Nation after 1945', *Journal of Modern History*, 1988, 60, p. 264; Gerlach, *op. cit.*, p. 226; M. Riedlsperger, 'Austria: A Question of National Identity', *Politics and Society in Austria, Germany and Switzerland*, 1991, 4, p. 61.

18 Bruckmüller, *op. cit.*, p. 221; Gerlach, *op. cit.*, p. 236.

19 See J. Bunzl, 'Austrian Identity and Anti-semitism', *Patterns of Prejudice*, 1987, 21, pp. 4–5; Riedlsperger, *op. cit.*, p. 55.

20 In 1991, 34 per cent of the Austrian population agreed that Austria was the first victim of Hitler's Germany; 39 per cent thought Austria shared responsibility for Nazi crimes; 32 per cent thought the Jews were exploiting the Holocaust for

their own purposes. F. Karmasin, *Austrian Attitudes toward Jews, Israel, and the Holocaust*, New York, Working Papers on Contemporary Anti-Semitism, American Jewish Committee, 1992, pp. 4–5.

21 F. Plasser and P. Ulram, 'Politischer Kulturvergleich: Deutschland, Österreich und die Schweiz' in Plasser and Ulram, *op. cit.*, p. 39.

22 See Wagner, *op. cit.*, pp. 124–43; E. Bruckmüller, *Österreichbewusstsein im Wandel*, Vienna, Signum-Verlag, 1994, p. 15.

23 E. Hanisch, 'Kontinuation und Brüche: Die innere Geschichte' in H. Dachs (ed.), *Handbuch des politischen Systems Österreichs*, Vienna, Manz, 1992, pp. 18–19.

24 In the early 1980s, 35 per cent of the German population said that in the case of war they were prepared to fight for their country. See also E. Noelle-Neumann and R. Köcher, *Die verletzte Nation*, Stuttgart, Deutsche Verlags-Anstalt, 1987, p. 61.

25 Bruckmüller, *op. cit.*, p. 27; E. Weinzirl, 'Meilensteine auf dem Weg zur österreichischen Nation' in Ferdinand Kaiser (ed.), *Täter Mitläufer Opfer – Sechzehn Reden über Österreich*, Thaur, Kulturverlag, 1993, pp. 60–1.

26 In 1989, 53 per cent of the Austrian respondents said they were 'very proud' of their nationality compared to 31 per cent of the Swiss, and 21 per cent of the Germans. See Plasser and Ulram, 'Politischer Kulturvergleich', p. 40; see also Noelle-Neumann and Köcher, *op. cit.*, p. 28.

27 On Haider and the FPÖ see H.-G. Betz, *Radical Right-Wing Populism in Western Europe*, New York, St Martin's Press, 1994; F. Plasser and P. Ulram, *Radikaler Reichspopulismus in Österreich: die FPÖ unter Jörg Haider*, Vienna, Fessel/GfK Institut für Marktforschung, 1994; see also J. Haider, *Die Freiheit, die ich meine*, Frankfurt, Ullstein, 1993.

28 In 1993, only 5 per cent of the population considered themselves more as European than Austrian citizens; another 16 per cent said they were both. *Gesellschaftspolitischer Monitor*, vol. 1, Vienna, Fessel/GfK Institut für Marktforschung, 1993, p. 25; see also Bruckmüller, *op. cit.*, pp. 48–58.

29 The official Swiss apology was part of a speech delivered by the Swiss Federal President, Kaspar Villiger, in May 1995. See '50 Jahre Frieden', *Neue Zürcher Zeitung*, international edition, 8 May 1995, p. 13.

30 C. T. Husbands, 'The Dynamics of Racial Exclusion and Expulsion: Racist Politics in Western Europe', *European Journal of Political Research*, 1988, 16, pp. 714–16.

31 F. Saint-Ouen, 'Vers une remontée du national-populisme en suisse? Les cas des vigilants genevois', *Annuaire suisse de science politique*, 1986, 26; G. Schiesser, 'Die Schweizer Auto-Partei', *Die Neue Gesellschaft/Frankfurter Hefte*, 1992, 39; J. Firschknecht, *Schweiz wir kommen – Die neuen Fröntler und Rassisten*, Zurich, Limmat, 1991.

32 Infosuisse, 'Ausländerpolitik und national Konsens', 1993, p. 6; D. Schloeth, 'Analyse de eidgenössischen Abstimmungen', *VOX*, 1994, 55, p. 16.

33 R. Eichwalder, 'Lebensbedingungen ausländischer Staatsbürger in Österreich', *Statistische Nachrichten*, 1991, 46.

34 See Bunzl, *op. cit.*; B. Kaindl-Widhalm, *Demokraten wider Willen? Autoritäre, Tendenzen und Anti-semitismus in der 2. Republik*, Vienna, Verlag für Gesellschaftskritik, 1990.

35 Karmasin, *op. cit.*, pp. 1–2; also C. Haerpfer, 'Xenophobie und Anti-semitismus 1992', Vienna, Institut für Konfliktforschung, 1992; A. Pelinka, 'Dismantling Taboos: Anti-semitism in the Austrian Political Culture of the 1980s', *Patterns of Prejudice*, 1993, 27; Bruckmüller, *op. cit.*, p. 158.

36 F. Plasser and P. A. Ulram, ' "Die Ausländer kommen!" ', *Österreichisches*

Jahrbuch für Politik 1990, Vienna, Verlag für Geschichte und Politik, 1991, p. 321; Bruckmüller, *op. cit.*, p. 154.

37 F. Lehner and B. Homann, 'Consociational Decision-Making and Party Government in Switzerland' in R. Katz (ed.), *Party Governments – European and American Experiences*, Berlin, de Gruyter, 1987; H. Kriesi, 'Direkte Demokratie in der Schweiz', *Aus Politik und Zeitgeschichte*, B23, 31 May 1991, pp. 45–6.

38 Plasser and Ulram, 'Politischer Kulturvergleich', pp. 33–4; C. Longchamp, *Unterstützung von Bundesrat und Verwaltung*, Bern, GfS-Forschungsinstitut der Schweizerischen Gesellschaft für praktische Sozialforschung, 1994, p. 15.

39 See R. Levy, 'Bürger in Bewegung' in P. Hugger (ed.), *Handbuch der Schweizer Volkskultur*, vol. II, Zurich, Offizin, 1992.

40 H. Kriesi, 'Political Power and Decision Making in Switzerland' in J. E. Hilowitz (ed.), *Switzerland in Perspective*, New York, Greenwood, 1991, pp. 487–9; Melich, *op. cit.*, pp. 268–81.

41 F. Plasser, P. A. Ulram and A. Graushuber, 'The Decline of "Lager Mentality" and the New Model of Electoral Competition in Austria', *West European Politics*, 1992, 15, p. 18; see also P. A. Ulram, 'Politische Kultur der Bevölkerung' in *Handbuch des politischen Systems Österreichs*, pp. 466–7.

42 See F. Scharpf, 'Economic and Institutional Constraints of Full-Employment Strategies: Sweden, Austria, and Western Germany, 1973–1982' in J. H. Goldthorpe (ed.), *Order and Conflict in Contemporary Capitalism*, Oxford, Clarendon Press, 1984, p. 282.

43 S. Barnes and M. Kaase, *Political Action: Mass Participation in Five Western Democracies*, Beverly Hills, Sage, 1979, p. 490.

3 Belgium and the Netherlands

Herman van der Wusten and Martijn Roessingh

INTRODUCTION

The Netherlands and Belgium have close linkages. In particular, together with the small state of Luxembourg, they formed the Benelux Union at the end of the Second World War, which was an important stepping stone in the construction of post-war European integration.[1] Since this period, the Low Countries have frequently been known as the Benelux states, and both Belgium[2] and the Netherlands[3] have in the past been viewed as models of political stability and moderation in spite of social divisions. However, in recent years the former has frequently been seen as a case study of the rise of divisive ethno-nationalisms,[4] and since the 1970s considerable attention has been paid to the demise/transformation of state-supported social pillars that legitimated the overarching social structures in both countries.[5]

The Netherlands and Belgium are very similar countries if painted on the wider canvas of the European political map: not big, highly developed, caught between major powers.[6] Braudel has shown them to have been at the receiving end when the centre of the emerging world economy moved from the shores of the Mediterranean to the North Sea around 1600.[7] Major parts of the Low Countries were sprinkled with towns and commercialised agriculture had already spread widely at the time. There was vivid interaction with cultural and commercial centres elsewhere in Europe: recall, for example, the travels of Renaissance painters, the contacts of Humanists and the spread of their printed works. The Netherlands from the time of their hegemonic status after the sixteenth century, and Belgium since the last stage of European expansion, have been involved in the administration of large colonial possessions.

But the Netherlands and Belgium also differ on a number of counts. The Netherlands have been spared a number of state life-threatening battles that have been more prominent in Belgium. The virtual absence of Protestantism in Belgium has paradoxically given free rein to the development of deep church–state conflict for prolonged periods of time. Early industrialisation in Belgium has set the stage for the emergence of a powerful socialist opposition at the start of modern mass politics. Both issues have drawn the lines for more existential battles within the Belgian body politic than was the case in the Netherlands during the crucial period of modern state-formation during the long nineteenth century. In the Netherlands Protestantism in different shades was most important from a religious point of view, the sizeable Catholic minority only gradually becoming emancipated during the last part of the nineteenth century. Various types of Protestants, liberals, initially conservatives, later Catholics discussed a long list of issues but divergent opinions were less threatening to state existence because the church-related institutions of Protestantism were less-encompassing and less ambitious vis-à-vis state power than in the case of the Catholics.[8] Socialism was a latecomer in the Netherlands as a result of late industrialisation. Consequently it found much of the political opportunity space for mass parties already occupied and was relatively less powerful than in Belgium. Finally the linguistic heterogeneity that has been a permanent feature of Belgian society has finally become a major problem for the Belgian polity during the twentieth century, whereas Dutch state-formation has not encountered divisive language issues.[9]

HISTORICAL ROOTS

The Netherlands

At the end of the sixteenth century, after the resistance movement against the Spanish imperial Habsburgs in the Low Countries had successfully liberated seven Northern Provinces, the new self-proclaimed Dutch republic became the hegemonic power in the emerging European state system.[10] After its short hegemonial period in the seventeenth century, the Dutch Republic of the United Provinces was superseded by other powers and entered a period of relative decline. In many respects, though, it was still one of the most developed countries in Europe (for example, as regards literacy). In the course of the nineteenth century the Dutch state elite made several, increasingly incisive, attempts to modernise by re-constituting its institutions and stimulating the economy. Partly as a consequence, local barriers were broken down. These developments set the stage for protracted conflicts between the various religious groups in the country.

The Dutch population has been religiously mixed ever since the introduction of Protestantism. The struggle for independence in the sixteenth to seventeenth centuries was partly fought against Catholic oppression. The leading circles in the republic were on the whole inspired by more tolerant and latitudinarian versions of Protestantism, though stricter and more emotive strands found support among the artisans and common folk. Catholicism had remained widespread in the Netherlands: the southern provinces were homogeneously Catholic, but pockets of Catholics could be found elsewhere. The Catholic faith was hardly encouraged: Catholics did not qualify for the higher positions in the country and no open practice of the faith was allowed. But there was no active suppression either.

Modernisation aroused religious antagonism particularly between latitudinarian and more orthodox Protestants in the context of the broadly based Reformed Church. This church was regulated by law although it was not a state church. The latitudinarian Protestants on the whole supported political Liberalism, a weakly organised party of notables. The orthodox Protestants fragmented into a number of mutually antagonistic religious institutions, but they also organised the first mass political party in the country overarching some of these differences; another sizeable orthodox Protestant party emerged alongside. Catholic emancipation had been under way since mid-century, but politically organised Catholicism emerged only towards 1900. A major socialist party developed during the first two decades of the twentieth century when it settled at somewhat less than 25 per cent of the total electorate. The socialists were only gradually incorporated into the main national positions of power due to their own hesitations and the refusal of others. But they began to take part in the municipal governments of the major cities from the First World War on.

As the various conflict cleavages in the Dutch population became more apparent through efforts at mass mobilisation, the liberal elite tried to counter these divisive tendencies.[11] There were efforts to re-emphasise the importance of the royal family, to re-launch an invigorated colonial mission, and to impose sanitised versions of presumed national history, a good example of what has been termed the 'invention of tradition'.[12] During the Boer War, Dutch opinion notably coalesced in a denunciation of the British and an all out support of the valiant Boers, descendants of Dutch settlers. But these trends were countered by orthodox Protestants underlining the Protestant nature of the nation, and re-telling the fight against the Spaniards with their own heroes. The Catholics cautiously countered, denouncing some of the major events as acts of piracy and cold blooded murder.[13]

The education issue became the major focus of conflict between orthodox and latitudinarian Protestants after it spilled over into national politics. It took half a century to settle this problem by a constitutional provision and new law (1870–1920). This opened the way for completely subsidised private education, provided that nationally set quality standards were met. This initiated the framework for a wide range of settlements on how to provide modern services. It re-inculcated a preference for broad based coalitions, proportionality and qualified autonomy in the Dutch body politic that is still important.

Church conflicts and their spillover into the sphere of politics encouraged drives to organise each population segment in its own camp. The availability of state subsidies further supported this notion. The top positions in the organisations of every camp were mutually linked. Certain key persons occupied several of those positions simultaneously and institutions for regular consultations were created. In this way, pillars (*Verzuiling*) were formed. Due to several 'construction errors', the pillars were never the neat all-encompassing bearers of the Dutch state. The orthodox Protestants, the real architects of the scheme, were involved in constant internal quarrels giving rise to extra organisational forms and occasional breakaways. The Catholics were in the end the best approximation of the ideal type. The socialists hesitatingly followed in the footsteps of their confessional brethren, but could never bring themselves to develop the whole array of institutions that was needed to bring a real pillar to life.[14] This applied even more to the liberals, who for a long time showed a distinctive disdain – though in the end they erected a number of more weakly demarcated organisations. The Netherlands showed traces of a *Kulturkampf* in the late nineteenth century, but after a while settlements were created that mingled efforts at 'cultural apartheid' with voluntary organisation aimed at 'sovereignty in one's own circle' as the orthodox Protestants labelled it. The Catholics tapped a longer standing tradition as they spoke of the 'principle of subsidiarity', a concept that recently made a rebirth in the context of European integration.

As the pillars became the mainstays of the Dutch state, they incorporated a traditional attribute of Dutch politics: a keen eye for workable compromise after a prolonged public stand on principles. As the era of mass politics dawned, the politicians' role of combining principled stands with flexible policy making was facilitated by the modest involvement of the average citizen in politics. The Dutch electorate has been characterised as 'aloof' and 'passive'. It implies that citizens have their primary interest elsewhere and become politically mobilised only on rare occasions and for short periods. Through the emergence of the pillars, the formation of the modern state apparatus was significantly shaped by an intricate web of relations with intermediate structures closing the divide between state and non-state spheres. This process was reinforced by the inter-war depression period and the war, which triggered corporatist mechanisms of cooperation between employers associations, trades unions and state. This process set the terms for post-war economic policy and social peace and prosperity.[15]

Belgium

The Belgian state was formed from the southern parts of the imperial (now Austrian) Habsburg possessions in the Low Countries. After the Napoleonic wars, the victorious powers had initially merged the Low Countries into a single buffer state, but in the 1830s the southern part of the new kingdom broke away. Even before the international settlement of the question in 1839, the Belgian constitution of 1831 created a 'unitary and decentralised' state, with a strong central government, but with considerable competencies and autonomy for the existing 2,500 communes and nine historical provinces. It was widely regarded as one of the most liberal constitutions of Europe and its character remained fundamentally unchanged until 1970. A linguistic border was present: the population in the southern part of the country (40 per cent), which industrialised relatively early, spoke French and Walloon dialects, while the northern population spoke Dutch dialects. But many French-speakers lived in the cities of the north where they formed the elite.

Until the 1960s, Belgian political life was dominated by a religious and a socio-economic cleavage. These two cleavages produced three political families: the liberals, the Catholics and the socialists. During the nineteenth century the most important division concerned religion and focused on state–church relations. Following a period of strong economic growth, the liberals came to power during the 1840s, but their attempts to reduce the influence of the Church in education provoked a reaction on the part of conservative Catholics. Although a network of state schools was created, Catholic influence was strong enough to limit its extension. The Catholics gained political power in the 1870s and 1880s and have since remained the central political formation. A second cleavage became politically activated when the socialists entered the political arena, following the introduction of universal male suffrage. Starting before 1900, the socialists established a broad array of cooperatives, unions, and societies – as did the other two political families. For every type of organisation (hospitals, sports clubs, universities, insurance companies, and so forth) Catholic, socialist and liberal varieties came into existence. The state itself also encouraged the formation of pillars by the arrangement of subsidised service-provision.

When he was developing his theory, Lijphart considered Belgium (together with the Netherlands) to be a perfect example of the consociational model of decision making in terms of the breadth of its coalitions, and minority vetoes.[16] The continuous search for political compromise, however, ensures that public involvement (in the form of elections or in other ways) hardly predicts the direction of policies.[17] Important decision making, such as the formation of new coalitions following elections, is done behind a veil of secrecy. Top level negotiations have often been located in old and secluded castles and may involve up to 100 days of talks. The result of this consensus-seeking is usually a complex package deal, which the rank and file of the parties and the grassroots support has to accept in full or reject completely. Belgian politicians are at the same time involved with their electorate as intermediaries with the civil service (more so than their Dutch colleagues). This creates clientelistic networks but at the same time prevents an unbridgeable distance between political decision making and the electorate. Suspicion of politicians is substantial and the Belgian electorate generally remains passive.

Over time, the traditional cleavages became intermingled with linguistic strife. Belgium had always been French in its symbols, and in the social dominance of the French language in social life. Initially, the political system did not facilitate the entrance of the language issue into the political arena. Power was in the hands of only a few French-speaking people who at the same time dominated political and economic life. Moreover, the concept of Flanders, and of the Flemish as an ethno-national community, had hardly developed by then, let alone any concept of a Walloon or Francophone community. After the introduction of universal adult male suffrage in 1893, the Flemish representatives within each political family slowly improved their status. Consequently some laws were passed that aimed at the equal status of both languages on the national territory as a whole. The growing importance of the Flemish voter and the shift of economic investment patterns towards the Flemish part of the country worried some Francophone leaders, leading to occasional defensive responses which usually stressed Belgian unity on the basis of the French language. During the 1930s, unilingualism in the two regions of Belgium, instead of bilingualism in the whole of Belgium, emerged as the preferable arrangement in both linguistic groups. For the Flemish, unilingualism enabled the protection of the Dutch-speaking character of the northern part of the country. To the French-speakers learning Dutch was unacceptable, and French-speakers in Wallonia were certainly willing to sacrifice the French-speakers in the Flemish cities to protect the French-language character of the rest of Belgium.

MODERN CHALLENGES

The Netherlands

As in many other countries of the western world, the 1960s were a period of transition in the Netherlands. Changes in political culture were in many respects more profound than those triggered by the painful Second World War experience. The pillarised state–society combination had blossomed to such an extent that its institutions had passed the point of perfection. The organisers of the services in the different spheres of life (education, health care, housing, leisure) became more and more professionalised, losing contact with their ideological brethren in other spheres, and increasingly tuned to their professional colleagues of other persuasions in the same sector. In the long run, the integrated pillars dissolved making way for sectoral concentrations of interrelated organisations that teamed up with specific government departments and services in municipal administrations. Collectively defending their turf, they continued to quarrel over internal allocation rules; but these struggles increasingly became negotiations between experts devoid of strong links to popular movements. In education, organisational professionals have long referred to themselves as the 'pedagogical province', slipping in a classic Dutch territorial metaphor for one expression of strong functional segmentation.

At the same time, further modernisation had spread the disenchantment of the world that accompanies secularisation. This deeply affected the political ideologies of Christian Democrats and socialists. Despite a last upsurge of ideological posturing by the socialists and soul-searching debates in the inner circles of orthodox Protestants and Catholics (who finally merged into a single Christian Democratic party during the 1970s), political culture among both the elites and the wider public tended to become deprived of overarching belief systems. A new party launched in 1966 – the Democaten'66 (later commonly known as D66) – stepped into the tradition of radical liberalism that had been without a political home for a while. It captured part of the middle-class post-materialist green vote. Its political fate has been highly volatile over the years, but its continuing existence (in the mid-1990s, it is the fourth largest party) indicates an important feature of the current phase of Dutch politics. The other development is the spectacular growth of the more traditional liberal party – the People's Party for Freedom and Democracy (VVD) since the 1960s. Taken together, the two wings of liberalism now capture the largest share of the votes for the three major political families (liberalism, Christian Democracy, socialism). On the other hand, the 1994 elections left the Christian Democrats in opposition for the first time in three-quarters of a century.[18]

This process was accompanied by less self-evident links between decision-making elite groups and 'their' parts of the population at large. But the strong sectors and their multitude of organisations, and the entrenched territorial administrations of municipalities and provinces, make for an intricate web of administrative relations where decisions are not quickly or easily taken. The remaining national predilection with consensual relations and proportionality now make for even more long-drawn-out policy processes. Round tables are the order of the day; meetings continue into further meetings. When finally all the 'noses point in the same direction', action can be taken. On the whole, deals that have been made are honoured. The chances of further encounters are simply too large given the smallness of the country. As policies develop issue by issue in an apparently random way, the technique of forging compromise and agreement becomes the craft of politics. The public at large, never very much enamoured by the spectacle politicians provide, is hardly involved in day-to-day politics. The legitimacy of the polity remains high, but it does not imply approval for specific politicians or policies. It is the structure of government that is accepted, especially the provision of services.

On various occasions during the last few years, politicians and administrators have become so deeply involved in their mutual relations in order to produce sufficient 'carrying capacity' for a shared decision, that they apparently lost their feel for popular sentiment. Severe beatings in the polls have been the fate of municipal socialist aldermen who were restructuring their inner cities to create an inviting environment for international companies with apparent neglect of the daily concerns of their traditional electoral support. Local referenda in the two big cities (Amsterdam and Rotterdam) recently dealt a deadly blow to the plans for metro-government in which their politicians had invested a major part of their ambitions for five years.

After the demise of pillarised society, the Netherlands had to deal with some major challenges. The increasing costs of the welfare state could no longer be squared with the levelling off of economic growth, economic restructuring aggravated labour market problems and the country was faced with a sizeable population of new immigrants. After the usual waverings and hesitations deals were struck in 1982–3. The corporate mechanism between central employers, trades unions and government again proved viable after severe signs of erosion. The cabinet started to govern with 'No nonsense' as a slogan and the worst problems were solved. After an initial outcry of some organised interests, public reaction was remarkably unruffled. Since that time, there has been repeated comment that corporatism is on the retreat, but it is by no means certain that this is the case. Although spectacular deals are no longer struck, there are continuous efforts by employers' associations, trades unions and government to at least co-arrange their public stands on major issues of social and economic policy. As everywhere else, it is increasingly difficult for each of the different partners to act as unified actors because central ideologically driven aims have become less salient.

Immigrants from the colonies and guest workers invited in the 1960s, together with their families and descendants, have added a new element to the Dutch population. Obviously a lot of now autochtonous Dutch have been immigrants in the longer term, but the difference between autochthonous Dutch and some of the others is nevertheless marked in a number of ways. Initially, the official reception pattern of these new immigrants was very much derived from the experience of pillarised society and the welfare state. Every group got its own state-inspired (and subsidised) apparatus, a professional elite of intermediaries between state and Dutch society, on the one hand, and the new group on the other, was created. In the long run, the rules of pillarised society even facilitated the emergence of fully subsidised schools on the basis, for example, of Islam – though with the vital requirement that they should comply with the general curricular rules and the qualification requirements of the teachers.

Politically, most efforts to organise separate immigrant parties floundered after they had been given the right to vote in local elections (the Dutch state again following the rule of broad access and proportionality). Their preferences have on the whole been with the major Dutch parties, particularly the Social Democrats. Intermarriage rates with the Dutch population are up and demographic behaviour is adjusting to Dutch patterns. However, there are still serious problems with school careers and work. And a radical right reaction has emerged since the early 1980s, though it is divided between several parties. The most notable party in recent elections has been the Centre Democrats (CD), which in 1994 won over 10 per cent of the vote in Rotterdam and 7.9 per cent in Amsterdam. Support is concentrated in the poorly endowed neighbourhoods of big cities, and among young unreligious poorly educated males.[19] They are the co-victims of economic restructuration with the immigrants.

Remnants of pillarised and corporatist society occasionally still show up, although the further modernisation of Dutch society has taken away much of their force. The current stage of Dutch political culture is still deeply imprinted with the tradition of pragmatic, broad compromise after principled stands. In the United Provinces such compromises were struck between the members of narrow elite groups in different parts of the country. In the current period the number of interested professional parties in every major decision is very large indeed. Technical argument has replaced debate in small elite circles and public rhetoric aimed at mobilisation and justification. Although the number of participants in decisions has increased, public debate has not. As the public on average is still passive and has directed its attention elsewhere, no great harm is done. On occasion, however, outbursts of civil protest show the considerable gap between administrators, experts and governed.

Foreign policy too tends to attract little public interest. During the seventeenth century the Netherlands was for a short while the pivot of the emerging European state system. Hegemonial powers display a know-how that is uncommon in others. They thus provide the models of modernisation of their era. They also need a flexible attitude to the outside world to manipulate it to their own advantage as their power resources are not sufficient to completely dominate the international system. This ingrained self-assured pragmatism is the kernel of the hegemon's position in the world.[20] After the period of hegemony there is the post-hegemonial trauma that can be quite sustained. The British have suffered from this for a long time and the Americans may well enter a prolonged period of uncertainty. For the Dutch it is all a very long time ago. Traces of the hegemonial attitude may perhaps still be grasped from a willingness to pose as a front-runner for just causes in the international world, but the old pragmatism surrounding such postures frequently dictates early retreats. When the going gets tough the resources for sustained action are lacking. Wavering between heroic inclinations and fear of the consequences results.[21]

In an open country like the Netherlands, external links have always significantly contributed to the political culture. As the time of a preserved field for high politics and diplomacy has now largely passed, this is more than ever the case. The colonial empire has provided opportunities for many to become acquainted with very different cultural environments. Whatever cruel exploitation and racist outlooks may have resulted, the colonial experience also opened windows. The earlier trickle of people back and forth between colonies and motherland resulted in significant migration flows at the time of decolonisation. In the late 1940s and 1950s a large group of Dutch and of Dutch citizens of mixed Dutch–Indonesian ancestry were repatriated, plus a smaller group of Moluccans who had served in the colonial army. This last group remained committed to an independent state on the Moluccan islands, now part of Indonesia. They hardly adjusted to their new situation, and some spectacular terrorist acts on Dutch soil followed in the 1970s. Surinamese independence in 1975 induced a significant part of the population of that colony to emigrate to the Netherlands.

After its hegemonial period, the Netherlands for a long time refrained from active involvement in international affairs. Around 1900 the passive neutral stance of a small country was increasingly replaced by international involvements within a neutral framework. The Hague hosted the first international Peace Conferences and acquired the seat of the International Court of Justice.[22] This period ended with the First World War, in which the Netherlands with some difficulty preserved its neutral status. The German occupation during the Second World War made it absolutely clear to the foreign policy-making elite that neutrality was no longer a viable option. As a result, the Dutch were very active in bringing about the Benelux Union, and the different institutions of international post-war cooperation at all levels (UN and IMF/World Bank, NATO, West European integration). However, the relatively prominent place of Dutch policy makers in those first years has now largely subsided, occasionally giving rise to sour comments on lost status.

Debate about the international status of the country is not widespread in the Netherlands. The earlier military integration in NATO has been accepted without much ado.[23] Only in the years around 1980 did the issue of new intermediate missiles arouse a powerful grass roots protest movement, but even then membership of NATO was hardly questioned. West European integration has progressed without much opposition. Recently the debate about loss of identity and sovereignty if an ever more closely integrated Europe were to come about, has been shallow. Integration is seen as a fact of life, an economic necessity, and attitudes are utterly pragmatic. Maastricht is a city in the south and nothing else. Interest in Europe as shown in turnout in the European Parliament elections is weak and falling, and politicians show little interest in taking a lead on these issues.

Belgium

The linguistic issue resurfaced in Belgium during the second half of the 1950s and the beginning of the 1960s. This resulted partly from the fact that regional differences on important political questions showed up time and again in these years. Examples were the suspicions of differential collaboration during the Second World War, the diverging opinions concerning the king's behaviour in those years, and the shift in the concentration of economic activity towards Flanders. The language problem also gained in prominence because other burning issues were resolved. This applies to the educational question and to the creation of the mechanisms that would enable the emergence of the post-war corporatist welfare state. Compared to the Netherlands, the resolution of the education question came relatively late in Belgium – once more emphasising the more serious tension in church–state relations.

Around 1960 the political system was temporarily freed of ideological strain between the major political formations. In the space that was created, regional differences could be considered more important and regionalist parties blossomed. Subsequent elections showed an increasing support for regionalist parties: up to 44 seats out of 212 in the Chamber of Representatives by 1974.

While the Walloon and the Flemish movements both had their roots in social dissatisfaction, their backgrounds were substantially different. After the war, Flanders remained preponderantly Catholic and Wallonia and Brussels preponderantly non-Catholic. Political support for the Catholics always remained higher in Flanders. The socialists, on the other hand, have their strongest support in Wallonia. The same applies to the communists. The regional stronghold for the liberals is somewhat less clear, although, apart from the 1970s, their showing in Brussels has always been particularly strong. The impact on regionalism was evident. As Claeys puts it:

> in opposition to the Flemish regionalist movement, which essentially [demanded] cultural autonomy in a country where Flemish predominance [was] insured in other spheres by the law of numbers, the Walloon region-alist movement [demanded] economic and political autonomy, the only means to achieve the transformation of Walloon society in a direction which [reflected] the Socialist and lay conception of the majority of its population.[24]

The regionalist parties reflected these basic political profiles: the Flemish Volksunie (People's Union) was generally much more conservative in socio-economic terms than the Mouvement Populaire Wallon (Walloon People's Movement), typically initiated by a former Labour Union activist. Brussels got its own regionalist party (of French-speakers).

The electoral shift towards the regionalist parties of the 1960s signalled to the three traditional parties the political importance of the regionalist sentiment in a situation in which the party system, as in the rest of Europe, had started to 'defreeze'. It implied that the pillars were tottering due to the diminished loyalty of significant numbers of traditional supporters. Initially, the main parties attempted to arrive at a compromise through classical means of pacification, ranging from putting the issue in cold storage, to introducing some legislation and negotiating agreements between senior leaders. During the negotiations the new regional parties acted as extremist flanks (so-called whipping parties) for the traditional parties. Fixation of the language border in 1962–3 and strengthening of the language regulations were insufficient to placate the regionalist sentiment, however. Ultimately a systemic regionalisation along both economic and cultural lines resulted.

The reforms created cultural communities which could wield authority in the fields of personal and cultural affairs and economic regions which were to have authority in economics and infrastructure.[25] However, the two kinds of territories over which these new institutions had power did not coincide.

Brussels, which is a mainly French-speaking city surrounded by Flemish territory, is the main problem. The Flemish are unwilling to accept that Brussels becomes part of the French-language territory and they want to restrict its size (suburbanisation gives it an 'oil-stain'-like appearance, as they point out). The French-speakers are unwilling to have Brussels incorporated into Flanders, and they do not like to have individual choice (such as the change of language or the change of address through suburbanisation) restricted by state laws. Unwilling to relinquish their claims, the Flemish have made Brussels their regional capital, while the French-language community includes both the French-speakers in the Brussels area and in Wallonia.

Given the long history of conflict and cooperation between the main pillars, it is not surprising that it took until the end of the 1980s before education was finally transferred to the cultural communities. The total budget allotted to the communities and regions increased after 1988–9 to 32 per cent of the total state budget; they then employed 40 per cent of the civil service.[26] Ultimately, and almost inevitably, the emerging federal structure was officially recognised in the constitution by a law passed in parliament during 1993. The position of Brussels region as a separate entity with all necessary guarantees was finally secured.

The traditional parties have now regained most of their ground. From 1974 onwards, the electoral importance of the regional parties has steadily declined from 44 seats in parliament to 13 in 1991. The overall trend, therefore, seems to point at a decline of ethno-national sentiment among the Belgian electorate, with Belgium as the main focus of identity. Recent polls indicate a large majority of Belgians (60–80 per cent) who refer to Belgium as their 'motherland' with only small numbers mentioning either Flanders or Wallonia first, but contrary evidence has also been presented.[27] A breakaway regional party in Flanders has made some inroads during the last years. This Vlaams Blok is the manifestation of right-wing sentiment. The thrust of its programme and the orientation of its following are far more geared to anti-immigrant attitudes than to the further elaboration of Flemish separatism.[28]

However, if regionalisation has been accepted by the traditional parties to maintain their support, this has been at the cost of their disappearance as state-wide units. Under regionalist pressure, the traditional parties have all split up: first, in 1968–9 the Catholics; in the years that followed, the Liberals; and, by 1980, also the Socialists. In 1984, even the Communist Party had broken up. Differences in support for the pillars between the various regions resulted in Flemish demands gaining more influence in the Flemish Catholic Party and Walloon demands being incorporated in the French-language Socialist Party. In this way the whole political spectrum became reorganised along linguistic–regional lines.[29]

The impact of this development on the political culture of Belgium has been strong. The combination of regional strongholds for the pillars with linguistic interests in a regionalised Belgium proved a potent mixture, in which almost every issue could turn into a point of linguistic conflict. More issues were brought up and more issues took on a regionalist flavour. Moreover, the traditional parties ceased to be 'national parties', that is, parties which have a considerable electorate on both sides of the linguistic border. This was different from other cleavages. It prevented the Belgian population from showing their views on the linguistic conflict. Although they can still choose between Catholic and Liberal Party viewpoints, and even between more or less regionalist parties, they generally cannot choose between the Flemish and Walloon point of view. Pacification of conflicting ethno-national views could no longer be achieved within the parties. This is crucial in the Belgian context, because of the importance of the political parties. The Belgian polity has often been called a 'particratie'.

In sum, Belgium has often been considered to be a case in which consociationalism is tested as a solution for ethno-national conflict. There was nothing automatic in this process. As noted by McRae in the beginning of the 1970s,

> [t]here is . . . a notable difference in tone between religious-ideological argument and linguistic argument in Belgium. Religious-ideological debate may be sharp, even hostile, but the differences are long established, understood, accepted, and tolerated, if not always treated with respect. Linguistic differences are bitter, intolerant, and reveal little reciprocal understanding.[30]

The territorial nature of the solution, however, differs fundamentally from traditional consociational methods, as practised for instance in the Netherlands. Indeed, the continuing dynamics of regional devolution within this context of consociational decision making are, to a large extent, contained in the process itself.[31] Every crisis is solved by further devolution.

Until recently, Brussels suffered from the prolonged ambiguity of its position. From a numerical point of view Brussels was not very interesting to the two main players in the game, the socialists and the Catholics, as neither had their electoral base in that region. Even after being upgraded to a region, Brussels' position is hardly enviable as its fiscal base is not sufficient to its tasks as capital of Belgium and of Europe, and the compensation it receives remains too small. Its fiscal base is further eroded by the departure of wealthier inhabitants. At the same time, the city has strongly internationalised at both sides of the income scale. Eurocrats and former labour migrants, occasionally from the same countries, are concentrated there. But Brussels remains one of the unifying elements in the Belgian polity. In Belgian terms the city is largely a French element enmeshed in Flanders. This diminishes Flemish incentives to pursue all-out independence.

A second unifying element, the monarchy, received a blow following the death of King Boudewijn (Baudouin) in 1993. From 1951 onwards Boudewijn had built up a tremendous amount of knowledge regarding the

Belgian political scene and also had gained substantial popularity with the population. Particularly after elections, when coalitions had to be constructed, he supposedly wielded considerable influence behind the scenes, although the precise extent of his influence remains unclear. Since it was based on experience and respect and not so much on constitutional powers (which are limited), the new king, Albert II, has to rebuild this influence from the start.

A third unifying element is the international orientation of Belgium, which is hard to over-emphasise. Belgium's capital is at the same time the effective 'Capital of Europe', and a large part of the European civil service is found in Brussels. Furthermore, its economy is amongst the most open in the international system and it benefits greatly from the common market. Generally, unity is considered necessary in this context. It is often questioned whether a divided Belgium could compete as effectively on the international markets and whether the benefits it gains from its political position as home to the effective European capital might be lost if disunity would proceed too far. Moreover, the country often sees itself as an example for the rest of Europe, in particular when it comes to the organisation of political and cultural diversity within one political system. Furthermore, Belgium hosts NATO and is a reliable member of this alliance. The country has of course many reasons to be oriented towards international cooperation in security matters, as its territory has traditionally been an arena for international violent conflict by the Great Powers, such as during the Napoleonic wars, the First World War and the Second World War.

However, with the sub-state units of Belgium gaining increasing powers to organise even the international affairs in their fields of competence, it remains to be seen to what extent the central Belgian institutions can control the external relations of the state. The long-standing political culture in Belgium has enabled the devolution to the sub-state units to proceed peacefully, but the territorial implementation of the consociational principle has nonetheless set in motion a process of differentiation between the two main parts of Belgium which has been hard to control. In the end, the raison d'être of the Belgian state may disappear in the clouds of devolution. Perhaps even more important, however, is the fact that the habit of prolonged and secret negotiations leading to complex and sophisticated packages of detailed and carefully balanced solutions may have prevented a violent outbreak of the linguistic conflict, but at the same time may have alienated the Belgian citizens from their politicians. The Belgian electorate has been called apathetic.

CONTINUITIES AND CHANGE

Conditioned by their modest size and geographical situation between three traditional European great powers, the Netherlands and Belgium have developed open political cultures that have in modern times been imprinted by comparable systems of polarisation and consociational decision making and extensive corporate welfare states. The Dutch tend perhaps slightly more to the Protestant nations of Northwestern Europe, the Belgians are perhaps a bit more at ease with the Catholic nations of Southern Europe, but the political cultures of the Low Countries are broadly similar on the European canvas.

Some subtle differences remain. The Dutch state is a bit larger, older, and it has a past as a great power. Politically, the Dutch encounter the outside world with a bit more pretence. The Belgians, though, have become the major hosts of the European institutions and they seem in their more self-effacing way at least as able to pursue their interests.

In the 1960s both polities had to accommodate appreciable change. The ensuing political transitions went in different directions. In the Dutch case the pillars for the most part broke down, though some parts remain. A form of pragmatic liberalism, which was the original mould in which the pillars were raised, again gained the upper hand in the political culture. In the Belgian case, the pillars themselves were finally restructured along regional lines. Major parts of the political culture remained intact, but regionalisation may bear the seeds of the ultimate destruction of the Belgian state. In both cases there seems to be a considerable gap between the world of politics and the population at large in terms of the involvement in policy making. The average voter has significant reservations about the world of politics in both countries. The bridging mechanism in the Dutch case is more clearly the correct provision of services by a technocratic bureaucracy, and in the Belgian case the clientelistic networks that politicians maintain. The nature of popular reluctance to be involved in politics is also different. Compared with the European average the Dutch proclaim a relatively high interest in politics, but they simultaneously stay aloof if they can (for example, party membership is low). Belgians on the whole express a low interest in politics. In 1990 the *Eurobarometer* survey found that 13 per cent of Dutch people expressed a 'great deal' of interest in politics compared to 6 per cent of Belgians (Community average 11 per cent); and only 11 per cent of Dutch people expressed no interest in politics compared to 31 per cent of Belgians (Community average 22 per cent).[32]

European cooperation is now the self-evident background of the existence of both polities. Possible further inroads in their autonomy that might jeopardise their continued survival in roughly their present form do not arouse anxiety and consequently do not figure prominently on Dutch or Belgian political agendas. This in itself is an interesting aspect of these political cultures. It does not imply that the Dutch and Belgian populations are particularly enamoured with the prospect of further European unification. Particularly in the 1990s they express less support for European unification than the population of the original six member states as a whole.[33]

The question of how to cope with considerable numbers of recent immigrants, however, troubles many: policy makers, some of those who meet with immigrants in their daily lives and perceive that they compete under conditions of scarcity in labour and housing markets, and also some who dislike cultural differences. Xenophobic attitudes are generally related to the size of recent immigration. With comparable proportions of immigrants, more Belgians than Dutch showed such attitudes in 1994 according to the *Eurobarometer* survey. Whereas 22 per cent of Belgians were high on the xenophobia index and 41 per cent low, in the Netherlands the scores were 11 and 51 per cent respectively (xenophobes in these polls are people who state that there are too many non-EC foreigners in their country and that they find people from other nationalities or race disturbing).[34] Both countries have anti-immigrant parties represented in parliament, the Belgian one the larger and the better organised. Whilst the chances that this reaction will decisively remould the political cultures in either Belgium or the Netherlands remain remote, the question of how these cultures will further evolve as a result of this immigrant experience is another matter.

NOTES

1 This chapter concentrates on the political cultures of the two larger countries, the Netherlands and Belgium. An overview of Luxembourg's political history can be found in J. Newcomer, *The Grand Duchy of Luxembourg. The Evolution of Nationhood 963 AD to 1983*, Lanham, University Press of America, 1984.

2 For example, A. Lijphart, 'Introduction: The Belgian Example of Cultural Coexistence in Comparative Perspective' in A. Lijphart (ed.), *Conflict and Coexistence in Belgium: The Dynamics of a Culturally Divided Society*, Berkeley, Institute of International Studies, University of California, 1981.

3 For example, A. Lijphart, *The Politics of Accommodation*, Berkeley, University of California Press, 1975. Lijphart developed an alternative model for a stable, democratic polity to the predominant model in the Anglo-American literature of the 1960s. This model of consociational democracy was originally constructed to explain the Dutch experience, then generalised for a number of smaller European political systems (notably Austria, Switzerland, the Netherlands and Belgium) and then used as a possible prescription for difficult cases elsewhere in the world (e.g. Lebanon, South Africa, Northern Ireland).

4 M. A. Roessingh, *A State of Tension: Ethnonationalism and Political Systems in Europe*, Amsterdam, University of Amsterdam Press, 1996.

5 On the idea of pillars/consociational democracy see P. H. Claeys, 'Political Pluralism and Linguistic Cleavage: The Belgian Case' in S. Ehrlich and G. Wootton (eds), *The Three Faces of Pluralism: Political, Ethnic, and Religious*, Farnborough, Gower, 1980; L. Huyse, 'Political Conflict in Bicultural Belgium' in Lijphart, *op. cit.*, 1981; Lijphart, *op. cit.*, 1975; A. Lijphart, *Democracy in Plural Societies: A Comparative Exploration*, New Haven, Yale University Press, 1977; K. D. McRae, 'Introduction' in K. D. McRae (ed.), *Consociational Democracy: Political Accommodation in Segmented Societies*, Toronto, McClelland and Stewart Limited, 1974; H. Post, *Pillarization: An Analysis of Dutch and Belgian Society*, Aldershot, Gower, 1989.

6 For political and socio-economic overviews see: E. H. Bax, *Modernization and Cleavage in Dutch Society. A Study of Longterm Economic and Social Change*, Groningen, Universiteitsdrukkerij, 1988; P. Berckx, *150 Jaar Institutionele Hervormingen in België; door ruime federale macht naar een nieuwe Belgische*

48   *Herman van der Wusten and Martijn Roessingh*

eendracht, Antwerp, Kluwer Rechtswetenschappen, 1990; L. Huyse, *Passiviteit, Pacificatie en Verzuiling in de Belgische Politiek,* Antwerp, Standaard, 1970; H. Knippenberg and B. de Pater, *De eenwording van Nederland: schaalvergroting en integratie sinds 1800,* Nijmegen, Sun, 1988; H. Knippenberg and W. van der Ham, *Een bron van aanhoudende zorg; 75 jaar Ministerie van Onderwijs en Wetenschappen,* Assen, Van Gorcum, 1993; E. H. Kossmann, *De Lage Landen 1780–1980: twee eeuwen Nederland en België,* Amsterdam, Elsevier, 1986; E. H. Kossmann, *The Low Countries 1780–1940,* Oxford, Clarendon, 1978; J. van Miert, *Wars van clubgeest en partijzucht: liberalen, natie en verzuiling, Tiel en Winschoten 1850–1920,* Amsterdam, Amsterdam University Press, 1994.

 7 F. Braudel, *La Méditerranée et le monde méditerranéen à l'époque de Philippe II,* Paris, Colin, 1949.
 8 On the impact of religion see H. Knippenberg, *De religieuze kaart van Nederland. Omvang en geografische spreiding van de godsdienstige gezindten vanaf de Reformatie tot heden,* Assen, Van Gorcum, 1992; J. M. G. Thurlings, *De wankele zuil: Nederlandse Katholieken tussen assimilatie en pluralisme,* Deventer, Van Loghum Slaterus, 1978.
 9 On the impact of language see V. Lorwin, 'Belgium: Religion, Class, and Language in National Politics' in R. Dahl (ed.), *Political Opposition in Western Democracies,* New Haven, Yale University Press, 1966, pp. 147–87; K. D. McRae, *Conflict and Compromise in Multilingual Societies: Belgium,* Waterloo, Ontario, Wilfried Laurier University Press, 1986.
10 E. H. Kossmann, *The Low Countries,* Oxford, Clarendon, 1978, offers the most extensive modern historical work on the Dutch and Belgian polities in a longer time frame.
11 N. C. F. van Sas, 'Fin-de-siècle als nieuw begin. Nationalisme in Nederland rond 1900' in *Bijdragen en Mededelingen betreffende de Geschiedenis der Nederlanden,* 1991, 106.
12 E. J. Hobsbawm and T. Ranger (eds), *The Invention of Tradition,* Cambridge, Cambridge University Press, 1983.
13 M. Kuitenbrouwer, *Nederland en de opkomst vam het moderne imperialisme. Koloniën en buitenlandse politiek,* Amsterdam, De Bataafsche Leeuw, 1985.
14 P. de Rooy, 'Begeerten en ideelen' in P. de Rooy, *De rode droom. Een eeuw sociaal-democratic in Nederland,* Nijmegen, Sun, 1995, pp. 8–91.
15 See J. M. M. van Amersfoort and H. van der Wusten, 'De cultuurgeografie van Nederland na 1945' in B. de Peter, G. A. Hoekveld and J. A. van Ginkel (eds), *Nederland in delen. Een regionale geografie I,* Houten, De Haan/Unieboek, 1989, pp. 83–104.
16 See Notes 2, 3 and 5.
17 W. Dewachter, *Besluitvorming in Politiek België,* Leuven/Amersfoort, Acco, 1992.
18 On these elections see V. Mamadouh, N. Passchier and H. van der Wusten, 'Herzelfde maar toch verschillend. De verkiezingskaart van Nederland na de aardverschuiving', in G. Voerman (ed.), *Jaarboek Documentatiecentrum Nederlandse politieke partijen 1995,* Groningen, Universiteitsdrukkerij, 1996, pp. 149–67.
19 F. J. Buijs and J. van Donselaar, *Extreem-rechts: aanhang, geweld en onderzoek,* Leiden, LISWO, 1994; J. van Donselaar, 'Post-war Fascism in the Netherlands', *Crime, Law and Social Change,* 1993, 19.
20 This is one of the views expressed and developed in Peter Taylor's new book on the functioning of the three hegemonial powers, the United Provinces, the UK and the US, in the world system of the last centuries. P. J. Taylor, *The Way the Modern World Works. World Hegemony to World Impasse,* Chichester, Wiley, 1996.

21 J. J. C. Voorhoeve, *Peace, Profits and Principles: A Study of Dutch Foreign Policy*, The Hague, Nijhoff, 1979.
22 A. Eyffinger, *The Peace Palace-Residence for Justice – Domicile of Learning*, The Hague, Carnegie Foundation, 1988.
23 A. van Staden, *Een trouwe bondgenoot: Nederland en het Atlantisch bondgenootschap 1960–1971*, Baarn, In den Toren, 1974.
24 Claeys, *op. cit.*, p. 175.
25 The restructuring of the Belgian state is a very complicated process. Good overviews and particular insights are in Berckx, *op. cit.*; M. Covell, 'Belgium: The Variability of Ethnic Relations' in J. McGarry and B. O'Leary (eds), *The Politics of Ethnic Conflict Regulation*, London, Routledge, 1993; R. Senelle, 'Constitutional Reform in Belgium: From Unitarism Towards Federalism' in M. Forsyth (ed.), *Federalism and Nationalism*, Leicester, Leicester University Press, 1989; E. Witte, 'Belgian Federalism: Towards Complexity and Asymmetry', *West European Politics*, 1992, 15. See also S. Newman, 'Losing the Electoral Battle and Winning Policy Wars: Ethnoregional Conflict in Belgium', *Nationalism and Ethnic Politics*, 1995, 4.
26 W. F. J. Dewachter, *De Dualistische Identiteit van de Belgische Maatschappij*, Amsterdam, Koninklijke Akademie van Wetenschappen, Noord-Hollandsche, 1992, p. 18; *Res Publica: tijdschrift voor politicologie*, 1993, pp. 570–2.
27 A. Coppé, *Polemiek rond België*, Leuven/Amersfoort, Acco, 1992, pp. 98–9; Dewachter, *De Dualistische Identiteit*, p. 29.
28 C. Mudde, 'One Against All, All Against One! A Portrait of the Vlaams Blok', *Patterns of Prejudice*, 1995, 29; M. Swyngedouw, 'The Extreme Right in Belgium: The Breakthrough of the Extreme Right in Flanders', *Regional Politics and Policy*, 1992, 2.
29 W. F. J. Dewachter, 'Changes in a Particratie: The Belgian Party System from 1944 to 1986' in H. Daalder (ed.), *Party Systems in Denmark, Austria, Switzerland, the Netherlands, and Belgium*, London, Pinter Publishers, 1987.
30 McRae, *Consociational Democracy*, pp. 20–1.
31 Roessingh, *op. cit.*
32 *Eurobarometer, Trend variables 1974–1993*, May 1994, pp. 161–4.
33 *Eurobarometer*, *op. cit.*, pp. 50–70.
34 Data from *Eurobarometers*; A. Melich, 'Comparative European Trend Survey Data on Racism and Xenophobia', paper presented at ECPR Bordeaux workshop, 1995.

4 Britain

Roger Eatwell

INTRODUCTION

While flirting during the 1990s with 'Britishness' as a substitute for new political ideas, John Major became fond of proclaiming that his nation could trace its monarchy back over 1,000 years, while its Parliament dates back over 700 years. His central vision of contemporary Britain was inspired by people watching the sun set over the village cricket ground, before retiring to the pub for warm beer and amicable conversation between teams and locals. These are revealing images, for they highlight both the widespread belief that the nation has deep roots and the way in which it is typically constructed in essentially male, 'green and pleasant land', southern English terms – ignoring notably different Irish, Welsh and Scottish traditions, let alone the myriad sub-cultures which have made up Britain.[1] It also reveals the association of Englishness with the acceptance of the rules of the game and small scale social pastimes, governed by long tradition rather than passion or rationality: what sane person could plan a game which in its ultimate form lasts for five days, often without a conclusive result (unless England is playing)?

These images have parallels in many older academic studies, including the pioneering opinion poll work on political culture carried out by Almond and Verba at the turn of the 1960s.[2] This saw Britain as a model of stable democracy, a 'civic culture' which derived its strength from social values rather than a clearly codified constitution. Crucial to Britain's strength was a high level of consensus, and the tendency of individuals to belong to overlapping social groups. Another alleged key feature was a balance between a willingness to participate and deference towards authority. Together, these traits worked to prevent the emergence of unbargainable demands and helped to ensure compliance by groups which did not share power. If Almond and Verba's work was greeted by little immediate academic response within Britain, this was mainly because it seemed to do little more than provide quantitative (and sometimes jargonated) evidence to support existing mainstream beliefs.[3]

Yet there were many problems with this and similar work, as later critics were only too keen to point out – including serious problems with the general behaviourist approach and vague definitions of key concepts. However, in the discussion which follows the argument will concentrate more on three substantive questions. The first concerns what factors helped to make national identity, a topic largely ignored in works on political culture. The second concerns the accuracy of the classic view of British political culture which was developed during the 1950s and early 1960s. And the third looks at changes which are necessary to this picture in the light of subsequent developments, changes which have produced a potential for dramatic political change.

THE MAKING OF THE BRITISH NATION

In the past, the predominant view among historians and social scientists has been that English – and especially British – identity was constructed during the post-Enlightenment era. However, recent historiography has tended to push back the date when national identity first began to emerge, although without arriving at a new consensus.[4]

Some historians trace the origins of Englishness to the culture which emerged after the arrival of Anglo-Saxon invaders 1,500 years ago. By 731 AD, the Venerable Bede had completed his *History of the English Church*, a book which helped give legitimacy to Alfred the Great (d. 899), who styled himself the King of England, and more generally to Anglo-Saxon state-building in Wessex. After the Norman conquest (1066), yet further progress was made in creating a consolidated state, extending further north, and increasingly able to raise significant revenue. By the sixteenth century a centralised government had encompassed Wales, and the 1707 and 1800 Acts of Union formally incorporated Scotland and Ireland respectively into the highly centralised 'United Kingdom' – though Scotland retained aspects of a separate state, and resistance to Anglicisation remained strong, especially in the Catholic areas of Ireland.

There was nothing automatic about this process, but several factors can be highlighted. The first, often under-stated, factor concerns the role of the Church which even before the Reformation helped to define Englishness in terms of values, for example civilised codes of war. The rise of Protestantism was especially important, as it was accompanied by a growing sense of the English as the chosen people, and the pursuit of freedom as a specifically English characteristic. Protestantism's rise also coincided with a rapid expansion of the printing presses, which helped disseminate the Word in the vernacular – as well as furthering the use of the English language. War too played its part. A handful of historians have highlighted the constant threat of Viking raids before the Norman conquest as a unifying factor. More commonly, the focus has been on the major wars which were fought against Spain and especially France. The post-Revolutionary wars fought virtually without a break between 1793 and 1815 have been identified as especially important in Linda Colley's highly influential argument that popular British identity developed rapidly during the eighteenth and early nineteenth centuries.[5]

However, in order to fully understand the emergence of national identity and consciousness it is also necessary to look more closely at social and political processes. From an early stage, the English monarch's power was circumscribed in notable ways. The Magna Carta (1215) made it clear that the king was not above the law. The Glorious Revolution led to the Act of Settlement (1688), which established the consent of Parliament as the basic principle of political authority rather than the Divine Right of Kings, more typical of continental sovereignty. England also differed in the sense that it never experienced classic feudalism. Indeed, Alan Macfarlane has argued that the practice of free men peacefully selling labour and land significantly pre-dated the Reformation.[6] The argument highlights important reasons why Britain had the first Industrial Revolution, but it overstates the centrality of commercial values (and glosses over a notably 'ungovernable' side to the English, often stressed by more left-wing historians). Admiration for the lifestyle of the landed aristocracy, including its paternalist values, remained strong, and after the seventeenth century there emerged a cult of the gentleman and the peaceful countryside – traits which helped to forge a link with the emerging bourgeois elite.[7] On the other hand, the aristocracy became aware of the new power of business and its more specifically British roots (much of the aristocracy admired continental manners and style). An osmosis therefore took place around ideas of common national identity,[8] aided by a growth of civil society which brought the groups together. The result – especially in southern England – was a form of 'gentlemanly capitalism', associated with banking more than industry (a development which has frequently been identified in recent years as a primary cause of Britain's failure to sustain a high level of economic growth).[9]

By the early nineteenth century, the main building blocks of Britishness were in place. Ethnicity could not be central in a multinational state – though the English language was a powerful force of cohesion. Rather, there were five main elements. The first was a religious component: Britain was a Protestant Isle, illuminated by true religion. Second, and partly linked to Protestantism, was a belief in the superiority of the British Parliament, symbol of liberty. Third was the demonisation of the Other, namely France, which was symbolic of both Catholicism and autocracy. Increasingly after the French Revolution, this component developed into a fourth pole: namely, the identification of the British with moderate and pragmatic forms of thought – an interesting development as British, especially Scottish, thinkers like Adam Smith had been in the van of the eighteenth-century Enlightenment. In its Conservative–Burkean form, the emphasis was on tradition and organic metaphors; in its Whig–Liberal form, the central theme was more balance and the inevitable movement towards progress. The idea of progress was also central to the final major pole of identity, namely the association of Britishness with trade and prosperity – a myth which had a very real basis, for while the British population more than doubled from 16 to 41 million during the nineteenth century, GNP rose by eleven times.[10]

Two frequently stressed aspects of British identity only developed fully in the late nineteenth century. The first was the cult of the constitutional monarchy. The British dynastic line had changed several times and had strong European links. With the possible exception of George III, the Hanoverian line was not popular. Certainly there seems to have been little real affection for Queen Victoria in her early years: she spoke German to her husband and for a time became virtually a recluse after his premature death. The celebration of monarchy was developed by the Conservative Prime Minister, Benjamin Disraeli, and others after the 1860s with the conscious intent of providing ceremonies and symbols which would help marry the growing working class to the system. The monarchy itself also showed an increasing interest in promoting good works in order to boost its appeal.[11] The celebration of the empire came late, too. In the mid-nineteenth century, many saw colonies as an economic millstone, diverting attention from Britain's central free trade mission. But by the turn of the twentieth century, politicians – especially Liberal Unionists like Jo Chamberlain and others within the Conservative Party – saw social imperialism as a means of attracting the working class. The growth in the provision of education after 1870 was a major facilitating factor, as it opened new channels for propaganda. For decades, school atlases highlighted the great swathes of the world which made up the greatest empire the world has known, while history lessons taught of the virtues of British rule.[12] The latter was not presented simply in terms of the economic benefits it would bring Britain. There was a more moral aspect: the myth of the White Man's Burden to civilise 'heathen' peoples and the virtues of Pax Britannica. Whilst the record of British imperialism is unquestionably mixed, in general there was a fair degree of reality behind the myth[13] – though empire undoubtedly encouraged a form of racism in domestic attitudes.

The late nineteenth century, therefore, offers fertile ground for the study of what Hobsbawm and Ranger have called the 'invention of tradition', but it is important to stress a point made by Anthony Smith – namely the existing texture of national myths.[14] English identity was not something plucked from the air, or which had simply existed among elites for centuries. The popular use of Boadicea can be traced at least as far back as the Armada (it had a Welsh variant too). Robin Hood has even older roots. So too has the cult of King Arthur. These myths clearly point to the deep-rooted tendency to identify Englishness/Britishness with liberty and high principle on the one hand, and threats from outside on the other. It is difficult to measure the extent of their social penetration, but there are good grounds for thinking that they helped shape popular consciousness well before 1800.

One of the most important questions concerning the development of nineteenth-century political culture is: why did radical socialism and mass popular movements fail to become major forces? One common explanation holds that radicalism, like the Chartist movement, was 'stifled by middle class solidarity';[15] but this type of argument overstates middle-class hegemony. Another left critique claims that the main phase of working-class radicalism came to Britain before Marxism could give it a body of doctrine which could help it develop consciousness: this gave time for elites to offer reforms which helped defuse extremism.[16] This line offers more fertile insights, underlining the generally shrewd nature of modern British political leaders – though at times, Disraeli being a good example, they were motivated by opportunism rather than grand principle. However, the approach does not fully bring out crucial macro and meso influences which helped prevent radical consciousness emerging.

It is important to remember that national identity had largely emerged before the rise of liberal democratic, let alone socialist ideas: it was essentially tied to demobilising rather than mobilising myths. British people were subjects not active citizens. Later, grand ideological visions, especially when linked to violent means, were seen as un-British. Moreover, the Industrial Revolution took place over a relatively long period of time, and did not produce the sudden spurts which often produced dangerous anomie elsewhere. There was unquestionably violence, such as machine breaking, but new forms of civil society emerged which helped tame this – especially religious movements in the industrial areas of the north, or Wales (it has often been said that the British labour movement owed more to Methodism than to Marx).[17] Trade unions too came to play an important part in working-class socialisation after they were legalised in the second half of the nineteenth century. Although a more aggressive form of unskilled unionism was emerging by 1900, the union movement in general was founded on the belief that concessions could be wrung from employers, especially as most sectors of the British economy remained relatively strong. For most unionists, social class was a sense of 'us' and 'them' more than a form of political consciousness, especially an internationalist socialist one which could have meant British workers making financial sacrifices for others.

In the early twentieth century, a further factor helped tie the working class to the nation. This was a growing portrayal of a German economic and military threat (Germany overtook Britain's GNP in the late nineteenth century). This trend reached a peak during the First World War, when the beastly 'Huns' were depicted as authoritarian militarists, capable of the worst bestialities, such as raping nuns and mutilating children.[18] The fact that vast numbers of Britons voluntarily fought in this horrifying war says much for the strength of national consciousness. And the fact that sacrifices were made relatively equally across classes and regions unquestionably furthered a sense of common identity. However, it is important to deconstruct British sentiment in 1914, to view it through individual eyes. There were undoubtedly jingoistic nationalists. But there were others, like socialist miners in South Wales, who fought in the First World War for very different principles – to destroy the German beast. Some may even have seen the war as necessary to preserve economic gains: certainly before the war a kind of national socialism had been emerging in a section of the working class.

War did not mean the death of mainstream socialism: indeed, especially after the Bolshevik Revolution, there were clear signs of new radicalism emerging. In order to maximise national solidarity and further the war effort (for instance, by allowing women into factories), representatives of the trades unions were accorded notable positions of power in a corporatist wartime arrangement, formalising a tendency which was to remain strong in British politics until the 1980s.[19] The development came at an opportune time. The pre-war era had witnessed considerable disorder, including a major threat of war in Ireland, a violent women's suffrage movement and considerable trade union discontent.[20] There was no bourgeois–English hegemony for these people at least. Indeed, the very nature of politics was changing from an essentially religious-based one to a class-based one.[21] In part, this reflected socio-economic change, including the rise of a new group of managers less committed to the old aristocratic-paternalist values, which had helped ease the transition to modern society. But class sentiments were also crystallised by a conscious change of vocabulary among political elites as the vote was extended to the working class, beginning with the Second Reform Act in 1867.

The Labour Party had major advantages in this new form of politics. It had been set up in 1900 by a coalition of unionists and socialists (terms which were far from synonyms). The former provided money and a strong local organisation in most areas: they also provided an ethic of class loyalty which helped the party survive internal schisms. The latter helped give the party an ideology, which focused around a commitment to nationalisation that became embodied in Clause 4 of the party's 1918 Constitution – though the party's leaders, notably Ramsay MacDonald, shrewdly played down radicalism in order to attract Liberal voters. Most Labour Party leaders also mixed the language of class with that of the nation, for around a third of the working class voted Conservative even after the vote had finally been extended to all males over 21 and most women in 1918 (women achieved equality in this sphere in 1928).[22]

The Conservative Party too was a complex mix. In 1914, it had a strong business and laissez-faire wing, which included recent converts from the Liberals. But it had a stronger and older Tory wing, which had its origins in the Anglican church and in the aristocratic values of *noblesse oblige*. During the 1860s and 1870s Disraeli had helped revamp this last sentiment by associating the party with social reform and the fight against a nation divided between rich and poor. But at the turn of the twentieth century the Conservatives had split badly over the issue of whether to use Imperial-preferential tariffs to finance reform. Further divisions stemmed from the fact that a notable wing of the party seemed willing to accept armed rebellion against the British Liberal Government by the Protestants in Ireland who opposed the granting of Home Rule to a united Ireland. The First World War, therefore, was a godsend to the party, helping it to unite behind a new wave of nationalism.[23]

For the Liberals, the war was disastrous. At the turn of the century, a group of Liberals, like David Lloyd George, had begun to adopt more collectivist policies and employ their own language of class to attract a section of the working class. But during the war, Lloyd George's ambition to be Prime Minister had split the party. When he took his followers into an electoral coalition with the Conservatives immediately the fighting ended, the rump Liberals found themselves squeezed between the politics of class and strident nationalism. The British first past the post election system does not favour third parties, unless they can concentrate their vote locally – as Labour could with its deep industrial-union roots. It was therefore a relatively small group of Labour MPs which found themselves the 'Official Opposition' by 1919.[24] Subsequently, many have seen the emergence of a dominant Conservative–Labour two party system as virtually inevitable given changes in the class structure. But whilst it is important not to overstate the 'high politics' side of these developments, there was a vital political side to the shaping of party politics – especially, to adapt Benedict Anderson's much-used term, the competing imagined communities of class and nation employed by the two 'winning' parties.[25]

There was similarly nothing inevitable about the election of Labour's first majority government in 1945. It is true that the 1930s had seen widespread unemployment, and at times in the 1920s class tensions had been sharpened, most notably during the somewhat misleadingly entitled General Strike in 1926. But these were also years of new ribbon house building, and a rapid growth of popular new leisure products like the radio and small cars – especially in southern England, though the country in general was coming out of recession by the late 1930s. It is interesting to note that the first opinion polls were carried out at this time. They show clearly that the Conservative (strictly 'National', as it included a handful of others) Government was set to be re-elected had it not been for the outbreak of war – although, intriguingly, there was a notable strand of opinion which was opposed to the government's appeasement of the fascist dictators, but which lacked a strong political lead.

Crucial in transforming Labour's fortunes at this time was a dramatic change in macro culture. The war undoubtedly strengthened nationalism, with its myths of the Dunkirk spirit and Britain standing alone against fascism before the USSR's and America's entry into the war in 1941. But there was another major side to wartime propaganda, which became ever more important as victory beckoned: namely, the stress on the need to make a new, reformed Britain – a form of propaganda which effectively combined nationalism, idealism and a sense of economic interest. This, and the presence in government of Labour ministers and the forging of ever-greater corporatist structures with the unions, created a sense of legitimacy and effi-cacy that carried the party to its greatest ever election victory.[26]

In 1951 Labour lost office, though in a curious general election which saw it win more votes than the Conservatives. This reflected the popularity of the extensive programme of reforms which it had carried out since 1945, and the full employment which had accompanied it (a trend which brought many women into the labour force on a permanent basis). Predictably, the incoming Conservative administration made few changes to this legacy during its thirteen years of ensuing government. Between 1950 and 1960, GNP grew at a rate of 2.7 per cent per annum, relatively high by historic British standards, and living standards rose notably. Indeed, this era is often characterised by a (mis)quote of Prime Minister Harold Macmillan: 'You've never had it so good'. It was these years which formed the backdrop to the first major social science studies of British political culture.[27]

THE CLASSIC VIEW OF BRITISH POLITICAL CULTURE

It is helpful to follow the analysis of Almond and Verba, and closely related works, as a means of establishing a basic overview of what could be termed the 'classic' view of British political culture during the 1950s and early 1960s. Typically, three aspects were highlighted as underpinning the civic culture.

Homogeneity

British society was seen as remarkably homogenous in a variety of ways. The English language was virtually universal. Britain was relatively urbanised and industrialised; only 3 per cent worked on the land. High taxa-tion and death duties, together with the creation of a welfare state and the achievement of full employment, had removed some of the extremes of wealth and poverty – especially the latter. Transport communications were good and there was an extensive national rather than regionally-based media, both print and broadcast. Indeed, Britain seemed to have a remark-ably 'national' political system, with general elections fought on wide programmatic platforms and the two main parties attracting at least a notable minority of the vote in all areas.[28]

This analysis pointed to important comparative differences. For example, Britain's small and relatively efficient agricultural sector helps explain why the EU's Common Agricultural Policy, from which Britain has benefited little in financial terms, has been a long standing bone of contention. But it also had notable blind spots. The most serious concerned the lack of emphasis on social class, which figured prominently in most studies of voting behaviour, as around 66 per cent of the working class voted Labour and 80 per cent of the middle class supported the Conservatives. Probably the main explanation for this lacuna was the essentially American perspective which underpinned many political culture studies, though there was a streak in British culture too which tended to deny the working class a separate sphere. Many of the 1960s new television programmes such as *Coronation Street*, or films like *A Kind of Loving*, were notable for their pioneering portrayal of ordinary life. The sociological theory of embour-geoisement also diverted attention from working-class values – at least until the mid-1960s, when it became clear that the argument ignored powerful socialisation factors, like membership of trades unions, basic workplace practice, or the fact that most affluent workers still lived in working-class communities.[29]

A second major omission concerned English sub-cultures (for instance the Liberal south-west), and especially Welsh and Scottish cultures – though this was more understandable. It has become fashionable to see Britain as a multinational state, but the Second World War and Labour's reforms had helped cement unity.[30] Moreover, Wales and Scotland were not socio-economically homogenous areas, and in Wales there were notably different linguistic patterns (few spoke Welsh in South Wales, or along the Marches). This had been a factor in helping to prevent a united and powerful separatist movement emerging, though at times poor leadership within the Scottish National Party and Plaid Cymru contributed to their lack of appeal. Nevertheless, there was a feeling of alternative identity in Wales and espe-cially Scotland which more multiculturally attuned studies would have picked up. Among the key factors which helped strengthen this identity in Scotland were clear symbolic differences (like its own patron saint, bank notes, and sports teams) and the fact that union with England left a distinct Scottish church, legal system and educational structure.[31]

Consensus

The second element in the classic view was the stress on consensual political values. Britain had never seen a major communist movement; whilst wartime cooperation with the USSR helped to boost the Communist Party, no party representative sat in the House of Commons after 1950. Fascism fared even worse electorally, failing to win a single seat even in local government. Moreover, by the 1950s, the two mainstream parties pursued remarkably similar policies in many areas. This was the age of 'Butskellism', a term coined from the names of successive Labour and Conservative Chancellors of the Exchequer in 1951 (Hugh Gaitskell and Rab Butler). Butskellism referred to the high level of agreement in three key areas of policy: accep-tance of Keynesian micro and macro economic management techniques to secure full employment (in practice around 2–3 per cent unemployment); support for an extensive programme of nationalisation, including both service and productive industries; and acceptance of a relatively extensive welfare state.[32]

Once again, there were unquestioned strengths in this analysis. Certainly the Conservatives had a long tradition of denying that they had an ideology, and Labour's socialism was characterised by piecemeal pragmatism rather than grand ideological vision. However, behind the consensual façade, there were notable divisions and sub-cultures. The communists may have been weak electorally, but they were strong in some unions, as was the non-communist left. Whilst anti-fascism became a defining part of British identity after 1945, there were recurring signs of animosity towards newly arrived non-white immigrants and a potential for racist politics – although the introduction of a Commonwealth Immigration Act in 1961 defused some of the political pressure. Moreover, Butskellism managed to coexist with an adversarial two party system, which frequently encouraged criticism rather than consensual problem solving.

The politicisation of Britain's first application to join the EEC in 1961 reflects both the dynamics of this process, and the underlying divisions within the main parties. In 1945, most British leaders looked more to the Commonwealth and the USA for economic and political cooperation. Within Labour circles, there were also fears about 'Europe' being dominated by the political right. Whilst some Labour leaders by the turn of the 1960s were increasingly seeing Europe as a means of reducing American influence and modernising the economy, Europe had not become a highly divisive issue within the party – unlike debates over Clause 4 (which committed the party to nationalisation) and a proposal to commit the party to unilateral nuclear disarmament. Within the Conservative Party, on the other hand, there were notable splits over Europe. One group wanted to find a major new post-imperial role in Europe, and to lessen links with America which had proved a fickle ally during the 1956 Suez expedition. But others saw Europe as a threat to national sovereignty, or as a betrayal of kith and kin in the Commonwealth countries with which Britain still traded extensively. Labour's bitter denunciation of the EEC was, therefore, partly designed to heal its own wounds, while giving it a weapon with which to attack the Conservatives. This was a fateful decision in terms of public opinion: previously, there had been a vague sympathy for union. Politicisation, combined with France's veto in 1963, hardened British attitudes against Europe.[33]

Deference

The third main aspect of the classic view was the identification of a notable deferential streak in British culture, the product of a society which had modernised relatively peacefully over a long period of time and which had retained strong aspects of earlier cultures. Deference was particularly manifest in the high levels of support which existed not just for the monarchy, but for the totally unelected House of Lords (life peerages were introduced in 1958). Even many within the working class expressed a preference for an MP who was the son of a lord over a working man. This type of social deferential view was one of two major explanations put forward by social scientists for working-class Conservatism (the other main explanation was that more affluent workers chose the Conservatives through economic self-interest).[34]

Britain at the turn of the 1960s was still very much an Establishment-based society, with most top positions being held by males who had gone to private school and Oxbridge. In 1963 the Conservatives even managed to choose as Prime Minister a man who was a member of the hereditary aristocracy, Lord Home (who resigned his title in order to be able to find a seat in the House of Commons). But arguments about deference raise a particularly large number of issues. Methodologically inclined social science critics pointed to the fact that it was difficult to define and operationalise. Besides, no matter how deference was defined, its explanatory power often seemed weak: for instance, many 'deferentials' voted Labour. Similarly, on some tests, British people were less deferential than, say, Americans.[35]

Even more importantly, a case could be made that – to the extent deference existed – it was largely the product of elite performance. Certainly polls showed a remarkable desire for strong leadership (59 per cent of Conservatives and 53 per cent of Labour supporters),[36] which clearly had implications in the event of leadership failure. In 1959, Macmillan had been 'Supermac', but by the mid-1960s there was a growing tendency to criticise political leadership – a trend encouraged by a combination of more aggressive television reporting and growing economic problems.

THE DECLINE OF THE CIVIC CULTURE

The argument linking the previous section is that there were serious problems in the classic depiction of Britain's political culture. Although Almond and Verba noted the importance of history, they proceeded to produce a remarkably ahistorical picture, omitting major meso and macro factors, such as the influence of class and political leadership. At best it was a picture of southern England in the 1950s. This last point is underlined yet further by adapting the framework used in the preceding section to consider developments since the 1960s.

Homogeneity

It is important not to overstate the problems of the classic view in terms of an underlying sense of common British identity. A study carried out in the early 1980s argued that 'pride of nation is conspicuous among Britons', with 86 per cent very or quite proud to be British, and only 8 per cent declaring themselves not very proud – one of the highest positive ratings of all the countries studied.[37] However, there is no question that since the 1960s Britain has become much less homogenous in a variety of ways.

One way concerns the continuing, albeit erratic, growth of Welsh and especially Scottish nationalism. There is no doubt that an important element of this stems from the work of intellectuals and others deliberately seeking to foster national consciousness: symptomatically, the unofficial Scottish anthem, *Flower of Scotland*, which immortalises victory over England, was written in the 1960s. But they have had fertile soil in which to till. This is not simply a question of the fact that there is a deep-rooted sense of difference from the numerically and culturally dominant English (in the 1990s, England has a population of over 46 million, Scotland has 5 million and Wales 3 million). Although both are subsidised by the British Exchequer, continuing relative economic decline has reinforced anti-English feeling in Wales and Scotland; and in Scotland the discovery of offshore oil in the 1960s has given calls for independence greater economic credability. The belief that small nations can find a new role within the European Union has given Welsh and Scottish nationalism further legitimacy. The result has been a notable growth in support for the Scottish National Party, and spectacular decline in support for the Conservatives, who in 1955 had won half the vote in Scotland, but under Margaret Thatcher came to epitomise the uncaring face of England. In the 1994 European elections, the nationalists gained 32.6 per cent of the vote, and have the potential for further progress given Labour's confusion over plans for devolved government.[38]

Britain since the 1960s has become a more multicultural society in another notable way. Although the 1961 Commonwealth Immigration Act heavily limited further immigration, on occasion (such as the expulsion of Uganda's Asians) new non-white groups have continued to arrive, while a relatively high birth rate has further expanded the size of this community. The 1991 census indicated that 5.5 per cent of the population came from these ethnic groups, with the most important hailing from Indian sub-continent backgrounds and the next largest from the West Indian ones. As they have primarily settled in or around England's large cities, in some areas they make up a notable minority, though in no parliamentary constituency do they yet account for a majority. Notable differences are beginning to emerge within these groups. For instance, among those from the Indian sub-continent, there is a growing middle class, and family structures are strong. Among Afro-Caribbeans, education achievements are often low, and unemployment high (a 1996 study found that 62 per cent of black Londoners between the ages of 16 and 24 were out of work, compared to 20 per cent of whites).[39]

Mounting unemployment more generally has also contributed to a growth in social inequality, for British welfare benefits have become low by European standards. Moreover, although the unemployment rate has fallen back from its 1980s peak of well over 10 per cent, many people now find themselves in low paid or short-term employment, receiving little protection from trades unions or government legislation. Sociologists debate whether it is legitimate to speak of a large 'underclass', but there is no doubt that a significant minority live in relative poverty, accompanied by weak family relationships and an absence of any serious sense of community. At the other end of the spectrum, there is a growing 'overclass', often working in dynamic areas of the tertiary economy. Adjusting for inflation, the number of people paid over £100,000 in 1995 prices has grown tenfold since 1980; many benefit on top of their basic salaries from various major perks, which have recently vastly increased differentials between many top managers and the average worker. Many of these people are concentrated in south-eastern England, though it is too simplistic to make a division between a declining industrial north and prosperous south. There are notable pockets of afflu- ence in the former, for instance parts of Cheshire; and there are many poor areas in London, and parts of Cornwall.

Consensus

The classic view saw consensus as a major strength in the British political system. However, increasingly during the 1970s, this view came under chal- lenge. Symptomatic of this sea change was the way in which the leading American political scientist, Samuel Beer, turned from admiration to the conclusion that Britain was really characterised by 'pluralistic stagnation'. Beer had in mind the way in which Britain's liberal corporatist system, which had if anything been strengthened by the 1951–64 Conservative govern- ments, encouraged a failure to take tough economic decisions, especially by according unions excessive veto powers – though the argument also pointed to a loss of political initiative and dynamism.[40] Others held that the problem was more the related one of 'overload': the government had taken on too many responsibilities, partly to buy off pressure groups and appease sections of public opinion.[41] As it could not fulfil many of these, the result was loss of legitimacy.

Such arguments appealed especially within the 'New Right' wing of the Conservative Party, which gained notable influence after Mrs Thatcher became leader in 1975. Thatcher was not an intellectual, and her policies were a strange mix of laissez-faire and authoritarian-nationalist, but she launched a powerful attack on the old Butskellite consensus. After she became Prime Minister in 1979, a new set of concerns came to dominate the policy agenda, including income tax cuts, privatisation, and a concern with inflation rather than unemployment as the key economic target.[42] Labour too moved away from Butskellism, initially in the direction of highly radical policies such as withdrawal from the European Union and extending state controls. The result was a major split and the creation of the new Social Democratic Party during 1981, which in the 1983 general election ran only just behind Labour in terms of the popular vote (though the electoral system gave Labour the vast majority of the Opposition seats). Labour subsequently moved back to more moderate ground, especially after Tony Blair became leader in the 1990s. Indeed, the party ditched much of its statist rhetoric, weakened its historic links with the unions and at times seemed almost Thatcherite.[43] In particular, Labour committed itself to tax cuts, though opinion polls have consistently shown since the early 1980s that people are willing to pay somewhat higher taxes to fund specific welfare programmes, notably the health service and education.[44] Labour has also only half-heartedly picked up the issue of major constitutional reform (the Liberal Democrats have taken this more to heart), though again there is notable poll evidence that this is popular with an important section of the electorate. Meanwhile, Mrs T. had been pushed from office after the disaster of the highly inequitable poll tax, a policy very much associated with her forceful leadership. She was succeeded by John Major, who tried to nudge his party towards a more consensual style, though without any of the grand vision of the type which had characterised Thatcher.

Notable ideological divisions remain, however, not least within the parties. Nowhere is this more true than in attitudes towards European unity. In spite of Britain obtaining opt-outs over the Social Chapter and EMU, the Eurosceptic wing of the Conservatives became ever-more concerned about the possibility of a federal Europe: by 1995 there was even serious talk of a British withdrawal.[45] There is no doubt that many hold sincere anti-EU views, and there are unquestionably real problems relating to merging a strong unitary state like Britain into a federal Europe. But there has also been an element of electioneering in the Eurosceptic position. In spite of winning the 1992 general election, the Conservatives have fairly consistently lagged behind Labour in 1990s opinion polls. But Thatcher had shown, especially at the time of the Falklands War in 1982, that nationalist rhetoric was popular. As opinion polls have continued to show widespread British opposition or indifference towards the EU, the issue has clear electoral attractions. A *Sunday Times* poll published on 17 March 1996 showed that only 30 per cent thought Europe had been good for Britain, and only 21 per cent wanted to go ahead with a single currency in the near future. Although the Labour Party has taken a more positive line towards the EU, this has been tempered by an unwillingness to give public opinion a strong lead – and by notable remnants of a left-wing which still sees 'Europe' as a capitalist club.

The Conservative Party is in more danger of a serious split than at any time since before the First World War. Should this take place, there seems considerable potential for a nationalist, or 'respectable' racist party. On several occasions small groups, like the National Front, or British National Party, have shown signs of having significant support in some urban areas. There are widespread myths which encourage hostility to ethnic groups, including the belief that they constitute a significant percentage of the population: a poll published in the *Independent on Sunday* on 7 July 1991 found that one in three whites think there are more than 10 million 'blacks' in Britain (the real figure was nearer 3 million). Racist groups have failed to prosper mainly as a result of their fascist leadership, the electoral system, and strong local and national anti-fascist campaigns.[46] However, a poll in the *Daily Express* on 8 August 1995 showed the potential for a major crack in the party system: 9 per cent said they would definitely vote for a British

Le Pen type party and another 17 per cent said they would seriously consider doing so. The main sign of hope was that racism was much less strong among the young, and in general there is growing evidence of the acceptance of multiculturalism. But should Britain introduce certain forms of proportional representation in the near future, there is considerable potential for a racist or radical nationalist party to make major inroads.

Deference

At the time that Almond and Verba wrote their classic work, a series of notable changes was taking place in British society. Education was becoming less authoritarian, as were most families (at least those which remained together, for the 1960s saw growing signs of family breakdown). Access to universities was broadening, especially for women and people from ordinary backgrounds. Youth culture stressed the questioning of old ways. It is easy to ignore a silent majority not significantly affected by these trends, but most people were now being socialised in a way which made deference a more marginal feature.

An important study in the 1970s noted that there had been a decline in deference, and argued that there was considerable potential for protest outside the conventional political channels – though the underlying discontent was rarely directed against the political system *per se*.[47] Alienation was more from mainstream parties, or particular leaders. However, since the 1960s there have been periodic outbreaks of social violence which reflect a more fundamental discontent with the state of society and the political process. It is true that the miners' strike of 1984–5 now seems light years away, and the poll tax riots of the late 1980s were aimed at a specific policy. But periodic inner city rioting by ethnic minorities and young whites reflects a more persistent feeling of anomie and alienation. The Henley Centre for Forecasting's report in May 1995 found deep-rooted pessimism about the implications of globalisation and widespread alienation from the government and political institutions (64 per cent of British workers felt very or fairly concerned about losing their jobs, one of the highest figures in Europe).

Since the 1960s, there has been a notable divergence within the electorate between one group, primarily in the educated non-productive middle class, which has moved towards post-industrial values, and another, mainly working-class group which has increasingly been characterised by economic instrumentality.[48] The latter group has become increasingly alienated from governments which fail to produce significant real increases in living standards. This claim might seem at odds with the Conservatives' repeated electoral victories after 1979, but these had much to do with suspicions about Labour's economic policies and the force of Thatcher's personal, albeit nationally divisive, appeal. The 1960s evidence that many people seek strong leaders remains powerful: polls consistently showed after 1992 that a key factor in the slump of the Conservatives' standing was Major's inability to provide a sense that he was in control and that he had a clear vision of the future. More generally, mounting reports of corruption and sleaze have led to ever-greater suspicion of politicians of all colours. On 23 September 1996, the *Independent* published a poll which indicated that whereas in 1973 39 per cent of people believed that 'politicians are in politics for what they can get out of it', the 1996 figure was 66 per cent. Criticism of the monarchy too has grown, though the Queen herself remains popular. An *Independent* poll published on 18 February 1996 showed that whereas in 1990 70 per cent thought the monarchy would still exist in 50 years time, by 1996 the figure had halved. The young especially were less monarchist, a reflection of a wider tendency for nationalism to be less strong in this age group – though other studies of young people tend to show that there are few if any great ideologies in which they believe.

CONTINUITIES AND CHANGE

In 1900, the British economy had been overtaken in size by the United States and Germany, but there was a sense in which British power was still at its zenith. One hundred years later, illusions of grandeur are not totally dead. Yet there is a growing awareness that 'Great Britain' has become a misnomer. When Britain joined the European Economic Community, sections of elite opinion believed that a new world role could be found as leader of Europe. But approaching the turn of a new millennium, Britain's relationship with 'Europe' remains troubled. Many British people seem remarkably resistant to taking on a new layer of European identity – although a growing number of Welsh and Scots see 'Europe' as a means of breaking the stranglehold of the *English* state, and trades unions and others throughout the land are increasingly looking to Europe as the coming sphere of political activity.

The constitutional challenges to the British state posed by the EU and internal micro-nationalism are reinforcing a series of centrifugal social tendencies. Society seems more divided than at any time since 1945. Social class and religion no longer provide a major sense of belonging, or guiding norms. Old ideologies which sought to forge a united nation now seem discredited. In the 1980s, 'One Nation' Conservatism was replaced by the belief that 'there is no such thing as society', while in the 1990s leaders of the Labour Party have competed to advocate formerly right-wing beliefs, including the reform of the universal benefits welfare system. Old symbols of unity, such as the Crown or Parliament, similarly have lost their power to unite: they now inspire abuse as much as awe. Politicians are treated with contempt: the leading tabloid newspaper, the *Sun*, even asked on 29 July 1993, 'Will the country be any worse off without MPs? No, of course not. . . . What we want is action not words.'

It is important not to over-interpret limited or short-term data, but there are signs that two divergent attitudinal trends are capable of being mobilised. First, there is a nationalist strand, including a notable authoritarian and racist streak. Second, there is a liberal strand, seeking greater participation and guarantees of new constitutional rights, including for women and ethnic minorities. The latter group seems to be potentially larger, but whilst this strand of opinion has received some succour from the Liberal Democrats, Labour has concentrated more on developing moderate economic policies to attract voters and business and financial interests. Labour has been especially cautious in talking of European federalism, though it has committed itself to specific EU policies, like the Social Chapter. Tony Blair has exercised considerable powers of leadership in taking the party ever further away from old shibboleths, but he has lacked the ability to offer the public a grand vision of the future. The rise of Britain's civic culture owed much to leadership. Failure in this sphere has recently furthered its decline.

NOTES

1 This chapter follows the common practice of using 'Britain' to exclude Northern Ireland, which is part of the 'United Kingdom': Northern Ireland has a notably different value structure and party system.
2 G. Almond and S. Verba, *The Civic Culture*, Princeton, Princeton University Press, 1963.
3 D. Kavanagh, 'Political Culture in Great Britain: The Decline of the Civic Culture' in G. Almond and S. Verba (eds), *The Civic Culture Revisited*, Boston, Little, Brown, 1980, p. 127. NB: this is an excellent short critique.
4 For a good introduction to approaches focusing on the earlier periods see A. Grant and K. J. Stringer (eds), *Uniting the Kingdom?*, London, Routledge, 1995.
5 L. Colley, *Britons: Forging the Nation, 1707–1837*, London, Pimlico, 1994. See also R. Samuel (ed.), *Patriotism: The Making and Unmaking of British National Identities*, 3 vols, London, Routledge, 1989.
6 A. Macfarlane, *The Origins of English Individualism*, Oxford, Blackwell, 1978. Cf. R. H. Tawney, *Religion and the Rise of Capitalism*, London, John Murray, 1929.
7 Cf. B. Moore Jnr, *The Social Origins of Democracy and Dictatorship*, Harmondsworth, Penguin, 1966, who points to the triumph of bourgeois values and the related rise of democracy.
8 L. Greenfeld, *Nationalism: Five Roads to Modernity*, Princeton, Princeton University Press, 1992, esp. pp. 27ff., argues that this sentiment first developed within a group of new aristocrats, who reacted against excessive privilege.
9 P. J. Cain and A. G. Hopkins, *British Imperialism*, London, Longman, 1993; W. A. Rubinstein, *Capitalism, Culture and British Decline in Britain*, London, Routledge, 1993; and M. Wiener, *English Culture and the Decline of the Industrial Spirit*, Harmondsworth, Penguin, 1985.
10 On the British ideological tradition see W. H. Greenleaf, *The British Political Tradition*, Vol. 2, London, Routledge and Kegan Paul, 1983.
11 V. Bogdanor, *The Monarchy and the Constitution*, Oxford, Oxford University Press, 1995; D. Cannadine, *The Decline and Fall of the British Aristocracy*, New Haven, Yale University Press, 1990; and F. K. Prochaska, *Royal Bounty: The Making of a Welfare Monarchy*, New Haven, Yale University Press, 1995.

12 J. M. McKenzie, *Propaganda and Empire*, Manchester, Manchester University Press, 1990; R. Colls and P. Dodds (eds), *Englishness: Politics and Culture 1880–1920*, London, Croom Helm, 1987.
13 See P. Marshall (ed.) *The Cambridge Illustrated History of the British Empire*, Cambridge, Cambridge University Press, 1996.
14 E. Hobsbawm and T. Ranger (eds), *The Invention of Tradition*, Cambridge, Cambridge University Press, 1983; A. D. Smith, *National Identity*, London, Penguin, 1991.
15 C. Townshend, *Making the Peace: Public Order and Public Security in Modern Britain*, Oxford, Oxford University Press, 1993, p. 1.
16 See Kavanagh, *op. cit.*, p. 128.
17 See E. P. Thompson, *The Making of the English Working Class*, Harmondsworth, Pelican, 1970.
18 K. Haste, *Keep the Home Fires Burning*, London, Allen Lane, 1977; G. Messinger, *British Propaganda and the State in the First World War*, Manchester, Manchester University Press, 1992.
19 K. Middlemas, *Politics in Industrial Society*, London, Deutsch, 1979; T. Smith, *The Politics of the Corporate Economy*, Oxford, Martin Robertson, 1979.
20 G. Dangerfield, *The Strange Death of Liberal England*, St Albans, Granada, 1970.
21 A. Briggs, 'The Language of "Class" in Early Nineteenth Century England' in A. Briggs and J. Saville (eds), *Essays in Labour History*, Vol. 1, London, Macmillan, 1960.
22 J. M. Winter, *Socialism and the Challenge of War*, London, Routledge and Kegan Paul, 1974; see also R. Barker, 'Political Myth: Ramsay MacDonald and the Labour Party', *History*, 1976, 61.
23 E. H. H. Green, *Conservatism in Crisis*, London, Routledge, 1995.
24 P. F. Clarke, *Lancashire and the New Liberalism*, London, Cambridge University Press, 1971; cf. T. Wilson, *The Downfall of the Liberal Party*, London, Collins, 1966.
25 B. Anderson, *Imagined Communities*, London, Verso, 1983, uses the term 'imagined community' to refer to nations, but some Conservatives saw class as essentially a myth and deliberately employed nationalism as a counter.
26 P. Addison, *The Road to 1945*, Cape, London, 1975; R. Eatwell, *The 1945–51 Labour Governments*, London, Batsford, 1979; K. O. Morgan, *Labour in Power, 1945–51*, Oxford, Clarendon Press, 1984; and H. Pelling, *The Labour Governments, 1945–51*, London, Macmillan, 1984.
27 V. Bogdanor and R. Skidelsky (eds), *The Age of Affluence*, London, Macmillan, 1971. For a general history of these and subsequent developments see P. Clarke, *Hope and Glory: Britain 1900–1990*, London, Allen Lane, 1996.
28 On homogeneity see also J. Blondel, *Voters, Parties and Leaders*, Baltimore, Penguin, 1966.
29 The major voting study was D. Butler and D. Stokes, *Political Change in Britain*, London, Macmillan, 1964; on the embourgeoisement theory see J. Goldthorpe, *The Affluent Worker in the Class Structure*, London, Cambridge University Press, 1969.
30 H. Kearney, *The British Isles: A History of Four Nations*, Cambridge, Cambridge University Press, 1989.
31 J. Brand, *The National Movement in Scotland*, London, Routledge and Kegan Paul, 1978; C. Harvie, *Scotland and Nationalism*, London, Allen and Unwin, 1977; A. Butt Philip, *The Welsh Question*, Cardiff, University of Wales Press, 1975.
32 S. Beer, *Modern British Politics*, London, Faber, 1965; R. T. McKenzie, *British Political Parties*, London, Macmillan, 1966.

33 M. Camps, *Britain and the European Economic Community, 1955–63*, London, Oxford University Press, 1964; R. Jowell and G. Hoinville, *Britain into Europe: Public Opinion and the EEC, 1961–75*, London, Croom Helm, 1976; and S. George, *Awkward Partner*, Oxford, Oxford University Press, 1994.

34 R. T. McKenzie and A. Silver, *Angels in Marble*, London, Heinemann, 1968; and E. Nordlinger, *The Working-Class Tories*, London, MacGibbon and Kee, 1967. On rates of change see S. Rothman, 'Modernity and Tradition in Britain' in R. Rose (ed.), *Studies in British Politics*, London, Macmillan, 1966.

35 R. Jessop, *Traditionalism, Conservatism, and British Political Culture*, London, Macmillan, 1974.

36 Nordlinger, *op. cit.*, esp. p. 17.

37 M. Abrams, D. Gerard and N. Timms (eds), *Values and Social Change in Britain*, Basingstoke, Macmillan, 1985, p. 17.

38 On nationalism see Note 31; see also B. Crick (ed.), *National Identities. The Constitution of the United Kingdom*, Oxford, Blackwell, 1991.

39 *Observer Review*, 25 August 1996. See also P. Gilroy, *There Ain't No Black in the Union Jack*, London, Routledge, 1992; J. Solomos, *Race and Racism in Contemporary Britain*, Basingstoke, Macmillan, 1993.

40 S. Beer, *Britain Against Itself*, London, Faber, 1982; cf. Beer, *op. cit.*; P. A. Hall, *Governing the Economy*, Cambridge, Polity, 1986.

41 M. Olson, *The Rise and Decline of Nations*, New Haven, Yale University Press, 1982; A. King (ed.), *Why Is Britain Becoming Harder to Govern?*, London, BBC, 1976.

42 A. Gamble, *The Free Economy and the Strong State*, Basingstoke, Macmillan, 1994; D. Kavanagh, *Thatcherism and British Politics: The End of Consensus?*, Oxford, Oxford University Press, 1990.

43 I. Crewe and A. King, *The SDP*, Oxford, Oxford University Press, 1995; E. Shaw, *The Labour Party since 1945*, Oxford, Blackwell, 1996.

44 R. Jowell, *British Social Attitudes: The 11th Report*, Aldershot, Dartmouth, 1994, esp. p. 1. NB: there is some debate about whether people give pollsters 'caring' answers, but vote in a self-interested way.

45 M. Sowemimo, 'The Conservative Party and European Integration, 1988–1995', *Party Politics*, 1995, 2.

46 C. Husbands, *Racial Exclusion and the City*, Allen and Unwin, London, 1983; R. Eatwell, 'The Extreme Right and British "Exceptionalism"' in P. Hainsworth (ed.), *The Extreme Right in Europe and the USA*, London, Pinter, 1997. See also R. Cohen, *Frontiers of Identity*, London, Longman, 1994.

47 A. Marsh, *Protest and Political Consciousness*, London, Sage, 1977.

48 J. E. Alt, *The Politics of Economic Decline*, Cambridge, Cambridge University Press, 1979; cf. R. Inglehart, *The Silent Revolution*, Princeton, Princeton University Press, 1977. See also A. Heath, R. Jowell and J. Curtice (eds), *Labour's Last Chance: The 1992 General Election and Beyond*, Aldershot, Dartmouth, 1994.

5 France

James F. McMillan

INTRODUCTION

To study political culture is to study the beliefs, values, assumptions (spoken and unspoken) and modes of action to be found within a given polity. In the context of modern France, this means exploring conflicts as much as consensus, because different cultural communities in France have disagreed about the meaning of Frenchness and retained their own identities, derived from collective memories and a distinctive sense of the past – a past remembered and reconstructed less as history than as myth. To investigate French political culture, in the first instance, is to explore the politics of memory in France.[1]

It is, second, to explore the relationship between the French people and the French state. It is of course possible to stress the diversity of France – of what Ferdinand Braudel called 'the dazzling triumph of the plural, of the heterogeneous, of the never-quite-what-you-find-elsewhere'. For Braudel, geography explains at least as much about France as history.[2] Such an approach, however, leads inevitably to an emphasis on regional studies rather than on national political culture. Here it is necessary to concentrate on what distinguished the French experience from that of other countries. The relationship between the French and the state was indubitably distinctive, above all because of the impact of the French Revolution, which opened up a chasm between *les deux France* – between those who identified with the Revolution and those who opposed it.

The struggle to impose the Republic as the embodiment of the revolutionary tradition dominated the political history of France well into the twentieth century.[3] The eventual success of that enterprise (particularly under the Third Republic, 1870–1940) ensured that the political culture of France was moulded largely in accordance with the triumphant republican tradition. The latter is therefore the principal focus of the present chapter, but the question needs to be posed as to how far that tradition has retained its potency and its relevance in contemporary France.

THE ANCIEN RÉGIME AND THE FRENCH REVOLUTION: RUPTURES AND CONTINUITIES

Before 1789 the person of the king was sacred and the royal will was deemed to be identical with God's will. Similarly, in his person the monarch represented both the state and the nation and was thus the sole embodiment of unity. The social order was both hierarchical, divided into three distinct estates (clergy, nobles and the Third Estate), and particularistic, consisting of a multitude of corporate bodies, which, if requested by the king, might send delegates to an Estates-General to give advice – though this was emphatically not a proto-parliament. By the 1760s, the monarchy was having to contend with the power exerted by a popular press and public opinion. That, however, is not to suggest that the order was already doomed or that a new political culture shaped by the doctrines of the Enlightenment and constructed around a reformed monarchy could not have emerged organically.[4]

Momentously, the royal attempts at reform backfired when on 17 June 1789 the Third Estate transformed itself into a 'National Assembly', enshrining the principle of popular sovereignty and launching a constitutional revolution. In August 1789 the revolutionaries issued their Declaration of the Rights of Man and the Citizen which stated explicitly that 'all sovereignty emanates essentially from the nation' and that 'The law is the expression of the general will'. It is true that not all of the past was to be repudiated immediately: most men of 1789 did not initially intend to abolish the monarchy and it was 1793 before the Jacobin radicals executed Louis XVI. From the outset, however, it was clear that the revolutionaries intended to remake the world anew. With Rousseau for their mentor, they set about dismantling the corporate society of what they now contemptuously dismissed as the 'ancien régime' and replacing it with a new social order based on individualism and equality before the law. The bond between individuals became citizenship and their membership of a nation committed to the principles of liberty, equality and fraternity.[5]

Effectively, as Lynn Hunt has argued, the Revolution invented modern politics by evolving not only new forms of political practice and social relations but also a new political language and symbolism.[6] Terms which evoked the Old Order, such as 'aristocrat' or 'privilege', quickly acquired heavily negative connotations. Others such as 'nation', 'patrie', 'constitution', and 'virtue', in Hunt's phrase, 'served as revolutionary incantations'. Revolutionary symbols, such as the liberty tree, the liberty cap, and the tricolour cockade permeated everyday life. Revolutionary festivals expressed in ritual the new sense of national community. The revolutionaries even devised a new revolutionary calendar, which took as its starting point the inauguration of the Republic.[7] Through these activities, revolutionaries such as Robespierre sought to mobilise the 'crowd' behind the Republic of Virtue and to take forward a revolution that was as much cultural as political.

Those who refused to identify with revolutionary values were branded 'enemies of the people' and subjected to the rigours of the Terror.

If the principal legacy of the Revolution was one of conflict, in two important respects it maintained a degree of continuity with the past. The first concerns the role of the state in promoting the national interest and fostering national unity. *Etatisme*, embodied in a cult of bureaucracy supposedly dedicated to the public good, has thus served as a counter-weight to fragmentation and has been accepted by virtually all sides of the political divide. The form of regime (the *pays légal*) may be the object of bitter contestation and undergo drastic change but the state (the *pays réel*) represents true, 'eternal' France. For the right, the state evokes the tradition of the monarchy which was responsible for the creation of France. On the left, the state is synonymous with the revolutionary tradition and the recog-nised instrument for the establishment of the Republic 'one and indivisible'. Bonapartists (who might be either authoritarian or left-wing) identified strongly with a state which Napoleon's centralising reforms had done so much to shape. Indeed, it may well be the case, as Eugen Weber has suggested, that the very intensity of ideological conflict in France owes much to the need for political parties to find something to argue about in a situation where the left as much as the right sought to exploit and extend the central power of the state.[8]

A second – and related – area of continuity and consensus is the realm of foreign policy. The pursuit of *grandeur* and territorial expansion were long-standing objectives of France, which since the time of Louis XIV had been the foremost military power in Europe. Although the revolutionaries rejected sordid conquest, these aims were subsumed into a crusade to export the principles of 1789 by means of revolutionary war. Napoleon began his ascent to the imperial throne in the army of the Republic; even as Emperor, he continued to invoke the ideology of the nation-state as the inspiration behind his redrawing of the map of Europe. His defeat at Waterloo in 1815 finally ended the dream of a French-dominated Europe but the mystique of French *grandeur* manifestly lived on.

REMEMBERING THE REVOLUTION

The Old Order continued to have its adherents, who repudiated not only the excesses but the 'principles of 1789' themselves. French conservatives saw the Terror as confirmation of Edmund Burke's views about the dangers of a politics based on abstract principles and which ignored deep-seated custom. They concluded 'popular sovereignty' led straight to the tyranny of the mob. The Revolution therefore gave rise to a powerful counter-revolutionary tradition expressed in the writings of such as Louis de Bonald and Joseph de Maistre, for whom the notion of country could not be separated from that of king and the practice of the Catholic religion.[9] Understandably, a powerful channel for the diffusion of such views was the Catholic Church which was probably the biggest single loser by the Revolution. By the middle of the nineteenth century, Catholic thinking encompassed a general condemnation of 'the Revolution', understood as the forces of subversion at work in the modern world.[10]

Opposition to the Revolution was by no means confined to reactionary intellectuals and diehard Bourbon loyalists among the aristocracy and clergy. The role of ordinary peasant women in resisting Jacobin de-Christianisation policies is particularly worthy of note.[11] Also, just as most revolutionary activity was concentrated in Paris, so most counter-revolutionary activity was to be found in the provinces, which rejected the capital's pretensions to determine the destiny of the whole nation. In the Vendée, peasants provoked by the administrative upheavals caused by the Revolution and resentful of the new bourgeois office-holders who had bought up Church property, took up arms in defence of Catholicism and in protest at attempts to conscript them.[12] For republicans, these *chouans* were religious maniacs who were the dupes of the local clergy and nobility. In counter-revolutionary mythology, by contrast, the Vendean peasants were celebrated as the real people of France; nor did Catholic martyrology easily forget the rebels drowned in the river Loire, among whom were 148 priests.

The year 1815 may have brought the revolutionary era to a close, but the restored Bourbons (1814–30) were never able to command the loyalties of those who continued to identify with 'the principles of 1789'. However, lines of fracture were still to be discerned within the revolutionary tradition itself. It was one thing to be in favour of 'popular sovereignty', quite another to translate this concept into viable institutions. Not all opponents of arbitrary monarchy were democrats. The initial intention of the men of 1789 had been to establish a liberal state which would marry the Revolution and the monarchy, and this remained the preferred solution of liberals like Guizot, who tried to repeat the experiment under the Orleanist regime (1830–48).[13] Citizenship might be for everyone (or at least all adult males), but only men of property should have the right to engage in political activity.

For republicans, however, only the creation of a viable democratic Republic could give authentic expression to the aspirations of the sovereign people. And, according to the Jacobin ideal, the Republic was envisaged as a polity in which the legislature, as the embodiment of the will of the nation, exercised supremacy over the executive. This was in marked contrast to the Bonapartist tradition, which sought to incarnate the popular will in a single figure, a 'man of destiny', who stood above party and personified national unity and national greatness. Bonapartism advocated plebiscitary, 'Caesarean', democracy rather than parliamentarism, and as the experience of the Second Empire (1852–70) was to show, it was to remain a powerful ideological current in nineteenth-century France.[14]

Finally, by storming the Bastille in 1789, the 'revolutionary crowd' announced the entry of the masses into the political arena in a recognisably modern way. Traditionally, risings of the urban populace had been precipitated by food shortages, and elements of the bread riot were not absent in the events of the 1790s. In the context of the Revolution, however, popular intervention on the part of the *sans-culottes* – the ordinary working men who wore trousers rather than the knee-breeches sported by the upper classes – was designed both to rescue the Revolution from the threat of possible counter-revolution and to force revolutionary governments to take up more radical positions. Popular politics also raised the question of popular violence: was the participation of the people inevitably accompanied by recourse to the barricades and the call for Terror to be adopted as an instrument of government in the name of the popular will?[15] The nineteenth century was to be replete with reminders – in 1830, 1848 and 1871 – that the revolutionary tradition was also one of insurrection.

Thus when republicanism began to re-emerge as a credible political alternative in the 1830s and 1840s, it was beset with internal divisions.[16] Educated by historians like Jules Michelet, the new generation looked to the Republic to inaugurate a higher form of civilisation. The more moderate wing, however, was prepared to settle for the introduction of what it called 'universal' (male) suffrage. The radical tendency wanted social as well as political reform. The issue of revolutionary violence was another source of tension, since the moderates were uneasy with the legacy of 1793, while the radicals refused to repudiate actions which were justified as a necessary response to the threat to the Revolution posed by challenges from its enemies both at home and abroad. A minority wing of extreme republicans, animated by the perpetual conspirator Blanqui, openly identified with the insurrectionary tradition and wanted to see the July Monarchy overthrown by force.

When republicans had a second chance at founding a viable democratic Republic after the Revolution of February 1848, they once again botched the job.[17] The Second Republic introduced manhood suffrage, but only a third of the electorate voted for republican candidates. Worse still, the June Days, a flare-up of the insurrectionary tradition in the shape of a social revolt on the part of desperate artisans, labourers and small businessmen which was savagely repressed by the forces of order, triggered memories of the violence and anarchy of the 1790s and provoked a decisive shift to the right. The principal beneficiary of this turn of events was the Bonapartist Pretender, Louis Napoleon, who exploited his opportunities first to become President in December 1848 and then to restore the Empire in 1852. As Emperor, Napoleon III came closer than many republican historians admit to fulfilling the Bonapartist dream of reconciling the principle of liberty with the principle of order and restoring France to former glories as a Great Power. But for the military disaster of the Franco-Prussian War of 1870–1, the political culture of France might have owed more to the Bonapartist than to the republican tradition.[18]

IMPOSING THE REPUBLIC: THE POLITICAL CULTURE OF THE THIRD REPUBLIC

As Eric Hobsbawm has explained, the late nineteenth century was the crucial phase in the historical process which he and Terence Ranger have felicitously called 'the invention of tradition'.[19] The rulers of most European states, conscious of the need to establish their legitimacy in an age of mass politics, resorted to new methods of manufacturing loyalty to the state and of heightening a sense of social solidarity and political identity. At the core of the French endeavour to turn 'peasants into Frenchmen'[20] was the attempt to inculcate a new 'civic religion' – republicanism itself – as the kind of 'spiritual principle' which Ernest Renan deemed necessary to the creation of national unity in his famous lecture on the idea of the nation delivered in 1882.

The education of the nation's children was thus the new regime's top priority and it immediately set about creating a national system of elementary education that was free, compulsory and, above all, run by the state rather than the Church. State-trained primary schoolteachers – the *instituteurs* and *institutrices* – were extolled in republican propaganda as the evangelists who would bring the gospel of republicanism to the peasant masses. Patriotism was the chief virtue of the manuals on morality and the history textbooks prepared by Ernest Lavisse, who firmly believed that the victory of Prussia over France in 1870 was attributable more to the Prussian schoolteacher than to the Prussian army.[21] From the history books, new generations were taught to appreciate the Revolution as the greatest event in French history and the establishment of the Republic as its logical outcome.

A related strategy was the creation of new rituals and public festivities. By far the most important of these was Bastille Day, the first of which was held in 1880. It proved an enormous success – except among supporters of the monarchy – since it allowed people to celebrate as they had not done in the ten years since the fall of the Empire. Based on traditional religious festivals which mixed the sacred and the secular, Bastille Day was a deliberate blend of official ritual and unofficial pleasures intended as much as the new secular schools to shape the development of a democratic and republican culture. Similarly the great exhibitions of 1889 (the centrepiece of which was the construction of the Eiffel Tower) and 1900 were meant to be demonstrations to the world that technical progress went hand in hand with the establishment of republican democracy.[22]

The erection of statues and monuments was a further way of glorifying the Republic and enhancing its appeal in the popular mind. Maurice Agulhon has written of the regime's 'statuomania', manifested in the busts of Marianne and the statues of local republican leaders which mushroomed throughout France.[23] The adoption of the *Marseillaise* as the national anthem likewise encouraged adhesion to the concept of the *patrie* promoted by the republican leadership, serving to foster linguistic unity and cultural integration in a country where, as late as the 1890s, significant numbers of the population spoke patois rather than French.[24] The ubiquity of the tricolour also served as a powerful symbol of the Republic and embodiment of the republican tradition.

If the Republic wished to rally friends, it was also quite happy to make enemies. The demonisation of political opponents was a strategy favoured by French democrats under the Third Republic as much as by Bismarck in the Second German Reich. The Third Republic, too, waged a *Kulturkampf* against the Catholic Church, which was singled out as the most pernicious and active threat to the realisation of republican ambitions to remake the nation in the image of 1789. 'Clericalism, there is the enemy!', proclaimed Gambetta, and no republican, whether moderate or radical, disagreed with him. Anti-clericalism became perhaps the single most prominent feature of French republican political culture under the Third Republic.

It was no accident that when republicans took over the Republic in 1879 they immediately embarked on a programme of anti-clerical legislation (which centred largely on extending the control of the state over education but also included the reintroduction of divorce in 1884) with the objective of bringing about the secularisation of both the state and society. The attack was renewed even more ferociously at the turn of the century in the aftermath of the Dreyfus Affair when the radical republicans came to power and, with socialist support, proceeded to attempt to ban the religious orders from teaching, broke off diplomatic relations with Rome and in 1905 passed a law separating Church and state which unilaterally ended the Concordat established between Napoleon and the Pope in 1801. Catholics were ruthlessly excluded both from political office and from the state bureaucracy, though – to the angst of the more virulent priest eaters – they could not entirely be kept out of the army or the diplomatic corps.[25]

The point should also be made that this quarrel between the Republic and the Church was by no means confined to high politics. It was replicated in the villages throughout provincial France in antagonisms between the parish priest, who denounced the 'godless' Republic and its governance by a cabal of atheists and freemasons, and local schoolteachers and free thinkers who saw themselves as the protagonists of science and sons of the Revolution. The dispute was also one of temperament – anti-clericals tended to have a healthy suspicion of authority (except as represented by the 'Jacobin' state) and in particular they disliked the Church's claims to interfere in people's private lives over questions of sexual morality. Jealousy of the alleged influence of priests over women was another staple theme of anti-clerical discourse.[26]

Whatever the source of their hostility to the Church, all anti-clericals agreed that Catholicism was forever compromised by its associations with the ancien régime. As the Jacobins had maintained back in the 1790s, Catholicism stood for fanaticism and counter-Revolution and was completely incompatible with true – meaning republican – patriotism.[27]

Even during the First World War, at a time when political conflict was supposed to have been suspended by adherence to the 'sacred union' proclaimed by President Poincaré, anti-clericals continued to accuse the Church of disloyalty to the nation, notably by following the directives of the Pope, Benedict XV, who was alleged to be a sympathiser with the cause of the Central Powers.[28]

Anti-clericalism is relevant to another – and much less commented upon – feature of the political culture of the Third Republic: its sexism. The democratic politicians constantly vaunted the virtues of 'universal' suffrage, without noting that it was universal only for men. Republican misogyny was rooted in the Enlightenment view of woman as 'other': only man was a complete human being. Women's biology marked them out as different and provided a scientific basis for the construction of an ideology of femininity which represented them as inferior.[29] Sexual equality was unnatural, and during the Revolution the Jacobins adhered to the Rousseauist maxim that the public sphere was required to be exclusively masculine – particularly under a Republic.[30] Besides, as the example of the Vendée showed, women were all too likely to be on the side of superstition and reaction. Michelet taught the next generation of republicans that women's intrusion into politics could only result in disaster.[31] This was the crucial argument adduced against votes for women in the Senate in 1922, when it threw out a suffrage bill which had been passed by the Chamber of Deputies in 1919.[32] French women obtained the vote only in 1944, after the Nazi Occupation and when the Third Republic was no more.

The Third Republic lasted as long as it did because it succeeded in convincing the crucial elements in French society – the peasant masses and the various rungs of the bourgeoisie in a society which experienced less rapid socio-economic change than neighbouring Germany – that it was the regime best equipped to look after their material interests. The relatively small urban working classes remained outside this 'republican synthesis',[33] their alienation expressed by the CGT, whose leadership rejected parliamentary action in favour of direct action and the revolutionary general strike.[34] Most workers, however, were not members of the CGT and even many of those who were ignored the exhortations of their leaders not to participate in the 'fraud' of democratic elections, and voted for the socialist party, the SFIO, in the years before 1914. The socialists themselves claimed to be a revolutionary Marxist party and in conformity with a resolution of the Second International in 1904, steadfastly refused to enter into 'bourgeois' coalition governments. Yet in their own way, both the socialists and the workers were profoundly republican and could be relied upon to rally to the republican banner in times of crisis, as was proved most impressively in 1914.[35] After 1920, it was the self-allotted role of the Communist Party (PCF) to call for the overthrow of 'bourgeois democracy'. However, despite their rhetoric of class war, the communists too came to affirm their fidelity to the republican tradition both in the era of the Popular Front in the 1930s and in the Resistance during the Second World War.[36]

It was a different story on the far right, however. The republic's universalist rhetoric rang hollow for those elements in French society whose identities and traditions it repudiated. Catholics, understandably, continued to refuse to identify with a concept of the nation which made them out to be unpatriotic. They preferred to think of France as the 'eldest daughter of the Church', loyal to the memory of Saint Louis and Joan of Arc. Joan rather than Marianne was their ideal, since she epitomised the Catholic linkage of patriotism with religion. From the late nineteenth century a strong Catholic campaign was mounted to reclaim Joan from the republican tradition in which she was represented as a daughter of the people betrayed by the great ones of Church and state, and to portray her as a Catholic martyr. Rome delivered its verdict in 1920, when Joan was canonised as a Catholic saint.[37]

Catholics, however, deceived themselves as to the extent to which France remained a fervently Christian nation. By the turn of the century many areas were effectively de-Christianised. The region around Paris, the Centre, the Limousin and the Charentes, were areas of particularly low levels of religious practice and the Mediterranean and its hinterland were not much better. In 1850 in the diocese of Orleans a mere 2 per cent of men and 11.6 per cent of women made their Easter duties. In Chartres, the figure for men in 1900 was 1.3 per cent. Religion flourished only in select regions: the Massif Central, Brittany, Flanders, Alsace-Lorraine, the Franche-Comté, the Basque country and the environs of Lyons. Nevertheless, the nineteenth century saw a strong re-Christianisation of the French countryside, and it would be a mistake to underestimate its appeal to countless thousands of French men – and more especially French women – who expressed their rejection of republicanism in ostentatious displays of religious adherence such as mass pilgrimages to Lourdes. The twentieth century also witnessed a religious revival in the period between about 1930 and 1960, though decline has been dramatic since the 1960s.[38]

The extreme right presented republicans with a bigger headache than Catholicism. By 1900, they could rejoice that they had seen off the challenges from Legitimists, Orleanists and Bonapartists – the 'Old Right' – but they had more difficulty dealing with the much more combative and aggressive 'New Right' which surfaced at the time of the Boulangist episode in the late 1880s and became a permanent fixture of the French political scene from the time of the Dreyfus Affair. This 'revolutionary' right appreciated the need to attract popular support but vehemently rejected the Republic and republican political culture. Instead, it sought to rally the masses to the doctrines of 'integral nationalism' as preached by renegade republicans such as Paul Déroulède and Maurice Barrès, and by the monarchist Charles Maurras, the guru of the main organisational expression of integral nationalism, the *Action Française*.[39]

Integral nationalism had more in common with German *völkisch* nationalism than with the French republican idea of the nation. Its ideal was 'my country right or wrong' and it demanded unswerving adherence to the nation as the supreme good. Such a commitment, allegedly, arose out of a sense of identification with the national soil and the cult of one's ancestors. As such, it could only be made by people who were 100 per cent French, and not by 'alien' elements within the population – Protestants, Jews, freemasons and naturalised Frenchmen. Thus integral nationalists were as concerned with 'the enemy within' as with external threats and developed a political culture that was characterised not just by hatred of democracy and the Republic but by xenophobia and racism. Anti-semitism, in particular, was its stock in trade, out of a hope that the masses could be seduced from socialism and republicanism and mobilised behind the slogan *La France aux Français!*[40] Though little came of the attempts to bring together nationalists and dissident socialists and syndicalists, the rise of the New Right paved the way for the emergence of a specifically French fascism in the period between the wars which, though never organised into a single movement, contributed powerfully to the sense of crisis which pervaded French democracy in the 1930s.

Thus it was not the 'Republic one and indivisible' which confronted Germany in 1939–40, but a nation riven by ideological divisions over the identity of France. The defeat of 1940, followed by the establishment of Vichy and the Nazi Occupation, revealed the full extent of *les guerres franco-françaises*. The anti-Dreyfusards and revolutionaries of the right welcomed the catastrophe as a 'divine surprise' which could be turned to the advantage of all those who favoured a 'National Revolution', the watchwords of which were 'family, motherland and work' rather than 'liberty, equality and fraternity'. Marshal Pétain opted for collaboration with Nazi Germany, though he did not go far enough for out-and-out collaborationists who wanted France to be part of the Nazi revolution. A Légion des Volontaires Françaises contre le Bolchevisme (many of whom were militants in the fascist PPF created by the ex-communist Jacques Doriot) went to the Eastern Front in German uniform to fight communism. Anti-semitic laws were passed by Vichy to exclude Jews from public life in France and the regime also collaborated in the Nazi Final Solution, furnishing 76,000 Jewish deportees for the death camps. Joseph Darnand's Milice ruthlessly hunted down Jews, freemasons and communists. Frenchman also exploited Frenchman through the operation of a black market. The years 1940–4 were dark years, and they continued to cast their shadow over French political life long after the Liberation in 1944.[41]

POST-1945: TOWARDS A NEW POLITICAL CULTURE?

The shock of 1940 was not easily overcome. Whereas the memory of the First World War was one of national solidarity and of a great victory (albeit a victory purchased at an inordinate price in human lives and injury), the Second World War inflicted a deep scar on the collective consciousness of the French nation. At the Liberation, France was effectively in a state of civil war, as those who had opted for Resistance – foremost among them the PCF – exacted revenge upon those whom they branded collaborators and traitors. A post-war purge involved some 10,000 summary executions.[42]

On the other hand, on becoming head of the provisional government which assumed power in 1944, General de Gaulle, symbol of French determination to fight on after 1940, sought both to marginalise communist influence and to rebuild national unity around the Republic. To foster the myth of *la France résistante*, he deliberately downplayed the significance of the Vichy regime and represented the great mass of the nation as loyal to France and united in a desire to defeat the Nazi enemy. He also emphasised the continuity between the Allied victory of 1945 and that of 1918, paying tribute to Clemenceau and Foch on Armistice Day, 1945.

For de Gaulle, to resuscitate the Republic was not to go back to the party squabbles and weak governments which had bedevilled French politics under the Third Republic. A referendum held in October 1945 suggested that 95 per cent of the electorate (which for the first time included women) agreed with him. Yet when, after long parliamentary wrangles, a constitution was finally agreed for the Fourth Republic in November 1946, the new regime bore some striking resemblances to its republican predecessor. Once again, both the politicians and the electorate preferred to vest supreme authority in an elected National Assembly rather than a presidential figure. The experience of Vichy, not to mention almost two years of a virtual de Gaulle dictatorship, had reinforced republican fears regarding authoritarian and personalised rule.

The main difference between the Fourth Republic and the Third was at the level of personnel and parties: with the Vichyite and fascist right excluded from national life, the political scene was dominated by the parties which had distinguished themselves in the Resistance – the communists, the socialists and the MRP, a new Christian Democrat party which did much to end the association of Catholicism with the reactionary right. But though it carried out important work of social and economic reconstruction and paved the way for a new role for France in European politics (by the 1960s, French GDP was close to overtaking that of Britain), the Fourth Republic was beset by the same problems of ministerial instability which had plagued the Third Republic. Further handicapped by the problems of disengaging from empire, which was not surrendered willingly (witness the Indo-China war and the bloody, tragic and ultimately futile attempt to retain Algeria), the regime never succeeded in establishing a consensual political culture.

Only under the Fifth Republic has France – apparently – shaken off the ideological baggage with which it had been weighed down since 1789. When de Gaulle, profiting from the threat of a military takeover in 1958, once again returned to power he ensured that this time a new constitution was drawn up in accordance with his own ideas for strong government. The Fifth Republic was designed more as a presidential than as a parliamentary regime – a tendency reinforced in 1962 by the introduction of direct presidential elections. At the same time, however, the 1958 Constitution was a curious hybrid which preserved essential elements of the republican tradition, notably the need for the prime minister and the government to command a majority in the National Assembly.

Many commentators thought that these arrangements would not outlast the passing of de Gaulle (who quit the political stage in 1969), not least because they were initially denounced by the left as a violation of republican principles and practice. Instead, the new institutional framework gradually won acceptance by the left as well as the right. François Mitterrand, one of the bitterest critics of the 'permanent *coup d'état*' of 1958, was elected the first socialist president of the Fifth Republic in 1981 and went on to rule in presidential style for two full seven-year terms of office until 1995. Moreover, on two occasions under the Mitterrand presidency (in 1986–8 and 1993–5) it proved possible to establish 'cohabitation' arrangements between the socialist president and right-wing governments backed by right-wing majorities in parliament. In retrospect it can be seen that under the presidencies of Pompidou (1969–74) and Giscard d'Estaing (1974–81), France became a neo-liberal democracy governed not so much by the left or right as by the centre. The Mitterrand presidency, which began amid high hopes on the left for the imposition of a genuinely socialist agenda, merely confirmed the trend.[43]

Thus after 1958 (the events of May 1968 notwithstanding) France seemed to escape from the cycle of permanent crises, upheavals and revolutions which were for long the most characteristic features of its political culture. French 'exceptionalism', deriving from the working out of the revolutionary tradition, would appear to be no more. In the Fifth Republic, the French have created a democratic regime in which there can be alternation of power at the level of both the presidency and parliament and the problems facing France – particularly those associated with the management of the economy – are typical of Western democracies.[44]

These political trends have been further accentuated by changes in French society. At the end of the Second World War a third of the workforce was still employed in agriculture; by 1970 the figure was 14 per cent and by the early 1990s the proportion had fallen to one twentieth (by which time over 60 per cent of the workforce were in the tertiary sector). Traditional France – the France of small peasant farmers and small businessmen – has vanished and in its place has emerged a new nation of employees and wage-earners, managers and technicians, which looks much the same as other advanced Western countries. The long post-war boom which lasted 30 years – the *trente glorieuses* – saw growth rates averaging over 4 per cent in the 1950s and 5 per cent in the 1960s, and was accompanied by the transition from an economy protected by high tariff barriers to one exposed to international competition. When recession came in the mid-1970s it merely reinforced the trend towards integration into a wider European and world market.

FRANCE AND EUROPE

Yet France remains recognisably different. A major reason for this is her ambition to be recognised as a major player on the stage of world politics. French national identity continues to be shaped by a myth of national greatness, as may be seen most clearly in French relations with Europe in general and Germany in particular.[45]

Since the revelation of Prussian military might in Bismarck's wars of the 1860s, the obsession of French policy makers has been how to assert French primacy in Europe in the face of a demonstrably stronger Germany. The verdict of 1870 was never accepted and there was some satisfaction when it seemed to have been reversed by the outcome of the First World War and the Treaty of Versailles. By the 1930s, however, it was apparent that French preponderance was largely illusory, not least because the sacrifices required to obtain victory in 1918 had been excessive and could never be demanded again.

In a post-war world order dominated by the two superpowers of the United States and the Soviet Union, France, like Britain, was unmistakably reduced to the rank of a second-rate power, obliged after further military failures to give up its empire in the Far East and in North Africa. In Europe, the policy makers of the Fourth Republic were as always preoccupied above all with Germany – or more specifically, after the onset of the Cold War, with West Germany. Wisely, after initially flirting with a hard-line attitude, they opted for rapprochement and economic cooperation and thus opened the way to the creation of the European Economic Community by the Treaty of Rome in 1957.

On his return to power in 1958, General de Gaulle built on the foundations laid by the Fourth Republic and made close ties with Bonn the key to his policy on Europe. Initially opposed to the establishment of the EEC on the grounds that French industry needed to be protected from foreign competition, de Gaulle came to embrace the 'Common Market' as both vital to the modernisation of the French economy and beneficial to French agricultural interests through its Common Agricultural Policy. Though fond of invoking French grandeur in his rhetoric, de Gaulle recognised that France could never on her own be the Great Power she once had been. If she were to be great again, it would have to be in association with other European states, and in particular with West Germany. This, however, held out the enticing possibility of constructing a 'European Europe' or a 'Europe from the Atlantic to the Urals' which could be an effective alternative to the 'Atlantic' Europe that had emerged as a result of American control of the NATO alliance against the Soviet threat and American economic preponderance in the West. De Gaulle's Europe was to be a Europe of nation states (what he called an *Europe des Etats*).

Under Giscard and more especially Mitterrand, however, the French made a much stronger commitment to a federalist Europe. Mitterrand and Jacques Delors, the President of the European Commission and formerly French Minister of Finance, were the prime movers behind the Single European Act of 1987 and the Maastricht Treaty of 1991. It was no accident that Mitterrand's Euro-enthusiasm was intensified by the reunification of Germany in 1990, which revived French paranoia about the emergence of a Fourth German Reich. For France, Europe has been the key both to the containment of her more powerful neighbour and the vehicle for exercising influence in the world beyond her own capacity but in keeping with her self-allotted 'civilising mission'.

CONTINUITIES AND CHANGE

As is clear from French foreign and defence policy, it is an exaggeration to suggest that the French have entirely escaped the burdens of their past. The most potent symbol of France's determination to be recognised as a world power is the all-party commitment to a French nuclear bomb.[46] The sinking of the Greenpeace ship *Rainbow Warrior* in Auckland harbour in July 1985 by agents of the French secret services (almost certainly acting under the orders of the Minister of Defence Charles Hernu and possibly even with the compliance of President Mitterrand himself) testified to the lengths to which the French would go to carry out nuclear testing in the Pacific.[47] It was entirely in character that on becoming President of the Republic in 1995 Chirac should immediately resume the nuclear tests on Mururoa Atoll and persevere with them in the face of world-wide protest – though French reaction was much more muted.

On the other hand, the French are by no means united in the belief that the best way to fulfil their leading world role is through a commitment to the construction of Europe. The referendum held in September 1992 to ratify the Maastricht Treaty produced a bare majority for the pro-Europeans: 51 to 49 per cent. Significantly, those in favour tended to be the better-off and the better-educated: the unemployed and the urban and rural poor voted against Maastricht, their fears articulated by the National Front at one political extreme and the PCF at the other. Voting in the referendum was undoubtedly influenced by general attitudes to Mitterrand and the economic situation, but opinion polls seemed to indicate a more fundamental dimension to French doubts. For instance, a poll in *L'Express* on 25 September 1992 found that 40 per cent thought that French identity was menaced by European Union. A series of subsequent polls has shown that whilst commitment to the creation of a more truly united Europe remains strong in many parts of French society, there are major doubts about the future, including the impact of the convergence criteria for EMU. Although the major demonstrations and strikes during 1995–6 can to some extent be seen as part of a long tradition of street confrontations over political and economic issues, they did also highlight fears that the new Europe would require significant cuts, including welfare.

However, the main theme of the anti-Maastricht lobby has been the threat posed to France by a supra-national Europe dominated by Germany rather than France. Dissident voices, which include those of the Gaullist Philippe Séguin of the Gaullist RPR and the socialist Jean-Pierre Chevènement, can now be heard within all the mainstream political parties claiming that French interests are being sacrificed to those of German bankers and industrialists and calling for a return to nineteenth-century notions of the nation-state and the Republic. Philippe de Villiers, a member of the once strongly pro-European UDF, quit in 1994 to found a new party, the Mouvement pour la France, to continue his anti-Maastricht crusade beyond the referendum and the European elections of 1994 (in which his anti-European candidates polled 12 per cent of the vote) into his bid for the presidency in 1995. The successful presidential candidate, the opportunistic Jacques Chirac, stopped short of adopting the full-blown Euroscepticism of his colleague Séguin, but played the nationalist card in the campaign by promising a referendum before France adopted the Single European Currency. In office, Chirac has reaffirmed his commitment to Europe but it is evident that he lacks the federalist faith of his predecessors Mitterrand and Giscard d'Estaing. The 'certain idea of France' beloved of General de Gaulle is by no means entirely a thing of the past.

Other ghosts of the past continue to haunt the contemporary political scene. In recent years the French have been obliged to confront unpleasant truths about the experience of Vichy and the Occupation. In 1987, the trial of Klaus Barbie, the Gestapo chief in Lyon responsible for the torture and death of the Resistance hero Jean Moulin, allowed the defence not only to draw comparisons between Nazi crimes against humanity and atrocities committed by the French in their colonies, but also to brand the Resistance itself as a source of disunity and violence. The reassuring myth of *la France résistante* developed by de Gaulle (long discounted by non-French professional historians) was exploded before public opinion. The long-running saga of Paul Touvier had the same effect. A prominent member of the Lyon Milice, Touvier had been twice condemned to death after the Liberation, but having been protected by elements within the Catholic Church was finally arrested only in 1989. A further five years elapsed before he was convicted of crimes against humanity in 1994, after protests which followed a legal judgement of 1992 ruling that he did not need to stand trial.

Still more sensational was the scandal surrounding René Bousquet, the Vichy chief of police who had been mainly responsible for the round-up and deportation of Jews from France to Auschwitz in 1942, who was found murdered on 8 June 1993. The public was shocked to learn of his long-standing friendship with the President of the Republic, François Mitterrand, who in a book published in 1994 was revealed to have been involved in right-wing student politics in the 1930s and to have been a sincere admirer of Pétain before he joined the Resistance in 1943.[48] The dismay and the disillusion on the left was enormous and helped to accelerate the disintegration of the Socialist Party, which was perhaps the most remarkable political development of the first half of the 1990s.

Similarly, the rise of the National Front under the leadership of Jean-Marie Le Pen is a salutary reminder that the racist and xenophobic right has not vanished from the political scene. On the contrary, Le Pen – whose party had polled a mere 0.4 per cent of the vote in the 1981 legislative elections – won 15 per cent of the votes in the first round of the presidential elections of 1995, many of them cast by workers (30 per cent voted for Le Pen) in the larger cities hit by the recession and susceptible to Le Pen's denunciations of immigration as the cause of unemployment and crime. During late 1996, his party's opinion poll rating was approaching 20 per cent. Le Pen's attacks on immigrants and the political class in general have found a powerful echo in a country which has notable socio-economic problems in many areas, including high unemployment and rising crime. He has also benefited from the breakdown of traditional class lines and a more general dealignment from mainstream parties.

The full impact of the National Front is to be measured not just in terms of the size of its own support but by the extent to which other political parties – not excluding the communists – have been obliged to respond to its agenda by taking a tougher stand against immigrants themselves. The parliamentary right, galvanised by the combative Charles Pasqua, Minister of the Interior in the 'cohabitation' administrations of 1986–8 and 1993–5, pushed through a new law on nationality in 1993 which denied the automatic right to French nationality to the children born of immigrant parents. Pasqua further pressurised Mitterrand into permitting a constitutional amendment which limited entry to France for foreigners and asylum-seekers and ruthlessly ordered police harassment in immigrant neighbourhoods.

Intolerance, of course, is by no means confined to the right in France. The Jacobin tradition itself, as we have seen, has denied pluralism and demanded 'assimilation' in the name of a homogeneous nation-state, often with disastrous consequences.[49] In recent years socialists and feminists have contested the right of Muslim girls to wear their headscarves to school on the grounds that these symbolised the oppression of women and were an affront to the secular and assimilationist ideals of the Republic. (This *affaire du foulard* was a great embarrassment to Lionel Jospin, the socialist candidate in the presidential elections of 1995, when he was Minister of Education back in 1989.) Poll evidence seems to indicate that a significant minority of the French are opposed to multiculturalism: a *L'Express* poll on 25 October 1991 found that whilst 59 per cent thought the diversity of origin of the French population was a rich feature of national identity, 37 per cent were opposed.

The decision by the government to commemorate during 1996 the 1,500th anniversary of the baptism of Clovis, allegedly the first king of 'France', highlights further divisions. A poll in *Le Monde* on 19 September 1996 found that 40 per cent of the French thought it a good idea, whereas another 40 per cent were opposed. Among the opponents were a notable number of those on the left, who disliked the involvement of the Catholic Church and feared the commemoration's impact in terms of legitimating radical nationalism. The debate on what it means to be French is still ongoing, and even if it no longer centres on the survival of the Republic, it is still animated by the politics of memory.

NOTES

1 The essential work on this theme is P. Nora (ed.), *Les Lieux de Mémoire*, 7 vols, Paris, Gallimard, 1984–93, a treasure-trove of suggestive articles on memory and commemoration. In English, see R. Gildea, *The Past in French History*, New Haven, Yale University Press, 1994; and J. R. Gillis (ed.), *Commemorations: The Politics of National Identity*, Princeton, Princeton University Press, 1994, especially for H. Lebovics, 'Creating the Authentic France: Struggles over French Identity in the First Half of the Twentieth Century'. See also J. Bridgford (ed.), *France: Image and Identity*, London, ASCMF, 1987.

2 F. Braudel, *The Identity of France, vol. 1., History and Environment*, London, Fontana, 1988, p. 38.

3 The excellent new history by R. Tombs, *France 1814–1914*, London, Longman, 1996, is written from this political cultural perspective. See also H. Le Bras and E. Todd, *L'Invention de la France*, Paris, Hachette, 1981. On French political traditions in general, S. Hazareesingh, *Political Traditions in Modern France*, Oxford, Oxford University Press, 1994.

4 See K. M. Baker (ed.), *The French Revolution and the Creation of Modern Political Culture, vol. 1. The Political Culture of the Old Regime*, Oxford, Oxford University Press, 1987. Also, F. Furet, 'L'Ancien Régime' in F. Furet and M. Ozouf (eds), *Dictionnaire critique de la Révolution française*, Paris, Flammarion, 1988.

5 C. Lucas (ed.), *The French Revolution and the Creation of Modern Political Culture*, vol. 2, Oxford, Oxford University Press, 1988.

6 L. Hunt, *Politics, Culture and Class in the French Revolution*, Berkeley, University of California Press, 1984.

7 M. Ozouf, *La Fête révolutionnaire*, Paris, Gallimard, 1976.

8 E. Weber, 'Left, Right and Temperament' in *My France: Politics, Culture, Myth*, Cambridge, Mass., The Belknap Press, 1991.

9 J.-F. Sirinelli, *Histoire des Droites en France*, 3 vols, Paris, Gallimard, 1992, is now the most comprehensive survey of the politics, culture and outlook of the French right.

10 G. Cubitt, 'God, Man and Satan: Strands in Counter-Revolutionary Thought among Nineteenth-Century French Catholics' in F. Tallett and N. Atkin (eds), *Catholicism in Britain and France since 1789*, London, The Hambledon Press, 1995, p. 135.

11 Cf. S. Desan, *Reclaiming the Sacred: Lay Religion and Popular Politics in Revolutionary France*, Ithaca, Cornell University Press, 1990.

12 C. Tilly, *The Vendée*, New York, Wiley, 1964; D. Sutherland, *The Chouans: The*

Social Origins of Popular Counter-Revolution in Upper Brittany, 1770–1796, Oxford, Clarendon, 1982.

13 P. Rosanvallon, *Le Moment Guizot*, Paris, Gallimard, 1985.

14 F. Bluche, *Le Bonapartisme: aux origines de la droite autoritaire (1800–1850)*, Paris, Nouvelles Editions Latines, 1980; B. Ménager, *Les Napoléons du peuple*, Paris, Aubier, 1988.

15 There is now an excellent tutorial on this theme by William Doyle available from the TLTP Consortium (Southampton and Glasgow Universities).

16 G. Weill, *Histoire du parti républicain en France, 1814–1870*, Paris, Alcan, 1900.

17 M. Agulhon, *The Republican Experiment 1848–1852*, Cambridge, Cambridge University Press, 1983, is the best short account.

18 Cf. J. F. McMillan, *Napoleon III*, London, Longman, 1991.

19 E. J. Hobsbawm, 'Mass-Producing Traditions: Europe, 1870–1914' in E. J. Hobsbawm and T. Ranger (eds), *The Invention of Tradition*, Cambridge, Cambridge University Press, 1983.

20 E. Weber, *Peasants into Frenchmen: The Modernization of Rural France, 1870–1914*, Stanford, Stanford University Press, 1976.

21 P. Nora, 'Ernest Lavisse. Son rôle dans la formation du sentiment national', *Revue historique*, 1962, 22.

22 R. Sanson, *Les 14 juillet. Fête et conscience nationale, 1789–1975*, Paris, Flammarion, 1976; C. Rearick, *Pleasures of the Belle Epoque: Entertainment and Festivity in Turn-of-the-Century France*, New Haven, Yale University Press, 1985.

23 M. Agulhon, *Marianne into Battle: Republican Imagery and Symbolism in France 1789–1880*, Cambridge, Cambridge University Press, 1981; and M. Agulhon, *Marianne au pouvoir: l'imagérie et la symbolique républicaines de 1880 à 1914*, Paris, Flammarion, 1989.

24 E. Weber, 'Who Sang the Marseillaise?' in *My France*.

25 For discrimination against Catholics, see M. Larkin, *Religion, Politics and Preferment in France since 1890*, Cambridge, Cambridge University Press, 1995.

26 See T. Zeldin (ed.), *Conflicts in French Society: Anticlericalism, Education and Morals in the Nineteenth Century*, London, Allen and Unwin, 1970.

27 R. C. Cobb, *The People's Armies*, New Haven, Yale University Press, 1987, pp. 442–79.

28 J. F. McMillan, 'French Catholics, rumeurs infâmes and the Union Sacrée, 1914–1918' in F. Coetzee and M. Shevin-Coetzee (eds), *Authority, Identity and the Social History of the Great War*, Oxford, Berghahn Books, 1995.

29 Cf. L. Schiebinger, *The Mind Has No Sex? Women in the Origins of Modern Science*, Cambridge, Mass., Harvard University Press, 1989; G. Fraisse, *Reason's Muse: Sexual Difference and the Birth of Democracy*, Chicago, University of Chicago Press, 1994.

30 L. Hunt, *The Family Romance of the French Revolution*, Berkeley, University of California Press, 1992.

31 On Michelet, see T. Moreau, *Le Sang de l'histoire: Michelet, l'histoire et l'idée de la femme au xixe siècle*, Paris, Flammarion, 1982.

32 S. C. Hause with Anne R. Kenney, *Women's Suffrage and Social Politics in the French Third Republic*, Princeton, Princeton University Press, 1984.

33 The phrase was coined by S. Hoffmann in his edited book *France: Change and Tradition*, London, Gollancz, 1963.

34 J. Julliard, *Fernand Pelloutier et les origines du syndicalisme d'action directe*, Paris, Seuil, 1971.

35 A. Bergounioux, 'Socialisme et République avant 1914' in S. Berstein and O. Rudelle (eds), *Le Modèle républicain*, Paris, Presses Universitaires de France, 1992.

36 D. Brower, *The New Jacobins: The French Communist Party and the Popular Front*, Ithaca, Cornell University Press, 1968.

37 J. F. McMillan, 'Reclaiming a Martyr: French Catholics and the Cult of Joan of Arc, 1890–1920' in *Martyrs and Martyrologies. Studies in Church History*, 1993, 30.

38 R. Gibson, *A Social History of French Catholicism 1789–1914*, London, Routledge, 1989; G. Cholvy and Y.-M. Hilaire, *Histoire religieuse de la France contemporaine*, 3 vols, Toulouse, Privat, 1985–8.

39 Z. Sternhell, *La Droite révolutionnaire, 1885–1914*, Paris, Seuil, 1978.

40 P. Birnbaum, *'La France aux Français'. Histoire des haines nationalistes*, Paris, Seuil, 1993.

41 H. Rousso, *The Vichy Syndrome. History and Memory in France since 1944*, Cambridge, Mass., Harvard University Press, 1991.

42 P. Novick, *The Resistance versus Vichy. The Purge of Collaborators in Liberated France*, London, Chatto and Windus, 1968.

43 An incisive survey of the post-war history and political culture of France is R. Gildea, *France Since 1945*, Oxford, Oxford University Press, 1996, which has a good, up-to-date bibliography on the themes covered in this final section.

44 On the 'exceptionalism' debate, see F. Furet, J. Julliard and P. Rosanvallon, *La République du centre. La fin de l'exception française*, Paris, Calmann-Lévy, 1988; and G. Flynn (ed.), *Rethinking the Hexagon: The New France in the New Europe*, Boulder, Westview, 1995.

45 See in general R. Tiersky, *France in the New Europe*, Boulder, Westview, 1994.

46 J. Howorth, 'The Defence Consensus and French Political Culture' in M. Scriven and P. Wagstaff (eds), *War and Society in Twentieth-Century France*, Oxford, Berg, 1991.

47 D. Porch, *The French Secret Services. From the Dreyfus Affair to the Gulf War*, London, Macmillan, 1995.

48 P. Péan, *Une Jeunesse française*, Paris, Fayard, 1994.

49 M. Silverman, *Deconstructing the Nation: Immigration, Racism and Citizenship in Modern France*, London, Routledge, 1992.

6 Germany

Ekkart Zimmermann

INTRODUCTION

There are few nation-states whose political culture presents as much of a puzzle as the German one. Among its most remarkable forming characteristics are: a history of more than 1,000 years (the German Reich officially was founded by Otto the Great in 962); more than a dozen distinct 'tribes' within whatever her boundaries were over time; up to a dozen capitals widely defined in her history (including Berlin, Bonn, Frankfurt, Vienna, Regensburg and Prague); more than five radically different regimes over the last 150 years; her remarkable late nineteenth-century economic growth (which in less than fifty years surpassed British supremacy); more neighbours around her than any other European state; a territorial expansion, after the Munich agreement of 1938, almost as great as that of the over-stretched nineteenth-century Bismarck empire; the experience of unconditional surrender in 1945 and persisting historical guilt relating to the Nazi era; the ensuing Allied occupation (including their attempts to rebuild a democratic political culture); and the division of Germany into two states by 1949, only for them to be suddenly reunited in 1989. What sort of political culture could be expected from such a country? And what are the implications of the continuing process of reunification with an East Germany which in many ways had developed a very different political culture, at just the time that major doubts are beginning to emerge in some quarters about the future of Germany's 'wonder economy' and political stability? Is Germany today truly a stable democracy, as was widely believed by the 1970s; or are older doubts about its culture, of the type voiced by Almond and Verba, still relevant?[1]

The current political culture of (West) Germany is primarily a fourfold function of historical experiences. The first stems from the failures and catastrophes resulting from two non-democratic empires, with the Nazi regime leading not only to war but to genocide as well. The second great formative experience was the disaster of the Weimar Republic (1919–33) and the associated economic, political and mental deficiencies. The third stems more from the experience of developing the economy, especially the conflict-management corporatist and welfarist arrangements which helped ensure relative industrial peace in the post-1945 era, thus furthering economic efficiency. The last, but by no means least, of these experiences is the persistence of local democratic traditions often embedded in closed milieus: it is misleading to portray the German tradition as essentially authoritarian, ignoring important sub-cultures, such as the liberal and social democratic ones.

Learning from historical mistakes and failures seems to be the essence and strength of West German political culture. For East Germans, learning now requires an even wider perspective, in particular the ability to take on board the failure (and crimes) of its economic and political system from 1949–89 and of the astonishing success of West Germany. But there is a new problem for West Germans too; if they can only draw *negative* lessons from the political culture of East Germany, does this imply that East Germans will derive the right conclusions set by the positive example in the West? The answer must be left open, though we can point to some structural clues and preliminary results.

THE LEGACY OF HISTORY

An important starting point in order to understand German political culture is the Reformation: the almost 50:50 split between Protestants and Catholics had major implications. The territorial principle of *cuius regio eius religio* (meant to defuse the religious conflict by having only the ruler decide about the religion 'chosen') had two devastating effects. First, it nourished rather than controlled religious divisions and dissent, though this was not always visible on the surface. Second, authoritarian structures of government were strengthened by extending them even to religious matters, with the Church in effect becoming part of the state bureaucracy. As a consequence of these religious cleavages the German territories experienced major wars that lasted for two generations in the first half of the sixteenth century, and during 1618–48 became the battleground of European religious and hegemonic war, which led to the death of one-third of the population. The country was devastated, and more than 300 'German' states sprang up in the territory of the Holy Roman Empire following the Westphalian peace in 1648.

During the nineteenth century, Germany re-emerged as a modern state. In opposition to the universal values proclaimed by the French Revolution (and carried forward by the Napoleonic armies deep into Eastern Europe), German nationalism centred around the *völkisch* concept of common descent ('blood'), and an organic idea of the state following Hegel, Fichte and Adam Müller. Moreover, nation-building, to incorporate the other major German states (including Bavaria, Württemberg and Saxony), took place with blood and iron, against external enemies rather than through internal revolution or evolution. The key figure in this process was

Bismarck, Prime Minister of Prussia, the king of which was crowned the new German Emperor in 1871 after the defeat of France (some German-speaking lands, including Austria and parts of Eastern Europe, remained outside the new Reich). However, rapid economic development, combined with social and political divisions, posed major problems for the German Establishment, especially after the departure of Bismarck. Although Germany had a parliament, the *Reichstag*, considerable power lay in the hands of Kaiser Wilhelm II (in Weber's words, the 'crowned dilettante', a man who referred to the Reichstag as the '*Schwatzbude*'), his entourage, the pan-German ultra-nationalists and the coalition of landed aristocracy, especially the Prussian *Junkers*, as well as heavy industry which was a notable feature of German development (Heinrich Mann in *Der Untertan* (1914) gave this somewhat feudal society its classical literary representation).[2] By 1900 aggressive social imperialism was increasingly the option which many in this group perceived as a way of defusing the growing socialist movement, and integrating Catholics into a Protestant-led state. The *Kulturkampf* against the Roman Catholic Church as well as laws against the socialist movement simply had proved a failure, in contrast to the social reforms (1883–9) which helped integrate part of the new working class. Nevertheless, the new Germany was in many ways a socially ghettoised state.[3]

Yet there were many other societal and political developments taking place in nineteenth-century Germany that could have allowed for different future options.[4] The much-cited interpretations of Wehler and Fischer, with their stress on the ruthlessly expansionist nature of pre-1914 German elites, tend to look at history from its end point, in a sort of backward looking teleology.[5] In another major interpretation, Blackbourn and Eley have argued against a peculiarly German *Sonderweg*, which allegedly marginalised the liberal middle class.[6] In their view, other nations were facing just as many obstacles and crises on route towards modernisation. Blackbourn even speaks of a *Verbürgerlichung* of society rather than a feudalisation of the bourgeoisie. Certainly, much German-bashing is based on a lack of serious comparisons with other countries. For instance, in terms of modern bureaucratisation and religious secularisation (especially in education) Germany was a leader, rather than a laggard; more central to the argument, 'its degree of limited democratisation is not at all unusual' up till 1918.[7] Britain, commonly seen as the oldest of the democracies, lacked universal male franchise at this time and considerable power resided in the unelected House of Lords (especially before its reform in 1911, which took away much of its power).

Perhaps the crucial point about German development is the particular mixture of relative modernisation in some spheres of life, combined with ideologically reactionary and racist tendencies in other areas. Certainly, the latter helps explain the absence of a major outcry against Nazi anti-semitic policies. Although strong anti-semitism was by no means unique to Germany, in other countries it faced a strong humanistic counter-tradition –

most notably after the Dreyfus Affair in France. The relative absence of such countervailing forces tells us more about the Holocaust than the attempt made during the 1980s by the leading conservative historian Ernst Nolte and others to 'relativise' it as one among many genocides, and essentially modelled on terror developments in the Soviet Union – a claim which led to a bitter polemic among academics and in the media.[8] Perhaps the final word in this 'debate' should go to the historian Jürgen Kocka, who asked why Germans would want to be compared with Russians on this topic, when in general they entirely shun any comparison with Russian culture and history.

A comparative analysis of the Great Depression which began in the late 1920s also reveals that the German case was not unique, in terms of length and, in part, the depth of the trough. What was unique was mass electoral polarisation (which produced not only a large Nazi Party but also the most important Communist Party in Western Europe), the heavy dissent amongst the elites and the strong anti-system consensus which reflected deeper-lying values. Thomas Mann in 1918, with his praise of German 'culture' against Western superficial 'civilisation', expressed a common view, which was just as typical as that of the ultra-radical critique of democracy which came from people like Kurt Tucholsky and Carl von Ossietzky. Within 10 years, Mann was to become a defender of the Republic, reflecting the possibilities for change. But relatively few liked Weimar; even Stresemann, the most influential figure in the 'golden' period between 1924 and 1928, called himself a 'republican by reason' (not by heart).[9]

The Weimar Republic itself had many shortcomings, of which three failures were crucial. First, with few exceptions, the population believed that it had been betrayed on the home front as Germany had made great gains in the east and was still fighting on foreign soil in the west in 1918 (the stab-in-the-back legend). This meant that for many Germans the military retained considerable influence and respect: indeed, the wartime Field Marshal Hindenburg was elected President in 1925 (and re-elected again in a run-off against Hitler in 1932), a kind of substitute for the Kaiser who had fled into exile at the end of the war. Second, the Social Democrats were not radical enough when taking power in 1919.[10] Thus the old economic structures (and mentality) of the Prussian Junker state survived just as much as the Prussian state bureaucracies. Third, the Social Democrats lacked both the ability and the will to hold on to power in a political vacuum created by the onset of the Great Depression after 1928.[11] Their electoral strength had drastically faltered from 29.8 per cent of the parliamentary seats in 1928 to 20.4 per cent in November 1932, though their voters were more resistant to Nazi challenges than those of the liberal parties of the centre. The Social Democrats left the Grand Coalition government in 1930 over a relatively minor issue of financing the social security scheme, leaving Germany to be governed nationally by a series of increasingly unstable and authoritarian centre-right coalitions (while behind the scenes lurked the growing power of the army and other interests).

The 'Weimar coalition' between the Social Democrats, the Centre Party and the German People's Party lasted in Prussia, the dominating state within the German Reich, for more than a decade before Chancellor Papen, in a coup-like measure, dissolved it in summer 1932 – which was to set a precedent for the Nazi destruction of local government after 1933. Another miscalculation on the part of right-wing elites paved the way for the next step to the German catastrophe. When forming a coalition with the Nazi Party in January 1933, the anti-democratic forces in the German National People's Party believed they could use Hitler as an instrument against the communists and Social Democrats. Once economic and political control was won back, Hitler could be dismissed (this interpretation broadly corresponds to the Marxist Bonapartist theory of fascism). But Hitler broke these shackles and used the conservatives' economic power for expansionary warfare. When it turned out that the war was to be lost and the economic base of the conservatives in the east would be routed through defeat on the battlefield, small pockets of resistance against Hitler developed. But these were brutally wiped out by him after the failed coup attempt of July 1944 (more than one thousand were executed or killed in a bloody revenge). The final blow to the landed economic and political interests in the east came from unconditional surrender in the Second World War and the occupation of the eastern territories by the Soviet Union.

Though Hitler never received more than 37.3 per cent of the Reichstag seats in free elections (July 1932), his legitimacy after obtaining power rose dramatically until the years 1940–1.[12] His triumphant return to Berlin after victory against France in 1940 probably showed him at the highest point of support amongst the German population. Historians' estimations go well beyond 90 per cent, a figure that explains the sway this man held over Germany till 1945, despite the coming catastrophe that became visible from the winter of 1941 onwards. Part of this enormous success had to do with the antipathies of Germans against party politics in the 1920s and 1930s, part with the economic and military successes the Nazis achieved. More important, however, may have been the particular skills of Hitler and the Nazi Party. The Marxist philosopher Ernst Bloch in a succinct dialectical remark had already noted in 1930: 'Nazis speak deceptively, but to human beings, the communists speak plain truth, but of things.' The ideology of the *Volksgemeinschaft* with its alleged equality of all Germans in a *völkische Ständestaat* probably left a deeper imprint on the collective 'soul' than many would like to acknowledge.

1945–90: THE RISE OF THE WEST GERMAN 'MODEL'

In their classic – though much attacked – comparative work on political culture in the late 1950s, Almond and Verba observed a lack of participant attitudes among (West) Germans and a general tendency towards compliance.[13] Amongst Germans they found pride in economic achievements since the Hour Zero of 1945, but not in the new institutions of democracy. The extensive Allied re-education programme had some effect in diminishing lingering support for forms of authoritarianism at the end of 1945. But it was the 1950s economic miracle (which by 1961 had once again taken Germany to the top of the European league, in front of Britain) which was seen by Almond and Verba as the crucial change underpinning the new state which had been formed in 1949 as the Allies began to relinquish their hold over the western zones of occupation.

The revisiting of German political culture by Conradt in the 1970s demonstrated that pride in new political institutions had grown in a direction typical of Britain.[14] Unconventional non-violent political participation, such as in citizens' initiatives, social movements or protest demonstrations, emerged as just as standard a form of political participation as the conventional ones. The Basic Law (*Grundgesetz*) became almost as accepted as the Mercedes star ever was. Moreover, these new survey data referred to the period after the first oil shock of 1973 had hit the country. The Basic Law, which had been a source of national pride for only 7 per cent of Germans in 1959, was cited by 31 per cent in 1978 and 51 per cent by 1988 (other notable sources of pride were the economy, cited by 33 per cent in 1959 and 50 per cent in 1988, and social welfare programmes, cited by 6 and 39 per cent respectively).[15]

This growing constitutional patriotism (*Verfassungspatriotismus*)[16] became highly obvious when the West German Basic Law, which had supposedly been only a temporary measure, was adopted for the united Germany in 1990. The law had been specifically designed to prevent a revival of extremism, with features such as a symbolic President rather than a directly elected one, and a federal system with notable powers given to lower levels of government: these institutions had functioned well and thereby gained strong popular support. Yet there can be no doubt that this support and increasing trust has declined somewhat in the 1990s. There is growing party weariness (*Parteiverdrossenheit*), occasionally lower turnout (though from previously very high levels, typically 90 per cent in major elections), and a decline in the share of votes which the two major parties – the Social Democrats and Christian Democrats – capture.[17] In terms of standard indicators of political support, West German democracy was and is ultra-stable, notwithstanding the relatively high ranking in terms of political protest since the major waves of student protest in the 1960s and the challenge by West German terrorists in the 1970s.[18] This was terrorist anarchism, however, not supported by the workers or any other major group in society. In the end West German terrorism was merely a police problem, since the state had withstood the terrorist challenge and had not overreacted, although this was not always clear in the 'hot year' of 1977. Luck on the part of political leaders (the liberation of the Lufthansa aeroplane in Mogadishu and the suicide of terrorist leaders) was also involved.

In sum, Easton's hypothesis could not have been better corroborated than in the West German case: economic efficiency leads to specific support (pride in the economy) which then broadens into output-independent diffuse support for the political institutions.[19] Support for political institutions (in contrast to that for respective governments) has not seriously declined in any of the three economic downturns of 1973, 1980 or 1992. This is remarkable since the growth rates after 1968 were nowhere what they were in the two decades before. Although the first major economic crisis of 1966–7, and the Grand Coalition formed in response to it, gave rise to the right-wing extremist National Democratic Party (NPD), this failed to cross the 5 per cent electoral hurdle nationally (4.3 per cent of the vote in 1969): detailed studies of the NPD vote showed that it had often come from groups like the old, or small farmers, who were soon replaced by a new generation of voters. Revealingly, it largely collapsed subsequently, due to in-fighting, the recovery of the economy and a change in the political opposition by the conservatives in Bonn.[20]

The smooth transition from Christian Democrat-dominated coalitions during 1949–65, to the Grand Coalition, to a Social Democrat-led government after 1969, further underlined the democratic normalcy of the system. It is important not to ignore politically apathetic people for whom politics is a bad word (something of a German tradition), and who are open to protest-type mobilisation. Nevertheless, during the 1970s and 1980s there emerged widespread acceptance that West Germany had become a civic culture – even more so than Britain. The stability of West German society, which once again became apparent in handling the two oil price shocks of 1973 and 1980, allowed it to become more and more of an attractive model, mixing market incentives with state provisions and 'guaranteeing' its inhabitants a high (and increasing) standard of living. They responded with 'a growing commitment to democratic procedures . . . [turning] West German public opinion [into one of] the most democratic in Europe'.[21] Corporate instruments such as the concerted action between government and the key economic groups like the trades unions, wide political representation of special interest groups, the multifold political instruments of a federal republic, all these institutions and devices need to be mentioned here.[22] Basically the model was to trade in strikes for higher wages and side-benefits. By contrast, East Germany was close to bankruptcy in the 1980s due to cuts in Soviet oil supply and the exhaustion of her own resources. Thereafter she had to rely heavily on credit from the West and on her own surface brown coal, causing gigantic ecological damage.

The well-organised and affluent West German society turned out to be a highly successful model and attracted widespread interest in Eastern Europe, not least in East Germany. In its mixture of market elements and state provisions (*soziale Marktwirtschaft*) it became more attractive than the image of American society with its strong individualism and free market ethic. 'Either the DM comes, or we will come ourselves' was the slogan of the East German masses, once the Berlin Wall had fallen on 9 November 1989. However, German reunification did not simply stem from an admiration for West Germany's economy. The political opportunity structure had widened due to dissent amongst political elites (not only within East Germany, but above all between Gorbachev and Honecker), to rapidly decreasing repression and shifting mass alignments.[23] Once those masses had entered the stage and called for free elections and unification, constitutional rights became a secondary thing that was taken for granted or at least perceived as instrumental. Moreover, once this stage was reached, it again came as no surprise that the political professionals in Bonn – especially within the Christian Democrats, who by the late 1980s had once again become the cornerstone of government – out-manoeuvred any potential autonomous East German democratic elite group. Those civilian groups were unprepared to grab power. A democratic counter-elite could not and had not formed under totalitarian conditions. Political dissidents had either left the DDR or had become the long-term victims of repression.

FROM 1991 ON: INTEGRATING THE EAST AND OTHER PROBLEMS

In West Germany it took two decades for specific system support to emerge and then to change into a more diffuse support. Will it take as long to forge a new democratic civic culture in the 'new *Länder*'? In contrast to West Germans after the war, East Germans initially seemed to have few reservations about democracy:[24]

> overall, it is safe to conclude that political skills, cognitive mobilisation, and patterns of political communication among East Germans are more highly developed than those of West Germans in the 1950s ... the first successful democratic revolution in German history ... added a new sense of civic competence and democratic consciousness among East German citizens.[25]

Yet East Germans (*Ossis*) feel and will increasingly feel relatively deprived of material standards the West Germans (*Wessis*) have acquired over five decades. This holds in spite of (or perhaps because of) the Western welfare state that is smoothing the economic and political transition in the East (a system which is now in dramatic need of being overhauled). None of those cushions was available to West Germans after the Second World War.

Comparisons with the West German population and the political skills which are being acquired in parliamentary politics will lead to more political pressure, going beyond the growing vote for the re-baptised former Communist Party, the Party of Democratic Socialism (PDS).[26] On the other hand, that pressure will remain relatively marginal since East Germany comprises only one-fifth of the population with one-tenth of Germany's GNP. Even the dramatic electoral shift to the PDS in East Berlin during the Berlin Senate elections in October 1995, where it obtained 36.3 per cent of the vote and became the strongest party, does not challenge this analysis. Due to its excellent local networks, its stress on East German issues, the weak performance of the other parties in the East and the problematic economic situation, the PDS has become a people's protest party.[27]

West Germans also express feelings of relative deprivation vis-à-vis their economic position before unification. Many West Germans believe that they are entitled to their relatively high standards of living through their hard work, whereas they think of the East Germans as incapable of disciplined work, as demanding and not grateful for the enormous support they get. (The most cynical quip is only six words long: 'There is an *Ossi* at work . . .'.) A number of (often highly dubious) surveys show that East Germans claim to have more emotional personal relationships, are in greater need of and share more with their community and express more group feelings, whereas West Germans are perceived as cold and money-minded.[28] On the other hand, it seems as if East Germans are 'aping' West Germans where possible. This encompasses both consumer behaviour (for example, cars, do-it-yourself shops, changes in food and eating habits, sex videos) and political pressure *within* the democratic channels that have been learned about.

Behind these issues lie very different interpretations of the historic nature of East German political culture. One major hypothesis – emphasising the impact of the state socialist authoritarian socialisation – holds that, due to communist re-education effects and structural changes that took place during the communist regime (increased upward social mobility of the working class until the 1970s, extremely high participation of women in the workforce, discrimination against bourgeois elements, centrally-planned economy with no official unemployment and wide state-administered social benefits), East German political culture developed very differently from that in the West.[29] It was a system in which the 'principles of anti-fascism, democracy and socialism and fostered traditions of German working-class culture such as egalitarianism and social justice' were dominant; however, 'instead of realising these promises, the regime extended increasingly hierarchical and authoritarian patterns of traditional German culture into all dimensions of everyday life: in family, workplace, and polity'.[30] Moreover, all elements of social democracy were persecuted. The traditional *Obrigkeitsstaat* reappeared, this time in a Prussian variant of a German path to state socialism. Efforts from the 1970s onwards at reincorporating parts of the Prussian history in this sense failed. East Germans continued to live with a double identity as citizens of the DDR and as Germans, which brings us to the second hypothesis.

This second hypothesis maintains that due to a common history, to familial ties, West German visitors and, above all, the powerful effect of the West's media, a new political culture never fully developed. This cultural heritage or familial legacy hypothesis maintains that, in view of the economic and political problems in the DDR, any efforts at mass legitimation were largely futile. Further, any regime that loses close to 20 per cent of its population and an even higher fraction of its most qualified people within a decade as the DDR did up to the summer of 1961, when the Berlin Wall was erected to prevent the growing exodus, seems to be destined to go bankrupt eventually. While there is some evidence that regime legitimacy in the East paradoxically increased after building the wall (due to economic improvements, better supply of consumer goods and the closed exit options to much-needed specialists), after the second oil shock in 1980 economic conditions rapidly deteriorated due to further disintegration from the world markets and political failures by the leadership to offer reforms in time.

These different approaches offer competing visions of future developments. The *structural hypothesis*, or *legacy hypothesis of authoritarian state socialism*, predicts a lasting socialisation impact of the conditions and the regime in the East. Though the regime in propaganda terms was oriented towards 'democracy', equality and progress, the reality was quite different. People were confronted with permanent discrepancies between promising rhetoric and miserable performance. This created almost schizophrenic feelings towards the system and explains the rapid decline of regime support once the repressive card could no longer be played.[31] But irrespective of such critical attitudes and mass dissent towards the end, this hypothesis maintains that the long-term authoritarian socialisation patterns are dominant. The authoritarian, petty bourgeois and intolerant everyday life conditions of the red Prussian state have left a dominant impact on the populace,[32] turning its members into passive and inefficacious individuals with an accommodation-oriented personality structure longing for behavioural clues to follow, with strong beliefs in formal institutional rules, and law and order. The absence of religious authority also weakens the potential for building civil society; the general DDR climate was secular (at the end of the 1980s, 9 million claimed not to belong to any church, 6 million were Protestants, and 2 million Catholics).

The alternative, more optimistic *critical events hypothesis* assumes that the events of 1989 gave a notable boost to the democratic longings. Summarising and simplifying a number of studies in surveys carried out around 1990, East Germans seemed to have caught up surprisingly fast with West Germans in scoring on democratic values.[33] Obviously there was some anticipatory socialisation through information from the West, especially television which was widely watched in the East. The same explanation is used to account for the astonishingly rapid 'implementation' of the Western party system and the growth of some sense of party identification.[34] Figures have crumbled, however, during the 1990s. Abstractly, East Germans are still in favour of democracy, but not the West German-dominated political variant.[35]

Thus, the broad protest vote for the PDS becomes understandable. The

PDS ingeniously makes use of an easy explanation of reality, activating feelings of low political trust, of frustration and relative deprivation coupled with some socialist nostalgia (around 20 per cent in East Germany now would prefer the old system, especially the belief that the state should take care of widely defined needs, including the rights of women, who in many ways have lost out since reunification). At the same time, it works within the strong social networks that survived the regime change.[36] Moreover, the PDS's leader, Gysi, is highly charismatic, in contrast to the grey image of the Western parties in the East, the members of which were often highly implicated in the communist system (*Blockflöten*) – though clearly the PDS has strong links with the past, and many of its voters come from the 35–55 age group, who have often had ties with the communist regime and who have in many ways been the biggest losers of reunification. Perhaps most interesting is the PDS's appeal to the young, a group which the Western parties in general have not specifically courted and among whom unemployment rates are high. Although youngsters were distrustful of their own teachers under communism, some of their lessons in school about the 'despicable' West now seem to be bolstered by reality.

From a systemic point of view, the PDS seems to be extremely helpful in bundling this mixture of feelings; without it, the use of violent protest and total obstruction would be much worse. On the other hand, the PDS in government might deter investment in the East and almost certainly will perpetuate the crisis of adjustment and the transformation process, if not reverse it. Although participation in government could lead to a fall in PDS support, it would still add to the new *Länder's* economic woes. Economic adjustment has proved much more troublesome than many believed. East Germany was highly uncompetitive by Western standards. But in an increasingly global market, many West German firms do not see it as a sufficiently cheap source of labour; it is also relatively small compared to many new markets in South East Asia. (Mobility to the East has picked up, but in 1995 there was still a slight net population outflow to the West of about 20,000–30,000. Altogether 1.5 million people have left East Germany for the West since the opening of the wall.)

Eckstein has provided a succinct explanation here. In times of political transformation deep-seated patterns of behaviour and sentiments are not destroyed but rather re-awakened, an approach which has been specifically applied to the German case to argue that 'Cultural discontinuities reinforce those social structures and related dispositions which are most prone to survive such upheavals, such as family, bureaucracy, and governmental authority'.[37] In the East German case, this is the Red-Prussian authoritarian pattern of submissiveness to law and order and the state taking care of needs. This pattern continues to prevail to this day, though there are gradual attempts at political re-education.

Persistent support for the democratic parties or the democratic system is to be expected only from those clearly profiting from the economic changes

– especially the educated and more skilled, though many old people have also done well through changes in pension arrangements. *Support* will flow via economic performance, via *specific support* in the manner suggested by Easton. Only if higher and persistent levels of output accumulate (over more than a generation), can diffuse support for the values of the democratic game be expected to develop. This is even more manifest elsewhere in Eastern Europe, for example in the 20 per cent vote for the Communist Party in the election to the Russian Duma in December 1995, or the widespread support for Zyuganov in the 1996 presidential elections. The PDS vote in East Germany is a functional equivalent of the Russian voting pattern (though the PDS has learned more parliamentary skills and may change quite rapidly through its younger members).

The conditions necessary for developing diffuse support seem to be more difficult now than they were after the Second World War in the new Federal Republic. There was simply no capital stock in East Germany equivalent to what there was in West Germany after 1945 (80 per cent of relatively modern plant remained intact from the ravages of war) – especially after the exchange rates between the East German and the West German currency were set much too high, thus wiping out any hope of market competitiveness for East German firms.[38] Wages soon followed on this slippery path. Not only were the (West) German unions pushing for this, but there was also a widespread belief that mass migration to the West would otherwise have taken place.

But there is no need to worry about a collapse of East Germany or return to dictatorship. Adapting Wright's theory to the German context, it is likely that the mass of apathetic people will grow,[39] but it takes charismatic leadership on the part of the dissidents and absolute failure on the part of incumbents if this dissent is to have any system effect. On a comparative base, such a misperformance of German political elites is not to be reckoned with. Indeed, commentators have frequently remarked on both the relatively low level of East German problems and general quality of political leadership in Germany compared to the East European countries.[40] East Germans also increasingly can compare their lot and the lot of West Germans with those of other European countries and derive favourable conclusions from this. *Comparative pride* thus becomes a component of regime support. Chancellor Kohl knows about this, and repeatedly points out that the economic plight cannot be as bad as described by the political opposition, when such large numbers of Germans travel abroad each year, filling the German roads. Certainly one of the most important empirical findings of recent surveys is that East Germans perceive strong linear progress when asked about their own economic situation over the last five and the next five years – a marked contrast to West Germans, who speak first of a linear decline and then stagnation.[41] (The belief that the general economic situation is worse than the private one is now a finding common to Western democracies.)

All this grumbling, in particular in East Germany, needs to be taken seriously, but Easton's point remains pertinent. It will take time for diffuse support to become as widespread as in West Germany, perhaps as long as communist rule lasted in East Germany. Despite the highest growth rates in Europe (1993–5: more than 8 per cent), this is not a self-sustaining boom. Rather, forecasts for 1996 speak of about 3–4 per cent real growth for East Germany and 2 per cent for West Germany. During such a period of two generations of build-up of a new society in the East, the former West German society will also change dramatically. It will become even more differentiated, with many more multicultural traits – in a word, almost an immigration country, although the large majority of the population and politicians alike will attempt to prevent this. Inequality will be rising as will visible poverty. It will definitely be a less 'cosy' and protected life than in the past. The choice of Berlin as the new capital – only half-heartedly accepted by the population in the West and the Bonn parliament – clearly shows the problems of the country in growing together.

On the other hand, talking about 'internal unity' – which has become a favourite slogan of many politicians – is ridiculous given the multitude of German tribes and their traditions. The distance – for example, between Southern Germans and Northerners (in Bavarian shorthand 'Prussians') – will most likely remain greater than any West–East variation.[42] This will be so even more should the states of Saxony and Thuringia follow the Bavarian pattern of moving from a relatively backward to a high-tech society. The historical burden is much higher in those East German states, but talent and industriousness in the population is still there. Yet, wages are too high for a real boost in productivity (in 1995 average wage costs, taking into account productivity, were still 30 per cent higher than in West Germany; *Süddeutsche Zeitung* on 22 February 1996 even quoted a figure of 70 per cent). By contrast, after the Second World War real wage increases were below productivity growth way up into the 1950s; also, the DM was undervalued, and both factors contributed to the strong export boom. Now the opposite constellation exists with too high wages in spite of labour abundancy around Europe and the world. The implication is clear for the German worker (and other social groups as well), namely, falling real wages and a likely relative loss in social standing.

A final important issue related to political culture is whether to take to court those responsible for the gigantic secret service apparatus, in particular for crimes against humanity. In a way, old patterns are repeated. A narrowly legalistic form of thinking has not altered much in Germany through all its regime changes: hence in part its inability to exonerate itself from its involvement in Nazi Germany, which was largely a legally instated government – even some of its dictatorial powers were acquired under the Weimar Constitution. With the former communist political leaders dying out or producing various medical certificates to avoid facing justice, it is the minor officials who are now likely to be 'hanged' as the saying goes – although most of these will probably escape legal sanction if the past is anything to go by. Perhaps this is beneficial in some respects, since otherwise an even more resentful class of former functionaries might emerge. But if people are to learn from history, all this will have to become an issue of communal dialogue about the societal and personal factors which account for such forms of behaviour. Confession and repentance are perhaps not enough if the wounds are to be healed. It seems possible that something like an East German 'equivalent' to the 1968 West German student interrogation of the societal order of the Third Reich and the mentality of their (fore)fathers will be the result, especially as contemporary historians are now dealing with the extensive involvement with the Stasi. If not, legacies of the past will leave a collective imprint that mars political achievements around 1989–90 and economic gains thereafter.

CONTINUITIES AND CHANGE

What is the state of German political culture today? Is it a viable, resilient and healthy culture or are there more ominous portents? The complex nature of the situation can be seen by the pattern of xenophobic violence in the 1990s. There was a massive rise in 1991–3, partly to be explained by a situation of anomie, a lack of social and political control that created an opportunity structure for such behaviour, but there was a major decline in 1994–5.

Social and political scientists hesitate to give sweeping answers to questions of future developments, especially as the very concept of political culture is a complex and controversial one – and in Germany is particularly elusive on account of its many different formative influences.[43] On the other hand, such commentators should be more qualified than most – if not all – others in making overall judgements. What then are the prospects for German political culture? Two scenarios seem to be prominent here, though others can be debated.

First, if economic progress persists, if the adaptation of the economic engine of German society to new challenges both internal and external succeeds, then more and more diffuse support will be built up. Easton's analysis is still the best guideline here. Though circumstances differ vastly, the East German path could indeed follow the West German, while learning from the latter model at the same time. This comment is not meant to downgrade the mass orchestration of protest and the transformation of society that was achieved on the part of the East Germans alone, following the Polish model, encouraged by Gorbachev and benefiting from historical circumstances (opening of the Iron Curtain in Hungary, avoidance of violence during the demonstration in Leipzig on 9 October 1989, fall of the wall). But accepting conflicting interests as the base of society, understanding the mechanisms of aggregating those interests from below on a competitive base; understanding the fundamental role of bargaining and compromise and, finally and most importantly, accepting majority decision rule while guaranteeing rights to minorities – these political essentials are still mainly to be learned by East Germans from West Germans.

Second, what about the dangers of renewed nationalism? Here part of the answer rests with progress towards a European political union. The economic (and political?) drift amongst European partners is complicated and more difficult to predict than ever. However, outside pressures are at work too, which no longer come primarily from the military threat in Eastern Europe, but from the global Asian economic challenge: Europe may just be forced to move faster than some of the national political elites or their people may like. Adenauer wanted to contain German nationalism and Franco-German rivalry in a Franco-German rapprochement around which a united Europe eventually was to be built. In the future, too rapid and not sufficiently legitimised steps towards a common European currency might produce rather the contrary, namely renewed feelings of nationalism. Certainly recent opinion polls seem to show that the German government has some way to go in convincing people to give up the DM, which is a symbol of national pride. There are those like former chancellor Helmut Schmidt who proclaim that Europe has only *this* chance at fundamental economic progress, but there are others who repeatedly point at anti-European bureaucracy sentiments that are widespread everywhere in Europe, and at the too great diversity of the national economies.

Anxieties about a weaker currency are looming large in Germany. The Minister of Finance has suggested raising the stability hurdles for European countries *after* they have fulfilled the conditions for membership in the common currency club, in order to fight off any temptation from the Social Democrats to make currency fears the focus of their next electoral campaigns. (In fact, Germany herself missed the 3 per cent budgetary debt figure as a share of the GNP in 1996.) All these scenarios look somewhat paradoxical. On the one hand, they are at the core of what nationalism often is about: *perceived* economic advantages or disadvantages. On the other hand, *if* the steps towards a common currency work out, a sizeable net growth effect should result from this reduction of international economic transaction costs. Yet, Europe economically needs to be much more mobilised not to fall (further) behind in economic dynamics after South East Asia and the US.

Another theme is the middle-European position of Germany as an alleged local hegemon towards Eastern Europe. Even if economically true, for historical reasons quite a few people in Eastern Europe will not be too happy with such a scenario. The only antidote here seems to be substantial economic progress for these people so that they can feel the benefits of widening markets. Intellectuals like Botho Strauss, conservative historians and politicians may sometimes nourish *Mitteleuropa* ideas in an often unclear terminology with stylistic resemblances of past times. There is, however, very little support for that in the liberal public. It simply is not and most likely will not become one of those *Gramscian* ideas dominating the public discourse. Voting behaviour at the polls also is more oriented towards economic issues (unemployment and foreign competition) rather than towards any 'nationalist' notions focusing on Germany's peculiar position in the middle of Europe.

The worst scenario is as follows: progress towards European unification fails, economic problems overburden not only East, but also West Germany, political leadership instrumentalises those supra-national frustrations as well as 'challenges to the national identity' through further immigration. The temptation is there and the political leadership has certainly failed to take the lead in terms of explaining that Germany is now a multicultural society. But the population, according to consistent survey results, does *not* perceive such a scenario as likely to happen and would *not* back revived nationalism.[44] As long as there is consensus amongst the population and the political elites to follow the successful West German democratic model (and learn from the failures of Weimar and Nazi Germany), there are grounds to be optimistic for the future. If war, however, is to resume in and spreads from former Yugoslavia into more neighbouring places and if Russia threatens again (e.g. in the Baltic region or vis-à-vis NATO in general), then the temptation to revive nationalism is there. As before, Germany depends very much on what happens in her neighbouring states (and vice versa, of course), both in Middle and Western Europe, in Russia and increasingly with respect to Islamic fundamentalism in portions of the Mediterranean.

The resilience of political culture in West Germany should be strong enough not to err in its basic orientation, irrespective of (temporary) problems with the political personnel and its difficulties in handling the economy and making the thorough adjustment to the mixed economy and welfare state. Material and, more importantly, mental resources should be sufficient for this job. On the other hand, East Germans will have to make many adjustments. They do not have the trust in the system that has accumulated in the West over three generations and which by any international comparison must be considered rather high now.[45] Mentally, the bargain will be won if West and East Germans start to perceive unification as a positive-sum game rather than a zero-sum or negative-sum game. Reshuffling more than a trillion DM to the East by now is only possible politically with an underlying optimistic judgement. It stands for an enormous act of solidarity, apart from direct human investment in the East. Marx in some respects is still right: human needs are societal needs and therefore relative in terms. The question is, where will West and East Germans look for comparisons: into their own history only, towards each other, towards their neighbours, or even beyond? The mixture of these comparisons makes for satisfaction or dissatisfaction with the political and economic system, and in this mixture quite a few changes are to be expected.

In creating a political culture of 'balanced disparities'[46] there is no substitute for time. Even though history cannot repeat itself – for purely logical reasons alone, since other contingencies are involved now – becoming 'wise' through history (Jacob Burckhardt) is the best manner in which a 'joint' political culture can emerge in Germany.

ACKNOWLEDGEMENTS

My thanks go to Roger Eatwell, Thomas Saalfeld, Rolf Becker and Mark Thompson for their comments.

NOTES

1 G. Almond and S. Verba, *The Civic Culture*, Princeton, Princeton University Press, 1963; D. Conradt, 'Changing German Political Culture' in G. Almond and S. Verba (eds), *The Civic Culture Revisited*, Boston, Little, Brown and Co., 1980.
2 For the classic Anglo-American style attempt to trace Germany's problems to the nature of economic development and elite formation see B. Moore Jnr, *Social Origins of Dictatorship and Democracy*, Boston, Beacon Press, 1966.
3 D. Groh, *Negative Integration und revolutionärer Attentismus. Die deutsche Sozialdemokratie am Vorabend des Ersten Weltkrieges*, Frankfurt/Main, Ullstein, 1973.
4 T. Nipperdey, 'Probleme der Modernisierung in Deutschland', *Saeculum*, 1979, 30. This uses the crises sequence approach of L. Binder, J. S. Coleman, J. LaPalombara, L. W. Pye, S. Verba and M. Weiner, *Crises and Sequences in Political Development*, Princeton, Princeton University Press, 1971.
5 F. Fischer, *Das Bündnis der Eliten*, Düsseldorf, Droste, 1979; H.-U. Wehler, *Das deutsche Kaiserreich, 1871–1918*, Göttingen, Vamdenhoeck und Ruprecht, 1988.
6 D. Blackbourn and G. Eley, *The Peculiarities of German History*, New York, Oxford University Press, 1984.
7 R. Collins, 'German-Bashing and the Theory of Democratic Modernization', *Zeitschrift für Soziologie*, 1995, 24, 16.
8 On the so-called historians' debate (*Historikerstreit*), see H.-U. Wehler, *Entsorgung der deutschen Vergangenheit. Ein polemischer Essay zum Historikerstreit*, München, Beck, 1988.
9 See K. Sontheimer, *Antidemokratisches Denken in der Weimarer Republik*, München, Nymphenburger Verlagshandlung, 1968.
10 On the controversy around the *Rätediskussion* and the socialisation of the coal industry, cf. E. Kolb, *Die Weimarer Republik*, München, Oldenbourg, 1988; R. Rürup, *Probleme der Revolution in Deutschland*, Wiesbaden, Steiner, 1968; and H.-A. Winkler, *Weimar 1918–1933. Die Geschichte der ersten deutschen Demokratie*, München, C. H. Beck, 1993.
11 E. Zimmermann and T. Saalfeld, 'Economic and Political Reactions to the World Economic Crisis of the 1930s in Six European Countries', *International Studies Quarterly*, 1988, 32.
12 On Nazi voting see J. Falter, *Hitlers Wähler*, München, C. H. Beck, 1991.
13 Almond and Verba, *op. cit.*, 1963; cf. J. Street, 'Review Article: Political Culture – from Civic Culture to Mass Culture', *British Journal of Political Science*, 1994, 24.
14 Conradt, *op. cit.*; see also K. Baker, R. Dalton and K. Hildebrandt, *Germany Transformed: Political Culture and the New Politics*, Cambridge, Mass., Harvard University Press, 1981; R. Dalton, *Citizen Politics in Western Democracies*, Chatham, NJ, Chatham House Publishers, 1988; D. Fuchs, G. Guidorossi and

P. Svensson, 'Support for the Democratic System' in H.-D. Klingemann and D. Fuchs (eds), *Citizens and the State*, Oxford, Oxford University Press, 1995.

15 D. Conradt, *The German Polity*, New York, Longman, 1993, p. 55

16 The term was apparently coined by D. Sternberger, 'Verfassungspatriotismus' in *25 Jahre Akademie für Politische Bildung*, Tutzing, 1982, pp. 76–87.

17 See D. Fuchs, 'Trends of Political Support in the Federal Republic of Germany' in D. Berg-Schlosser and R. Rytlewski (eds), *Political Culture in Germany*, London, Macmillan, 1993; H. Rattinger, 'Abkehr von den politischen Parteien? Dimensionen der Parteienverdrossenheit' in *Aus Politik und Zeitgeschichte*, 1993, B11.

18 O. Listhaug and M. Wiberg, 'Confidence in Political and Private Institutions' in Klingemann and Fuchs, *op. cit.*; and E. Zimmermann, 'Political Unrest in Western Europe: Trends and Prospects', *West European Politics*, 1989, 12.

19 D. Easton, 'A Re-Assessment of the Concept of Political Support', *British Journal of Political Science*, 1975, 5.

20 See E. Zimmermann and T. Saalfeld, 'The Three Waves of West German Right-Wing Extremism' in P. Merkl and L. Weinberg (eds), *Encounters with the Contemporary Radical Right*, Boulder, Col., Westview, 1993.

21 R. Dalton, 'Communists and Democrats: Democratic Attitudes in the Two Germanies', *British Journal of Political Science*, 1994, 24.

22 P. Katzenstein, *Industry and Politics in West Germany: Toward the Third Republic*, Ithaca, Cornell University Press, 1989.

23 S. Tarrow, *Power in Movement. Social Movements, Collective Actions and Politics*, New York, Cambridge University Press, 1994.

24 Dalton, *op. cit.*, 1994; P. Gluchowski, F. Plasser and P. A. Ulram, 'Politisch-kultureller Wandel in Deutschland. Eine Übersicht über Veränderungen und Wandlungslinien' in F. Plasser and P. A. Ulram (eds), *Staatsbürger oder Untertanen? Politische Kultur Deutschlands, Österreichs und der Schweiz im Vergleich*, Frankfurt/Main, Peter Lang, 1993.

25 M. Minkenberg, 'The Wall after the Wall: On the Continuing Division of Germany and the Remaking of Political Cultures', *Comparative Politics*, 1993, 26, 63.

26 J. W. Falter and M. Klein, 'Die Wähler der PDS bei der Bundestagswahl 1994. Zwischen Ideologie, Nostalgie und Protest' in *Aus Politik und Zeitgeschichte. Beilage zur Wochenzeitung Das Parlament*, 1994, B51–2/94.

27 See also B. Westle, 'Unterstützung des politischen Systems des vereinten Deutschland' in P. Mohler and W. Bandilla (eds), *Blickpunkt Gesellschaft 2. Einstellungen und Verhalten der Bundesbürger in Ost und West*, Opladen, Westdeutscher Verlag, 1992; and W. Zapf, 'Zwei Geschwindigkeiten in Ost- und Westdeutschland' in E. Holtmann and H. Sahner (eds), *Aufhebung der Bipolarität – Veränderungen im Osten, Rückwirkungen im Westen*, Opladen, Leske and Budrich, 1995.

28 For instance, E. Brähler and H.-E. Richter, 'Deutsche Befindlichkeiten im Ost-West-Vergleich', *Aus Politik und Zeitgeschichte*, 1995, B40–1.

29 For instance, H. Solga and K. U. Mayer, 'Mobilität und Legitimität. Zum Vergleich der Chancenstrukturen in der alten DDR und der alten BRD oder: Haben Mobilitätschancen zu Stabilität und Zusammenbruch der DDR beigetragen?', *Kölner Zeitschrift für Soziologie und Sozialpsychologie*, 1994, 46.

30 Minkenberg, *op. cit.*, p. 60.

31 T. Kuran, 'Now out of Never: The Element of Surprise in the East European Revolution of 1989', *World Politics*, 1991, 44.

32 Cf. W. Engler, *Die zivilisatorische Lücke*, Frankfurt, Suhrkamp, 1992.

33 Cf. P. Bauer, 'Politische Orientierungen im Übergang. Eine Analyse politischer Einstellungen der Bürger in West- und Ostdeutschland 1990/1991', *Kölner*

Zeitschrift für Soziologie und Sozialpsychologie, 1991, 43; Dalton, *op. cit.*, 1994; M. Watts, 'A "Participatory Revolution" Among the German "Unification Generation"?', *European Journal of Political Research*, 1994, 25; and F. Weil (ed.), *Research on Democracy and Society. Vol. 2: Political Culture and Political Structure: Theoretical and Empirical Studies*, Greenwich, Conn., JAI Press, 1994.

34 H. Rattinger, 'Parteiidentifikationen in Ost- und Westdeutschland nach der Vereinigung' in O. Niedermayer and K. von Beyme (eds), *Politische Kultur in Ost- und Westdeutschland*, Berlin, Akademie Verlag, 1994.

35 Cf. Zapf, *op. cit.*

36 E. Noelle-Neumann, 'Problems With Democracy in Eastern Germany After the Downfall of the GDR' in F. Weil (ed.), *Research on Democracy and Society. Vol. 2: Political Culture and Political Structure: Theoretical and Empirical Studies*, Greenwich, Conn., JAI Press, 1994; E. Noelle-Neumann, 'Wo sind die Zeugnisse des Umlernens?', *Frankfurter Allgemeine Zeitung*, 13 December 1995; and *Der Spiegel*, 27, 1995.

37 H. Eckstein, 'A Culturalist Theory of Political Change', *American Political Science Review*, 1988, 82; Minkenberg, *op. cit.*, p. 56.

38 H. Siebert, *Das Wagnis der Einheit. Eine wirtschaftspolitische Therapie*, Stuttgart, Deutsche Verlags-Anstalt, 1993; and G. Sinn and H.-W. Sinn, *Kaltstart. Volkswirtschaftliche Aspekte der deutschen Vereinigung*, München, Deutscher Taschenbuchverlag, 1993.

39 J. Wright, *The Dissent of the Governed: Alienation and Democracy in America*, New York, Academic Press, 1976.

40 W. Seifert and R. Rose, *Lebensbedingungen und politische Einstellungen im Transformationsprozess. Ostdeutschland und Osteuropa im Vergleich*, Berlin, Science Center, 1994.

41 Seifert and Rose, *op. cit.*; Zapf, *op. cit.*

42 For amusing cultural anthropological insights about those differences see R. W. B. McCormack, *Unter Deutschen. Porträt eines rätselhaften Volkes*, Frankfurt/Main, Eichborn, 1993.

43 O. W. Gabriel, 'Politische Kultur aus der Sicht der empirischen Sozialforschung' in O. Niedermayer and K. von Beyme (eds), *Politische Kultur in Ost- und Westdeutschland*, Berlin, Akademie Verlag, 1994.

44 D. Fuchs, *Die Unterstützung des politischen Systems der Bundesrepublik Deutschland*, Opladen, Westdeutscher Verlag, 1989; P. Mohler and H. Götze, 'Worauf sind die Deutschen stolz? Eine vergleichende Analyse zur gefühlsmäßigen Bindung an das politische System der Bundesrepublik' in P. Mohler and W. Bandilla (eds), *Blickpunkt Gesellschaft 2. Einstellungen und Verhalten der Bundesbürger in Ost und West*, Opladen, Westdeutscher Verlag, 1992; E. K. Scheuch, 'Die Suche nach der Besonderheit der heutigen Deutschen', *Kölner Zeitschrift für Soziologie und Sozialpsychologie*, 1990, 42.

45 Dalton, *op. cit.*, 1994, p. 472.

46 Almond and Verba, *op. cit.*, 1963, p. 476.

7   Greece

Nicolas Demertzis

INTRODUCTION

The way fellow Europeans think of Greece is usually a strange mixture of
an idealised past and a series of confusions about, even ignorance of,
Greece's more recent history. On the one hand, their vision is inspired by the
Classical tradition, of the glories of Athens and the other city-states, which
forms an important part of a common European heritage. On the other
hand, an incomplete knowledge of modern Greece is quite widespread. For
example, everybody knows that democracy was created in Classical Greece,
but it is hardly known that modern Greece has one of the longest parliamentary traditions in the West: in 1864 the male population in Greece was
completely enfranchised, whereas in 1880 the number of the disenfranchised
in Great Britain – supposedly a latter day font of democracy – was as high
as 40 per cent.

European knowledge of Classical Greece is often partial, or highly selective. Its tradition was mixed: certainly not all the city-states were
democracies, and in Athens 'democracy' was a male preserve and perfectly
consistent with slavery. However, the main focus of this chapter is not the
Classical tradition, or ancient Greece. Rather, the point is to identify a more
modern Greek political culture which begins to emerge in the nineteenth
century. History is vital to understanding modern Greek identity, but it is
debatable whether any major insights are gained by beginning in the mists of
time, or with the foundations of Europe's first major civilisation. The crucial
point is to understand tensions within modern Greek culture, for instance,
its more democratic, outward looking side, and its more holistic Orthodox
religious aspect. Without this background, it is difficult to understand the
nature of contemporary Greek political culture – the main subject of this
chapter.

EARLY NATIONALISM, THE ORTHODOX LEGACY AND ATROPHIC CIVIL SOCIETY

As with all European countries, Greece's road to modernity had its own peculiarities. Founded in 1830, the Greek state developed from the 1821–7 revolution against the Turks, who had ruled the area for centuries and whose long-standing presence in the Balkans to this day makes it difficult to draw a neat boundary of 'Europe' along Greece's eastern boundary. That revolution, typical of the separatist Eastern nationalist movements,[1] was an historical case where an ethnic population under the domination of one of the great modern multiethnic empires undertakes the project of independence by appealing to the ideal of the nation. In Greek nation-building, the idea of the nation precedes the formation of the state, which, in turn, transforms this nation into a political entity.[2]

The making of the Greek state was feasible both because of the Ottoman weakness in the southern part of the Balkan peninsula and external intervention by England, France and Russia aimed at keeping the 'Eastern Question' under control. In addition it was affected by major competition and conflicts among the Greeks caused by great social inequalities, especially between peasants and landowners. The rationale of the Greek movement of independence was marked by the articulation of two different discourses: a nationalist–separatist discourse and a popular–egalitarian discourse with localist overtones. Although in the beginning the revolution was both national and social-agrarian, it ended with the traditional elites as the victors of that inner struggle. Thus a more conservative form of nationalism prevailed in the discursive practices of early Greek statehood.

Yet Greek nationalism was, and still is, far from unequivocal. On the one hand there existed those who defined the nation in terms of the Classical heritage and the new Enlightenment ideals such as freedom, rationality and secularisation. On the other hand, one may find the proponents of the resurrection of the Byzantine empire who understood nation in terms of Orthodox Christianity. This bifurcation caused numerous intense debates, social upheavals, policy disorientation, and feelings of insecurity, angst and ambiguity. For instance, the great dispute concerning the name of the modern Greeks: should they call themselves 'Hellenes' or 'Romii'? (The latter term comes from the 'Romans', which is the way the Byzantines referred to themselves; this debate was linked to the linguistic question of the constructed and Classical-like *katharevusa* and everyday *romeika*.) The Hellenic designation referred to an outward-directed image of the nation as the immediate heir of the Classical culture, whereas the Romeic designation had strong connotations with the Orthodox religious origins of the Greeks.[3] By the same token, in spite of their radical-liberal character, when compared with their West European counterparts the concepts of citizenship and Greekness in the first revolutionary constitutions were conterminous with the ideas of Christian believers.[4] One could pick up plenty of similar instances from Greek political history; however, the point to underline is that early Greek nationalism was not only more 'cultural' than it was 'political' but it created highly ambivalent collective identities as well. Moreover, the concept of 'Hellenic-Christian civilisation', introduced much later, has never managed to reconcile this ambivalence effectively.

Though 'invented' and 'selective',[5] they both have pertinent effects on contemporary Greek political culture. But the two clashing traditions are of different types in many ways. Although the linguistic side represents an important social continuity, the Hellenic and Enlightenment tradition has been less grounded in popular culture: for the most part, it has been cultivated from above by elites. Contrariwise, the Byzantine and Ottoman religious and political tradition has been much more ingrained in everyday habitus, a term borrowed from Bourdieu to refer to the orchestration of activities based on practical consciousness.[6] This tradition is distinguished by a particular intersection of instrumental and consummatory orientations (where the former relate to empirical ends and the latter to more transcendental and integrative values).[7] On the one hand (and to use two Weberian terms relating to traditional authority), the 'patrimonial' political domination of the Byzantine empire and the 'sultanist' type of Ottoman power, as well as the familial and communal kind of social organisation and economic production, diminished the possibility of a contractual idea of citizenship, which was to become so important in much of Western Europe. That was due to the personified, though not entirely arbitrary, style of politics of both empires. The lack of institutionalised political procedures that would guarantee natural and civil rights and duties was the chief reason for the shaping of instrumental and defensive outlooks towards authorities. This was reinforced by the reality of everyday life, which resulted in the mistrust of any sort of secular power, and the belief that much of public life was based on nepotistic principles.[8]

On the other hand, the Orthodox conception of the self, with its mystic and communitarian overtones, was the basic theological context within which individuals were seeking for long-term justification and meaningfulness. Unlike the Catholic and the Protestant conceptions, where the relationship between man and God is mediated by reason and the law, the Orthodox Christian feels united with God in a non-mediated personal relationship. Consequently, a deep-going fatalism has grown out of this conception, but this has not led to a single consummatory vision which could harness the entire social energy. Partly, this was due to the elastic character of the Orthodox dogma which, contrary to many other Christian dogmas, has been flexibly adjusted to the day-to-day practical demands of life. The personified element made Orthodoxy more of a popular-religious practice than a prescriptively codified set of religious ethics, especially ones which required strict adherence.

The making of the Greek state and nation, including its parliamentary system, took place principally in a non-capitalist socio-economic environment.[9] Nineteenth-century Greece was an overwhelmingly agrarian society whose later economic development has been of a quasi-capitalist character. The latter is characterised by three notable factors. First, Greek economic capital has been more commercial and in general small business-based than industrial and productive. Second, most of the economic development has been mediated by the state as the principal mechanism of surplus distribution. And third, an institutionalised capitalist market *per se* has never been a major feature of Greek development. Thus neither a deep-rooted labour class nor a capitalist class in the proper sense have ever developed historically in Greece. Indeed, bourgeois culture is severely limited; instead, petty bourgeois patterns of life have tended to prevail.

Alongside these factors, clientelism and patronage have had major long-term effects which have been responsible for an atrophic civil society and an hypertrophic state. Atrophic civil society means the absence of strong intermediary 'bodies' between the state and the quasi-capitalist market of Greece, as well as the prevalence of the family as one of the central institutions of social, economic and cultural reproduction. In spite of their early appearance, for the most part parliamentarism and enfranchisement were the means for securing an essentially traditional mode of domination of various local elites rather than legitimating a social contract based on the logic of the market relationship. The institutional rules were ultimately subjected to a preferential clientelistic relationship between the central authority, the political elites, and the citizens. Thus the typical legal-contractual principles were subverted by an essentially non-modern mode of domination; consequently, particular state benefits have created expectations for personal and/or family aggrandisement rather than for collective development. By and large, legitimation was rendered, as it were, a face-to-face cause rather than one arising from the non-personal binding constitutional setting. Consequently, the state was the primary means for making clientelism possible under the regime of formal parliamentary democracy.[10]

Undoubtedly, many fundamental changes occurred in the economy and polity of twentieth-century Greece, especially after the Second World War. Contemporary Greece is an intensively urbanised, thoroughly consumer-oriented and Western-style country which since 1981 has been a full member of the European Union. Yet the unequal situation of a non-articulated civil society and an overriding paternalistic state remains as one of its most important structural features. Notable areas where this has manifested itself are in state–corporatist regulations of interest intermediation, in the absence of local activism and basic organisational structures of most political parties, in the populist style of governing, in the military interventions, up to 1967, in the subjugation of the Orthodox Church to the state, and in the gigantic public sector, as well as in the widespread grey economy which makes for the multivalent character of modern Greeks' social identity.[11]

All in all then, the fundamentals of Greek nation-building and statehood were an ambivalent selective tradition made up of Christian Orthodox and Classical–Enlightenment dimensions, and the state-centred organisation of economy and polity as well as a weak civil society. As we shall see, these fundamentals have pertinent effects on Greek political culture today, since they operate at the macro-analytical level of the *longue durée*.

CONTEMPORARY GREEK POLITICAL CULTURE

Apart from a number of previous pioneering works on the political system, political history and economy, research on Greek political culture only began essentially in the mid-1980s and much remains to be done. This research started with a comparative project on South European political culture,[12] and is characterised by a more or less firm attachment to the mainstream political culture theory of the 1960s, including a preference for quantitative methods at the expense of the qualitative ones, and the primacy of the national level as a unit of analysis over the sub-cultural one. But since then, some efforts have been made to complement this research profile with more integrative theoretical approaches inspired by a broad conception of culture, with more sophisticated qualitative methods, and with an emphasis on the political sub-cultural level of analysis.[13] The discussion in the rest of this chapter will seek to outline contemporary Greek culture against the background of this growing breadth of perspectives.

POLITICAL CLEAVAGES AND MAJOR SUB-CULTURES

As with any other case, Greek political culture is made up of sub-cultures; for most of the time their articulation has rendered it imperfectly integrated or even fragmented.[14] The political cleavages of the country have deep historical roots inherited from two traumatic periods: the National Schism of 1915–22 and the Civil War of 1945–9. The first gave rise to a right and anti-right coalition; the second to a communist or left and an anti-communist division. During the 1960s and definitely after 1974 the two cleavages overlapped so that the major political families corresponded to two major parties, with the left being still fragmented, isolated and minimal.[15] Thus the Third Greek democracy (1974 until the present) is more or less a 'tripolar party system with bipolar competition'. It should be noted that the cleavage between right and anti-right does not match the traditional right–left division that characterises most European political cultures (though with post-industrialism and other changes, this feature is declining). This is so because, for the most part, the respective identifications and loyalties correspond less to rival socio-economic collective interests than to competing forms of vertical clientelism – though especially during the 1990s the right–anti-right cleavage refers horizontally to separate social groups.[16]

In spite of the intense regional inequalities of Greek society, clientelism has also been one of the prime reasons for rural and urban cultures not

having been transformed into two major separate political sub-cultures –
though since 1974 the traditional patron–client form of clientelism has
largely been replaced by a party-bureaucratic form.[17] Another major reason
is the diffuse middle-class profile of this society and the increased levels of
conspicuous consumption supported by remittances from abroad, by foreign
loans and by grey economic activities. Last but not least, the strong
economic, sentimental and familial connections of urban dwellers who were
part of the massive internal immigration from the countryside during the
1950–70 period is one more reason why a clearer rural–urban split has not
opened up.

Quite a lot of work has been done recently, written in Greek mainly, on
the subject of women's political culture; although the old stereotypical
profile of women has been confirmed (i.e. less politically interested, more
alienated, etc.), this work brought some new facets to the fore. Given that
from 1971 to 1989 female employment increased from 27.7 per cent to 37.0
per cent, a certain relationship has been observed between systematic work
experience and participatory orientations in public affairs. Younger and
more educated women place themselves more to the left than male respondents of the same status; besides, there is among them an active minority
which has developed a special awareness of female gender that makes them
reject the male definition of politics and the public sphere. Nevertheless,
women's political issues remain underdeveloped compared to those of many
of the Western European countries.

By and large, Greece is an ethnically and religiously homogeneous
society, though this does not imply the absence of minorities, whose rights
and needs have only recently been given some serious thought. The oldest of
these minorities are:

1 the Muslim community in Western Thrace which to a great extent is self-
   defined as Turkish;[18]
2 the Slavophone population in (Greek) Macedonia which, although
   constituting little more than 1 per cent of the total population and thoroughly Hellenised, is a controversial group as far as the Greek
   government's Balkan policies are concerned;
3 the gypsy (Roma) minority which numbers no more than 120,000 people,
   who are almost totally Christianised and of Hellenic consciousness;
4 the Jewish community, which after the Nazi extermination and post-war
   emigration is small and well integrated into Greek society;
5 the Roman Catholics, the Protestants and the Jehovah's Witnesses, who
   are all small religious communities, the latter being the most oppressed
   because of its members' refusal to serve in the army.

Apart from these there are newer national minorities too, which mainly
come from the Middle East, Africa, the Far East, Albania and Poland.
Although racial, ethnic and religious discrimination in Greece seems far less
widespread than in other Western countries, the virtual absence of research

on the different groups' lives and political cultures means that this is an area about which little is known systematically. But one thing is certain: the identification of Hellenicity with Orthodoxy has made it difficult for various minorities to become fully integrated into the dominant political culture, and the concept of multiculturalism and ethnic pluralism remains underdeveloped.

MAIN POLITICAL CULTURAL FACETS

With reference to the national level, compared to both the European Union nations and the Southern European ones, Greeks appear to have an unusually high and constant *interest in politics*. In 1983 Greece ranked sixth among the 10 EC countries; in 1989 it advanced to fourth and by 1990 had almost overtaken the Netherlands for third place.[19] From 1985 Greek respondents have been the most interested in and positively oriented to politics among the Southern Europeans. The situation has remained almost unchanged since then and it is in accord with what has been described as Greek 'over-politicization'.[20] According to the 1990 data, as many as 59.6 per cent of Greek men were interested in politics whereas only 48.6 per cent of women were. Also, interest in politics in Greece is directly proportional to length of education, something which agrees with almost all comparative political culture research: 66 per cent of those with university education claimed an interest in politics compared to 49.7 per cent of those without tertiary education.

What did change, however, was the Greeks' *satisfaction* with the way in which democracy works in their country as well as with the life they lead. Whereas in 1985 and 1988 Greeks ranked fifth and fourth respectively in terms of satisfaction with democracy in their country, in 1992 and 1993 they ranked next to last (the Italians took last place), though in 1994 the Spaniards pushed them out of the penultimate place. The same trend appears as far as the index of overall life satisfaction is concerned, an index that is less influenced by short-term fluctuations; during the last five years Greeks have been characterised as being by far the most dissatisfied among the Europeans: in 1993 17.1 per cent of Greeks were not at all satisfied with their life whereas the next least satisfied were the Portuguese with 9.3 per cent.[21] It should be pointed out here that there is almost no difference between the degree of political interest exhibited by those who declare themselves to be satisfied with life and those who express dissatisfaction (54.4 per cent and 53.8 per cent respectively). Similarly, 58 per cent of those who are satisfied with the way democracy works are interested in politics, compared to 53.6 per cent of the dissatisfied ones.

It might be thought that as well as a tendency towards de-legitimation, these findings imply a protest potential too. This would be correct if it were not for the presence of some other notable and counteracting elements: these are, first, a relatively low index of *political efficacy* and second, a rising degree of *political alienation* and *political cynicism*. As a matter of fact, these elements have been growing since 1985; for instance, in 1990 though 54.5 per cent of Greeks were interested in politics either 'a great deal' or 'to some extent', 64.2 per cent declared that politics was so complicated that they could not understand it; at the same time 69.5 per cent were cynical towards politicians in general.[22] To be sure, such attitudes are not conducive either to conventional or to unconventional political action: in spite of low degrees of life satisfaction and high political dissatisfaction among the Greek public, the likelihood is that the combination of low efficacy and low trust will lead to withdrawal from politics. Yet so far this has not been the case; Greeks are still interested in politics and they still participate massively, although party dealignment and declining turnout is growing, especially among the young. Therefore, a 'paradox' comes out of this situation; as we know from the mainstream political culture theory, great political interest is not a symptom of either low political efficacy or high political alienation. How can a person be interested in something strange that they cannot understand?

One can find a way out of this paradox by placing the Greeks' meaning of politics and citizenship into its proper political cultural context which draws much from the selective tradition referred to above. That is, one should move beyond a quantitative analysis to a qualitative understanding of the particular ways in which most Greeks institutionalise the political. Of course this requires a separate book; it suffices here to recall the tradition of atrophic civil society, the preponderance of the family and the clientelistic statism. All these have contributed to the merging of the public and the private – a privatisation of the public and a publicising of the private. This makes for personification of institutions and of agencies of authority and for the replacement of political equality by a diffuse sort of assimilation. By the same token, rights are seen primarily as *ad hoc* claims and privileges, and civic obligations are chiefly viewed as external impositions upon a supposedly unbounded personal freedom.[23] Thus, by and large, politics is understood as a 'private' issue rather than a public one; the statist and clientelistic mode of domination fosters an essentially pre-modern atomistic and/or domestic conception of politics that collides with the modern democratic understanding of it. It is an atomism – not an individualism in the modern sense of the word – which in its ideal-typical condition is sustained before and beyond any socio-centric or contractual normativity and rationality;[24] this is so because the social and political self in Greece is constituted by means of reciprocal and yet asymmetric bonds within various reference groups which are principally organised on a personal basis following a concentric circle-like scheme. This primordial atomism is the basis of the limited *trust* among the Greek public which is conditional for the shaping of a civic culture (in a 1993 *Eurobarometer* study only the Italians and French among EU members trusted each other less). In many ways, the result is similar to the concept of 'amoral familism' in southern Italy, where the family is the key unit beyond the individual and 'honour' (*philotimo* in Greek) is the central concept guiding behaviour.[25] Needless to say, these sorts of orientations and practices are not conducive to the ideal of participatory democratic politics, based on reason, compromise and marginal bargaining.

A crucial aspect of any political culture is *political communication* at both interpersonal and mass level. As a symptom of the over-politicisation referred to above, *Eurobarometer* in 1993 showed that Greeks discuss political matters very much when they get together with friends, with only Danes and Germans ranking higher. Those who discuss politics most are men (though as age and education increase, the distance between men and women on interpersonal political communication decreases), more educated and younger people, managers and white-collar workers, and those who place themselves subjectively in the upper middle class. Another major source of influence in this context seems to be the extent to which the news media are used: the more Greeks follow the news the more they tend to talk about politics. As with all Europeans, television is the prime news medium for Greeks: 74 per cent in 1994 said that they watch the news on television every day (the average in the European Union at the time was 75 per cent).[26] Almost a third of the population listen to radio news and read newspapers every day, with the latter playing a less important role than in many other Western European countries. Thus one could maintain that although Greeks are television dependent they are not high media users in general when compared with the Northern Europeans.

THE GREEK ATTITUDE TOWARDS EUROPEAN UNION AND OTHER COUNTRIES

Attitudes towards European affairs depend both on short-term socio-economic fluctuations and longitudinal political cultural factors. By the end of the 1970s, the entry of Greece into the EC was a highly controversial issue for the public and the parties. A great deal of later foreign policy decisions were conditioned by that controversy. Measurements of the Greek interest in EC/EU politics started in 1982;[27] since then the percentage of those who are not interested in EC/EU politics ('not much' and/or 'not at all') decreases fairly steadily: 64 per cent in 1982 and 1986 and 39 per cent and 47 per cent in 1990 and 1994 respectively. Comparatively speaking, from 1982 to 1994 Greece ranks very high as far as the interest in EC politics is concerned: apart from 1988 and 1989 Greece is constantly to be found within the first three places. Also, together with Luxembourg, Greece comes second in the rankings of positive attitudes towards European integration and scores equally highly concerning the positive opinions of its respondents about whether Greece has on balance benefited from being a member of the EC/EU. As with other Mediterranean people, Greeks are more likely to express dissatisfaction with the way democracy works in their country than with the democratic deficit in the European Union. Whereas in 1993 65 per cent of the Greek respondents were dissatisfied with their country's democracy, only 37 per cent were not satisfied with democracy in the EC.[28] Perhaps even more revealing of their desire to identify with the new Europe, Greeks have consistently shown themselves to be among those most willing to identify themselves as 'European' as well as their own nationality.

To be sure, these favourable attitudes, which to some extent disprove the stereotypical idea of the profoundly xenophobic character of Greek political culture,[29] are counterbalanced by some traits which, of course, are not unique to the Greek public. One of them is a remarkable discrepancy between the affective and the cognitive component of the Greek attitude towards the EU. That is, although Greeks are positively disposed towards European affairs they appear to know very little about them; on the one hand it is a perceived information deficit, shared also by other Europeans, especially from the southern countries. Seventy-eight per cent of Greeks say they know little of the workings of the EU, the Community average being 71 per cent.[30] Greeks also exhibit the most limited awareness of European institutions; on a crucial question asking about the names of institutions of the European Community that they had heard of, 70 per cent of the Greek public replied 'don't know' whereas the EC average was 39 per cent and the next closest value of 60 per cent was that of the British, normally thought of as the most Eurosceptic and unaware in the Union.[31]

Perhaps the nature of *Eurobarometer* polling does not tap true feelings. Certainly the recent nationalist mobilisations ignited by the relationship between Greece and the former Yugoslavian Republic of Macedonia and directed, among others, against the European Union, is another major inconsistency of the Greek attitude towards Europe (these sentiments, and related issues like the growth of economic refugees, have not yet spawned a major new radical nationalist party, though the Political Spring won 4.9 per cent in 1993). Greece wants to be part of Europe, but there is a sense in which it is still distant and separate. Briefly speaking, there are three prime reasons for these inconsistencies. First, there is the local–global antinomy that marks the international system under contemporary conditions of economic, military and cultural rearrangements. Second, there is the traditional ambivalence of Greeks towards the West in general which, as we show, comes from the specificities of Greek nation-building; this ambivalence is expressed historically as a socio-psychological interchange between attraction and repulsion.[32] Third, and simultaneously, the favourable attitudes towards the European Union are nothing but a 'rationalisation' of a deep-rooted instrumental understanding of Greek membership; by and large, the EU is seen as the source of economic benefits that subsidise the poor public finance of the country.

There are also potential tensions with the EU over the admission of Turkey, or more generally improved relations with that country. This is not simply a question of the war with Turkey to gain independence, or even more recent territorial conflicts, notably over Cyprus. Although there is a diffuse instrumental support for the EU, Greeks are suspicious of other nations in general – a feature of a defensive attitude fostered by the state bureaucracy and rural sectors since the nineteenth century (though there has been more cosmopolitanism among Diaspora Greeks and the small but growing echelons of industrial and financial capital). It should be noted that contemporary Greece is the most distrusting member country in the EU, followed by Italy, Ireland, Spain and Portugal.[33] Greeks trust the French and the Spaniards more than any other EU nations, but this feeling is not mutual since the French and Spaniards trust Greeks very little. As a final point, it is interesting to note that Greeks appear to trust Americans less than most Europeans, probably largely a hangover from populist anti-American outlooks of the 1970s and the 1980s.[34]

CONTINUITIES AND CHANGE IN GREEK POLITICAL CULTURE

Normally, political cultures evolve quite slowly. Nevertheless whenever swift changes do occur they do not come out of thin air; there is always an inter-play between the stable and the unstable traits.

As mentioned earlier, from the 1960s to the early 1980s a number of changes took place in Greek society due to the process of modernisation. In a very short period, Greece ceased to be an agrarian society, without however becoming a profoundly industrial one; put another way, in terms of mentality, contemporary Greece is a post-agrarian rather than an industrial or post-industrial society, although it encompasses traits of the latter societal types. At its core, it became a state-centred petty bourgeois society marked by the domination of the tertiary sector. One of the principal aspects of modernisation was a rapid upward social mobility that resulted in a less cohesive form of extended family structure and generational differences. The high level of social mobility increased already existing relative deprivation between groups, a tendency which has continued to this day. These trends have been buttressed by both the clientelistic statism and the widespread grey economic activities. Moreover, they provided the ground for the development of populist political practices and anomic social behaviour before, after, and during the colonels' dictatorship (1967–74).

The most sound changes in Greek political life appeared after 1974; the abolition of the monarchy, the end of the politically exclusionary state of emergency that followed the civil war, the debasement of 'veto groups' such as the military and the para-constitutional cycles, the renovation of political personnel, the establishment of an open competitive political system, the pluralistic reorganisation of the party system, and the expansion of political communication are some of these changes – developments largely determined by the dynamics and the conjunction of transition to the republic.[35] Yet, as manifest as it might be, political modernisation did not transcend the continuity of the fundamentals of the country's political culture, i.e. strong nationalism, traditional patterns related to the legacy of Orthodoxy, and atrophic civil society.

It is precisely this merging of modernisation processes and traditional components that most scholars have in mind when they refer to the peculiarity of the Greek road to modernity. In fact, Greece seems to stand somewhere 'in between', with the crucial point being the need to explicate its 'in between' condition. So it is frequently argued that Greece is a *transitory society* and that its political culture is a transitional one characterised (in the terminology of Almond and Verba)[36] by a mixture of parochial, subjective and participatory orientations, with the latter steadily growing.[37] It is also argued that modernisation and tradition in contemporary Greece are so contrasted as to give rise to two opposing political cultural camps[38] and to a new political cleavage that tends to predominate over the other cleavages of the political system. According to these arguments, there are two incommensurable political cultures in Greece. One is indigenous, parochial, precapitalist, protectionist, populist, underdog and defensive; the other is liberal, outward-looking, and modernising. It is also argued that despite its earlier mastery, the traditional culture will sooner or later be marginalised by the modernising one, pressed by the rationalising imperatives of European unification.

In spite of important insights into recent changes, I do not think that these arguments do justice to the Greek case. It is my conviction that the transition thesis is overwhelmed by the evolutionism that has marked comparative politics of the past decades. Transition – not transformation – means that something moves towards a predetermined objective; this type of reasoning, however, cannot cope with contingencies and indeterminacies since it is embedded into the well-known ideal typical evolutionary scheme 'traditional–transitional–modernised society'. To characterise Greek society nowadays as transitional says too little, inasmuch as modern Greece was seen and understood from the outset as being somewhere in between.[39] As an analytical category, therefore, unless one wishes to over-generalise, 'transition' blurs rather than enlightens something which was taken into account by developmentalists themselves as early as the mid-1960s.[40]

Furthermore, interpreting contemporary Greek political culture in terms of the 'cultural dualism' described above seems to me to miss two crucial, interrelated points: first, by contrasting tradition with modernisation it neglects the fact that there is not one single tradition and that modernisation itself cannot exist outside a framework of some tradition; thus, tradition is not something negative by definition. Second, it views tradition and modernity as two pre-constituted and mutually exclusive rather than inter-constituted and interrelated cultural entities; for the point is not that there are two opposing political identities as much as that the contradiction between tradition and modernity penetrates all camps, any identity, and every individual or collective political actor.

On the whole, I think that the best conceptualisation of contemporary

Greek political culture comes from inventing, as a working hypothesis, the category of *inverted syncretism*. It is a category designed to deal more accurately with the articulation of modernity and tradition in Greek political culture. Originating in the sociology of religion and cultural anthropology, 'syncretism' was used by political scientists to mean the functional relatedness of heterogeneous traits whenever two different political cultures communicate. As a reinterpretation, syncretism is an acculturation process where the patterns of one culture are domesticated and conformed to the schemes of another and yet retain their original function. Thus in countries like Japan, Taiwan, and South Korea, where the traditional cultures were more instrumental than consummatory, syncretism took place because modernising patterns were assimilated to the traditional ones without however losing their original function.[41] In Greece an almost inverted process took place: retaining just a formal status, modernising patterns lost their original function while traditional ones remained intact or even became rejuvenated. Hence, the condition of inverted syncretism explains better both the change and continuity in Greek political culture referred to above.[42] The question however remains whether this condition can stand still in the highly complex environment of European unification and renewed nationalist pressures.

NOTES

1 J. Breuilly, *Nationalism and the State*, Manchester, Manchester University Press, 1985, pp. 107–11.
2 See P. M. Kitromilides, ' "Imagined Communities" and the Origins of the National Question in the Balkans' in M. Blinkhorn and T. Veremis (eds), *Modern Greece: Nationalism and Nationality*, Athens, Sage-ELIAMEP, 1990.
3 M. Herzfeld, *Ours Once More. Folklore, Ideology, and the Making of Modern Greece*, New York, Pella, 1986, pp. 18–21.
4 See A. Paparizos, 'Enlightenment, Religion and Tradition in Modern Greek Society' in N. Demertzis (ed.), *The Greek Political Culture Today*, Athens, Sage, 1994 (in Greek).
5 For these concepts see E. J. Hobsbawm and T. Ranger (eds), *The Invention of Tradition*, Cambridge, Cambridge University Press, 1983, pp. 1–14; and R. Williams, *The Long Revolution*, Harmondsworth, Penguin, 1961, pp. 66–8.
6 P. Bourdieu, *Outline of a Theory of Practice*, Cambridge, Cambridge University Press, 1977, pp. 78–87.
7 A distinction made by D. Apter, *The Politics of Modernization*, Chicago, University of Chicago Press, 1965, pp. 83–7, 250–1.
8 See N. Demertzis, 'The Selective Tradition of the Greek Political Culture' in Demertzis, *op. cit.*; D. Charalambis and N. Demertzis, 'Politics and Citizenship in Greece: Cultural and Structural Facets', *Journal of Modern Greek Studies*, 1993, 11; A. Pollis, 'Political Implications of the Modern Greek Concept of Self', *British Journal of Sociology*, 1965, 16; and J. K. Campbell, 'Traditional Values and Continuities in Greek Society' in R. Clogg (ed.), *Greece in the 1980s*, London, Macmillan, 1983.
9 N. Mouzelis, *Politics in the Semi-Periphery*, London, Macmillan, 1986.
10 J. K. Campbell, *Honour, Family, and Patronage*, Oxford, Clarendon, 1964,

pp. 213–62; N. Mouzelis, *op. cit.*, Part II; and C. Tsoucalas, 'On the Problem of Political Clientelism in Greece in the Nineteenth Century', *Journal of the Hellenic Diaspora*, 1978, 5; N. Mouzelis, 'Capitalism and the Development of the Greek State' in R. Scase (ed.), *The State in Western Europe*, London, Croom Helm, 1980; and 'Class and Clientelistic Politics: The Case of Greece', *Sociological Review*, 1978, 26.

11 R. Fakiolas, 'Interest Groups: An Overview' in K. Featherstone and D. Katsoudas (eds), *Political Change in Greece Before and After the Colonels*, London, Croom Helm, 1987; P. C. Schmitter, 'Still a Century of Corporatism?' in P. C. Schmitter and G. Lehmbruch (eds), *Trends towards Corporatist Intermediation*, London, Sage, 1979; Y. Papadopoulos, 'Parties, the State and Society in Greece: Continuity within Change', *West European Politics*, 1989, 12; G. Mavrogordatos, 'Civil Society under Populism' in R. Clogg (ed.), *Greece 1981–89. The Populist Decade*, New York, St Martin's, 1993; V. Macrides, 'Orthodoxy as a *conditio sine qua non*: Religion and State/Politics in Modern Greece from a Socio-historical Perspective' in *Ostkirchliche Studien*, 1991, 40.

12 See the issues 69A and 75A of *The Greek Review of Social Research*, Summer 1988 and 1990 respectively (in Greek).

13 For instance: N. Demertzis, *Cultural Theory and Political Culture*, Lund, Studentlitteratur, 1985; M. Pantelidou-Malouta, *Political Attitudes and Perceptions at the Onset of Adolescence. Political Socialization in the Context of Greek Political Culture*, Athens, Gutenberg, 1987; and *Women and Politics*, Athens, Gutenberg, 1992 (in Greek).

14 N. Diamandouros, 'Greek Political Culture in Transition: Historical Origins, Evolution, Current Trends' in R. Clogg (ed.), *Greece in the 1980s*.

15 See Papadopoulos, *op. cit.*, pp. 58–61 and G. Mavrogordatos, 'The Emerging Party System' in R. Clogg (ed.), *Greece in the 1980s*.

16 For the concepts of 'vertical' and 'horizontal' coalitions see E. Wolf, *Peasants*, Englewood Cliffs, NJ, Prentice-Hall, 1966, pp. 81–6.

17 V. Papacosma, *Politics and Culture in Greece*, Ann Arbor, University of Michigan Press, 1988, pp. 20–1; C. Lyrintzis, 'Political Parties in Post-Junta Greece: A Case of "Bureaucratic Clientelism"?' in G. Pridham (ed.), *The New Mediterranean Democracies. Regime Transition in Spain, Greece and Portugal*, London, Frank Cass, 1984.

18 F. de Jong, 'The Muslim Minority in Western Thrace' in G. Ashworth (ed.), *World Minorities in the Eighties*, Sunbury, Surrey, Quatermaine House, 1980.

19 *Eurobarometer*, June 1983, December 1988, June 1989 and December 1990.

20 See among others M. Spourdalakis, *The Rise of the Greek Socialist Party*, London, Routledge, 1988.

21 See *Eurobarometer* 1985, 1988, 1992, December 1993 and July 1994; and *Eurobarometer* March 1991 (Trend Variables 1974–1990) and June 1993; see also Ronald Inglehart, 'The Renaissance of Political Culture' in *The American Political Science Review*, 1988, 82.

22 P. Kafetzis, 'Political Crisis and Political Culture. Political Alienation and Involvement in Politics: An Incompatible Relationship?' in Demertzis (ed.), *The Greek Political Culture Today*.

23 A. Pollis, 'The State, the Law and Human Rights in Modern Greece' in *Human Rights Quarterly*, 1987, 9.

24 See C. Tsoucalas, ' "Enlightened" Concepts in the "Dark": Power and Freedom, Politics and Society', *Journal of Modern Greek Studies*, 1991, 9.

25 See Campbell, *op. cit.*, p. 186, etc.; and V. Vassiliou and G. Vassiliou, 'The Implicative Meaning of the Greek Concept of *Philotimo*', *Journal of Cross-Cultural Psychology*, 1973, 4.

26 *Eurobarometer* July 1994.

27 See *Eurobarometer* April 1993; Trends 1974–1992.

28 See *Eurobarometer* June 1993, pp. 7–9.

29 See Diamandouros, *op. cit.*, pp. 46–7, 59.

30 *Eurobarometer* December 1993, pp. 35–9.

31 *Eurobarometer* June 1993, pp. 3–5, A12.

32 On this see T. Lipowatz, 'Griechenland: Eine gespaltene Identitaet' in *Politische Psychologie PP-Aktuell*, 1994, 3.

33 *Ibid.*, p. 84, A50. Yet unlike Italians and Belgians, Greeks' trust is highest in people from their own country.

34 On this see J. Iatrides, 'Greece and the United States: The Strained Partnership' in Clogg, *op. cit.*; and 'Beneath the Sound and Fury: US Relations with PASOK Government' in Clogg (ed.), *Greece, 1981–89*. On the populist phenomenon in Greece generally see C. Lyrintzis, 'The Power of Populism: The Greek Case', *European Journal of Political Research*, 1987, 15.

35 See Papadopoulos, *op. cit.*, pp. 55–8; D. Kioukias, 'Political Ideology in Post-dictatorial Greece: The Experience of Socialist Dominance', *Journal of Modern Greek Studies*, 1993, 11; and N. Diamandouros, 'Transition to, and Consolidation of, Democratic Politics in Greece, 1974–1983: A Tentative Assessment' in Pridham (ed.), *op. cit.*

36 G. Almond and S. Verba, *The Civic Culture*, Princeton, Princeton University Press, 1963.

37 See for instance Papacosma, *op. cit.*, p. 28; and Diamandouros, 'Greek Political Culture in Transition', pp. 59–60.

38 See among others Diamandouros, 'Politics and Culture in Greece, 1974–91: An Interpretation' in Clogg, *Greece in the 1980s*, where one can find quite extended literature on Greek political culture.

39 This, however, does not mean that it is immovable.

40 E.g. Apter, *op. cit.*, pp. 13, 15, 20; S. N. Eisenstadt, *Tradition, Change, and Modernity*, New York, Wiley, 1973, pp. 17, 30–1, 37, 103–6 and 158–9; also F. Riggs, *Administration in Developing Countries: The Theory of Prismatic Society*, Boston, Houghton Mifflin, 1964, pp. 4, 11, 27 and 34–7.

41 See S. Huntington and J. Dominguez, 'Political Development' in F. Greenstein and N. Polsby (eds), *Handbook of Political Science*, Vol. III, Cambridge, Mass., Addison Wesley, 1975, especially pp. 18–19.

42 I think that inverted syncretism can be combined with Riggs' concept of 'prismatic situation' (*op. cit.*, pp. 24–30) which refers to the superimposition of modern political structures on traditional cultural patterns which fail to function autonomously and get embedded in traditional orientations.

8 Ireland

Brian Girvin

INTRODUCTION

On the island of Ireland there are two distinct political cultures. In the South (the Republic of Ireland or Eire) there is a fairly homogeneous population which is predominantly Roman Catholic, nationalist, and which has been independent of the United Kingdom since 1922. In Northern Ireland, which remains part of the United Kingdom, the majority Protestant, unionist and British population constitute another cohesive political culture. However, a minority of those who live in Northern Ireland do not identify with the majority political culture and consider themselves to be part of the nationalist political culture.[1] Furthermore, within the nationalist culture throughout Ireland there is a division over tactics between those who support peaceful political means and a minority who accept violence (there is a parallel split within the unionists).

Although the main focus of this chapter will be on nationalist Ireland, this does not entail any lack of importance for unionism. Indeed, this writer believes that the distinctness of unionist political culture and its importance has been seriously underestimated by most analysts until very recently. Notwithstanding this, there is a strong interrelationship between the two political cultures on the island, but it is one based on historical conflict, misunderstanding and dislike on both sides.[2] Indeed, an historical perspective – including the way a community is 'imagined' and its founding myths – is especially important to an understanding of contemporary Irish political culture.[3]

THE DEEP HISTORICAL ROOTS

At the heart of the distinctions between the two political cultures is national identity and a history of division and conflict. These divisions pre-date modern nationalism, but contribute to the form which the political cultures take. These modern political cultures have their origins in the historic failure of the English crown to fully integrate Ireland into the British state, as it did successfully with Wales and Scotland. The Normans arrived in Ireland in the twelfth century, but never fully conquered the Gaelic Irish. Indeed, by the fourteenth century Gaelic Ireland had absorbed the Normans to such a degree that it was said they were more Irish than the Irish themselves. The Gaelic world, based as it was on clan loyalty, was a highly fragmented one, and there is little evidence that a unitary state existed at any time under Gaelic control. However, the Normans are important because they brought the English crown into Irish political life. As the English state consolidated and expanded, Ireland became part of its geo-political considerations. Despite this, until the sixteenth century English control of Ireland remained weak: the only secure area of English control was the area around Dublin, the so called Pale.[4]

The English Reformation changed this and increasingly political difference in Ireland was refracted through religion. The seventeenth century is especially catastrophic in terms of Irish history and folk memory. It begins with the collapse of Gaelic Ireland which is followed by the Ulster Plantation. The 1641 Rebellion by the native Irish in Ulster is a response to this; in turn the Cromwellian wars in Ireland are a continuation of these conflicts. The wars of attrition in the seventeenth century culminate with the Williamite Wars and the Glorious Revolution which marks the end of Catholic Ireland's resistance to Protestant England. By 1700 the Gaelic elite had either been extinguished, or forced into exile or underground, while Irish Catholics generally had been dispossessed and outlawed.[5]

By the early eighteenth century a complex socio-political structure had emerged on the island, but it is possible to identify three specific sub-cultures.[6] The first of these was a small self-conscious Anglican (Church of Ireland) landed elite who dominated the political, economic and social life of the island from the end of the seventeenth century to the end of the nineteenth century. Their power and position was ultimately dependent on the military might of the British state. While this elite was also dominant in north-east Ulster, it was challenged by the Presbyterian (nonconformist) majority in that area. Presbyterians became increasingly radical and democratic during the eighteenth century, closely identifying with the Scottish Enlightenment. However, rural Ulster was also riven by sectarian conflict which further divided Catholics and Protestants. These tensions continue to characterise politics in many parts of Ulster to the present day.[7]

The majority of Irish people remained Catholic. Although wars in the seventeenth century had destroyed Gaelic Ireland, these conflicts created the basis for a new sense of Irishness suffused by Catholicism. Religion provided a notion of cohesiveness in the face of oppression, and this oppression provides the emotional links required for that very cohesiveness. Whether this identity can be considered to be nationalist is debatable, but the experience of Irish Catholicism during the eighteenth century marks it off as a separate and distinct sub-culture with quite specific values, norms and perhaps world view.[8] Catholicism helps to explain the difference between Ireland and Scotland and Wales: whereas the latter two regions could identify with Linda Colley's component parts of Britishness: Protestantism, the Empire and the Monarchy, this proved much more difficult in the Irish case – not least because the Protestant Irish never constituted more than 25 per cent of the population and never exercised cultural hegemony over the rest.[9]

The failure in the 1790s to achieve a union among the Catholic, Anglican and Presbyterian Irish on radical republican lines, led to separate developments during the nineteenth century for each group. The Act of Union which followed in 1800 integrated Ireland into the British state; but in contrast to Scotland and Wales Catholic Ireland never became an integral part of the British state or its political culture. The Irish were not British, nor was there a Catholic nationalist identity. There was a Catholic cultural religious identity which was often sectarian and anti-Protestant; but within Catholicism there was also a liberal movement for equal rights for Catholics *within* the United Kingdom. This movement for civil rights was transformed by Daniel O'Connell when he successfully mobilised Catholic opinion, which had the consequence of separating the political evolution of the Catholic Irish from the Protestant Irish and from the British (and Protestant) state. This led to the rise of an Irish Catholic nationalism which, between 1800 and 1850, changed the political landscape in Ireland beyond recognition.[10]

THE HARDENING OF IRISH POLITICAL CULTURE

It is during the first fifty years of the nineteenth century that the main characteristics of Irish political culture harden. O'Connell gave the new movement form and direction, but many of the trends are independent of his influence. Religion becomes the central characteristic of the political culture, but it is religion mixed with political nationalism. The religious element allowed nationalism to distinguish the movement not only from the British, but also from the substantial Protestant minority in Ireland. At the same time as Irish nationalism consolidated its hold over the Catholic population, Irish Protestants became British, particularly in the north-east region of the island. Both societies became quite homogeneous, successfully linking identity with loyalty to the political culture to achieve internal cohesion in the face of external threat. The British nature of Unionist identity is a qualified one, but it is nevertheless real.[11]

In the process of its development, Irish nationalism discarded the use of the Gaelic language and has been English speaking throughout its history. Despite subsequent claims that Gaelic was the language of Irish nationalism, the original language has decayed since the beginning of the nineteenth century. The society in which the political culture developed has also been an essentially rural one, and since the late nineteenth century one with a strong sense of proprietorialism. This rural, Catholic, English-speaking and proprietorial society imposed specific social norms on the political culture. These reflected the teachings of the Roman Catholic

Church, were patriarchal in nature and content, narrowly moralistic in family and sexual matters, and inculcated an anti-intellectual 'intellectual' environment.[12] This was also a society which was anti-liberal in ideology and culture. The main features of modern Europe, individualism, industrialisation and secularism, were eschewed by Irish society. The values embodied in the land and religion were considered superior to those of urban, secular and capitalist Europe. The logic of this distinct political culture was independence, on the grounds that Catholic nationalism could not find true expression in a Protestant-liberal state.[13]

Catholic nationalist Ireland remained estranged from modernity by the time of independence, whether this is expressed in economic, cultural, religious or political terms. Continuity was the main feature after independence. This can be better appreciated by the nature of Ireland's independence struggle. The demand for Home Rule (or devolved government) met with intense resistance from Protestant Ireland, which insisted on its right to remain within the United Kingdom.[14] By 1914 the island was facing civil war, with both sides armed and mobilised. The First World War postponed the confrontation, but in the event promoted further conflict. The 1916 Rebellion in Dublin (which provides the foundation myth for modern republicanism), the subsequent execution of the leaders of the revolt and the reaction of nationalist opinion to the British handling of this, and the conscription issue in 1918, led to Sinn Fein winning the majority of Irish seats in the 1918 general election. The war of independence which followed (1919–21) further polarised opinion within the island, radicalising nationalist opinion in particular. This radicalisation led to a civil war between the new government and the irreconcilable republican elements, after the Irish Free State was established in 1922. The republicans refused to recognise the new state, believing it fell well short of the republic they had fought for, and that it enhanced the partition of the island.[15]

The Irish Free State remained a predominantly agricultural society, with rural values retaining their dominance within the society. Security of tenure led to immobility in the countryside. Irish marriage rates were among the lowest in Europe and this can be accounted for in terms of stability on the land and the propensity for the surplus population to emigrate. This in turn contributed to the decline in population, which continued until 1961.[16] The stability of the society and the economy encouraged these trends, as did the social power of the Catholic Church. Society was informally regulated to a considerable degree during the 40 years after independence, but in contrast to many other European societies this regulation met with little opposition.[17] There were serious divisions after independence which resulted in the civil war, but the failure of the militants and their political marginalisation by 1924 indicates the strength of the culture's stability. The cohesiveness of the political culture prior to independence had given the nationalist movement strength; this cohesiveness was transferred to democratic institutions after independence. While Ireland was not a conflict-free society, as

nationalist ideologists sometimes asserted, conflict was very carefully mediated by the political and social elites to prevent the emergence of serious
social and economic cleavages within the society. This commitment to
stability and consensus was reinforced not only by the political actors in the
new state, but by the political culture which placed a very high premium on
stability, continuity and consensus.[18] This internal democratic stability was
reinforced by the borrowing of many British institutions by the new state. Its
parliament, legal system and civil service were modelled on those of the
United Kingdom, while a common currency, open labour market and free
trade reinforced both economic continuity and stability.[19]

The paradox in all of this is that a state born in revolution, with a strong
nationalist political culture and an ideology which is often anti-modern and
anti-British, adopted many of the political, social, economic and legal characteristics of this industrial and imperial state. There are a number of ways
to resolve the paradox. In the first place the 'revolution' was not revolutionary. The use of violence does not mean that the objectives of the
separatist movement were revolutionary. Certainly in social and economic
terms the insurrectionists, and their successors, did not embrace a policy
agenda which was either radical or revolutionary. Once political independence had been achieved the Church and a majority of the society accepted
the treaty which established the Irish Free State. One further reason for this
was the continuing proprietorial nature of Irish society up to 1970. Having a
stake in the society did not prevent this substantial section of society from
being separatists, but it certainly prevented any experimentation with the
social system.[20]

This is not to claim that independence was not important: not only was it
popular at the time, but unlike many successor states in Europe the Irish
Free State remained democratic and achieved political stability. There were
also institutional changes of some significance. When Fianna Fáil came to
power in 1932 it was committed to a radical shift in the relationship between
Ireland and the United Kingdom, an aim which was fully realised. In
economic terms a policy of protectionism was pursued which attempted to
achieve self sufficiency in industry and agriculture. In social policy welfare
provision was expanded, while there was a renewed emphasis on the need to
restore the Irish language. In foreign policy de Valera followed an increasingly independent policy, one which culminated in the declaration of
neutrality in 1939 at the outbreak of the Second World War.[21] Despite these
changes, the broad contours of the political culture remained much as they
had been for over a century. Independence enhanced and reinforced the
traditional nature of the political culture, removing the direct influences of
Britain on that culture. The 1937 Constitution, which replaced the British-
influenced 1922 one, institutionalised the central features of the culture. A
special place was reserved for the Roman Catholic Church, Articles 2 and 3
affirmed that the unification of Ireland was a constitutional aim, while
various other articles gave a pronouncedly Catholic character to moral and

property issues. In broad terms the Constitution codified the main elements of the political culture, embodying in the document the key elements of land, religion and nationalism. It was designed as a constitution for a republican Ireland, one that was stable, conservative and self sufficient.[22] It was a constitution drafted in the certainty that little of substance would change; a conservative constitution for a conservative people.

THE FAILURE OF TRADITIONAL IRELAND

The conditions under which the Constitution was framed began to erode after the Second World War and disappeared by the end of the 1950s. Unlike most of Western Europe, Ireland did not share in the economic expansion which occurred after the Second World War. Prior to this Ireland had not been particularly poor or disadvantaged in Europe, but became so between 1945 and 1970. In absolute terms, virtually every other state in Western Europe improved its economic performance in comparison to Ireland. This traditional society entered a crisis during the 1950s from which it was to emerge only during the middle of the 1960s, by which time circumstances and the international environment had changed radically.[23] In 1960 Ireland was still a remarkably homogeneous society, marked by a political system which, though democratic, was decidedly anti-liberal and moralistic.[24] The crisis which overtook Ireland in the 1950s provided the incentive for change. The agricultural economy virtually collapsed and traditional society came under considerable strain, while accelerating emigration threatened the continuation of the state itself. Although the crisis was economic in form, its content was far deeper. The traditional society could no longer provide for the economic, normative or emotional needs of the people.[25] In a context where Irish living standards were considerably lower than those in the United Kingdom, the pressure on the system increased. The changes were essentially economic, involving a break with the protectionist policies which had been in place since the 1930s. Economic nationalism was replaced by a renewed commitment to free trade.[26]

The economy became more open and increasingly committed to participating in European expansion. Furthermore, its structure became more industrial, though much of its industrial expansion was due to investment by foreign companies. Trade patterns also changed: whereas in the past the majority of trade was with the United Kingdom, by the end of the 1960s trade became more diversified both in content and destination. Ireland's social structure also changed under the pressure of industrialisation. Agriculture became less important and rural Ireland continued its depopulation, though this process was slow by northern European standards. Proprietors remained over-represented in the population when compared to other European states until well into the 1970s, and Ireland's social structure had more in common with states in southern Europe than with the more industrially advanced ones of the European Community.[27] This is a pattern which continued to prevail into the 1990s, though its impact has been weak-ening somewhat. In contrast with other small European states the Irish economy did relatively badly during the 1950s, and then took the next 30 years to recover from this setback.[28]

Economic change during the 1960s and 1970s destabilised the traditional community. As Garvin has noted, communalism has been a characteristic of Irish political life throughout the twentieth century. The pressure of economic development broke down some of the values which underwrote communalism, because these values were based on pre-industrial norms, notions of order and behavioural patterns. However, there was no one-to-one relationship between the imperative for economic development and possible changes in the political culture.[29] The decay in rural society was not uniquely Irish; however, the Irish crisis was more fundamental precisely because the values of its political culture were so entwined with rural values and ideology. Change then begins with strains in a society which can be plotted in a number of ways. New movements, ideas, cleavages and issues emerged which became nodal points for mobilisation, debate and opposi-tion. Where there is no challenge to existing values, where consensus is the norm, conservative parties rarely appear. Political conservatism was weak in Ireland because of the widespread identification with the norms of the polit-ical culture and there was no need for the self-conscious defence of traditional values.[30]

This homogeneous political culture based on an anti-liberal moral community (moral protectionism to accompany economic and diplomatic protectionism) began to break up by the end of the 1960s.[31] Growing indus-trialisation, economic integration and joining the European Community accelerated the process. These changes did not imply that Ireland would give up its specific historic identity or indeed that its traditional political culture would change in any radical fashion. However, the changes, though economic and therefore technocratic, had wider consequences. During the 1960s many European states experienced rapid social change, often expressed in changing lifestyles, individualism, pluralism and the dissolution of many traditional value systems and norms. The trend was particularly strong on moral questions, and in most states access to contraception, divorce and abortion became easier, church attendance dropped, often considerably, while the role of religion as a guide to behaviour declined.[32] Though there were noticeable differences between northern and southern Europe and between Catholic and Protestant societies in these matters, what was noticeable was a trend towards convergence between the differing states. When Ireland joined the European Community in 1973, most of its partners were moving very rapidly away from a traditional moral framework and developing one which was decidedly liberal, and which was at variance with the still dominant anti-liberal ethos of Irish political culture at that time.

It would be too strong to suggest that the European Community had a specifically liberal imperative, but individual member states and a commitment to universal norms of behaviour gave it an essentially liberal image. To the extent that this was the case, Ireland remained distinct. This in itself would not have proved decisive; after all, the European Community has never been in a position to impose moral uniformity on an individual state. Despite this, membership did have a significant impact on Ireland, especially in legal matters. On a number of occasions, decisions by the Court of Justice and the European Court of Human Rights have prompted Irish governments to change domestic legislation. Within Ireland itself, a number of factors were influencing opinion in a more liberal direction. Sections of the Catholic Church were deeply influenced by Vatican II and by what was believed to be a more individualistic approach to doctrinal and moral issues.[33] At the very least the reforms convinced many that pluralism was to be valued for its own sake and this in turn led to an acceptance of toleration, a factor historically absent from Irish political culture.

This was compounded by the conflict in Northern Ireland. The violence there had two effects: the first was to distance one section of opinion from the historic objective of national unity, especially if unity could only be achieved by force. But it also drew attention to the question of the Protestant tradition both north and south and the need to accommodate it. This led to serious debate concerning the legitimacy of the IRA and its use of violence, as well as to the Catholic nature of the southern state. Some of these concerns led to the deletion of Article 42 from the Constitution in 1972, an article which had proclaimed the special position of the Catholic Church in Ireland. It also led in the 1980s to Garret FitzGerald's 'Constitutional Crusade' and to the New Ireland Forum: each of which assessed critically various aspects of the nature of southern society in its relationship to Northern Ireland and the United Kingdom.[34]

TRADITIONAL VALUES AND SOCIAL CHANGE

Concern over violence in Northern Ireland changed opinion among some sections of nationalist political culture, but it could easily be compartmentalised as part of a process towards regulating the terms of the relationship between Northern Ireland and the Republic. More problematic was the question of reform for its own sake within the Republic. It was reported that significant sections of the governing Fianna Fáil party were opposed to any changes in the laws prohibiting contraceptives, despite the widespread evasion of the law by the early 1970s. In this area legal change was slow, despite a Supreme Court decision in 1973 to permit the importation of contraceptives for personal use. By the end of the 1970s, whatever changes had taken place in opinion, behaviour, or in the society were not influential among politicians. Indeed the traditional political elites were reluctant to engage in debate which might bring them into conflict with the Catholic Church and resisted change as a consequence.[35] Moreover, voting behaviour continued to express traditional patterns as late as 1969, and perhaps also up to 1977. If social change was taking place, its impact on the political system and the political culture remained slight.[36]

By this time, however, the Irish political map was being redrawn significantly. At the most general level there developed a 'reform consciousness' among educational, administrative and academic elites. This was reflected in the growing professionalisation of most of these bodies. Accompanying this, many interest groups emerged which lobbied on individual issues. Some, such as the National Farmers' Association, organised to defend the interest of traditional sectors of the economy, while others, like the women's groups, sought to redefine the political agenda in a new fashion. Furthermore, within the political parties there were signs of change also. The Labour Party began a move to the left, while Fine Gael assumed a liberal stance under the leadership of Garret FitzGerald. Fianna Fáil changed least and, under the leadership of Charles Haughey, became an expressly conservative party.

With the exception of the contraceptive issue, most of the politically contentious issues, such as the claim to Northern Ireland, the restoration of the Irish language, and moral questions, remained off the political agenda until the early 1980s. Yet polling evidence suggested that opinion had begun to change, sometimes quite dramatically, on some of these questions. Biever found at the beginning of the 1960s that opinion in Dublin was still essentially theocratic. A decade later, Mac Gréil's survey drew attention to the extent to which that homogeneous culture had broken along distinct cleavages.[37] Mac Gréil's data suggested that opinion was seriously divided on a large number of moral and political issues which, traditionally, had either not divided Irish opinion or where there was an overwhelming consensus.

The extensive survey carried out subsequently by Nic Ghiolla Phádraig confirmed that a shift in opinion was taking place at the national level, but it also showed that change was gradual and that secularisation was slow among many sections of Irish Catholicism. What these and other polls discovered was that church-going remained remarkably high by European standards, but they also highlighted the erosion in the belief system underlying this. In addition, these and other data hinted that there was a detectable decline in the anti-liberal and moralistic uniformity which had prevailed for over a century among Irish Catholics.[38]

But despite these changes, the political agenda has been dictated largely by the traditional political forces in the society and the extent of liberal mobilisation has been weak.[39] Progress or modernity are not unproblematic; there is no one way street in which a society moves from one end to another. Societies can get lost in the maze of streets, particularly if there is no street plan or, maybe more accurately, the plan is out of date and new buildings have been put up and now become obstacles. If societies operate as organic units, the past is carried through the present and contributes to the future. If the values of the past are described as traditions, they have an impact on the way change is accepted, rejected or modified. Modernisation is often taken to be in conflict with tradition, but in all but the most exceptional circumstances tradition is embodied in that process. It is also important to distinguish between *tradition* which is a set of beliefs, values and norms passed on from one generation to another, and *traditionalism*, which ascribes superiority to those values and insists on their retention to the exclusion of new values. In the latter form, tradition becomes conservatism and the defence of the past becomes a political imperative and a cause for political mobilisation. Traditions may change in response to change, but traditionalism is the elevation of traditions to the realm of ideological superiority.[40] Tradition itself is neither conservative nor radical: it is necessary to define the context in which it is invoked before its use can be assessed. Whatever the purpose, tradition imposes constraints on change and if change occurs at too fast a pace or if it runs against deeply ingrained beliefs in the political culture then tradition will be invoked to avoid or prevent change. From the point of view of change, tradition can be dynamic, whereas traditionalism preserves a static and normative society which must be defended against the modalities of the modern.[41]

But there is a deeper feature to this. Those who identify with traditional norms are often anxious about their future or that of their family or community. They also believe that they are under siege and need to organise to offset the consequences of this. In Ireland the most successful model for this organisation has been the farming community, partly because it has considerable influence within the political parties but also because its community has been seriously threatened by industrialisation and change. The defence of agrarian interests has been remarkably successful, whether the focus is on the Common Agricultural Policy or on the priorities in educational policy. In sharp contrast, Irish language enthusiasts have not been successful in invoking tradition to prevent the death of the language or the demise of the Gaeltacht. In this case tradition has not been successfully mobilised because, despite the constitutional priority which Irish has been given, the majority of the population have little more than a sentimental link to Irish, whereas rural Ireland benefits from a historic relationship with nationalism and the wider society. The other institution which has benefited from tradition has been the Fianna Fáil party which, under the leadership of Charles Haughey (1979–92), has adopted a consistently conservative political strategy. Central to this has been the defence of the Constitution in its original form. This has been closely linked to identifying the party with nationalism, the Church and rural values, all of which combined to give the party a strong conservative identity which has successfully mobilised traditional sections of the electorate during the 1980s.[42]

The changes which began in Ireland during the 1970s are relatively weak outside the economic sphere. By the end of that decade, however, a powerful reaction had set in against the modernising trends in society. The war in Northern Ireland revived the irredentist claim contained in the Constitution, and anti-British sentiment became widespread.[43] In political terms, Fianna

Fáil reasserted its nationalist and populist roots and achieved a landslide victory at the 1977 general election. Constitutional reform was postponed, while the 1960s promise of change disappeared. More profoundly, by the early 1980s a well-organised and financed lay Catholic lobby appeared, committed to reasserting traditional (Catholic) values. This movement was extremely successful in its objectives between 1982 and 1990. In 1983 it campaigned successfully for an amendment to the Constitution which outlawed abortion under all circumstances. In 1986 these organisations defended the constitutional ban on divorce and successfully identified its referendum campaign with traditional nationalist and religious symbols. Between 1986 and 1990 the anti-abortion groups used the courts to outlaw the circulation and distribution of information on abortion.[44]

These developments call attention to the role of tradition in the political culture. Because Irish political culture had its foundation in essentially traditional norms, it was relatively easy to mobilise opinion around their defence. Referendums during the 1980s also highlighted the continuing strength of traditional views. In 1983 the electorate endorsed, by a 2–1 majority, an amendment to the Constitution which prohibited abortion under any circumstances; in 1986 an attempt to remove the prohibition on divorce in the Constitution was defeated by 63.5 per cent voting against the proposal. The 1981 European Values Study reported that Irish respondents (of all ages) were far more likely to hold traditional views on religious and moral issues than their European counterparts. What these data show is that roughly one-third of the electorate take a liberal view on a range of issues, whereas between a half and two-thirds take a conservative position. While the conservative vote is not available on every occasion, it is more open to mobilisation by conservatives than by liberals. What this also shows is that tradition is not passive in this context, but confronts change, seeking to dominate it and give it a conservative character and direction. If change is inevitable in the modern world, this does not entail that change will inevitably move in a progressive or liberal direction. The evidence from Ireland in the 1980s shows the defensive character of tradition and its strength in preventing substantive change at any of the levels of political culture.[45]

THE NATURE OF CHANGE IN THE 1990s

If the 1980s can be characterised as a period when conservatives in Ireland successfully resisted the reform imperative, the first half of the 1990s tells a different story. Although change in the political system had been frequently predicted, it was not until the late 1980s that evidence for volatility appears. Between 1982 and 1992 the combined votes for the two largest parties declined from just under 85 per cent to 64 per cent. New political parties increased their vote and representation, reflecting a new volatility within the system. At the 1992 general election the Labour Party doubled its vote and its seats. More importantly perhaps, Fianna Fáil's vote fell below 40 per cent for the first time since 1927. This outcome questioned that party's ability to form a single party government, or indeed its dominance within the party system. The logic of these trends is that coalition government now appears to be the only option available for government formation. In 1989 Fianna Fáil accepted coalition as a temporary measure, but since 1992 the party has reluctantly had to accept coalition as a normal feature of politics.

Some of these changes can be explained by social and demographic changes. The 1990 European Values Study noted that inter-generational differences were becoming more pronounced. Age and education had important effects on Fianna Fáil support. Whereas 37 per cent of those who had third level education supported Fianna Fáil, this increased to 60 per cent among those who had not completed secondary school. However, this applied to voters aged 30 or over; only 32 per cent of those aged under 30 and who had not completed secondary school continued to identify with Fianna Fáil. Fianna Fáil is losing support among its traditional working-class electorate and is not gaining it elsewhere. Indeed, both Fianna Fáil and Fine Gael are losing support among urban voters, and are heavily dependent on a rural vote which is in decline. The changes which took place at the 1992 general election can be explained in terms of an electorate which is becoming more volatile, more attracted to new parties and, in urban areas, less willing to vote for traditional parties. It is the Labour Party and the smaller parties which benefited most from these changes in 1992.[46] Despite these trends, a referendum held to remove the prohibition on divorce in November 1995 was only narrowly passed, with 50.3 per cent voting in favour. Legislation has now been introduced to give effect to the result.

One of the consistent trends during the 1980s and early 1990s was that Fianna Fáil was more likely to take a conservative position on constitutional, nationalist and moral issues than other parties. The 1990 presidential election, which led to the election of the liberal Mary Robinson, demonstrated the ability of the liberal wing of Irish politics to mobilise a majority in a clear choice between liberal and conservative. On even the most sensitive issues, opinion also seemed to be shifting. Between 1981 and 1990 attitudes to abortion changed quickly, despite the constitutional amendment. Whereas less than half of those questioned in 1981 considered that abortion was acceptable when a mother's life was threatened, this had increased to two-thirds by 1990. This shift is significant as it predates the X case, and the decision taken by the Supreme Court in 1992 that abortion could be performed under certain circumstances within Ireland and within the meaning of the amendment which purported to outlaw any such intervention.

One consequence of this decision was that three referendums were held in November 1992 to clarify the status of the Constitution in matters relating to abortion. The outcome further demonstrated the extent to which opinion had changed. The right to travel was affirmed, as was the right to obtain information on abortion. However, an attempt to restrict the circumstances under which an abortion might take place was defeated by the combined votes of liberals and conservatives. Furthermore, in 1995 the new coalition government of Fine Gael, the Labour Party and the Democratic Left gave legislative effect to the referendum on information, despite the opposition of Fianna Fáil, the Catholic Church and the anti-abortion lobby. Changes are also evident elsewhere in the culture. A February 1995 poll reported that 59 per cent of respondents were in favour of removing the ban on divorce, while 35 per cent were opposed. The strongest support came from those under 50 years of age, living in urban areas and who were in non-farming occupations. Among the political parties, opposition was strongest in Fianna Fáil and Fine Gael, though both parties agreed to support change.[47]

Change can also be measured in respect of Northern Ireland. When one considers the strength of nationalism as a component part of Irish political culture, it is not surprising that over two-thirds of respondents agree that a united Ireland is an objective to be aspired to. Despite this, in the same survey 49 per cent believed it would never happen, while a further 24 per cent considered it would not happen for 50 years or more. Interestingly, whereas 56 per cent considered the Irish nation to comprise the 32 counties of the island of Ireland, 38 per cent believed that the Irish nation was limited to the 26 counties of the existing state. This latter figure has some importance in the context of the constitutional claim on Northern Ireland, and on current discussions to change this claim as a way of re-starting the peace process and further isolating the IRA. Polls taken more recently show a complex set of attitudes on Northern Ireland. There is considerable reluctance to give up the aim of a united Ireland, but significant support for changing the constitutional claim and including an aspiration to Irish unity. This draws attention to the continuing strength of traditional nationalist assumptions, but also highlights flexibility on the part of the electorate. There is also some evidence to suggest that respondents in the Republic are willing to postpone unity, if this helps the peace process in Northern Ireland. The weakening of the more fundamentalist view of Irish nationalism is accompanied by a more realistic view of the nature of Northern Ireland. In a 1987 poll respondents were asked what nationality they considered the Northern Irish to be: 33 per cent considered them to be Irish, 15 per cent British and 42 per cent thought them to be both British and Irish.[48] All of these matters are subject to debate and dispute within the Republic of Ireland but, precisely because they are so divisive, they highlight the extent of change over the past 25 years. Although the IRA ceasefire did not last, further changes are evident in public opinion in the Republic. In February 1996 it was reported that, for the first time, those who favoured Irish unity as the preferred solution to the conflict were in the minority.

CONTINUITIES AND CHANGE

The process discussed above is still under way. In comparison to other parts of Western Europe, Ireland retains many traditional values and norms. However, on a wide range of issues Ireland is not that different from its European neighbours. European integration has, in numerous ways, opened up the society to unprecedented external influence, and liberals especially support the cause of further integration. Notwithstanding this, the main dynamic for change is being provided by the society itself. New divisions have emerged in Irish society, and the electorate has increasingly divided along liberal and conservative lines in response to this. Although fluid, the issues and the context are clear on a number of major issues including abortion, Northern Ireland, European Union and NATO membership. The mobilisation process remains complex and different coalitions appear on each issue, but conflict on these issues has become routine in the life of the political culture. The Irish Constitution no longer reflects a consensus, but is the focus for division and conflict. It is at this level that the most serious divisions now appear: for many, the meaning of the political culture is embodied in the Constitution. The extent to which the Constitution is changed and the degree to which this proves acceptable to the majority will determine the future of Irish political culture. In question is the extent that a society with an anti-liberal and majoritarian tradition can adapt its political culture to accommodate change in Europe and in Ireland, while coming to terms with pluralism and diversity within the society itself. Irish political culture retains many traditional features and they are firmly grounded institutionally and at a mass level. However, change has accelerated and increasingly the electorate has demonstrated a capacity to recognise this and to act in response to it. This tension was evident at the November 1995 referendum on divorce. The prohibition on divorce was removed by a majority of less than 1 per cent. The strength of the opposition to change highlights the continuing importance of traditional values within the political culture. There will continue to be tension between the forces of change and those of tradition, but the importance of democratic politics provides the means for change to be accommodated within Irish political culture.

ACKNOWLEDGEMENTS

I would like to thank Chris Whelan and Jack Jones for access to various polls.

NOTES

1 R. Rose, *Governing Without Consensus*, London, Faber and Faber, 1971.
2 P. Bew, P. Gibbon and H. Patterson, *Northern Ireland 1921–1994*, London, Serif, 1995; J. Todd, 'Two Traditions in Unionist Political Culture', *Irish Political Studies*, 1987, 2; A. Aughey, 'Contemporary Unionist Politics' in B.

Barton and P. J. Roche (eds), *The Northern Ireland Question: Perspectives and Policies*, Aldershot, Avebury, 1994.

3   See B. Anderson, *Imagined Communities*, London, Verso, 1983; E. Gellner, *Culture, Identity and Politics*, Cambridge, Cambridge University Press, 1987.

4   C. Lennon, *Sixteenth-Century Ireland: The Incomplete Conquest*, Dublin, Gill and Macmillan, 1994.

5   B. Fitzpatrick, *Seventeenth-Century Ireland: The War of Religions*, Dublin, Gill and Macmillan, 1988.

6   H. Kearney, *The British Isles: A History of Four Nations*, Cambridge, Cambridge University Press, 1989.

7   D. W. Miller, *The Queen's Rebels*, Dublin, Gill and Macmillan, 1978; P. Brooke, *Ulster Presbyterianism*, Dublin, Gill and Macmillan, 1987.

8   A much stronger view on the nature of Irish identity has been developed by B. Bradshaw, 'The Invention of the Irish', *Times Literary Supplement*, 14 October 1994.

9   L. Colley, *Britons: Forging the Nation 1707–1837*, New Haven, Yale University Press, 1992.

10 B. Girvin, 'The Act of Union, Nationalism and Religion: 1780–1850' in J. Elvert (ed.), *Nordirland in Geschichte und Gegenwart/Northern Ireland – Past and Present*, Stuttgart, Franz Steiner Verlag, 1994; B. Girvin, 'Nationalism, Democracy and Irish Political Culture' in B. Girvin and R. Stürm (eds), *Politics and Society in Contemporary Ireland*, Aldershot, Gower, 1986.

11 A. Jackson, 'Unionist History' in C. Brady, *Interpreting Irish History: The Debate on Historical Revisionism*, Dublin, Irish Academic Press, 1994; E. Moxon-Browne, *Nation, Class and Creed in Northern Ireland*, Aldershot, Gower, 1983.

12 B. Chubb, *The Government and Politics of Ireland*, London, Longman, 1982, for a classic discussion of these themes.

13 Tom Garvin, *Nationalist Revolutionaries in Ireland, 1858–1928*, Oxford, Oxford University Press, 1987; L. Mjøset, *The Irish Economy in a Comparative Institutional Perspective*, Dublin, National Economic and Social Council, 1992.

14 A. T. Q. Stewart, *The Ulster Crisis*, London, Faber, 1969.

15 J. J. Lee, *Ireland 1912–1985: Politics and Society*, Cambridge, Cambridge University Press, 1989; D. Fitzpatrick, *Politics and Irish Life, 1913–22*, Dublin, Gill and Macmillan, 1977.

16 J. Lee, *The Modernisation of Irish Society 1848–1918*, Dublin, Gill and Macmillan, 1973; C. Ó Gráda, *Ireland: A New Economic History*, Oxford, Oxford University Press, 1994.

17 J. H. Whyte, *Church and State in Modern Ireland 1923–1979*, Dublin, Gill and Macmillan, 1980.

18 B. Kissane, 'The Not-so Amazing Case of Irish Democracy', *Irish Political Studies*, 10, 1995.

19 D. Keogh, *Twentieth-Century Ireland*, Dublin, Gill and Macmillan, 1994; J. F. O'Connor, 'Article 50 of Bunreacht na h-Eireann and the Unwritten English Constitution of Ireland' in J. P. O'Carroll and J. A. Murphy (eds), *De Valera and His Times*, Cork, Cork University Press, 1983.

20 D. Rottman and P. O'Connell, 'The Changing Social Structure of Ireland' in F. Litton (ed.), *Unequal Achievement: The Irish Experience 1957–1982*, Dublin, Institute of Public Administration, 1982.

21 B. Girvin, *Between Two Worlds: Politics and Economy in Independent Ireland*, Dublin, Gill and Macmillan, 1989, pp. 88–130.

22 D. Keogh, 'The Constitutional Revolution: An Analysis of the Making of the Constitution' in F. Litton (ed.), *The Constitution of Ireland 1937–1987*, Dublin, Institute of Public Administration, 1988; B. Girvin, 'The Republicisation of

Irish Society: 1932–1948', *A New History of Ireland*, Vol. VII (forthcoming: Royal Irish Academy).

23 K. A. Kennedy, T. Giblin and D. McHugh, *The Economic Development of Ireland in the Twentieth Century*, London, Routledge, 1988.

24 B. Girvin, 'Social Change and Moral Politics: The Irish Constitutional Referendum 1983' in *Political Studies*, 1986, 43; J. Lee, 'Society and Culture', in Litton, *op. cit.*, 1982.

25 J. A. O'Brien (ed.), *The Vanishing Irish: The Enigma of the Modern World*, New York, McGraw-Hill, 1953.

26 E. O'Malley, *Industry and Economic Development: The Challenge for the Latecomer*, Dublin, Gill and Macmillan, 1989.

27 M. Peillon, 'Placing Ireland in a Comparative Perspective', *The Economic and Social Review*, 1994, 25.

28 J. H. Goldthorpe and C. T. Whelan (eds), *The Development of Industrial Society in Ireland*, Oxford, Oxford University Press, 1992.

29 T. Garvin, 'Democracy in Ireland: Collective Somnambulance and Public Policy', *Administration*, 1991, 39.

30 B. Girvin, *The Right in the Twentieth Century: Conservatism and Democracy*, London, Pinter, 1994, pp. 1–23.

31 R. Breen, D. Hannan, D. B. Rottman and C. T. Whelan, *Understanding Contemporary Ireland: State, Class and Development in the Republic of Ireland*, Dublin, Gill and Macmillan, 1990.

32 R. Inglehart, 'Value Change in Industrial Societies', *American Political Science Review*, 1987, 81.

33 T. Fahey, 'Catholicism and Industrial Society in Ireland' in Goldthorpe and Whelan, *op. cit.*; P. Kirby, *Is Irish Catholicism Dying?*, Cork, Mercier, 1984.

34 G. FitzGerald, *All In a Life*, Dublin, Gill and Macmillan, 1991; D. H. Akenson, *Conor: A Biography of Conor Cruise O'Brien*, Montreal, McGill-Queen's University Press, 1994.

35 Whyte, *op. cit.*, pp. 377–418; Girvin, 'Social Change', *op. cit.*

36 R. Sinnott, *Irish Voters Decide: Voting Behaviour in Elections and Referendums since 1918*, Manchester, Manchester University Press, 1995, pp. 90–113.

37 B. F. Biever, *Religion, Culture and Values*, New York, Arno Press, 1976; M. Mac Gréil, *Prejudice and Tolerance in Ireland*, Dublin, College of Industrial Relations, 1977. It should be noted that Biever's fieldwork was carried out in 1962, while Mac Gréil's survey was confined to Dublin during 1972–3.

38 M. Nic Ghiolla Phádraig, 'Religious Practice and Secularisation' in P. Clancy, S. Drudy, K. Lynch and L. O'Dowd (eds), *Ireland: A Sociological Profile*, Dublin, Institute of Public Administration, 1986; M. Fogarty, L. Ryan and J. Lee, *Irish Values and Attitudes*, Dublin, Dominican Publications, 1984.

39 C. O'Leary and T. Hesketh, 'The Irish Abortion and Divorce Referendum Campaigns', *Irish Political Studies*, 1988, 3; J. P. O'Carroll, 'Bishops, Knights – and Pawns? Traditional Thought and the Irish Abortion Referendum Debate of 1983', *Irish Political Studies*, 1991, 6; B. Girvin, 'Moral Politics and the Irish Abortion Referendums 1992', *Parliamentary Affairs*, 1994, 47.

40 P. Keating and D. Desmond, *Culture and Capitalism in Contemporary Ireland*, Aldershot, Avebury, 1993.

41 The role of tradition is a complex one, and there is not enough room in this chapter to discuss it in detail; Girvin, *The Right in the Twentieth Century*, assesses its contribution to conservative politics; E. Hobsbawm and T. Ranger (eds), *The Invention of Tradition*, Cambridge, Cambridge University Press, 1983, offer some interesting insights.

42 P. Mair, *The Changing Irish Party System*, New York, St Martin's Press, 1987; B.

Girvin, 'Social Change and Political Culture in the Republic of Ireland', *Parliamentary Affairs*, 1993, 46.

43 B. Girvin, 'Constitutional Nationalism and Northern Ireland' in B. Barton and P. J. Roche (eds), *The Northern Ireland Question: Perspectives and Policies*, Aldershot, Avebury, 1994.

44 E. O'Reilly, *Masterminds of the Right*, Dublin, Attic Press, 1992; Girvin, 'Moral Politics', *op. cit.*

45 For a discussion see Girvin, *The Right in the Twentieth Century, op. cit.*

46 C. T. Whelan (ed.), *Values and Social Change in Ireland*, Dublin, Gill and Macmillan, 1994; M. Gallagher and M. Laver (eds), *How Ireland Voted, 1992*, Dublin, Folens/PSAI Press, 1993.

47 B. Girvin, 'Ireland and the European Union: The Impact of Integration and Social Change on Abortion Policy' in M. Githens and D. Stetson (eds), *Abortion: Rhetoric and Reality – Public Policy in Cross Cultural Perspective*, New York, Routledge, 1996.

48 Market Research Bureau of Ireland, *Eire Inniu: An MRBI Perspective on Irish Society*, Dun Laoghaire, MRBI, 1987; *Irish Times*/MRBI Poll, September 1992; *Irish Times*/MRBI Poll, May 1995.

9 Italy

Roger Griffin

INTRODUCTION

At the first meeting of the parliament of the newly united Italian kingdom in March 1861, Massimo d'Azeglio remarked: 'We have made Italy; now we must make Italians'. His words have been cited so often since as to become a cliché, a shorthand reflection of the widespread belief that – to use the words of Metternich on the eve of the Risorgimento which heralded the creation of the new state – Italy was, and remains, just a 'geographical expression'.

Let us start with the stereotypes, then. Chapters in books about Italians bristle with anecdotes and judgements to the effect that the Italians are characterised by an anarchic individualism, by a general disrespect for rules, by a widespread willingness to exploit loopholes in the system.[1] Such a 'national character' is hardly conducive to the emergence of a what Almond and Verba term a 'civic culture'. Indeed, in their summing up of this classic work, the authors concluded that 'The picture of Italian political culture that has emerged from our data is one of relatively unrelieved political alienation and of social isolation and distrust', adding that 'Italians are particularly low in national pride'.[2]

This damning verdict by 'outsiders' was published in 1963. In 1994 a team of predominantly Italian specialists published a collection which sought to produce a synoptic picture of 'the state of Italy'. An introductory section deals with 'sedimentations', historical factors which still continue to weigh heavily on the present. Clientelism, familism,[3] transformism, Machiavellism: it claims that as far as Italy is concerned 'these are the -isms which have become key words for historians and political scientists'.[4] The argument which unfolds suggests that the combined impact of these -isms, reinforced by the long-term impact of the 'Southern question' and the power of the Church, have made Italy's political habitat particularly inhospitable to liberal values. 'Familism', for example, which occurs when 'the interests of the family are prioritised over the other principal components of human co-existence', automatically leads to 'a relatively weak civil society and deeply rooted mistrust of the central State'.[5] Another essay on 'solidarity' judges that in terms of social integration and cohesiveness Italy 'is still far from achieving the modern levels of development of neighbouring European countries'.[6]

In his autobiographical novel *Christ Stopped at Eboli*, Carlo Levi recorded a powerful testimony of the inability of the fascist state, or indeed of any state in the long and tortured history of the Mezzogiorno, to win the allegiance of ordinary people. But if general portraits of 'the Italians' are to be believed, the malaise is not restricted to the south: it seems that Locke, Jefferson, Paine and their like were detained at Chiasso – the last Swiss town on the motorway travelling to Milan. In case such an observation raises spectres of a mythical 'national character' begotten by the peculiarities of the Mediterranean climate or Latin genes, we should briefly consider the historical background to such collective 'incivility'. Or would it be more accurate to say, the Italians' alleged collective failings? If we adopt an approach which is less obsessed by behaviourism and utopian ideals, and focus more on qualitative data, we may arrive at the conclusion that Italians turn out to have found partial solutions to some endemic problems of modern liberal democracies which other European societies are only now beginning to face up to.[7]

THE LIBERAL ATTEMPT TO MAKE ITALIANS

The situation faced by the first rulers of the newly united kingdom of Italy was paradoxical: it was Europe's newest nation-state, but at the same time it could be conceived as one of its most ancient nations. Once the Romans had subdued and incorporated the peninsula, they regarded it as 'patria' or fatherland, and everything beyond as part of a provincial or colonial empire. Despite the multiple invasions which characterised the Dark Ages, this Italian heartland retained enough territorial and cultural homogeneity for Dante in the twelfth century to treat it as what might now be called a 'submerged nation' destined to be united by an inspired ruler. The ensuing Renaissance established the enormous vitality of Italy as a 'cultural nation', much as the pre-unification Germany of Goethe and Schiller had been.

By the middle of the nineteenth century, the case for Italian unification seemed irresistible, at least to those imbued with 'progressive' thought. Its fragmentation into particularist states under various hues of oppressive rule, whether indigenous or foreign, meant that the cause of Italian unification could appeal to the liberal Romantic imagination as much as that of Greece had done a generation before. Yet, a vast gulf divided the *paese legale* – the new kingdom as it existed officially – from the *paese reale*, the 'real country'. For one thing the particularist states which were now formally united all had distinctive legacies. Some areas had a continuous history of foreign invasion and occupation going back to the collapse of the Roman Empire (and it was tempting to regard Roman rule over Italy's regions itself as a foreign occupation, as Carlo Levi was to discover a century later). In more recent times a decisive impact on the level of each state's economic and political 'modernisation' had been whether their most recent experience of non-democratic rule was under the Austro-Hungarian Empire, the Papacy, the Spanish Bourbons, or an Italian aristocrat (and even here there were considerable differences in the degree of oppression or 'enlightened' despotism). No part of the new kingdom could boast any experience of populist nationalist or proto-democratic movements to compare with those of Holland, England, the United States, France, Greece, or Switzerland.

What also hindered the emergence of even an embryonic civic or national consciousness was an extremely high level of illiteracy compared with such countries: over 60 per cent of men and 75 per cent of women, by the time Rome had been incorporated in 1871. As if this was not enough, by the same year only 0.6 per cent of the population outside Tuscany and Rome are estimated to have known Italian at all.[8] But if the educational and linguistic foundations for the diffusion of shared civic values at a national level had yet to be established, this problem faded into insignificance compared to two other major factors: the 'Roman Question' and 'the Southern Question'. Pius IX initially backed unification, but after the Kingdom of Italy had been established he used the full weight of the Vatican to challenge its legitimacy, including the formal instruction to Catholics not to vote.

The problem of the Mezzogiorno had equally deep roots. Centuries of feudal rule under foreign occupation had created a legacy of deeply antiliberal economic and social traditions which made the new kingdom of Italy a highly abstract notion for most southerners. The new state behaved with extraordinary insensitivity to the new province over which it arrogated jurisdiction thanks to Garibaldi's expedition to 'liberate' the south in 1860, not only imposing military service and raising taxes, but actually removing some of the meagre privileges which the peasantry had retained under the Bourbons. Also, the logic of the national economy was to siphon off resources towards the north, so that poverty in the south actually increased in real terms after 1861. The combined effect was to provoke a dramatic upsurge of the guerrilla-style resistance known as 'brigandage' which had first erupted in 1799 against both the Bourbons and the French 'liberators'. The state reacted by sending in the army to impose its authority by the ruthless use of force, creating practically civil war conditions in some areas till 1870.[9]

The failure of the new state to deal efficiently with the 'Roman Question' and 'Southern Question' was symptomatic of the third structural flaw of the Risorgimento: the inability to develop a political elite capable of creating a regime worthy of the term 'liberal', though this was how many politicians termed themselves. The electorate initially comprised males who were over 25, literate, and paid property tax. This meant that in 1861 only 1.9 per cent of the population was eligible to vote, and in the event a mere 57 per cent of them chose to use this right, which meant an effective electorate of 1 per cent. By 1882 this had only grown to 7 per cent, while a complex electoral law played into the hands of those who wished to manipulate it locally.

Inevitably, what emerged was an undifferentiated 'political class', made up overwhelmingly of nobles, landowners, businessmen, urban professionals, and industrialists, who manned (literally) all the nodal points of state power. The deputies it supplied naturally took to political horse-trading amongst themselves with little regard for the public interest. To pass any new laws thus involved the prime minister in a constant process of aggregating support on an ad hoc and personalist basis, a practice which came to be known as *trasformismo*. In the formative period of Italy's political life as a unified country, it had the fateful consequence of ensuring that immediate issues of bourgeois concern tended to take priority over long-term, genuinely national ones, and radical reforms were out of the question. The main concern of politicians was not the creation of a healthy parliamentary system to represent a mature civil society, but the promotion of the interests of the commercial classes from which they were drawn, the need to bring the already alarming national debt under control, the maintenance of internal order, and the consolidation of Italy as a European power, and hence, as the spirit of the times dictated, an imperial one. The attempts by Giovanni Giolitti in the years preceding the First World War to use *trasformismo* 'benignly' to lay the basis for a more democratic system ultimately ended in failure.

Neither Mazzini's nor Cavour's wishful imaginings – to use Benedict Anderson's fertile term[10] – of the new Italian nation had been borne out by the realities of post-unification Italy. The absurdities and contradictions which lay behind the construction of the Victor Emmanuel monument in Rome, intended to symbolise the heroic new Italy that had come into being with the Risorgimento, can justly be seen as epitomising just how compromised, botched (and sometimes farcical) the whole process of making Italians had been.[11]

ILLIBERAL ATTEMPTS TO MAKE ITALIANS

Given the conspicuous failure of the liberal regime to create a civic and national culture with a semblance of dynamism, institutional cohesion, and popular roots, it was inevitable that some of the most politicised in Italy saw liberalism itself as the chief obstacle to realising the promise of the Risorgimento. The first decade of the new century thus witnessed a variety of cultural and political campaigns of the extreme left and extreme right aimed at Italy's rejuvenation. The most significant was eventually to be the one led by a socialist revolutionary whose quest for an effective revision of Marx had led him in the direction of voluntarism, syndicalism, and nationalism. Benito Mussolini nevertheless just remained within the fold of orthodox revolutionary socialism till the interventionist campaign of 1914–15 created an alliance of forces bent on 'making Italians' through a collective national experience: the prospect of finally integrating the masses within the nation in a 'holy war' against the historical enemy, the Austro-Hungarian Empire and her war-mongering German ally, was irresistible. In November 1914 Mussolini threw in his lot with the interventionist cause, and took the first vital step towards developing his own highly eclectic and malleable synthesis of revolutionary nationalism and anti-Marxist socialism which would one day be known by the name of 'fascism'.

Fascism itself was not a coherent ideological force: its only common denominator was the myth of a reborn Italy based on a new type of state which would succeed where both liberalism and the experience of the First World War had failed, by finally completing the Risorgimento. In the 'New Italy' the people's energies would be harnessed so fully that all social, economic, and existential problems would be solved (what the philosopher Giovanni Gentile called the 'totalitarian state'). By eliminating divisive liberal pluralism through a single-party state, the anarchy of liberal economics through corporativism, the secularism and anomie of liberal individualism through a civic religion based on the fascist revolution and its leader, fascists convinced themselves that they would bring about a new type of order which would solve the contradictions of the modern age and create the first genuine democracy. The bond between the Italians and the state would no longer be based on the legal-rational one of choices made in the voting booth, but on the charismatic one created when individuals participated in the heroic destiny of the nation and thus became a genuine 'people' for the first time.[12]

However, fascism failed not only to turn Italy into the thoroughly modernised industrial power needed to become a Great Power, but to fascistise the masses. Whatever sphere is examined a gap can be seen between the regime's ideals and policy objectives and the reality, whether it is the wonders of the corporative system,[13] the creation of a 'civic religion' based on the fascist state,[14] the 'totalitarianisation' of Italians through the Italian Fascist Party,[15] the triumphs of the educational system, leisure, and youth organisations,[16] the strength of the armed forces, the opportunities for natives and settlers opened up by the conquest of Ethiopia, or, most conspicuously of all, the infallibility of Mussolini himself. Especially once the regime was manoeuvred into being the junior partner of Nazism, to the point of introducing the very type of anti-semitic legislation that the fascist press had always mocked, and the prospect of another world war moved ever closer, popular support for the regime melted away. By 1943 the civic religion had become a priesthood without a congregation, while the regime's impact on political culture had proved overwhelmingly negative.[17]

On the economic front, the totalitarian and corporativist policies of the fascist regime meant that it became extensively involved in the economy. It thus perpetuated the problem of the vast national debt, the uncontrolled expansion of the state, and the stunted development of a private commercial, industrial, and financial sector which it had inherited from the liberal regime. Nor did the new regime succeed in purging its 'new order' from the endemic vices of massive inefficiency and corruption: indeed, the single-party state created the ideal environment for these vices to be indulged and refined on an even greater scale. On the political front, fascism did much to reverse the push towards democratisation which had been felt in the aftermath of the war. Mussolini's manipulation of the various factions within fascism and of the conservative forces on whose collaboration he depended, meant that effectively he perpetuated the art of *trasformismo* on an even greater scale than ever before. Meanwhile the Italian populace, instead of being politicised by fascism, were actively depoliticised. 'Believe, Obey, Fight', one of the regime's many slogans, was a call for Italians to stifle any critical interest in what it did on their behalf and become willing, enthusiastic embodiments of the *homo fascistus*. In real terms this all too often meant apathy in the guise of conformism, and careerism in the guise of idealism. Not for nothing were the initials PNF (Partito Nazionale Fascista), stamped on the identity card, colloquially said to stand for Per Necessità Familiare ('for reasons of family necessity').

THE FIRST REPUBLIC'S ATTEMPT TO MAKE ITALIANS

The supreme paradox of Mussolini's attempt to make Italians was that it did finally have the effect of launching a powerful movement of national solidarity – one aimed at destroying fascism for ever. The armistice of September 1943 left Italy divided south of Rome between Allied- and Nazi-controlled areas. Millions of Italians north of this line faced stark choices: to fight alongside Nazis for the Salò Republic, to carry on with everyday life at the risk of being sent to German labour camps if captured in one of the random *rastrellamenti* ('rakings') of areas, or to join the Resistance.[18]

All over the north partisan units sprang up associated with political groupings: in order of importance these were the communists, the radical-liberal Party of Action, the Christian Democrats, the socialists, and the liberals, all pursuing different agendas for post-war Italy. Throughout Italy these parties set up local Committees for National Liberation, which in January 1944 led to the formation of a national committee, which by the end of the war had virtually become a provisional government. These forces had played a major role in accelerating the destruction of the Third Reich and in liberating the country. One result of this was that Italy, despite being an Axis power, could justifiably be treated by the Allies not as a country to be occupied and steered back to democracy, like Germany, but, more like France, as a country which had been temporarily occupied by fascism and then risen up against it. Moreover, the power of the Resistance movement provided a vital prerequisite for the country's rapid resurgence as a liberal democracy: the foundation myth of the new Italy was that the *paese reale* had risen heroically to free itself from dictatorship.

Voting on 2 June 1946 put an end to the monarchy and established the

constitution of the new Republic. Prominent amongst its founding principles was the outlawing of any attempt to refound a fascist party, and a
commitment to regionalism clearly designed to break the domination of
Rome and centralised power. Even more significantly, the Resistance myth
had allowed two of liberalism's potential enemies, the communists and the
Catholics, to present themselves as its bastions.[19] Yet in retrospect the first
elections set an ominous pattern. Of the 556 seats, the Christian Democrats
won 207, the Communist Party 104 and the Socialist Party 115, whereupon
the Christian Democrat Alcide De Gasperi formed a government with the
communists and socialists, and the small republican party.

Within a year, however, the Resistance alliance was in shreds. In a move
to defuse support for the right in the south, facilitated by the increasingly
chilly climate of the Cold War, the prime minister dropped his left-wing
partners. For the next four decades the DC (Christian Democrats) would
remain the undisputed ruling party, but a party forced by the mechanics of
the electoral system to hold power with a varying selection of coalition
allies, a situation which created a paradoxical blend of stagnation with
instability, strength with weakness, monopoly of power with ineffectiveness.
Twenty-eight governments and 12 prime ministers came and went between
1945 and 1970, while each administration sought to maintain ascendancy
by using ministerial positions and political appointments both inside and
outside parliament to buy support. Moreover, the DC was predisposed by
its anti-liberal roots to be suspicious of all genuinely pluralistic and secular
politics, and hence to see the state not as the institutional apparatus of civil
society, but as its own mechanism for upholding Catholic hegemony and
keeping out communism (thus it had few reservations about being the
custodians of 'Gladio', the elaborate counter-insurgency plans set up by the
Allies at the end of the war to ensure that Italy could protect itself from a
communist insurrection). In short, it had no more scruples about manipulating liberalism than it had about manipulating fascism. The important
difference was that it was now the senior party in any alliance, not the
junior one.

It was a situation which bred careerism and undermined the concept of
party loyalty or conviction politics, not just within the DC but in any party
which sought to exercise influence. Factionalism thrived as individuals jock-
eyed for influence and favours. By the same token, since the system suited all
parties, with even the communists allowing themselves to be bought off with
favours, there was no possibility for a clear-cut opposition party to emerge,
and any movement for electoral or constitutional reform was nipped in the
bud. This substitution of democracy by a corrupt 'party-ocracy' was further
encouraged by a peculiarity of Italian political parties. Sociologists have
shown how in post-war Italy membership of a party is rarely the expression of
deep political beliefs. Instead, parties have functioned primarily both as social
networks (and hence as a source of material advantage), and as a way of
affirming a sense of identity inherited as a birthright. Even for non-members,

voting has generally been less an opportunity to choose a government than a ritual reaffirmation of well-entrenched values and prejudices.[20]

Meanwhile, outside parliament, the judiciary and civil service, largely unreformed and unpurged since fascism, were a potential source of resistance to enlightened policies, and, since jobs had to be found to keep some politicians sweet and reward others, a tentacular *sottogoverno*, or shadow state, emerged made up of literally thousands of government agencies and quangos supposed to provide public services at every level of society. Politics became, as in pre-fascist times, a complex game played between members of an exclusive club, while the gap between the 'real' and 'legal' country yawned as wide as ever: state organs grew ever more sclerotic; the efficiency of para-state agencies declined as their personnel and numbers grew; the civil service, manned by a disproportionate number of tendentially illiberal officials recruited from the south, hypertrophied. Every new initiative to remedy structural problems, such as the Fund for the South or the Land Reform Boards, became a new source of patronage and the distribution of favours, draining vast amounts of state money in the process. To take just two examples, Catania's main hospital at one point had 1,200 employees for 1,500 cared-for patients, while the Ministry of Defence by 1949 somehow managed to have on its pay-roll 76,000 more staff in peacetime than it had under fascism. There was little incentive for anyone within the system to make books balance or cut expenditure, while the inefficiency and corruption endemic to the fiscal system enabled the richest in the private sector to pay derisory amounts of tax, so starving the state of a proper revenue. Inevitably, the national debt continued to spiral.

Other sores continued to fester. Needless to say the south, which had no experience of the Resistance and thus was impervious to the new Republic's foundation myth of anti-fascist solidarity, remained economically and socially backward, and a breeding ground for the worst forms of the abuse of authority and privilege compounded by the infiltration of organised crime into every centre of wealth and power. Regionalism, though built into the new constitution, only started to become more of a reality with reforms introduced in the 1970s (though not to the point of breaking the stranglehold of centralised authority).[21] Even the commitment to the outlawing of fascism was made a nonsense by the formation of the openly fascist *Movimento sociale italiano* (MSI) in December 1946. As if this were not enough, the state apparatus contained elements of an anti-communist right so radical as to be anti-democratic as well. This became abundantly clear when it emerged that the Minister of the Interior, De Lorenzo, had planned to stage a coup in 1964 and while in office had abused his authority to organise the tapping of citizens' phones on a scale of which the East German Stasi could have been proud.

For a time, the expansion of the Italian economy and the prospects of an improved standard of living underpinned a notable degree of social and political calm. However, gradually Italy was becoming more secularised and modernised, and pressures for change were building up which could not be accommodated within the old system, forcing them into the extra-parliamentary sphere. The wave of international student protest triggered by the Parisian 'Events of May' in 1968 ushered in a decade of unrest, fuelled by the considerable economic upheavals which ensued in the wake of the oil crisis of 1973 (the quadrupling of oil petroleum prices hit Italy particularly hard since it had no natural energy resources apart from some hydro-electric power). For years the news was dominated by student riots, strikes by school pupils and by public sector workers, industrial strife, deep public divisions over such issues as abortion and divorce, scandals over the corruption of party officials, and rumours about government involvement with the Mafia and the shadowy masonic lodge known as P2. The most serious symptom of the crisis of authority was the readiness of left and right extremists to carry out acts of terrorism to overthrow the state. The right deliberately resorted to sporadic acts of violence as part of a 'strategy of tension', aimed at destabilising democracy to a point where an authoritarian state became inevitable. It was symptomatic of the critical health of Italian democracy that during the 1970s and early 1980s, when this strategy was applied, neo-fascist terrorists were rumoured to have been operating in collusion with elements within the MSI, the police, the army, and the judiciary (rumours which subsequent research has fully borne out).[22]

Paradoxically, the first wave of the crisis forced the DC to make a crucial concession: in the 'historical compromise' of 1973 the communists were finally allowed once more to be coalition partners of the DC, a move which was to have profound repercussions for Italian regionalism. Three years before Italy had become a state made up of five special and 15 ordinary regions, and the strong presence of communists in local government ensured that the devolution of power and resources to the regions (and hence to more accountable authority) gradually became a reality. Moreover, economic and social stability slowly returned, and one historian could report that by 1982 the system was in many ways working well – though 'central government had at last given up the attempt to "make Italians"'.[23]

THE SECOND REPUBLIC: A FINAL CHANCE TO MAKE ITALIANS?

If in the 1970s the fabric of Italian society seemed to be tearing itself to shreds, the 1980s suggested that it had been stitched and patched together again. It was typical of the engrained complacency of the ruling elites, however, that, even though the 1970s had laid bare the deficiencies of Italy's electoral system and political culture, no movement was initiated within parliament to reform it. The DC was still the ruling party, and was still unashamedly embroiled in the contemporary equivalent of *trasformismo* to produce coalition governments. The state continued to hypertrophy in accordance with Parkinson's law, so that by 1992 there were 300,000 laws on

Italy's statute books compared to 5,587 in Germany, and while between 1989 and 1992 the GNP went up by 324 billion Lire, 230 billion of that had gone to government coffers, which was still not enough to dent the enormous national debt. As a result the average Italian worked from 1 January to 28 July for the state.[24] Meanwhile, abstentionism from elections and public disaffection from politics was at a record high.

Three factors were soon to emerge which would combine to bring about an unimagined rapid bout of change. The first was the growth of a radical regionalist movement in the north, which became a force to be reckoned with after the formation of the Lega Lombarda in 1984. The 'ethno-regionalism' (preached in terms which were frequently covertly racist) by the league combined a critique of the parasitic nature of the state powers in Rome and the mythical 'South' in general, with a celebration of the enterprise and dynamism of an equally mythical 'North'.[25] It was a formula which exerted a powerful emotive appeal for disaffected voters from Tuscany to the Alps, and found in Umberto Bossi a leader whose clean-cut image and outspoken scorn for the status quo generated a certain magnetism. By making the transition from a secessionist to a federalist regionalism, and aggregating the northern leagues into the Lega Nord in 1989, Bossi was able to enter mainstream politics as an advocate for a thorough-going overhaul of the system.

The dramatic disintegration of the Soviet empire not only precipitated the identity crisis in the Partito Comunista Italiano (PCI) experienced by all its European comrades, but meant that one of the most powerful sources of the mass appeal of the DC, its staunch anti-communism, suddenly became an anachronism. The PCI responded in 1991 by softening its image with a change of name to Democratic Party of the Left (PDS). This policy eventually led to a split in 1992 as a result of which hard-core Marxists formed their own party. The DC response to the regionalist challenge and the end of the Cold War ethos which had helped sustain it was initially complacent. But this complacency was shattered when a state crisis broke in 1992 which gave rise to the name 'Tangentopoli', or 'Kick-back City' (the suffix 'poli' to Italian ears evokes the goings-on in Mickey Mouse comics). A zealous team of financial and legal investigators led by a group of Milan magistrates started uncovering the full extent of the web of political corruption and circulation of 'funny money'. The ensuing revelations scandalised even many Italians.

As warrants for investigation rained down on the nation's political class, calls for electoral reform became irresistible, backed by the force of a popular referendum heavily supporting change. In April 1992 the old parties of the 'party-ocracy' were punished, their base eroded by parties associated with reform, such as the Lega Nord and the anti-Mafia La Rete. By the time of the next referendum on reform of April 1993, which even the DC had to back, 82.7 per cent voted to reduce the degree of proportional representation. The result was a hybrid: 75 per cent of votes would be attributed to single-member constituencies, the rest to proportional representation – though the much abused preference vote would disappear. The aim was to create a bipolar political system which would allow the prospect of some sort of alternation between major political parties on the lines of other liberal nations, an arrangement which many Italians see as the sign of a healthy democracy.

This principle was put to the test in the elections of March 1994. On one level the results showed that there had indeed been a legal revolution profound enough to justify talk of a Second Republic. New parties had emerged to woo the voter: the Partito Popolare and the Pact for Italy set up by some centrist DCs, the Democratic Alliance launched by some leftist DCs, the Alleanza Nazionale, formed by the neo-fascist MSI with the addition of some rightist DCs, and, most significantly of all, a shiny new centre-right party, the Forza Italia, brainchild of media magnate Silvio Berlusconi. The 'party-ocracy' was dead. Or was it? The Italian voter had not been confronted by a true bipolar system, but by 10 main parties which had grouped themselves into potential government coalitions: on the left the Progressive Alliance, a mixed bag made up of the PDS, La Rete, and others; in the centre the Popular Party and the Pact for Italy; and on the right the 'Pole of Freedoms' made up of Forza Italia, the Lega Nord and the Alleanza Nazionale. The extraordinary incompatibility of the bed-fellows in both the left and right groupings meant that if either of them were elected the leader of the dominant party would be forced to indulge once again in a modern version of *trasformismo*, albeit within a closed instead of an open coalition. This situation proves to have been even more extraordinary when the composition of the right-wing 'pole' is considered, which included the originally secessionist and anti-fascist Lega Lombarda[26] with the anti-federalist Alleanza Nazionale which, despite its renunciation of aspects of fascism, retained a neo-fascist agenda.[27] Before Tangentopoli, the Lega had been too particularist and anti-statist to have been a coalition partner with the DC, while the former MSI had been systematically excluded from coalitions through the whole post-war period.

Nevertheless, it was the motley Polo delle Libertà which triumphed in the elections. The new Italian government was formed by someone whose power base was not a traditional political constituency but a vast commercial empire. Berlusconi had only entered politics four months earlier at the head of the Forza Italia, a virtual reality party conjured out of thin air by the power of its founder's media empire.[28] Thus the new electoral system gave a working majority to three parties whose only common denominator was the fact that they were anti-communist, had never been contaminated by the 'party-ocracy', and were formally pledged to the creation of a new Italian Republic (albeit one conceived in very different terms).

The new Republic was meant to introduce the basis for a regular 'alternation' between left and right. Yet as one commentator put it, 'the pendulum stayed on the same side. . . . The alternation had been kept in the family: it was an alternation from right to right'.[29] The majority of voters who had kept the anti-communist DC in power automatically voted for the anti-communist 'Pole of Freedoms and Good Government'. Once more Italy had a prime minister forced to wheel and deal to keep his fragile coalition government together. Nor did this ploy guarantee stability, for within months not only had Bossi broken ranks, but Berlusconi himself was forced to resign. He had lost his grip on power through the combined effect of suspicions of the probity on which his business empire was based, misgivings about the close involvement of his financial and political interests, concern at his monopoly of the non-state Italian media, and popular protests against the austerity package which targeted the generosity of state pensions as part of the campaign to reduce the national debt. Before long the complex new voting arrangements were widely associated more with confusion than with greater democracy, the continued demolition of the Tangentopoli was encountering increasing public apathy, questions were being asked about the integrity of some of the very Milan magistrates who had blown the whistle on the venality of Italy's political masters, and charges that the state was in the hands of 'thieves' were as audible as ever before. By early 1995 the wind of change seemed to have blown itself out in Italy.

But lo and behold, in the 1996 legislative elections it was the centre-left 'Olive Tree' coalition which won by a narrow margin over the centre-right (which now called itself simply 'the Pole for Liberty'). For the first time in its history the leaky ship of the Italian state was being navigated by a disparate set of politicians dependent for their majority in parliament on the unreconstructed Communist Party. Another fly in the parliamentary ointment was the fact that the AN had increased its vote to 15.7 per cent, and its leader Fini was ominously enjoying even greater popularity than ever. Bossi's response of returning to a secessionist position by creating the Lega Padania was also ominous. It therefore remains to be seen how far this unexpected turn in Italy's political evolution heralds the creation of the dawn of a genuinely civic political culture.

CONTINUITIES AND CHANGE

There is little doubt that long after these words are printed commentators will still be struggling to make sense of the anomalies of Italian political culture and to determine whether the elections held in the aftermath of the 'earthquake' of 1992–4 actually marked the coming of age of Italy's political culture, rather than the umpteenth symptom of a protracted puberty crisis.[30] Perhaps Italy is caught in an interregnum of indefinite duration, in what is not the Second Republic but, to echo the title of one of Fellini's major films, Republic One and a Half. Yet even if the nation's new political class ultimately turns out to be as corrupt and undemocratic as the old, this should not be taken as a verdict on Italian political culture as such.

There are a number of sound academic reasons for revising the conventional picture distorted by decades of loose generalisations and prejudice, some of them rooted in a scarcely veiled 'Latino-phobia' on the part of Anglo-Saxon commentators. In the mid-1970s, for example, the Italian scholar Giacomo Sani wrote an elegant critique of the famous Almond and Verba account of Italy's woeful deficiency in civic virtues, which partly explains why their analysis was so comprehensively ignored inside Italy.[31] Sani ascribes its neglect to the fact that Italian scholars developed conceptual tools more appropriate to analysing their country's politics than the comparative one pioneered in *The Civic Culture*. He also stresses that since the defeat of fascism the majority of the nation's opinion makers and politicians have consistently upheld the fundamental rules of the liberal democratic game enshrined in the 1948 constitution, even those of parties historically opposed to it (notably the Catholics, communists, and neo-fascists). Furthermore, he maintains that the persistent tendency of Italians to mistrust the world of government and officialdom can be interpreted as a demonstration of the electorate's idealism and sound instincts, rather than disillusionment and cynicism.

Indeed, when the EU's *Eurobarometer* on long-term trends in public opinion reports that in 1993, as the First Republic crumbled away in the midst of a daily diet of corruption scandals, 25 per cent of Italians were still satisfied with the way their democracy worked (as opposed to 51 per cent of Britons), it could be argued that the figure is disturbingly high rather than low.[32] The European Commission's *Eurobarometer* report on the first year of the New European Union (1994) offers other data on Italian public opinion which suggest a more positive view of Italian maturity in political matters. At the same time, 55 per cent of Italians have no trouble seeing themselves as Europeans (third out of the 12 member states); 98 per cent support the unification of Europe (first); 76 per cent of Italians voted in the 1994 Euroelections (fourth); and 41 per cent of Italians were satisfied with the level of democracy in the EU (sixth).[33] If such comparative opinion polls are reliable and if the days of the sovereign nation-state are numbered,[34] then it is other political cultures – especially the British – that are in danger of being chronically underdeveloped, not the Italian one. In terms of national pride, xenophobia, and the capacity to be disturbed by the conflicting beliefs held by others, there is little to choose between Italy and Britain (81:79 per cent; 42:46 per cent; 8:11 per cent, respectively). However, attitudes to 'foreigners' may well undergo significant changes in the next decade as Italians come to terms with the full social, economic, and cultural implications of their country having been transformed from a country of mass emigration to one of mass migration. Slowly they will have to take on board the fact that the 'extra-communitarians' in their midst – which now number about 1.5 million between 'regularised' and 'clandestines' (about 2.5 per cent of the total population) – are there to stay. At present, while generally retaining their instinctive civility towards peoples of different ethnicity, few have made the mental leap of considering that a Maghreb African can be fully Italian in terms of citizenship while remaining culturally distinctive.

Another salutary qualification to received views is implicit in recent trends in the historiography of modern Italy.[35] Not only is the idea of a direct causal link between the weak liberalism of the Risorgimento and fascism under attack, but there is a new concentration on producing nuanced portraits of regional history which involves rethinking the categories of modernity and backwardness which so often have been applied crudely and misleadingly to Italy: after all *every* nation follows its own *Sonderweg* to modernity, which is always a complex blend of unique tradition with 'global' forces.[36] A bout of sustained 'revisionism' could eventually remove some distortions in the conventional account of Italy's transformation into a nation-state. A good example of such long-overdue reassessment is Robert Putnam's attempt to demonstrate that contemporary Italy can be divided into regions of advanced or underdeveloped 'civic virtues' which are ultimately a function of the degree to which a civic tradition had been able to grow up by the fourteenth century.[37] Even more sophisticated in its conceptual framework is Paul Ginsborg's article 'Italian Political Culture in Historical Perspective'[38] which rejects the overwhelmingly negative image of Italy of so many Italian and non-Italian commentators, arguing instead that political scientists should focus on the deeply conflictual processes which have actually shaped her political culture and stop lamenting that it does not resemble a highly idealised vision of the civic virtues of northern European democracies.

There are other considerations which might profitably be taken into account by those keen to point out the defects in Italy's political life. For one thing, public apathy and ignorance about politics is a symptom of every 'mature' modern democracy. It has even been interpreted as a sign that democracy is working: it leaves politics to professional politicians and thus allows the bulk of the population to lead apolitical lives. As for corruption, scandals calling into question the integrity of politicians great and small have rocked the political establishments of modern liberal democracies across the world. As Lord Acton pointed out so long ago, corruption may safely be regarded as endemic to all concentrations of unaccountable power, and unaccountable power is something which the modern state cannot help but engender.[39] Nor does Italy have a monopoly on the misappropriation of public funding, tax evasion, organised crime, or creating a black economy.

It is also arguable that Italy's alleged lack of civic values has some definite advantages when less prescriptive humanistic yardsticks are applied. *Campanilismo*, or a keen sense of local patriotism, may act as a prophylactic against the official nationalism to which state politicians would like Italians to convert *en masse*, but the retention of local customs, culinary habits, and dialects which go with them can serve as a bulwark against the erosion of identity and the sense of roots, a major source of the anomie and neurosis associated with modernisation. 'Familism', too, may undermine a more abstract sense of loyalty to civil society or the modern state, but it also ensures that the degree of institutionalisation and sheer neglect suffered in some 'more advanced' societies by marginalised groups – the mentally and physically handicapped, the homeless, the poor, the old, children – is minimalised. The persistence of religious culture may be a sign of 'backwardness' to convinced secular humanists, but at the same time it underpins a highly developed tradition of religious humanism which to some degree acts as a source of 'para-civic values'.

Such 'para-civic values' came into their own particularly when fascism attempted to create a 'totalitarian society' in which all Italians were to internalise the dictates of the state and the will of its leader. As Steinberg has convincingly shown,[40] Italian *'menefreghismo'* ('I-don't-give-a-damnism') and the inbred cynicism about orders from above which went with it meant that (in stark contrast to Germans with a hypertrophied sense of 'duty' to the state) even convinced fascists refused to comply with Mussolini's specific directives to cooperate in the measures through which the Nazis imposed the Final Solution in occupied territories: humanity prevailed over duty. The aftermath to the débâcle of 1943 produced many episodes of unsung heroism performed by farmers and 'ordinary Italians' who at enormous personal risk harboured escaped POWs and partisans. They were motivated by that instinctive hospitality, humanism, and selflessness which a mature 'civic society' can perhaps aspire to, or reinforce, but never create. The failure of Mussolini to make Italians by fascistising them is surely a tribute to the fact that in the main they have remained resistant to the demands of official nationalism to trade their individual sense of origins, place, family, and 'belonging' for a civic identity which is ultimately artificial.

The Italian journalist Luigi Barzini has taken this argument even further. He accepts that the way his compatriots blend anarchic individualism and hedonism 'makes all laws and institutions function defectively'. Yet it is precisely this cocktail which provides the spirit of the Italian *arte di vivere* (art of living) which he claims originally evolved to defeat the invasion and regimentation of their lives by outside forces, and which now has much to offer in a modern age bent on mass-producing iron cages of instrumental reason for us all to live in. 'Naturally more and more people flock to Italy each year . . . drawn to the place where the new perplexing problems of the contemporary world are familiar monsters, problems with which the natives learned to live long ago.'[41]

The question which remains tantalisingly open is whether there are any serious prospects for Italy to develop a mature national, though regionally diversified, civic culture which would enable it to play a full role in the new Europe.[42] It hardly needs pointing out that some of the larger member states of the EU can scarcely claim to be role models in this respect. For the foreseeable future the country seems doomed to remain polarised indefinitely between a cynical or impotent political class and a sceptical, disaffected electorate. Following deep-rooted survivalist instincts, most Italians may well stay stubbornly ensconced within their shell of familistic individualism and anarchic humanism as long as their sensors tell them that the external environment of public life remains polluted.

A judgement as astute as that of many a professional commentator was offered me by Augusto, one of the dying breed of Italy's traditional class of *contadini* (farmers working family land), and old enough to have lived through both the fascist and post-fascist attempts to 'make Italians'. Except when he was drafted into the army by Mussolini's regime or evading Nazi *rastrellamenti* (raids to root out partisans), he has spent the whole of his life in the tiny village of Martini set in the rolling hills of Piedmont, where gaping holes are now being rent in the once lush green quilts of vineyards as fields worked for centuries are left to fall fallow or give way to kiwi plantations and motor-cross courses. Waiting for his bank manager son to arrive back from work, he told me, 'They say that things are changing, but I think that it will take a generation for things to change.' A day may be a long time in politics, but in the life of a political culture even a generation is not.

NOTES

1 For example, L. Barzini, *The Italians*, Harmondsworth, Penguin, 1968; G. Procacci, *History of the Italian People*, Harmondsworth, Penguin, 1968; J. Haycraft, *The Italian Labyrinth. Italy in the 1990s*, Harmondsworth, Penguin, 1987; and P. Ginsborg, *A Contemporary History of Italy*, Harmondsworth, Penguin, 1990.
2 G. Almond and S. Verba, *The Civic Culture*, Princeton, Princeton University Press, 1963, pp. 402–3.
3 For a classic text on the anti-civic consequences of Italian familism see E. C. Banfield, *The Moral Basis of a Backward Society*, New York, Free Press, 1958.
4 P. Ginsborg (ed.), *Lo Stato d'Italia*, Milan, Mondadori, 1994, p. 45.
5 *Ibid.*, p. 78.
6 *Ibid.*, p. 88.
7 For criticisms of behaviourism, often used insensitively about the Italian case, see E. Pisani in M. Dogan and R. Rose (eds), *European Politics*, Boston, Little, Brown, 1971; and G. Sani, 'Italy' in G. Almond and S. Verba, *The Civic Culture Revisited*, Princeton, Princeton University Press, 1980.
8 M. Clark, *Modern Italy, 1871–1982*, London, Longman, 1984, p. 35.
9 For an overview of the 'Southern Question' see M. L. Salvadori, *Il mito del buongoverno. La questione meridionale da Cavour a Gramsci*, Bari, Einaudi, 1960.
10 B. Anderson, *Imagined Communities*, London, Verso, 1985.
11 See J. Dickie, 'La macchina da scrivere: the Victor Emmanuel Monument in Rome and Italian Nationalism', *The Italianist*, 14, 1994.
12 For example, R. Griffin (ed.), *Fascism*, Oxford, Oxford University Press, 1995, extracts, 5, 8, 13, 14, 15, 22, 28.
13 D. Roberts, *The Syndicalist Tradition and Italian Fascism*, Manchester, Manchester University Press, 1979.
14 See E. Gentile, *The Sacralization of Politics in Fascist Italy*, Cambridge, Mass., Harvard University Press, 1996.
15 See E. Gentile, *La via italiana al totalitarismo*, Rome, La Nuova Italia Scientifica, 1995.

16 V. De Grazia, *The Culture of Consent: Mass Organization of Leisure in Fascist Italy*, Cambridge, Cambridge University Press, 1981; and T. Koon, *Believe, Obey, Fight: Political Socialization of Youth in Fascist Italy, 1922–43*, Chapel Hill, University of North Carolina Press, 1985.
17 Clark, *op. cit.*, Part 3.
18 See G. Carocci, *Storia d'Italia dall'Unità ad Oggi*, Milan, Feltrinelli, 1986.
19 See Clark, *op. cit.*, Chapter 4; Ginsborg, *op. cit.*, 1990, Chapter 2. The Resistance myth on which the First Republic was based is set to come under extensive critical overhaul with the forthcoming publication of the last volume of Renzo de Felice's monumental biography of Mussolini, just when the Alleanza Nazionale is calling for 'pacification', a healing of the historical rifts between the partisans and the blackshirted defenders of the Salò Republic whom they want to be officially rehabilitated as patriots rather than traitors.
20 See P. Furlong, *Modern Italy: Politics and Policy-Making*, London, Routledge, 1994. On the implications for Italian 'political identity' see S. Parker, 'Electoral Reform and Political Change in Italy, 1991–4' in S. Gundle and S. Parker (eds), *The New Italian Republic: From the Berlin Wall to Berlusconi*, London, Routledge, 1995.
21 W. Brierly and L. Giacometti, 'National Identity and the Failure of Regionalism' in B. Jenkins and S. Sofos (eds), *Nation and Identity in Contemporary Europe*, London, Routledge, 1996.
22 See F. Ferraresi, *Threats to Democracy*, Princeton, Princeton University Press, 1996.
23 Clark, *op. cit.*, pp. 395–6.
24 This at least is the claim made in the draft Election Manifesto of Forza Italia (p. 72), published in February 1994.
25 See J. Dickie, 'The South as Other: From Liberal Italy to the Lega Nord', Supplement to *The Italianist*, 14, 1994.
26 On the Lega Nord see R. Mannheimer (ed.), *La Lega Lombarda*, Milan, Feltrinelli, 1991; and S. Allievi, *Le parole della Lega*, Milan, Garzanti, 1992.
27 See P. Ignazi, *Postfascisti?*, Bologna, 1995; and R. Griffin, 'The "Post-Fascism" of the Alleanza Nazionale: A Case Study in Ideological Morphology', *Journal of Political Ideologies*, 2, 1996.
28 M. Revelli, 'Forza Italia: l'anomalia italiana non è finita' in Ginsborg, *op. cit.*, 1994; and P. Statham, 'The New Politics of Intolerance', unpublished paper for European Consortium of Political Research workshops, 1995.
29 L. Bobbio, 'Dalla destra alla destra, una strana alternanza' in Ginsborg, *op. cit.*, 1994, pp. 654–61.
30 See, for example, S. Parker, 'Political Identities' in D. Forgacs and R. Lumley (eds), *An Introduction to Italian Cultural Studies*, Oxford, Oxford University Press, 1995.
31 G. Sani, 'The Political Culture of Italy' in G. Almond and S. Verba (eds), *The Civic Culture Revisited*, Princeton, Princeton University Press, 1980.
32 *Eurobarometer Trends, 1974–1993* (1994), pp. 29, 34.
33 *Eurobarometer: Report on Standard Barometer 42* (1995), Sections 9.6, 9.7, 10.5, 9.5, 3.1, 4.2, 4.3.
34 See M. Horsman and A. Marshall, *After the Nation-State*, London, HarperCollins, 1994.
35 For example, R. Putnam, *Making Democracy Work. Civic Tradition in Modern Italy*, Princeton, Princeton University Press, 1993.
36 See J. Davis, 'Remapping Italy's Path to the Twentieth Century', *Journal of Modern History*, 66, 1994.
37 Putnam, *op. cit.*

38 P. Ginsborg, 'Italian Political Culture in Historical Perspective', *Modern Italy*, 1995, 1.
39 See for example the chapter 'Democracy and Invisible Power' in N. Bobbio, *The Future of Democracy*, Oxford, Polity, 1987.
40 J. Steinberg, *All or Nothing: The Axis and the Holocaust*, London, Routledge, 1990.
41 Barzini, *op. cit.*, p. 368.
42 For example, G. Rusconi, *Se cessiamo di essere una nazione*, Bologna, Il Mulino, 1993.

10 Poland

Bogdan Szajkowski

INTRODUCTION

The analysis of Polish political culture in this chapter is not restricted to a narrow definition of this concept in terms of civic conduct. Such an approach would give us only a selective view and partial explanation of past and present political behaviour. Poland's geopolitical location at the crossroads of the European continent, its rich, diverse and deeply rooted political and social traditions, its complex political development and social structure, all lend themselves to a much broader approach to the analysis of the country's political culture. In order to understand the political culture of contemporary Poland we should seek to identify its roots, distinctive features and specific characteristics that have direct bearing on individuals' political attitudes and which form part of their shared experience of the political system.

The concept of political culture in Poland should be understood in a much wider sense than that usually used in respect of Western societies, where the emphasis is on public, and in particular political, participation. Polish political culture emphasises the sense and tradition of community belonging. The attachment to community as one of the main forms of social and political organisation is deeply imbedded in the Polish psyche and therefore underpins attitudes towards the state and its institutions. It stresses the notion of 'us' – a group of people sharing similar values, sense of identity, historical memory, interests and social life. The subjective element of the feeling of community – 'us' the people versus 'them' the state, its organisation and bureaucratic institutions – is an important aspect of boundary creation and maintenance. The retreat into these boundaries and values offers protection at turbulent times. In this sense, the patterns of political culture are predominantly conducted in informal communities, very often without connections with state institutions. High esteem for community goes hand in hand with the questioning and often the rejection of the state and its institutions. The perceived division between rulers and ruled is an entrenched element of Polish political culture.[1] These traditional and deeply-rooted divisions have been reinforced by more than four decades of

158   *Bogdan Szajkowski*

communist experience. The communists enjoyed power and privilege, but despite the oppressive apparatus at their disposal lacked authority.

One of the key aspects to understanding Polish political culture is the intertwining of Roman Catholicism and nationalism. It is perhaps the main defining and functional aspect of political culture in contemporary Poland. The symbiotic relationship between religion and nationalism also embraces patriotism, messianism, elements of fatalism and hope as well as realism and acceptance of reality, and a high degree of tolerance. However, it is a relationship which in recent years is showing notable signs of change.

ROMAN CATHOLICISM AND NATIONALISM

The Roman Catholic Church in Poland has been a national institution for centuries. Almost since the creation of the first Polish state in 966, the vigour and influence of Polish Catholicism have been closely linked with the fortunes, misfortunes and trepidations of the Polish nation and people.[2] The long historical association of Polish Catholicism and Polish ethnicity, as well as their reciprocal influence, has resulted in an almost inseparable integration of the Church and nationalism. For centuries the Church has exerted a considerable impact on popular attitudes towards political ideologies and institutions. The national identity of Poland has recently found its modern form through, and in conflict with, the state, which has been weakened continuously since the end of the seventeenth century.[3] Conflicts between the Church and the state developed into a mechanism that identified Catholicism with national identity; consequently the overwhelming majority of Poles perceive any threat to Catholicism as a threat to the existence of their national identity. In defence of the latter they therefore tend to congregate around the Church and religious values. Catholic practices have served as a powerful vehicle for the popularisation of the national creed.

The Polish state ceased to exist with the third partition of Poland in 1795, when Russia, Prussia and Austria shared the spoils after a period of growing encroachment which had led to a Polish revolt, inspired by French revolutionary successes. These partitions weakened both the authority of the state per se and the standing of state institutions of the occupying powers. At the same time, however, in many respects the partitions strengthened immeasurably the standing and prestige of the Church which, over the last 200 years, has become the most important national institution.

The fact that the creeds of the two most repressive and culturally aggressive partition powers – Prussia and Russia – were, respectively, Protestantism and Orthodoxy, made it remarkably easy for the Poles to identify Roman Catholicism with Polish nationality and to express their patriotism and longing for freedom through the Church's structures and religious symbolism. Romantic poets like Adam Mickiewicz (1798–1855), writing in exile, developed a messianic allegory in which Poland, the 'Christ of nations', suffered, was crucified, but would rise again for Europe's redemption.[4] During the years of Poland's occupation, the Church has been the guardian of the nation's language, history, traditions and culture. Clergy, drawn from all levels of society, participated actively in promoting cultural and patriotic values. But even earlier the Church had developed a strong constitutional role. Following traditions dating back to the twelfth century, and earlier threats to the integrity of the Polish state during the period between the death of one monarch and the confirmation of his successor, the Primate of the Roman Catholic Church normally replaced the person of the king.[5] He handled domestic and foreign policy in his capacity as *inter rex*; he further received foreign envoys, conveyed and supervised the progress of electoral sessions of Parliament and officially announced its choice of the new king. The rulers of Poland were also crowned and had their matrimonial unions blessed by the Primate, the latter taking precedence even over cardinals. After 1918 Poland's Constitution and the new code of canon law changed the legal position of the Primate. Nevertheless, in the public mind he remained head of the Church in Poland and the work of primates Edmund Dalbor (1918–26), August Hlond (1926–48) and Stefan Wyszynski (1948–81) went a long way towards perpetuating this image.

Thus in more recent times the state has been continuously faced with a rival authority whose national role stretches back to the Middle Ages and whose roots in society are very deep. Embedded in the national fabric, Polish Catholicism came to represent not only a system of religious beliefs and sacramental acts, but also the embodiment of Polish cultural values and traditions.[6]

Poland regained its independence in 1918, one of the series of states in Central Europe which emerged at the end of the First World War and the collapse of the old Austro-Hungarian and Russian empires. But two years later, during the Russo-Polish war, the Red Army occupied a sizeable part of eastern Poland and at one stage even threatened the capital. Somehow the exasperated Polish Army managed to defend Warsaw and eventually expelled Soviet troops. The victory in the battle of Warsaw has since been referred to in unofficial Polish history as the 'miracle on the Vistula' performed by the Black Madonna of Czestochowa, the Queen of Poland, the Defender and Helper of the nation in tragic situations, again acting as she did in the seventeenth century during the Swedish occupation of Poland. The icon of the Black Madonna kept in the Monastery of Jasna Gora (Bright Hill) has remained for centuries not only a religious symbol, but also a symbol of Poland's resistance to foreign tyranny, and few Poles would wish to draw any distinction between the two. It should be remembered that the cult of the Black Madonna reflects a type of religiosity with strong emphasis on Mariology, the Mother of God (*Theotokos*) and the Mother of the People. This in turn corresponds to the traditional position of the woman and mother in Polish culture, family and public life.

The ensuing treaty between Poland and the USSR, signed in 1921, took more territory than the Allies had proposed at the Paris Peace Settlement.

Poland had also been given back part of East Prussia by the post-war settlements, providing a vital corridor to the sea. But the settlement fired German revanchism and heightened traditional dislike of the 'Slavic' Poles. The brutal Nazi invasion of 1939 wreaked a terrible vengeance, which had its counterpart on the eastern frontier, for the preceding Nazi–Soviet Pact had effectively re-divided Poland between the two aggressors. Poles as well as Jews suffered terribly during the war, though there was no systematic policy of genocide aimed at Poles (and troubling questions remain about anti-semitic traditions in Central Europe, and local help given to the Nazis). Predictably, during their trials, Poles turned even more to the Catholic Church for solace and a sense of hope.

During the Russo-Polish war of 1920, the Polish communists had supported the invading Red Army: they regarded an independent Polish state as merely a transition to Poland's submersion in the 'international camp of social revolution where there is no problem of national borders'. Solutions like autonomy, independence and self-determination were merely connected 'with the evolution of a capitalist world'. The Polish communists, therefore, refused quixotically to have anything to do with the newly re-born Polish state. At the end of the Second World War, Polish communists were motivated less by a sense of internationalism, than by dependence on the USSR. A new Polish state was created, but it was not independent. This direct connection with Russia was a crucial problem in attempts to legitimise the communist regime. The second major obstacle was the fact that the new regime was, at least formally, guided by Marxism-Leninism, an outlook whose principles are fundamentally at odds with those of Catholicism.

The Catholic Church in Poland has always been the strongest Church in Eastern Europe. After its victory during the Counter-Reformation in the seventeenth century, it ruled unchallenged over the souls of the Polish people. The Church enjoyed exceptional influence and wealth, accommodating itself to changing political currents and circumstances. In 1945, the moving of Polish borders some 500 kilometres to the west (conceding territory to the USSR and regaining primarily Polish parts of Germany) meant that for the first time in Polish history, and uniquely in Eastern Europe, the Polish nation was religiously and ethnically homogenous.[7] The Church represented great power, uniting some 95 per cent of the population within its organisation and behind its ideology.

When the country fell under communist rule, a new era of direct encounter between the Catholic Church and communism began. The Church had a socially broad, coherent and uniform organisation,[8] much more efficient and certainly not inferior to that of the ruling communist party. Priests and nuns, through their day-to-day direct contacts with the people, maintained intimate knowledge of local affairs and thus had access to many secrets. They were a part of the Church's nation-wide intelligence network. Most importantly, however, the communists lacked the basis of social support which the Church had at its disposal. The peasants, who formed the majority of the population in the 1940s and who had originally benefited from the agrarian reform carried out by the new regime, became aware of the real agricultural policies of that regime almost immediately after its formation. As they opposed forceful collectivisation of their newly acquired land, they became the target of abuse, persecution and victimisation. They have remained the strongest and most faithful ally of the Church.

The communists claimed to have seized and wielded power on behalf of the workers, but a majority of these were of peasant stock. It is important to note that mass migration of the peasant population to towns has taken place in Poland since 1945. It is estimated that by the 1960s, 20 per cent of the inhabitants of Warsaw were born in the countryside, and in Wroclaw no less than 40 per cent. In other towns in the Recovered Territories and new towns like Nowa Huta the proportion has been even higher.[9] But these workers soon became disillusioned because of the ineffective economic policies of the new government.[10] The fact that the Church kept the allegiance of most of the 'ruralised' working class is extremely important for an understanding of the emergence, dynamics and politics of the Solidarity movement. Lastly, the intelligentsia, most of whom were members of the former landed gentry, and who after the war absorbed the remnants of that class, were naturally opposed to the communist regime. Even for those who were by no means religious, the Church offered the only opportunity of openly expressing their disapproval of the government by attending Sunday Mass. The Church pulpit became a unique source of the uncensored word, an opportunity for an expression of the national conscience in the material and non-material concerns of the people of Poland.

Its well coordinated social role became wider over the years and its work extended into practically all social and age groups. Many Poles, perhaps the majority, looked to the Church, in the absence of other legitimate mechanisms of politicisation, not only for spiritual guidance but also for political direction. The symbiotic relation between Polish national, cultural and democratic political traditions embodied in Polish Catholicism have been reflected during the communist period by another trend: that of political realism. This point has been succinctly put by one of the Church's spokesmen in the following terms: 'There is only one government possible here. . . . No one else can form an administration. Sometimes we [the Church] have to help them [the government] to stay in power. We don't want chaos any more than they do'.[11]

During the 1970s and 1980s, the Church had openly joined the overwhelming current of dissent. It became the main spokesman, as well as the arbiter between the communist regime and the majority of the population. The Church's support and expert advice proved instrumental for the creation of the Solidarity trade union movement in 1980. At that time religious symbolism used by the striking workers was the language for expressing the ideas of social emancipation, historical memory and the ancient struggle for national independence. During the period of martial law

(1981–3), and subsequently until 1989, the Church assumed the role of a mediator in one of the most profound social and political conflicts in the history of any of the communist countries of Eastern Europe, calling for a broadly based open discussion between the regime and the society. There can be little doubt that the Roman Catholic Church played an immensely important role in anti-communist resistance and the final demise of the communist system. The high respect for the Roman Catholic Church reflects the common view of the Church as an institution with community-like characteristics and features. In popular perception it forms an important part of the social fabric of the society rather than of the state.[12]

THE ROMAN CATHOLIC CHURCH AFTER COMMUNISM

Since 1989 the Roman Catholic Church has had visible difficulties in repositioning itself within the emerging, new democratic order. It is quite evident that after the advent of the pluralistic changes the Church has substantially lost its ability to shape and lead political discourse. This is primarily due to the lack of the propensity to innovate, to keep pace with the needs of the times, and to respond positively to the demands of the process of transformation from authoritarianism. The Church has shown that it could preserve the link to the past but could not lead into the future. It thus contributed to a widening cleavage between the Church and the state, which cut across other political divisions and intensified ideological conflict. Some scholars suggest that since 1989 the Church has attempted to fill the post-Marxist doctrinal vacuum with Catholic fundamentalism.[13]

Various opinion surveys have indicated for several years that Poles believe that the Church has become too powerful since the fall of communism. Some 95 per cent of Poles call themselves Roman Catholics, and weekly church attendance remains about 48 per cent, which is high even for Roman Catholic countries. But the approval rating of the bishops has dropped from about 90 per cent in 1989, when the Church was seen as a major force in bringing down communism, to 46 per cent in 1995. There are clearly signs of growing resentment to some actions and initiatives by the state, the Roman Catholic hierarchy and the clergy to enhance further the position of the Church – such as the addition of new impediments to divorce, and rules forcing soldiers to take part in 'field masses' and other religious observances.[14]

One of the most divisive and controversial issues in post-communist Poland has been the abortion legislation. The passage of the law on abortion in 1993 was accompanied by a long and bitter campaign, at times bordering on hysteria by its opponents as well as its supporters. The law allowed for abortion to be performed only if pregnancy poses a threat to a woman's life or health, if it resulted from rape or incest, or if the foetus was irreparably damaged. Anyone performing abortions in other cases faced prison terms of up to two years. The law was strongly supported by the Catholic Church as a step in the direction of a total ban, consistent with the Church's teaching. However, public opinion polls taken since 1990 show that between 18–26 per cent favour legalisation of abortion with no restrictions, 34–37 per cent favour legalisation with some restrictions, 21–26 per cent favour a ban with some exceptions, and 11–14 per cent favour a total ban.[15]

The introduction of religious instruction in state schools during the 1990–1 school year has been seen by some as another example of the Church's unwelcome influence on the post-communist society (most of the religious classes are conducted by nuns and priests).[16] However, opinion polls conducted in October 1995 show that most of the public accepted religious education in schools: some 67 per cent of respondents approved, while 30 per cent disapproved.[17]

The December 1992 Law on Radio and Television has been another area of controversy. It states that 'religious feelings of the audience, and in particular the Christian system of values, should be respected in broadcasting'. Several left-wing members of parliament petitioned the Constitutional Tribunal in December 1993, maintaining that the law infringes freedom of speech by arbitrarily choosing one value system over others. The tribunal, however, ruled that the Christian values mentioned in the law were to be interpreted as universal values, not as referring to any particular religion.[18]

The issue of the new Concordat between Poland and the Holy See[19] has been a subject of further divisions among public opinion. The document was signed in July 1993 but as yet not ratified by the Polish Parliament. The delay in ratification has been explained by the ruling Democratic Left Alliance as an articulation of the 'unease that the Concordat evokes in much of society'.[20] Many Poles believe that the document gives the Church too much influence over public life. An opinion poll conducted by the Public Opinion Research Centre (CBOP) in October 1995 shows that 34 per cent of the respondents supported its ratification, 27 per cent were against, while the majority of respondents, 39 per cent, declared indifference or had no opinion.[21] These figures underline the way in which the Church has lost some of its protective and integrative role since the fall of communism, but it still remains an important institution of Polish national identity.

DIALOGUE, TOLERANCE AND TRANSITION

Decommunisation in Poland proceeded in a negotiated and orderly manner. The Round Table dialogue that took place from February to April 1989 between the representatives of the government, the ruling communist party, and its supporting organisations on the one hand, and the still illegal Solidarity trade union movement on the other, symbolised national unity. It culminated in the Round Table Agreement based on compromise and mutual concessions that laid the foundations for the future shape of post-communist political institutions and the eventual dismantling of communist rule in the country. It demonstrated the willingness of all parties to search for peaceful solutions and to resolve a very difficult set of problems and issues through diligent negotiations. Solidarity's eventual victory in a partially-free vote in 1989 paved the way for the dismantling of communism in Eastern Europe, highlighted also by the collapse of the Berlin Wall and the bloody removal of Romanian leader Nicolae Ceauşescu. Poland, which went through several bloody clashes during the 45 years of communist rule (including the rising of 1956, centred on the town of Poznán), chose a different path under a Wałesa-brokered compromise with reform-oriented communists.

After 1989 no attempt was made to prevent those who had worked for or with the secret police or in the higher echelons of the party and the government from henceforth occupying a prominent role in public life. The first post-war non-communist Prime Minister Tadeusz Mazowiecki decided to draw a 'thick line' under the communist past, thus allowing everything to be written off. There was no attempt to examine the collective guilt of the communists or to dwell on historical justice and restitution. Mazowiecki's approach demonstrated not only the tradition of dialogue but also another important aspect of Polish political culture – the tradition of tolerance: 'A Pole can always strike a compromise with another Pole'.

Mazowiecki's 'thick line' left virtually the entire nomenklatura[22] system intact and inadvertently paved the way for the subsequent election of the Democratic Left Alliance (SLD), the successor of the former ruling communist party. It is undeniable that the state administration and economic systems could not function without the expert knowledge of the nomenklatura. A body of several hundred experts cannot be replaced overnight. They are the only experienced administrative workforce in the country and they cannot be replaced by hastily trained administrative specialists no matter how impeccable their previous career background. However, it should also be noted that the successful adaptation of the nomenklatura personnel into a new post-communist state and economic structures shows that the nomenklatura does not act out of ideological conviction, but follows its pragmatic instincts.

Since 1989, the problem of how to manage the transition to democracy has been one of the main problems of political culture in Poland. Over 40 years of communist rule has created an ethos of egalitarianism. The collectivist nature of communism has led to the homogenisation of society and a lack of clear social and political differentiation. The residues of homogenisation have produced a political environment in which political parties, an essential part and parcel of the democratic process, find it difficult to represent differing political and economic interests and generate sufficient trust, respect, loyalty or belief in institutions. The development of political parties in post-communist Poland has been closely linked to the parliamentary and electoral processes. Parliamentary and presidential elections have, however, further fragmented the party system. Moreover, they have produced the phenomenon of the politicisation of morality. This process appears to be a reversal of the moralisation of politics which shows signs of emerging in many Western European countries (parties re-emphasising the role of civic virtues, the family, etc.).

Although between 1990 and 1994, dozens of political parties registered their existence, most proved either ephemeral or irrelevant or both. The genuine political parties were those with a degree of public recognition and at least a minimum measure of coherent structure and organisational linkage between members and leaders. The new parties possessed few resources with which to spread their message to an electorate little versed in democratic practices, so parliamentary representation was the most effective way to gain the media exposure which is now the stuff of modern political campaigning. The successful parties were those with deputies in parliament. Even where parties were relatively well funded, this could not guarantee party development. Indeed, in the first four years following the communists' loss of power, no successful party was organised from the bottom up, i.e. as an extra-parliamentary force, with the exception of Social Democracy of the Republic of Poland (SdRP) – the descendant of the former ruling Communist Party, the PZPR. However, even parliamentary representation could not guarantee success. The 1993 election represented a defeat for the Solidarity-generated parties and for many other small groupings which had achieved a single seat. The victors were the SdRP and the Polish Peasant Party (PSL), two successor parties with continuity of structures and a bedrock of support. Both capitalised on society's widespread insecurity, increasing attachment to welfare-state values, and growing secularism, as well as benefiting from the fragmentation of the right-wing parties.

This election led to a considerable reduction in the number of parties and offered some hope for, though no guarantee of, a future consolidation of the party system. However, longer-term developments will depend not only on the ability of parties to put down roots in society, but also on future institutional relationships and achieving a greater stability of class forces and social cleavages, which are still being shaped by the process of socio-economic transformation – a process which at present is having major effects on many parts of society, not least by introducing greater differentials and a sense of insecurity even among those who have kept a steady job in the more free market environment of post-communism.[23]

GEOPOLITICAL DIMENSIONS OF POLITICAL CULTURE: ATTITUDES TO THE EU AND NATO

The 'Return to Europe' has featured highly on the popular and political agenda since June 1989. Membership of the European Union and NATO, symbols of economic prosperity, democratic success and security, has been viewed as a vital process in the 're-Europeanisation' of the country – a re-entry to a full and active membership of the European community of nations. It means the construction of 'normal' European institutions, parliamentary democracy, a market economy, and different social security systems.²⁴ More importantly in popular perception, it offers perhaps the only practical way out of the current political, economic and strategic predicaments. The attraction of the EU and NATO, which stems from their successful operation in the economic, political and security spheres, could not be matched by any other grouping elsewhere.²⁵ Membership of the European Union has been seen by Polish public opinion and politicians as particularly important.

The Polish public's attitude towards membership of the EU is to a large degree shaped by a combination of myths, stereotypes, anxieties and hopes. According to opinion polls conducted by the CBOS since 1993,²⁶ Poland's aspiration to membership of the EU enjoys an overwhelming, consistent public support. In March 1996, 75 per cent of respondents declared they would vote 'yes' in a referendum on this issue. However, between 1993 and 1995, the percentage of those favouring an immediate integration declined from 41 per cent to 27 per cent. A growing number of respondents indicate a more distant 5–10-year perspective of integration (an 18-point increase since 1993). It can be argued that this trend reflects a growing degree of maturity in understanding the complexities and costs of the integration process as well as increased knowledge about the EU, its processes and policies. The level of understanding of these is still on a very low level. Polls shows that the number of respondents who consider the process of Poland's integration with the EU as a complex and difficult one has expanded significantly.

In general, the public expects that integration with the EU will bring more benefits than losses. The percentage of those expressing this opinion has, however, decreased from 50 per cent in 1993 to 35 per cent in 1995, while the number of those expecting mixed results has increased from 23 per cent to 32 per cent, respectively. This change does not necessarily mean the weakening of support for integration. Rather, it indicates that the basis for this support is becoming more rational, as Poles are becoming more pragmatic and tend to assess different values and events through the prism of their impact on the economy and individual living conditions. In general, Poles expect that the country's integration with the EU will have a positive impact on their material status, attitude towards work, efficiency, enterprise, frugality, and the level of knowledge and education. A closer examination of opinions on the impact of integration on specific areas demonstrates a significantly lower level of optimism. Most common are concerns related to its consequences for the spheres associated with the protective function of the state – public health care, welfare, education, culture and – first and foremost – the public sector of the economy and agriculture. Interestingly enough – in spite of these concerns – many respondents believe that the integration will help reduce unemployment.

Another aspect of public opinion on European integration concerns beliefs related to the inevitability of this process. The feeling that it is an irreversible 'historic necessity' arouses anxiety in some groups, stemming from the fear of the unknown. Many people are afraid that they will lose control over their lives and/or that Poland will have little influence on the course and results of the integration process set out by the Maastricht Treaty. In June 1994, a majority (52 per cent) believed that the integration would not limit Poland's sovereignty. A year later, 55 per cent were ready to support replacing Polish zlotys with a common European currency. However, many Poles do not approve of the limitations which a full integration would impose on certain attributes of Poland's sovereignty. In 1995, 58 per cent did not want the European Council to make decisions regarding Polish foreign policy, a figure which rose to 67 per cent in relation to the Polish army. It should be noted, however, that the Polish public, in comparison with the public in the countries of Western Europe, has only minimal knowledge of the EU decision-making mechanism. Therefore, resistance should be considered an indicator of the need for better public education on this subject, which has not had a sufficient lead in this area.

There are some good omens for the prospects of building more fundamental support. Recently, more and more Poles have come to believe that the growing relationship with the EU has been beneficial to both sides (5 per cent in 1993, 11 per cent in 1995). An explanation of this trend should be sought in the improved public perception of Poland's international standing. An increasing number of respondents believe that Poland is gradually becoming an attractive partner for the West. Another indicator of the public's growing positive assessment of Poland's position in relations with the West is the change in opinion about the motives of those EU members who favour enlargement to include some Central and Eastern European states: 25 per cent in 1994 and 31 per cent in 1995 believed that those countries expected the enlargement to strengthen the EU. Nevertheless, there is undoubtedly a significant minority who think that supporters of enlargement within the EU are essentially driven by their own self-interest: this figure could grow notably if there are not more signs that the EU is willing to help in tangible economic ways.

Membership of the North Atlantic Treaty Organisation has been the stated goal of Poland since 1989. Successive Polish governments have stressed that for Poland, Europe and North America are one security zone. Consequently, the US presence in Europe and its European commitments are part of the main premises of security and stability of the European continent. European security should rest on the existing structures which have been pragmatically developed and adapted to the changing environment. Each of these structures has its own possibilities and its own field in which to work. Poland wants to make them more complementary.[27] Polish governments have in particular sought to join and preserve a NATO characterised by a real, integrated military strength and a continuing transatlantic partnership between Europe and North America.[28] This policy has inevitably caused tensions with Russia, which has in the past seen Poland as a buffer zone and a crucial part of the Warsaw Pact. Moreover, whilst

Russian attitudes towards the West remain ambivalent, there are clearly Russian fears that Polish policy is partly motivated by a desire to put up a new cultural curtain situated on Poland's eastern frontier.

Among the public at large immediately after 1989, there was a balance between those favouring joining NATO and those pursuing neutrality. But beginning in 1993, the number of those favouring NATO membership started to grow. One poll in 1996 found that some 72 per cent of respondents regarded Poland's integration with NATO as the most favourable security arrangement.[29] Only one in ten favoured neutrality as the best policy option. This change is quite understandable given the Russian public opposition to the expansion of NATO expressed in 1993; political instability to the east which has produced notable votes for Russian nationalists like Zhirinovsky in 1993 and after; and the fact that Russia still retains considerable military force, which could be used to restore a greater Russia – not least as a way of rallying domestic public opinion in the event of continuing economic or political crisis. However, public support for NATO does not automatically translate into a favourable assessment of the Western commitment towards Poland. Almost half (47 per cent) believed that in case of a direct threat to her security, Poland could not count on Western assistance (29 per cent expected such assistance). Moreover, the Polish public is less supportive of integration with NATO when presented with its possible consequences. Only 49 per cent would vote 'yes' in a referendum on this issue if foreign troops were to be stationed in Poland (30 per cent would vote 'no'); and only 12 per cent favoured NATO membership if it entailed deploying nuclear weapons in Poland.

Curiously, political preferences are not a significant factor in public attitudes towards Poland's membership of the Alliance. Demographic characteristics also do not seem to exert a strong influence here, though support is strongest among the educated and weakest among farmers and unskilled workers. However, there are a relatively large number of 'Don't knows' among the less educated, which may skew the results. It is not clear whether this reflects a genuine indecision, or a more fundamental problem of opinion polls in picking up views on sensitive issues, or ones which people have not thought carefully about.

CONTINUITIES AND CHANGE

Clearly Poland has undergone notable changes since the 1970s. The old communist regime has been overthrown largely by internal opposition, in which the Catholic Church as well as Solidarity played a notable part. However, whilst still important in everyday life, the Catholic Church is not the force it was. People are experiencing the impact of rapid socio-economic change without the protective umbrella that it once offered much of society.

New parties which have emerged are not securely based, and Lech Wałesa's defeat in the 1995 presidential election shows that there is still life in a rejuvenated form of moderate communism. Given the many unknowns in the Polish situation, including the likelihood of achieving long-term economic growth which will help all, there undoubtedly remains potential for party system change, including the incursion of more populist parties, especially if led by charismatic leaders who can gain media access. Radical nationalism has not so far gained a significant foothold, which is partly a reflection of the problems faced by all new parties, but this situation also reflects a strong desire to be accepted as part of the West. Whether this situation will continue in the event of Poland failing to join the EU, or at least be accorded significant economic benefits in the near future, is another matter.

Attitudes to Germany are another issue which could develop notably in the next few years. There are growing fears of German economic imperialism, even of the revanchist claims of the growing strand of nationalism in German mainstream politics. In some ways this encourages rapid entry to the EU and NATO, and the construction of a general system of both military and political security which will give Poland a direct say in developments. But memories of the war are far from dead, and fear of Germany – coupled with fear of Russia – could encourage an insular mentality which could fuel political forces which would work against Poland's return to the European home. There is still much to play for.

NOTES

1 F. Millard, *The Anatomy of the New Poland*, Aldershot, Edward Elgar, 1994, p. 3.
2 For further discussion of the relationship between religion and nationalism in Poland see B. Szajkowski, *Next to God... Poland: Politics and Religion in Contemporary Poland*, New York, St Martin's Press, 1983.
3 P. G. Lewis, 'Obstacles to the Establishment of Political Legitimacy in Communist Poland', *British Journal of Political Science*, 1982, 12, p. 129.
4 T. Garton Ash, *The Polish Revolution*, London, Coronet Books, 1985, p. 3.
5 Under Polish law at that time the Primate was traditionally the Archbishop of Gniezno and Warsaw, the first among the country's senators and as such he presided over the Senate.
6 V. Chrypinski, 'Church and State in Gierek's Poland' in Maurice D. Simon and Roger E. Kanet (eds), *Background to Crisis: Policy and Politics in Gierek's Poland*, Boulder, Westview, 1981, p. 239.
7 There are no official statistics on ethnic minorities in Poland since the war. The main minority groups in 1991 were Germans (2+ per cent), Ukrainians (c.1 per cent), and Byelorussians (0.5+ per cent). Only a very small number (c.3,000) Jews remain, most who survived the Holocaust having left after 1945.
8 Only limited statistical data on religious denominations has been published in Poland since the war. According to available figures the membership of the Roman Catholic Church at the end of 1989 comprised some 36 million (94.6 per cent) of the population. The Roman Catholic Church had 8,458 parishes/congregations in 1989, compared to 6,716 in 1976, and 21,699 priests compared to 19,456. Data from *Rocznik Statystyczny – 1977*, Warsaw, Glowny

Urzad Statystyczny, 1977, p. 23; *Kosciol Katolicki w Polsce 1918–1990*, Warsaw, Glowny Urzad Statystyczny, 1991, pp. 53–4.

9 Polish sociologists refer to this phenomenon as the 'ruralisation of the towns' or the 'ruralisation of the working class', because the bulk of the migrants from the countryside became workers. A survey conducted in 1970 showed that 63 per cent of the blue-collar workers and 37 per cent of white-collar workers who had taken up residence in towns in the preceding decade had come from the rural areas.

10 It should be remembered that with the exception of Silesia, which has its own specific religious tradition, Polish religious culture has a plebeian character even in the new working-class towns. Hence the strong union with the local parish, the mass participation of the people in the erection of 'their' church, and the integrating cultural role of the parish and the priest who enjoys substantial prestige.

11 T. Sebastian, *Nice Promises*, London, Chatto and Windus, 1985, p. 191.

12 Much the same can be said about the reasons for the high social standing of the army.

13 A. Flis, 'The Polish Church as an Enemy of Open Society', unpublished manuscript.

14 In the *Soldier's Prayerbook* (1994) Brigadier General Kazimierz Tomaszewski, second in command of the Warsaw Military Region, instructs his subordinates:

> It would be inadmissible to set any such precedent as exclusion from an honour company for reasons touching differences of religion. . . . Refusal to follow the standard is a refusal to carry out an order. . . . Participation in the Ceremonial Roll Call at a Field Mass is a duty, and if you are an unbeliever or a member of another faith, you may refrain from active participation in prayers. Only carry out the commands that are given to you without any public display of the fact that you are dissatisfied.
>
> (See *Gazeta Wyborcza*, 31 December 1994–1 January 1995.
> Quoted by Andrzej Flis, *op. cit.*)

15 J. Karpinski, 'Poles Divided Over Church's Renewed Political Role', *Transition*, 1996, 2, p. 13.

16 Religion was taught in schools immediately after the end of the Second World War and for about a year after the 'golden October' in 1956 which brought about a limited liberalisation.

17 'Kwestie ideologiczne: prywatyzacja, bezrobocie, aborcja, konkordat' (Ideological questions: privatisation, unemployment, abortion, concordat), Public Opinion Research Centre (CBOS), Warsaw, January 1996. See also Karpinski, *op. cit.*

18 Karpinski, *op. cit.*

19 The 1925 Concordat between the Republic of Poland and the Holy See had been unilaterally declared null and void by the communist authorities in 1945. Poland established diplomatic relations with the Vatican in July 1989, but negotiations for a new Concordat started even earlier. The Concordat states that church and state are 'autonomous' and 'independent', commits the state to allow religious education in schools and kindergartens, and recognises Church marriages as legally binding in civil law. See: Andrzej Korbonski, 'A Concordat – But no Concordat', *Transition*, 1995, 1.

20 *OMRI Daily Digest*, 22 July 1996.

21 Karpinski, *op. cit.*

22 The nomenklatura list (a listing of positions to be filled by the Communist Party organs) in 1988 included around 900,000 positions. In addition to dominating enterprise management, the Communist Party controlled the state

administration, education, local government, the judiciary and the legal and medical profession, the diplomatic service and media personnel.

23 F. Millard, 'Poland' in B. Szajkowski (ed.), *Political Parties of Eastern Europe, Russia and the Successor States*, Harlow, Longman, 1994, p. 236.
24 A. Krzeminski, 'W kolejce do Europy', *Polityka*, 1991, 12.
25 B. Szajkowski, 'The Polish Association Agreement: An Overview of Institutional Arrangements' in A. Evans and P. Falk (eds), *Transformation and Integration: The New Association Agreements*, Umeä, University of Umeä, 1992, pp. 309–10.
26 'Polish Attitudes Towards Poland's Integration with the European Union', findings based on CBOS Polls, 1993–1995, Public Opinion Research Centre (CBOS), Warsaw, April 1996.
27 H. Suchocka, 'Poland's European Perspective', *NATO Review*, 1993, 41, pp. 3–4.
28 B. Szajkowski, 'New Poland in the New World Order', Inaugural Address to the Third International Conference on Polish Affairs, *Poland... Between Two Worlds*, St Mary's College (University of Detroit), Orchard Lake, Michigan, October, 1993.
29 'Polish Attitudes Toward Poland's Integration with NATO', findings based on CBOS Polls, 1993–1996, Public Opinion Research Centre (CBOS), Warsaw, April 1996.

11 Portugal and Spain

António Costa Pinto and Xosé M. Núñez

INTRODUCTION

Seen from the outside, the Iberian peninsula appears as a geographical, social and historical unit, divided into two different states. But Spaniards and Portuguese have in the past rarely made such comparisons – though the entry of both states into the European Community in 1986 marked the beginning of growing reciprocal appreciation. For many Spaniards, Portugal has been a kind of 'accident' of Spanish history which does not deserve attention. Spain is for many Portuguese the historical enemy, and a continuous referent in affirming their national identity. Behind these stereotypes lies a complex mix of similarity and difference.

Both countries are usually catalogued as 'Mediterranean' lands. They have enjoyed 'glorious' imperial pasts, but were latecomers to the process of European industrialisation. Late modernisation was accompanied by the emergence of weak democratic systems, characterised by the overwhelming predominance of traditional hierarchies in the rural areas and the inefficiency of the state in terms of – to use Eugen Weber's term – 'nationalizing' the peasants and turning them into citizens.[1] Social tensions during the inter-war period led to the establishment of dictatorial regimes, which survived until 1974–5. Subsequently, both countries have become consolidated democracies, integrated into the European Union – thus ending two centuries of isolation. The result is that Portuguese and Spaniards are among the most enthusiastic supporters of the European project.

Apart from the obvious imbalance in size and population (10 million inhabitants in Portugal, 39.5 million in Spain today), other differences are noteworthy. First, while Portugal has been almost an ideal type of ethnocultural homogeneity since the Middle Ages, Spain is characterised by great regional divergences (both in terms of culture and development) resulting in its 'national problem' becoming one of the main factors of twentieth-century Spanish history. Second, the imperial heritage lasted in Portugal until 1975; Spain lost her last overseas colonies in the 1890s (though she retained a troubled protectorate in Morocco). Third, Spain experienced the tragedy of a civil war (1936–9); and General Franco's subsequent authoritarian regime was far more brutal than the Salazar dictatorship in Portugal. Fourth, the Francoist dictatorship undertook the task of economic modernisation during the 1960s, while Portugal's took place more after the 1970s. The combination of past massive repression and economic take-off created among many Spaniards a kind of passive conformity towards the political regime, whereas Portugal's backward character and the upsurge of anti-colonial revolts in the colonies, paved the way for an army-led breakdown of the dictatorship. The initial semi-revolutionary nature of Portugal's transition process was very different from the end of the Francoist dictatorship, thanks to reluctant agreement between reformist-oriented former supporters and the democratic opposition movements (though threats from sections of the army and police lingered on, surfacing most notably in the 1981 abortive coup).[2]

THE MAKING OF TWO STATES AND DIFFERENT NATIONS

Spain

Spain is one of the oldest states in Europe, its origins lying in the unification of the kingdoms of Aragón, Castile and Navarre between 1480 and 1512. After 1492, Castile undertook ambitious overseas expansion in Europe and the Americas, becoming one of the most important powers during the sixteenth and seventeenth centuries. This 'Golden Age' lived on in the memory of many, not least nationalist historians, who saw Spain as a great force in creating Western (Catholic) civilisation; it also led to a belief – still persistent today – that Spanish was an 'old imperial' language, understood by everyone.

However, political unification implied neither cultural homogenisation nor real strengthening of the state apparatus. By the end of the eighteenth century, Spain was still marked by the strong survival of different traditions, political privileges and legal codes. Habsburg Spain maintained the traditional formula of an 'aggregative monarchy', that is, the existence of different 'kingdoms' united by a common Crown and the principle of dynastic loyalty, and whilst the Bourbon dynasty (which occupied the Spanish throne after the Wars of Succession in 1714) undertook a French-style state-centralising policy, its impact on regional identities was less than expected. In spite of the predominance of the official Castilian language, many territories not only kept their languages and traditions, but also very distinct legal codes.[3] In some cases, notably the Basque provinces and Navarre, they also retained their own political institutions, such as governing assemblies and collective territorial privileges (the *Fueros*). In Catalonia, although the traditionally autonomous self-governing institutions were abolished in 1714, a strong community sentiment persisted.[4]

The structural elements which contributed to the nineteenth- and early twentieth-century relative failure in nation building are the object of frequent disputes among historians. Nevertheless, it can be argued that the following set of factors were crucial to the development of modern Spanish political culture(s).

First, there was little industrial development, though there were notable pockets in specific regions (the Basque country, Catalonia, Asturias). The consequence of this was the emergence of very important territorial imbalances, which correspond neither with centres of political decision making nor with the geographical recruitment of the ruling elites (the latter being predominantly of Andalusian or Castilian origin).[5]

Second, political divisions sharply marked the transition from the ancien régime to the liberal state. To the permanent confrontation between absolutist monarchists (who after 1833 became Carlists) and liberals, must be added the growing division within Spanish liberalism between moderates and progressives (from 1850 the democrats and republicans emerged among the latter). The moderate liberals were characterised by their strong centralism, and therefore the period of moderate predominance (1833–68) was one of restructuring the Spanish state into a liberal-centralist one, closely following the French Jacobin model.[6] Hence, progressive liberals became fierce defenders of 'provincial' and local liberties – a trait which linked them with the Carlists.

Third was a set of state failures.[7] One aspect concerns an ill-endowed education policy, which failed fully to impose one national language or disseminate a set of homogenising civic-patriotic values (the latter reflects a wider failure to agree on myths and symbols, for example the national flag). Illiteracy rates were also among the highest in Europe. Also, the Spanish army never fulfilled a 'nationalising' role. The reason for this was that military service was not obligatory for all citizens, only affecting those who lacked financial means to elude it – a system which made the army an 'enemy' of the lower classes. Moreover, the absence of clear enemies after the War of Independence against Napoleonic France in 1808–13 made it difficult to coalesce national sentiment around defence of the army. A final factor concerns the fact that civil servants' loyalties were linked to the different political factions or parties which held office. In 1918 it was legally established that state jobs were permanent, but *amiguismo* (personal influences) became a permanent and socially accepted norm of public behaviour. A lack of satisfaction with an inefficient state, and lack of confidence in its capability to achieve reform from above, became deep rooted in the Spanish population.

A fourth factor was the permanent instability of Spanish politics, and especially the fact that political representation until 1923 was manipulated by state-orchestrated clientelism. With the exception of brief periods of real democratic government, politics prior to 1931 were constantly characterised by the contradiction between relatively advanced modernisation of the political system (Spain was among the first states to adopt universal male suffrage in 1890, and its laws of association and freedom of speech were liberal), and the everyday political practice.[8] This usually led to anti-system politics and revolutionary attempts by the whole spectrum of the opposition, and therefore to a permanent situation of latent civil war. The *politics of exclusion* became a contradictory feature of Spanish political culture after the nineteenth century, very much accentuated by increasing social polarisation during the first third of the twentieth century. The parallel consequences were the radicalisation of the workers' movement (especially after the Russian Revolution in 1917) and the increasing authoritarian response which was adopted by large sectors of the upper-middle classes, the Catholic-influenced establishment and the army. The permanent weakness of the Spanish lower-middle classes, crushed between the two opposite poles, was decisive in paving the way to the final confrontation in the Civil War.

It is also important to consider attitudes towards 'Europe', which varied notably. While the reactionary, Catholic-oriented tendency which emerged in the first two decades of the nineteenth century regarded the continent above the Pyrenees as an atheistic matrix of liberal thought, the liberal-democratic trend held that Spain had to 'recover' its lost link to Western Europe. Especially after the 1898 defeat by the United States, Spanish intellectuals became totally obsessed with the relationship with Europe. In the inter-war period, and especially during the second Spanish Republic (1931–6), liberal-democratic pro-European views tended to dominate the Spanish government, particularly through a new generation of intellectuals who had studied in Germany or France and who became supporters of the full integration of Spain within international society (a view expressed, for example, by Salvador de Madariaga).[9] Nevertheless, the fascists and the Catholic radical right remained loyal to the attitudes towards Europe held by previous traditionalists, which were combined after the 1920s with a diffuse appeal to a cultural imperialism towards Latin America (the myth of 'Spanishness'), aimed at counteracting European views, and even the danger of regional separatism. The Spanish Civil War meant the imposition of this second trend of thought on the first, including the suppression of growing peripheral Basque, Catalan and Galician nationalist movements.[10]

Portugal

Although Portugal shared some of the same weaknesses vis-à-vis nineteenth-century state construction, it enjoyed a different starting point. Its frontiers had remained basically unchanged since the late Middle Ages; there were no national or ethnic-cultural minorities and no Portuguese populations in neighbouring countries; similarly, there were no religious or ethnic-linguistic minorities.[11] Moreover, the period in which the kingdom was integrated into a Catholic peninsular monarchy (1580–1640) constitutes an important point of reference in Portuguese national identity. The reconquest of independence in 1640 is even today celebrated as one of the fundamental moments in the affirmation of the national identity against the principal external enemy: the Castilian-Spanish.

Anti-British nationalism decisively marked the genesis of the Portuguese liberal movement in 1820. The first liberal triennium was also characterised by difficult relations with Brazil, which culminated in Brazilian independence in 1822.[12] This period witnessed the beginning of a major discourse on decay and regeneration, whose essential traces would be taken up again and again by future generations: the grandiosity of the Middle Ages and the discoveries, followed by decline in the sixteenth century, highlighted by the Inquisition, by the abandoning of productive activities in favour of living off the colonies, and finally by the loss of independence in 1580; this continuous decay, which the reconquest of independence in 1640 had been unable to halt, could now be offset by the regenerative impulse of internal reforms necessitated by the definitive loss of economic control over Brazil.

From the seventeenth century onwards, Portuguese imperial power had been complemented by her political and economic dependence on Britain. Tensions with Britain increased dramatically in the 1880s, leading to the emergence of the first strong anti-British sentiments in modern public opinion.[13] The British foiled Portuguese aspirations to what is now Zimbabwe, forcing her to abandon intentions to unite Angola and Mozambique. This episode cemented modern Portuguese nationalism, symbolically marking what became Portugal's main foreign policy characteristic up to the 1970s, namely the defence of her colonial heritage. In fact, one could say that 'the identification of the colonial empire with nationalism in Portugal provides a kind of functional equivalent to the divisive nation-state issues' found in other European societies at the time.[14]

In the second half of the nineteenth century, Portugal could be categorised as a non-industrialised country governed by a stable 'oligarchic parliamentarianism'. Despite representing a system of oligarchic liberalism in a predominantly rural society with a strong clientelistic streak, the liberals created a modern centralised state, and also consolidated fundamental freedoms. But widespread illiteracy meant that the masses were never truly integrated, and local cultures remained strong. Attempting to exploit the African colonies whilst timidly advancing an industrialising policy based on import substitution, this oligarchic and clientelistic liberalism began to come apart at the turn of the century. The emergence of the republican movement, which mobilised large sections of the urban middle and lower-middle classes, until then excluded from politics, was expressive of this crisis.[15] But the republican project cannot be separated from the objective of overcoming localisms and transforming the popular masses into citizens. And though the final balance does show an overall failure, the integration instruments that were produced (the symbols and rituals of the nation) were destined to triumph in the long term.

The Republican Party had an extremely flexible programme with a great capacity to exploit themes such as nationalism, anti-clericalism, the expansion of political participation, the right to strike, and other demands made by a feeble labour movement. On the eve of the 1910 revolution it united a political constellation which ranged from a moderate electoralist faction to Jacobin authoritarians. In October 1910 the constitutional monarchy was overthrown in Lisbon by republicans, backed by a section of the armed forces. Portugal thus became one of Europe's first republics. The republicans sought a 'mass nationalisation' of the parochial rural areas still dominating Portuguese society. A new national flag and anthem, a new civil liturgy with its own holidays, a model of 'citizen building', a populist-type political mobilisation, and an accentuated 'nationalisation' of teaching programmes, characterised the 1910 rupture. Adopting a populist strategy, the republicans made themselves into the spokesmen for a nationalism that would 'regenerate the fatherland', linking the monarchy to the idea of dependence on Britain and economic backwardness.

However, Portugal's entry into the First World War in 1916 had disastrous consequences politically and socially, and seems difficult to understand, given nationalist attitudes to Britain. The main motivation was the hope for a place at the winners' table, though recent research has exposed the hidden agenda that looked to military intervention in Europe as a means of mobilising public opinion around the new regime. Among the most serious consequences of participation, was the impact on the growth of an authoritarian, traditionalist and corporatist nationalism among intellectual and military elites.[16]

THE AUTHORITARIAN LEGACY

Spain

After the Civil War, the exile of thousands left Spain intellectually impoverished, while the intensity of the Francoist repression virtually eliminated dissent. Spain underwent hard times during the immediate post-war period, partly as a result of the autarchic economic policy copied from fascism. Spanish industrial output did not recover its 1929 level until 1950, though the war had left most industry intact.[17]

Initially, Franco maintained a close relationship with the fascist powers. Spain did not enter the war – partly because of Germany's rejection of Spain's imperial demands (the French part of Morocco, for instance) – but some volunteers fought on the Russian front until 1944, when Franco realised the Germans were heading for defeat. In response to the diplomatic and economic blockade imposed by the Allies, Franco introduced some changes – such as diminishing the cruelty of repression, and the appointment of prominent Catholics as key ministers. Moreover, from 1948 on, Spain acquired new geostrategic importance as a result of the Cold War. Although not fully accepted as an equal partner in the democratic world, an authoritarian Spain was preferred to a potentially 'communist' one. Spain duly received financial help from the Western powers and opened its doors to American forces (although it was not allowed to enter NATO, as Portugal did). Spain was also allowed to join the main international organisations, like the UN, and foreign ambassadors returned to Madrid.

The Francoist regime began to evolve in the direction of an authoritarian state characterised by a Catholic corporatist and anti-liberal ideology. This was accompanied by a decline in the more overt fascist trappings (especially the *Falange Española*, which after 1937 merged with the Carlists and other right-wing organisations to form the official state party) and the increasing influence of the neo-Catholic technocrats linked to the *Opus Dei*. The latter were anti-liberals, but they stressed the need for efficiency and modernisation, maintaining that there was no contradiction between economic progress and political authoritarianism accompanied by a certain degree of social-Catholic reformism.[18]

These developments were accompanied by an attempt to 'renationalise' Spain by forbidding the public use of languages other than Castilian, and extending through the school system, the mass media (especially television after 1957), and new social phenomena like football, a sense of nation. This programme was accompanied by the state's refostering of myths incarnating Spanish resistance against the Roman Empire or the Napoleonic invasion of 1808, the Christian reconquest and the unifying role played by the Catholic faith, and the 'Golden Age' of the overseas empire. Emphasis was also put on the Civil War as a 'Crusade' against the 'anti-Spain', a strand symbolised by the construction of a pharaonic temple dedicated to the memory of the war (the so-called 'Valley of the Fallen' [*Valle de los Caídos*] near Madrid).

It is difficult to measure the impact of Francoist 'renationalisation'. The vast growth in Spanish language television audiences and the extension of literacy seem to have considerably eroded regional loyalties and traditions. Nevertheless, the success of the 'nationalising' programme seems to have been limited, particularly in those areas where peripheral nationalist movements had existed before 1936: the Basque Country, Catalonia and, to a lesser extent, Galicia. The combination of cultural repression and previous nationalist feelings paved the way for the emergence in 1959 of the Basque nationalist ETA, which from the mid-1960s onwards adopted the strategy of terrorism it has maintained until the present. The state's legitimacy was not accepted by significant sectors of the Basque and Catalan populations, and this phenomenon became especially acute at the beginning of the 1970s.[19]

Measuring the impact of 'nationalising' propaganda is also made difficult by rapid socio-economic change. After 1959, the Francoist regime drastically changed its economic policy, and through the 'Stabilisation Plans' paved the way for the entry of major foreign investments, the move towards a free market economy, the massive arrival of European tourists and the migration to the newly industrialised urban centres and other European states of peasants who sent back foreign currency which contributed to financing Spanish industrial development. The result was that between 1955 and 1975, the percentage of the active population occupied in the tertiary sector went from 25.9 to 39.2 per cent, overtaking for the first time the percentage of the population in agriculture (from 46.1 to 23 per cent), while the industrial sector rose from 21.6 to 27.4 per cent.[20]

The speed of this modernisation provoked deep changes in values and mentalities. Although the regime did not implement new measures of political liberalisation during the 1960s, apart from some secondary aspects (such as limited reforms concerning the freedom of the press and workers' participation in labour relations), it was unavoidable that the new social problems created by these changes would provoke the emergence of political opposition. This often focused around university students, industrial workers, and some areas of peripheral nationalism. Nevertheless, none of these foci were strong enough to provoke the break-up of the regime before the death of General Franco in 1975.

Nor did the government adopt a 'European' policy of further democratisation. On the contrary, the Francoist regime during the 1940s and 1950s had insisted on the idea of Spain being the sole defender of a 'crusade' against the disruptive values of European culture represented by communism and secularisation. This official attitude did not change after Spain's failure in 1962 to be accepted as a member of the EEC. The main reason for applying for membership was the defence of Spanish exports and to encourage modernisation; it was not intended as a first step towards liberalisation.[21]

The legacy of the Francoist period for Spanish political culture can be summed up as follows. There was the political *passivity* of the new social strata created or reinforced by the massive modernisation process in the 1960s, which offered a perspective of social mobilisation without any ingredient of political participation. As a consequence of this, Spaniards tended to give preference to *domestic and family well-being*. There was also a certain degree of *preference for political stability*. These features clearly overlap with those mentioned for the preceding period, but the difference was that the Franco dictatorship practically eliminated the tendency to radicalisation/polarisation. The self-justifying image often offered by anti-Francoist activists tends to hide an important aspect: the Spanish population neither rose against the government, nor did it vote against the coming of democracy in the 1976 referendum. Most Spaniards welcomed democracy, but they did so passively.

Portugal

Established following a military coup in 1926, Oliveira Salazar's 'New State' (1933–74) profoundly marked Portuguese politics. Salazar was a corporatist Catholic who was able to consolidate his regime from the basis of a shaky military dictatorship. He did so without challenging international alliances, particularly the one with England, and focused his attentions primarily on maintaining Portugal's colonial empire.[22] Throughout this long period, changes at the level of institutions and of decision-making machinery proved very limited. It was only when Salazar was replaced by Marcello Caetano, in 1968, that a series of reforms took place, and the part of the political elite associated with the old dictator was removed.

Salazarism did not represent a clean break with the fundamentals of modern Portuguese nationalism. What Salazarism did was to consolidate and 'massify' the late nineteenth-century 'national regeneration' emphasis on the colonial dimension as the heart of Portuguese identity – a Portugal small in Europe but large in global terms. Two important dimensions were later added: the reconciliation between traditionalist Catholicism and the 'nation', and corporatism – henceforth both considered as encompassing a 'national tradition' which had been threatened and almost destroyed at the turn of the century by the secularising adventures of 'imported' liberalism.[23] Catholicism re-emerged tightly woven into the 'nation's' historic formation through its ritual and through official discourse, thus reinforcing the idea of Portugal's medieval genesis in the process of the 'Christian reconquest' of the Arabs. Beyond the immediate function of 'eliminating class conflicts', corporatism became the official ideology. With an 'organic' medieval Portugal as a paradigm, the image which the 'New State' hoped to foster was that of 'a society without conflicts', be these political, social, local or cultural.

With the 'New State', the movement to 'reinvent the past' took a qualitative leap forward. Any memory of Arab culture or of cultural diversity in general was either the target of disdain or was covered by silence. The north, the 'Christian cradle of nationhood', was valued above all. It was symbolically represented by Guimarães, a small northern city which had been the first seat of the medieval kingdom. The preservation strategy for national monuments consisted of the notably efficient reconstruction of all symbols of the 'Christian reconquest', particularly of castles as well as military fortresses in general. National heroes from the time of the nation's foundation or its maritime conquests became the objects of well-programmed graphic, cinematographic, and monumental development. An eminently 'organicist' conception dominated the image that the regime tried to project of itself and of the country. As far as propaganda was concerned, it could be said that the project of the integralist radical right, blessed by social Catholicism, was applied.

The myth of the 'empire' was also central to the ideology of the 'New State' and the effort to create a colonial mentality through the school apparatus and propaganda reached its height during the 1930s–40s. The survival of the colonies was at the heart of the nationalism of the *Estado Novo*, and it was the key variable in the dictatorship's foreign policy, which was clearly fearful of any Nazi or Italian fascist expansion outside Europe. After the Second World War and in anticipation of the resistance to decolonisation,

Salazar changed the 'imperial' rigidity of the 1930s, favouring a more 'pluri-racial and pluricontinental' model. As the international scene turned progressively hostile, colonialism gradually became 'the regime's fifth essence' and 'replaced corporatism' as the ideological heart of the *Estado Novo*.[24] The Franco dictatorship suffered international isolation after the Second World War, but Salazar's was rapidly integrated in the international order. This he owed to his neutrality during the war, to his military conces-sions to Britain and the United States, and to the rapid onset of the Cold War. Thus Portugal joined the UN (after an initial veto by the Soviet Union) and was a founding member of NATO.

It was not easy for the regime to adapt itself to the new international scenario resulting from the war – especially with regard to the dominant position of the United States, a country which the dictator had always feared and mistrusted. This feeling was heightened as Africa's decolonisa-tion commenced and Portugal's colonial policies suffered their first international condemnations from the UN's Afro-Asian bloc, foreshadowing the beginnings of the pro-independence guerrilla movements. But the regime continued to survive, cultivating (like Francoism) an external image of a benign authoritarianism, an 'anti-communist bulwark of Western civilisa-tion', while efficiently reining in the internal opposition. After suffering a period of internal turmoil when, in 1958, the dissident general Humberto Delgado obtained significant results in the presidential 'elections', the regime was to go through an even more serious coup attempt launched in 1961 by members of the military establishment. Having neutralised the conspiracy, Salazar embarked 'rapidly and forcefully' upon the colonial war which would erode the regime, shattering it 13 years later.

Up to the end of the 1950s, the structure of Portuguese society had changed little. In 1960, 43 per cent of Portugal's active population worked in the primary sector, 22 per cent in the secondary, and only 34 per cent in the tertiary sector; only 23 per cent lived in towns with populations of over 10,000. With an extremely high illiteracy rate, the very ideologised school system reached only a few. Technical scientific training reached even fewer. In the rural world, the Catholic Church was the most powerful socialisation instrument. This would significantly change in the 1960s, though the rural legacy would be felt until the 1980s, when Portugal underwent a 'second wave' of urbanisation (which left only 12 per cent on the land by 1992). One of the classic themes in academic work on Spain's transition to democracy has been the modernising economic boom in the 1960s. During the same period, although more modestly, Portugal also took a modernising leap. One economic historian has written, with perhaps a little overstatement, that Portugal 'stopped being dominated by the primary sector; the tertiary one took over, marking the passage from a peasant society Portugal to another, post-industrial, one, that never knew the characteristics of an industrial society'.[25]

Economic development was marked by the progressive openness of the country's economy, by EFTA membership, and rising foreign investment. At the same time that emigration to more developed parts of Europe from the rural interior was on the rise, a new urban middle class was growing, whose values had little in common with the official ideology. The 'tourist boom' and the money the emigrants sent home would multiply the effects a few years later.

But the colonial war was the determining element in the transition to democracy, as it led to the progressive isolation of Caetano, the last prime minister of the authoritarian regime, and rendered his attempts at reform inconsequential. This factor also determined the unexpected nature of the regime's overthrow by the military, surprising the authoritarian elite, civil society and even the (underground) opposition. The 'imperial myth', re-affirmed over and over again by the regime, became stronger as the 1960s wore on, but its echo within Portuguese society was much less than is generally supposed. Indeed, although the decolonisation was quick and dramatic for the thousands of Portuguese who had to abandon the African colonies, it did not provoke the rise of significant radical movements. With the transition to democracy and decolonisation, what was perhaps the central element of Portuguese nationalism came unravelled.

THE DEMOCRATIC EXPERIENCE

Portugal

The fall of the *Estado Novo* in the coup d'état on 25 April 1974 resulted in a period of crisis that lasted until 1976. The abrupt nature of the fall of the authoritarian regime led to the emergence of social movements that quickly dismantled the previous authoritarian institutions. They were aided by a deep state crisis and by the creation of parallel powers based in the armed forces. Moreover, a political purge movement removed and in some cases exiled hundreds of former members of the political police and administrative elite of the *Estado Novo*.[26]

In 1975, political radicalisation on the left reached its zenith. The occupation of land in the south began; the great economic groups were nationalised; important company directors left the country; and the Catholic Church's official broadcasting station was occupied and turned into the mouthpiece of the revolutionary left.[27] Thus the conditions were created for the political fulfilment of one of the main themes of the ideological discourse of the radical right since the turn of the century: capital (Lisbon) versus province, Catholic north versus 'red' south. This dual political culture was a constant element of Portuguese conservative and traditionalist thought.

With the anti-leftist political offensive of the summer of 1975, came the first relatively successful mass mobilisation of the provinces since the middle of the nineteenth century. Local notables and Catholic churchmen played an important role in the centre and north of the country. In Lisbon it was the Socialist Party of Mario Soares, together with members of the armed forces belonging to the moderate left, that led the movement which came to a head on 25 November 1975. This date was crucial in containing the pre-revolutionary wave and in establishing a *de facto* representative democracy.

The independence of Angola in 1975 established the end of the Portuguese colonial empire. Decolonisation marked the radical right with an unprecedented ideological trauma, which was aggravated by a factor that remains exceptional from the comparative perspective – namely, the rapid integration of the thousands upon thousands of white ex-colonials. These *retornados*, who could have created upheavals in the political system, did not do so and the irreversible decolonisation provoked a wave of mutual countercharges, evident in the abundant literature published at the time.[28]

The turn towards Europe of Portuguese external policy, following the hesitations of 1974 and 1975, was carried out with the practically unanimous support of the democratic parties not only for economic motives, but fundamentally for political motives: to consolidate democracy. This widespread support was consolidated in the 1980s by the timely coincidence of a triple movement: an accelerated social change; economic growth; and the influx of community funds. This coming together of factors delayed the development of any possible isolationist nationalism.

Throughout the 1980s, Portuguese society grew away from the double legacy of the authoritarian regime and the revolutionary period of 1975. Some compromises between the largest right-wing and the largest left-wing parties, the PSD and the PS, and Portugal's entry into the EC in 1986 (only the Communist Party rejected it) brought about significant changes in the country's economic and political panorama, including an increase in foreign investments, an influx of subsidies for improvement to infrastructures and the conversion of weak sectors such as agriculture.[29] At the internal level, the revision of the Constitution in 1989 eliminated the principal of nationalisation and agrarian reform, and the process of privatising the vast state sector was initiated. Gauges such as inflation and unemployment (4.5 per cent) showed improvements between 1986 and 1991. Of course, the negative effects of EC membership only began to be felt after 1991, with the progressive opening of frontiers putting pressure on the weakest sectors of Portuguese industry and agriculture. It was, however, in this atmosphere of economic growth and unanimity about EC membership, that the old quarrels inherited from 1975 would be dissolved with the 1989 revision of the Constitution.

Up to 1985, the successive governments produced by elections were either minority or coalition governments. However, in 1987 the PSD, the largest centre-right party, obtained 51.3 per cent and was thus able to form the first one-party government and was the first to complete its mandate. In 1991, this majority was reconfirmed. The PSD's domination of the right, with the CDS fighting for survival without moving to the far right, literally destroyed even the smallest space for extremist representation. The CDS, which during the process of transition and consolidation of democracy played an essential role in the 'democratisation' of an authoritarian sector of the Portuguese right more associated with Salazar's regime, has been the great 'victim' of the right-wing electorate's pragmatism, more supportive of the strong, populist leadership of Cavaco Silva, Secretary General of the PSD and Prime Minister from 1985 to 1995.

The progressive economic integration into Europe profoundly changed the structure of the country's economic partnerships: neighbouring Spain, for example, went from being an insignificant commercial partner in the late 1970s to one of the most important in the early 1990s. And in internal politics, to take another example, membership in the European Union would constitute a base for calls for 'regionalisation' in a small state with a centralist tradition, and without historical or culturally legitimate decentralising pressures. In this last respect, what stands out is the moderate but rapid development of the only legitimate poles for decentralising pressure, which were quickly included in the 1976 constitution that created the autonomous regions of Madeira and the Azores. On the mainland, there was sporadic debate on the question of regionalisation, with the political parties wavering between the centralist model or moderated decentralisation. Nevertheless, pressures for regionalisation have increased, especially in the years following Portugal's membership in the European Community, most notably after the socialists' return to power in 1995 – though the issue divides both left and right.

Although much less so since the 1980s, Portuguese society continues to manifest a (modest) divergence in favour of materialist values, when compared to the dominant post-materialist trend in Europe. The values associated with social well-being and immediate social needs also play a central role, as opposed to social and political participation, where the values of authority are still greater than the European average.[30] However, public surveys and intellectual output on 'national identity' agree on one point: the Portuguese are not undergoing a national identity crisis. National identity remains strong, but this has not affected the majority's general belief that EU membership is a good thing.

In 1978, three years after decolonisation, 20 per cent of the Portuguese still believed that Portugal could not survive without the ex-colonies. That same year, there was little awareness of the importance of joining the EEC. Only at the very end of the 1970s did opinion polls note increasing belief in the need to join the European Community. Between 1980 and 1991 the figure for those who thought membership a good thing grew from 24 to 71 per cent.[31] In 1993, 65 per cent of the population thought that Portugal had benefited a great deal by joining the EU, in terms of economic development. As in other countries in southern Europe, there seems to have been a strong relationship between 'Europeanism' and weak 'national pride' among the middle classes, and weak 'Europeanism' and strong 'national pride' among the least educated and rural lower classes.[32] Regarding the Maastricht objectives, most Portuguese approved in general, although a majority, when questioned explicitly about a European federal system, opposed this option.

When the negative impact of European Union membership began to be felt in the early 1990s, particularly in rural areas, some new farmers' movements appeared, mostly dominated by the right-wing parties and pro-protectionist movements. Portugal's obligation to open her market progressively may, as one author said, open a political space for a nationalist 'Poujadisme'.[33] Towards the end of 1992 these trends would be aggravated by the first signs of the economic recession that announced the end of the 'golden age' stemming from Portugal's admittance into the EC. The more recent changes of the CDS, towards an anti-European nationalism, and its electoral results in 1995 (9 per cent) were a clear sign of the availability of that space.

Such nationalist sentiments have not yet been combined effectively with anti-immigrant sentiment. The overall number of immigrants was relatively low until the late 1980s: 50,000 in 1989, most of them Africans, representing 0.5 per cent of the population.[34] In spite of this, racist acts multiplied at the end of the 1980s and caused the first violent incidents involving groups of skinheads. In recent years, some 'qualified' immigrants have been coming in, from Brazil for example, causing some signs of mounting xenophobia in a society which had not known significant foreign communities. Moreover, these numbers rose considerably at the beginning of the 1990s, and indeed they were probably already much higher than the official statistics would admit. According to the Interior Ministry, legal and clandestine immigration in 1993 was something like 250,000, close to 2.5 per cent of the country's population. And 1992 and 1993 would see public opinion echo with the first violent confrontations with immigrants, mostly black Africans, on the outskirts of Lisbon. However, the immigration/racism factor is not yet significant in comparison to some other countries.

Spain

The first period of democratic transition in Spain (1975–8) has often been characterised as a successful achievement of political engineering based on agreement between the anti-Francoist opposition and the reformist sectors within the Francoist regime.[35] The first general elections held in 1977 had shown that the Spanish electorate was far more moderate than previously supposed. The Communist Party, which had counted on widespread support as a reward for its past oppositional role, remained far behind the more moderate Socialist Party (PSOE), which under the charismatic leadership of Felipe González evolved towards social democracy in 1979–80. On the right, the majority was obtained by the *Unión de Centro Democrático* (UCD), under the charismatic leadership of former Falange member Adolfo Suárez: this was a coalition of Christian Democrats and liberals, supported by many reformist sectors from Francoist backgrounds and local elites previously dependent on the state apparatus. As well as the key role played by political elites in the approval by referendum (December 1978) of a new Constitution, no less important was King Juan Carlos I, who had been designated successor by Franco in 1969 and who directed a complicated process of bargaining and acted as a focus of loyalty.[36]

There followed a period (1978–82) which was still characterised by the difficulties in achieving a full democratic consolidation, partly because of the violent offensives conducted by some groups (the far right, some terrorist-oriented sectors of the extreme left, radical Basque nationalism) in order to provoke a break-up of the emerging pluralist 'consociational democracy'. This was partly linked to problems of restructuring the state in order to satisfy regional autonomy demands in Catalonia, the Basque Country and (to a lesser extent) Galicia. This gave rise to a more decentralised system composed of 17 'autonomous communities', which can be considered as mid-way between the federal model and the Italian decentralising model.[37]

Spain's new regional structure seemed to be the definitive solution for the 'national problem'. Nevertheless, two factors contributed, and still contribute, to the lack of definitive stabilisation of the system of autonomous communities. First, there is the problem of incorporating Catalan and especially Basque nationalism, which aim at a deeper autonomy within a multinational state. Second, has been the problem of the improvised and ambiguous distribution of powers between the town councils, the autonomous communities and the central government. Some of these problems seem on the way to being resolved, following the post-electoral agreement signed in 1996 between the party in office, the liberal-conservative Popular Party (PP), and the main Basque and Catalan nationalist parties.[38] Even so, the rapid creation of regional administrations has frequently led to duplicity of bureaucracies. Moreover, there have been growing tensions between town councils' demands for finance and higher units of government, resurrecting the old nineteenth-century 'municipalism'. A third problem stems from the rise of regionalisms all over Spain. To a certain extent, these are a new incarnation of pre-war regional movements, though today they protest against 'unfair' discrimination by the state in favour of Catalonia or the Basque Country, which are often accused of lack of solidarity. But there is now a further factor encouraging the emergence of 'autonomist regionalisms': the fact that the consolidation of a decentralised political system created a new political arena which offered regional elites a wider field for achieving power and controlling resources. In other words, regional administrations imposed from above, which very often did not correspond to majority regional consciousness, created the necessity of promoting regionalism on the part of both traditional and new regional political elites.

The failed military coup in February 1981 marked a notable point in the ending of the second phase of the transition to democracy, as well as making visible the weaknesses which were still present: popular demobilisation (no mass resistance took place against the rebellion, which was aborted by the opposition of the king), the Spaniards' lack of concern with politics, and finally the strong Francoist nostalgia, particularly among the army and some branches of the state, like the police, which had not been purged. The sudden break-up in 1982 of the UCD expressed the extent to which the political scene was still characterised by its lack of stability and structural articulation. Localist options, groups of notables and personal loyalties made it difficult, especially for the right-wing groups, to achieve a consolidated party organisation until the beginning of the 1990s. The situation on the left was considerably better, since the PSOE abandoned its Marxist principles and adopted a more 'Europeanised' stance, which made it possible to achieve an overwhelming general election majority in October 1982.

From then on, the third phase of the democratic transition can be distinguished, and it may be called that of the *definitive democratic consolidation* – a phase favoured by the further modernisation which took place during the 1990s. Nevertheless, there are still a number of issues which are in dispute, especially the model of the state (decentralised, federal or confederal) to be adopted. Nor has a completely stable framework of labour relations been achieved, in spite of the progressive institutionalisation of the two main workers' trades unions (the socialist-influenced General Workers' Union and the communist-influenced Workers' Committees): the period 1988–94 witnessed two general strikes and many sectoral labour conflicts. Finally, the successive political scandals which have characterised the first half of the 1990s, concerning almost all political parties with governing responsibilities, but which especially damaged the public image of the Socialist Party, are another sign of the difficult adaptation of old social behaviour patterns. Corruption and clientelism are by no means exclusive of Spain (one only needs compare the Italian case), but the difference is that in a young democracy, destabilisation may arise from a generally held conviction among the population that 'politics is corruption'.

Nevertheless, the socialist governments (1982–96) have decisively contributed to the deepening of democracy in Spain. The progressive institutionalisation of the political party system and the channelling through the constitutional framework of most political and social conflicts; the implementation of an extensive welfare state, which has made it possible to reduce poverty and inequality; the large increase in education expenditure, which has virtually eliminated illiteracy; the new creative dynamic which has characterised the culture, arts and sciences in Spain; and the democratic education of new generations, are undoubtedly clear signs of consolidation, though not yet of democratic *maturity*. No significant extreme-right parties exist. The very low level of immigration (2.3 per cent of the active population in 1993, 3.6 per cent of the Madrid population in 1994) made it impossible for the extreme right to convert its message in a broadly accepted manner, as has happened in other European states.[39]

However, it is well known that political cultures are not only a product of present circumstances but the fruit of family, education and political social-isation since childhood. In this sense, the political habits and mentalities shaped during Francoism and before are still present,[40] even in the behaviour of younger generations of Spaniards. In this sense, most special-ists agree today on the survival of the following characteristic features of Spanish political culture.[41]

First, there is passivity and fear of instability: Spaniards tend, even today, to prefer what is known. This proves a real obstacle to opposition parties in elections, though the defeat of the socialists in 1996 may contribute to a greater acceptance of political change. Second, there is little interest in poli-tics; on the contrary, most people value the private sphere. Spaniards are among the least politically interested readers of newspapers, which makes them strongly dependent on television. Thus the images of party leaders are often more important than the content of their programmes. Third, there is the persistent importance of political clientelism, friendships and favouritism which carry over into all walks of life. Although the importance and, above all, the social tolerance towards this have considerably decreased recently, a high level of cynicism persists. Fourth, there is the extreme diver-sity of regional political sub-cultures, which sometimes makes it difficult to refer to one overall Spanish model. Moderation, high levels of political consensus and preference for a two-party system are characteristic features of Catalan politics, which reveal clear signs of democratic maturity. On the other hand, Basque politics are characterised by their polarisation and high level of penetration within family life (particularly among the nationalist voters, who, during the Franco years, built up networks based on family, friendships, cultural societies, etc.), while Galician, Balearic or Canary Islands' politics are still characterised by the strong persistence of variegated forms of political clientelism, particularly in the rural areas.

Attitudes towards Europe have changed enormously since 1975. The young Spanish democracy sought entry to the European Community because of the symbolic value attributed to it: to become 'Europeans' meant to consolidate democracy and to close a dark period of Spanish history characterised by political and cultural isolation from Europe. The negotia-tions for Spain's entry lasted from 1977 to 1986, and were full of obstacles – especially over other members' fears of Spanish competition in agriculture, fishing or tourism. But in spite of the disillusionment brought about by the realisation that behind the pan-Europeanism lay strong economic interests, integration within the EC was greeted with enthusiasm by most Spaniards, even if it also implied that Spain had to become a member of NATO. Opposition to the conditions imposed upon Spain by the Maastricht Treaty has arisen sporadically, but no significant anti-EU movements exist, except some left-wing-oriented peripheral nationalist parties (among them, the most important is the Galician Nationalist Block, which holds the EU responsible for the dismantling of such crucial sectors of the Galician economy as fishing). Almost all Spanish parties, including most Basque and Catalan nationalists, are strongly pro-European. The latter see the EU as the model for an overall European federalisation which will increase their level of self-government, while reducing the influence of present-day nation-states.[42] Some sectors of the Spanish economy are suffering heavily from the restrictions imposed by Brussels, especially parts of agriculture, but in democratic Spain, to say 'no' to Europe is identified by most citizens with reactionary, Francoist-like positions. Most Spaniards do not want a return to isolation, since in the Iberian peninsula this has historically meant authoritarianism and backwardness. At the end of the 1980s, 73 per cent believed that the Civil War was a 'shaming' episode from the past which had to be forgotten: it was time to look forward.[43] Present disillusions with 'Bundesbank imperialism' have given rise to certain doubts, but this has not fundamentally affected support.

CONTINUITIES AND CHANGE

Spain and Portugal belong today to the southern part of the European Union, but it would be quite inadequate to view them as peripheral countries. The social values, customs and mentality of the younger generations are similar to those predominating among their British or German counterparts, though with the obvious peculiarities which characterise overwhelmingly Catholic areas (for example, in the importance attached to family ties). High rates of unemployment in Spain, which especially concern the young, and the costs of restructuring backward economic activities in Spain and Portugal, such as agriculture and fishing, have contributed to lessen the European enthusiasm of the second half of the 1980s. But no significant tendencies exist which aim to restore the cultural frontier at the Pyrenees, as it was 50 years ago.

In spite of the increasing reciprocal knowledge, as well as economic interconnection, between Spain and Portugal after 1986, it is difficult to deduce from this that anything like an 'Iberian identity' exists. Portuguese national feeling today is still among the strongest in Europe, while in Spain a complex mosaic of mixed 'twofold identities' emerges from the opinion surveys, which means that a Spanish national identity permanently competes with peripheral ones.[44] Present disputes about regionalisation in Portugal seem minor in comparison with the careful balance of territorial power which it was necessary to establish in Spain after 1975. Conversely, the strong Jacobin outlook of Portuguese national identity makes it very difficult even for well-informed Portuguese intellectuals to perceive the complexity of 'other' neighbouring identities. To take an example, the Portuguese obsession with Spanish 'imperialist ambitions' over the whole peninsula is for most Spaniards incomprehensible; on the other hand,

Galician nationalists' frequent calls for 'help' from Portugal have never found an important echo on the Portuguese side, which views Galicia as a kind of 'ethnic relict' of the pre-national past of Portugal.[45]

Nevertheless, these problems of mutual understanding turn into cooperation between Spain and Portugal when their interests are confronted with those of others in the framework of the European Union. Both states are dependent on the positive counter-effects that their entry into the EU has brought to them; their currencies are deeply interrelated as far as fluctuations are concerned (although in this respect Portuguese currency is heavily and involuntarily dependent on the 'health' of the Spanish currency), and their economic ability to join the 'hard core' of the EU in monetary and closer union will be very much interrelated. Paradoxically, the need to escape from peninsular isolation through European partnership may have brought about as an unexpected consequence a better reciprocal knowledge of two neighbouring states whose relationship had been characterised by a lack of mutual confidence since the Middle Ages. This probably relates to the fact that 'national' state interests have become geographically wider, and may serve as a lesson for Eastern European countries which are on the eve of joining the EU.

NOTES

1   E. Weber, *Peasants into Frenchmen*, Stanford, Stanford University Press, 1976.
2   See J. J. Linz and A. Stepan, *Problems of Democratic Transition and Consolidation: Southern Europe, South America and Postcommunist Europe*, Baltimore, Johns Hopkins University Press, 1996.
3   On the lack of law codification see B. Clavero, *El código y el fuero. De la cuestión regional en la España contemporánea*, Madrid, Siglo XXI, 1982.
4   See J. Fernández Sebastián, *La génesis del fuerismo*, Madrid, Siglo XXI, 1991; and R. M. Artaza Montero, *As Xuntas do Reino de Galicia no final do Antigo Réxime (1775–1834)*, Coruña, Fundación Barrié de la Maza, 1993.
5   See A. Carreras and J. Nadal (eds), *Pautas regionales de la industrialización española (siglos XIX y XX)*, Barcelona, Ariel, 1990; J. Nadal, *El fracaso de la revolución industrial en España, 1830–1913*, Barcelona, Ariel, 1974; L. Prados de la Escosura, *De Imperio a Nación. Crecimiento económico y desarrollo en España (1830–1930)*, Madrid, Alianza, 1991.
6   See J. M. Jover Zamora, *La civilización española a mediados del siglo XIX*, Madrid, Espasa-Calpe, 1992.
7   B. de Riquer and E. Ucelay-Da Cal, 'An Analysis of Nationalisms in Spain: A proposal for an integrated model' in J. G. Beramendi, R. Máiz and X. M. Núñez (eds), *Nationalism in Europe: Past and Present*, Santiago de Compostela, Universidade de Santiago de Compostela, 1994, vol. II; X. M. Núñez, 'Questione nazionale e crisi statale: Spagna, 1898–1936', *Ricerche Storiche*, 1994, 24; B. de Riqueur, 'La debole nazionalizzazione spagnola del XIX secolo', *Passato e Presente*, 1993, 11.
8   See J. Varela Ortega, *Los amigos políticos. Partidos, elecciones y caciquismo en la Restauración (1875–1900)*, Madrid, Alianza Editorial, 1977.
9   J. M. Quintana Navarro, *España en Europa, 1931–1936*, Madrid, Nerea, 1993.
10 See I. Sepúlveda, *Communidad cultural e hispanoamericanismo, 1885–1936*,

Madrid, UNED, 1994; J. G. Beramendi and R. Máiz (eds), *Los nacionalismos en la España de la II República*, Madrid, Siglo XXI, 1991.

11 See A. Costa Pinto and N. Monteiro, 'Probleme der nationalen Identität in Portugal', *WerkstattGeschichte*, 1994, 8. See also D. Stanislawski, *The Individuality of Portugal. A Study in Historical-Political Geography*, Austin, University of Texas Press, 1959.

12 See V. Alexandre, *Os sentidos do império. Questão nacional e questão colonial na crise do Antigo Regime*, Oporto, Afrontamento, 1993.

13 See N. Teixeira, *O Ultimatum Inglês. Política externa e política interna no Portugal de 1890*, Lisbon, Alfa, 1990.

14 See H. Martins, 'Portugal' in M. Scotford Archer and S. Giner (eds), *Contemporary Europe: Class, Status and Power*, London, Weidenfeld and Nicolson, 1971, p. 63.

15 P. Tavares de Almeida, *Eleições e Caciquismo no Portugal Oitocentista (1868–1890)*, Lisboa, Difel, 1991.

16 N. Teixeira, *O Poder e a Guerra. Objectivos nacionais e estratégias políticas em Portugal, 1914–18*, Lisbon, Estampa, 1996; see also A. Costa Pinto, 'Crises and Early Authoritarian Takeover: Portugal' in D. Berg-Schlosser and J. Mitchell (eds), *Crises, Compromise, Collapse. Conditions for Democracy in Interwar Europe*, London, Macmillan, 1997.

17 J. Fontana (ed.), *España bajo el Franquismo*, Barcelona, Crítica, 1986; J. L. García Delgado (ed.), *El primer Franquismo. España durante la II Guerra Mundial*, Madrid, Siglo XXI, 1989; F. Portero, *Franco aislado. La cuestión española 1945–1950*, Madrid, UNED, 1989.

18 See M. Ramírez Jiménez, *España 1939–1975. Régimen político e ideología*, Barcelona, Guadarrama, 1978; J. J. Linz, 'From Falange to Movimiento-Organization: The Spanish Single Party and the Franco Régime, 1936–1968' in S. P. Huntington and C. H. Moore, *Authoritarian Politics in Modern Society*, New York, Basic Books, 1970. See also A. Botti, *Cielo y dinero. El nacionalcatolicismo en España*, Madrid, Alianza, 1992.

19 H. Johnston, *Tales of Nationalism: Catalonia, 1939–1979*, New Brunswick (NJ), Rutgers University Press, 1989; G. Jáuregui, *Ideología y estrategia política de ETA*, Madrid, Siglo XXI, 1981; J. G. Beramendi and X. M. Núñez, *O nacionalismo galego*, Vigo, Edicións A Nosa Terra, 1995.

20 C. Molinero and P. Ysàs, *El régim franquista. Feixisme, modernització i consens*, Vic, Eumo/Universitat de Girona, 1992, p. 52.

21 W. Bernecker, 'Del aislamiento a la integración. Las relaciones entre España y Europa en el siglo XX', *Spagna Contemporanea*,1993, 4.

22 A. Costa Pinto, *Salazarís Dictatorship and European Fascism. Problems of Interpretation*, New York, Columbia University Press, 1995.

23 R. W. Sousa, *The Rediscoverers. Major Writers in the Portuguese Literature of National Regeneration*, University Park, Pennsylvania State University Press, 1981; M. Braga da Cruz, *As Origens da Democracia Cristã e o Salazarismo*, Lisbon, Presença, 1980; M. de Lucena, *A Evolução do Sistema Corporativo Português*, vol. 1: *O Salazarismo*, Lisbon, Perspectivas e Realidades, 1976.

24 B. Sousa Santos quoted in M. Braga da Cruz, *O Partido e o Estado no Salazarismo*, Lisboa, Presença, 1988, p. 45.

25 A. José Telo, 'Portugal, 1958–1974' in H. de la Torre (ed.), *Portugal y España en el cambio Político (1958–78)*, Merida, UNED, 1987, p. 88.

26 K. Maxwell, *The Making of Portuguese Democracy*, Cambridge, Cambridge University Press, 1995; M. Braga da Cruz, *Instituições, Política e Processos Sociais*, Lisbon, Bertrand, 1995; A. Costa Pinto (ed.), *Modern Portugal*, Palo Alto, Sposs, 1997; A. Costa Pinto, 'Dealing with the Legacy of Authoritarianism: Political Purge in Portugal's Transition to Democracy

(1974–76)' in S. U. Larsen (ed.), *Modern Europe after Fascism, 1945–1980s,* New York, SSM-CUP, 1997.

27 N. Bermeo, *The Revolution Within the Revolution. Workers' Control in Rural Portugal,* Princeton, Princeton University Press, 1986; P. Manuel, *Uncertain Outcomes: The Politics of the Portuguese Transition to Democracy,* New York, the University Press of America, 1995.

28 A. Costa Pinto, 'The Radical Right in Contemporary Portugal' in L. Cheles, R. Ferguson and M. Vaughan (eds), *The Far Right in Western and Eastern Europe,* London, Longman, 1995.

29 C. S. Costa, 'Cinco anos e meio de integração da Portugal na CEE: das dúvidas do momento de partida à autoconfiança reencontrada' AA, VV (1991), *Portugal em Mudança. Ensaios sobre a actividade do XI governo costitucional,* Lisbon, Imprensa Nacional, 1991.

30 J. Vala, 'Valores socio-políticos' in Luís de França (ed.), *Portugal, valores europeios, identidade cultural,* Lisboa, IED, 1993, p. 257.

31 M. Bacalhau, *Atitudes, Opiniões e Comportamentos Políticos dos Portugueses, 1973–1993,* Lisboa, FLAD, 1995; *Les Européens vus par eux-mêmes,* Luxembourg, CEE, 1986.

32 de França, *op. cit.,* pp. 270–5.

33 See M. Rebelo de Sousa, 'Seis anos-do Estado à sociedade' AA, VV (1991), *op. cit.,* pp. 33–4.

34 Cf. Parlamento Europeu (1990), *Relatório de Inquérito sobre o Racismo e a Xenofobia,* pp. 67–8.

35 M. Redero San Román (ed.), *La transición democrática española,* Madrid, Marcial Pons, 1994; R. Morodo, *La transición política,* Madrid, Tecnos, 1984; R. Garcia Cotarelo, A. de Blas Guerrero and J. Felix Tezanos (eds), *La transición democrática española,* Madrid, Sistema, 1989; R. Cotarelo (ed.), *Transición política y consolidación democrática. España (1975–1986),* Madrid, CIS 1992; M. Caciagli, *Elecciones y partidos en la transición española,* Madrid, CIS-Siglo XXI, 1986; J. Maravall, *La política de la transición (1975–1980),* Madrid, Taurus, 1982.

36 See S. Juliá, 'Raíces y legado de la Transición', in AA, VV, *Memoria de la Transición,* Madrid, El Pa's, 1996, pp. 457–9.

37 F. J. Llera, *Los vascos y la política,* Bilbao, UPV, 1994; J. Solé Tura, *Nacionalidades y nacionalismos en España,* Madrid, Alianza Editorial, 1985.

38 A. Hildenbrand, 'El Estado de las autonomías diez años después de la Constitución de 1978: un balance de la descentralización política en España', *Mélanges de la Casa de Velázquez,* 1990, XXVI.

39 See J. L. Rodriguez Jiménez, *Reaccionarios y golpistas,* Madrid, CSIC, 1994; X. Casals, *Neonazis en España,* Barcelona, Grijalbo, 1995; X. M. Núñez, 'A imigraçâo e a extrema-direita em Espanha', *Risco,* 1994, 21.

40 A. De Miguel, *Sociología del Franquismo,* Barcelona, Euros, 1975; FOESSA, *Informe sociológico sobre el cambio político en España, 1975–1981,* Madrid, Euramérica, 1981.

41 J. Vidal Beneyto (ed.), *España a debate. I: La política,* Madrid, Tecnos, 1991.

42 K. J. Nagel, 'Stateless Nations of Western Europe and the Process of European Integration: The Catalan Case' in Beramendi, Máiz and Núñez, *op. cit.*

43 Quoted in Bernecker, *op. cit.,* p. 73.

44 M. Garc'a Ferrando, E. Lopez-Aranguren and M. Beltráum, *La conciencia nacional y regional en la España de las Autonomías,* Madrid, CSIC, 1994.

45 P. Vázquez Cuesta, 'Portugal–Galicia, Galicia–Portugal: un diálogo asimétrico', *Colóquio-Letras,* 1995, 137–8.

12 Russia

Stephen White

INTRODUCTION

Men, as Marx once remarked, make their own history: but they do not make it as they choose. Nations, one might equally suggest, create their own destinies: but they do so in a way that is shaped by their historical past. How long, for instance, has the state been in continuous existence? Has there been a tradition of public organisation, or of citizen activity at a more local level? For how long has there been a parliament with real powers, elected by a relatively open process? Has economic life, both business and labour, been closely regulated by the state or has it been largely autonomous? Has the press been relatively free, and the judiciary relatively independent? Have the rights of religious and national minorities been respected? What knowledge have ordinary people had of the process of government, and to what extent have they been willing to identify with the institutions that have supposedly represented their interests?

In the Soviet and Russian case, it has sometimes seemed that the historical past all but determined a pattern of authoritarian government that has lasted – in varying forms – up to the present. For Richard Pipes, to take a notable commentator, a statist or patrimonial system has existed in Russia, 'whatever the regime and its formal ideology', since at least early medieval times. He sees the origins of communist rule in the USSR 'primarily in terms of Russian historical experience': for although Marxism had authoritarian implications, the form it took in regimes that were based upon it depended largely upon their indigenous political traditions, which in Europe were liberal but in Russia largely totalitarian.[1] Writers like Tibor Szamuely and Robert Conquest have taken a similar view; for Zbigniew Brzezinski, taking matters still further, Soviet communism represented not just the continuation but the restoration of tsarist patterns of rule after the feebleness and indecision of the later Romanovs.[2]

There was, of course, another view: either that the Russian past was less authoritarian than such writers suggested, or that its authoritarian past had little relevance to the Soviet rule that succeeded it. For some comparative historians, for instance, the Russian government was subject to checks from its society in a way that was not essentially different from the rest of Europe; there were particularly close parallels with the Prussian form of absolutism on which it was explicitly modelled.[3] For Alexander Solzhenitsyn, writing more polemically, Russia's distant past had been subjected to the 'distorting effects of fervent radical thought in the West' in terms of which Russia's modern development had been interpreted, 'not as something peculiar to communism, not as a phenomenon new to human history, but as if it derived from primordial Russian national characteristics established in some distant century'. This, for Solzhenitsyn, was more than historically unfounded: it was 'nothing less than a racist view'.[4]

In this chapter I shall consider three of the issues to which this distinctive experience gives rise. In the first place, I shall be concerned with the inheritance of tsarist rule; second, with the impact of communist government; and third, with the complex process of change that has taken place since 1991. Despite the hopes that were entertained for some time after the end of Soviet rule, it will be suggested that there has been a 'metamorphosis of power'[5] rather than a change of system, and that the relationship between government and the wider society can still be understood within a tradition that has privileged executive authority as against citizens and the institutions through which they have sought to act. And it is political cultural factors of this kind that can in turn help to explain the very different nature of 'transition' in post-communist Europe: in some countries (such as the Czech Republic) to a stable multiparty capitalism, in others (such as Russia) to a rather different hybrid in which government remains authoritarian, the value system is strongly welfarist, and the economy is an administered if no longer a centrally planned one.

THE IMPACT OF THE PAST

After early state forms centred around Kiev and Novgorod, modern Russia began to establish itself in the fifteenth century around the principality of Moscow. Its religion was Orthodox, a part of Eastern Christianity: the Russians, it was said, had embraced Christianity rather than Islam as it allowed them to drink. The political traditions of the Moscow principality were centralist and authoritarian, unlike those of Novgorod and Pskov, where city assemblies played some role in government: but they were annexed and their municipal institutions dissolved in 1478 and 1510. And it was expansionist: described as the 'gathering of the lands' by Soviet historians, the state gradually extended its control by conquest or annexation into Siberia from the sixteenth century onwards, into Ukraine and Belorussia in the eighteenth century, and into Central Asia and the Caucasus in the nineteenth.

Perhaps because its frontiers were open, there was a premium on military strength (the military budget was a large one by the standards of the time, and the army itself was the biggest in Europe). There was little emphasis upon representation, although a form of elected local government began to establish itself in the 1870s, and in 1906 an elected Duma was wrung from a reluctant Emperor – very late by the standards of the rest of Europe and North America.

Formally speaking, the Duma had a considerable range of powers. It could enact and amend legislation; it could appoint and dismiss government officials; it had the right to consider national and departmental budgets; and it had general supervisory rights over the apparatus of government. Its real powers were much more limited. It had no right to make changes in expenditure connected with foreign loans, the army and navy, the imperial household, or the ministry of internal affairs (about two-thirds of government spending was thus removed from its control). Ministers, moreover, were responsible to the Tsar, not to the Duma, and the Tsar alone had the right to appoint or dismiss them. Ministers could be questioned by members of the Duma, but they could refuse to provide an answer or provide one at a later date if they found this more convenient. Indeed it almost seemed, wrote the historian and statesman Paul Milyukov, that 'the more a minister succeeded in antagonising the Duma, the more reliable he was considered to be in the contest between the old regime and the Russian democracy'.[6]

The Duma's influence over the conduct of government, these limited powers notwithstanding, appears to have been increasing in the later tsarist period, and in 1915 its unremitting pressure led to the resignation of four ministers. In the view of some Western scholars the Duma would, in fact, have developed into a fully-fledged Russian parliament if war and revolution had not prevented it from doing so. This remains debatable; what is certainly clear is that the Russian Empire was governed, as late as the early twentieth century, by a scarcely-modified autocracy, and that it was the only major European country of which this could still be said.

It was, moreover, a form of government that drew upon the support of a very limited section of the population. The right to vote was a very restricted one by comparison with other major countries at the same time: even in 1910 only 2 per cent of the adult population participated in national elections. Moreover, deputies were drawn to a much greater extent from aristocratic and landed circles. Direct comparisons are difficult, but the evidence that is available suggests that 51 per cent of deputies to the Duma in the early twentieth century were of noble background; in France the corresponding figure was 11 per cent, in Germany 12.9 per cent, in Britain 15.4 per cent and in Italy 16.5 per cent. In all of these countries, by contrast, a professional or commercial middle class was much more strongly represented – though there have been arguments about the extent of such variations and whether they help explain the political development of these respective countries (in particular whether there was a German *Sonderweg* which left the middle class relatively weak).[7]

What about popular attitudes and values? Again, it is difficult to establish such matters retrospectively, but the evidence also suggests that levels of political literacy were low even by the standards of the time. One aspect of this was what has been called 'naive monarchism'. The popular uprisings of the seventeenth and eighteenth centuries, for instance, were almost never directed against the Tsar himself, but rather against the boyar aristocracy who were supposed to have misinformed him. There was a widespread 'pretender phenomenon', with at least 20 spurious claimants to the throne in the seventeenth century and more than 40 in the eighteenth century (the unfortunate Peter III was raised from the dead on at least 16 occasions).[8] Equally, there was a very shaky understanding of the political process. In the elections to the Third Duma in 1907, for instance, employers sent their clerks, husbands and their wives to vote for them, and some put letters, insurance policies or even bad verse into the ballot box rather than the voting papers they were supposed to have brought with them.[9] Later still, in 1918, there was no serious attempt to defend the Constituent Assembly when the Bolsheviks dissolved it and brought Russia's 'constitutional experiment' to an early end.

This political culture was, in turn, the product of a distinctive social structure. One of its most important features was the lack, as compared with Western Europe, of a balance between monarchy and aristocracy. Russia had no feudal system, at least in its 'classic' European form, and there was no counterpart to the complex network of reciprocal obligations, of monarch to noble and of landowner to serf as well as vice versa, within an overall framework that was defined by contract. It was this balance, and the need to regulate it, that developed in Western Europe into the rule of law, and it was the need to discuss and occasionally renegotiate the balance that encouraged the growth of representative institutions. In Russia, by contrast, the landed gentry or *dvoryanstvo* failed to establish an institutional expression of their common self-interest, and were unable to limit the exercise of monarchical power as their counterparts had done in Western Europe. On the contrary, the nobility were in effect 'nationalised' through the Table of Ranks, adopted in 1722, which converted them into a service class whose membership was defined by the state. The Table of Ranks remained in effect, with some modifications, up to 1917.

At least one further feature of the pre-revolutionary political culture deserves attention: the communal, collectivist traditions of rural society.[10] The village commune or *mir* was a social as well as an economic institution: it was responsible for the collection of taxes and the redistribution of land, it despatched recruits to the armed forces, and carried out a variety of legal duties including the issuing of passports, and sending people into exile or banishment. Village responsibilities were exercised through an assembly in which all heads of households were represented, and in which decisions were normally taken unanimously. What Lenin called the peasants' 'instinctive, primitive democratism'[11] was further reinforced by the traditions of the Orthodox Church: particularly its doctrine of *sobornost*, a community of believers among whom love and truth were collectively located, and its close association with the state through the Holy Synod, in effect a ministry of religion. This, in turn, made it easier for political controls to be established after 1917 in what mainstream Western European thought has usually regarded as the private sphere – beliefs and values, the arts, family life and social interaction more generally – though this is clearly not true of fascism, or the more authoritarian forms of Catholicism.

THE IMPACT OF COMMUNISM

The Bolshevik Revolution, and subsequent defeat of the counter-revolutionary forces, established a regime that, in many respects at least, sought to change the traditional culture it had inherited. Church and state were separated, and religious practice was always legal; but the communist society of the future was supposed to be an atheist one, and party members were required not simply to be irreligious but to oppose 'superstitions' of this kind. More positively, the communist society of the future was supposed to be one of political and social activism; and it was to be an enlightened society, with high levels of education and cultural consumption. It was to be a society without national or ethnic tensions, as 'working men had no country'. And it was to be a society of gender equality, with women voting, working and earning on the same basis as their male counterparts. Eventually, the 1961 Party Programme promised, there would be a 'classless social order' with 'complete society equality' in which the great principle would finally be realised: 'From each according to his ability, to each according to his needs'.[12]

An enormous effort was made, after 1917, to ensure that these objectives were carried into practical effect. The education system played a part, as the focus of political youth movements as well as the institution through which the new regime propagated its own view of history and other school subjects. A network of propagandists spread across the country, offering regular expositions of the party point of view at the workplace and (for party members themselves) a rigorous system of political instruction. Most important of all, the mass media were expected to 'bring the party's word to the masses' and not just reflect developments at home and abroad. Newspapers, for instance, were briefed regularly and instructed on the campaigns they should prioritise, and the people they should mention (or not mention). Television news typically began with pictures of combine harvesters bringing in a record crop, before passing on to the unemployment and social division of the capitalist world. And there was 'visual propaganda', including posters, 'red corners', statues of Lenin and 'boards of honour' with pictures of an area's most outstanding workers.

There has been a good deal of evidence of behavioural change over the Soviet period – evidence, for some Western scholars, that Soviet citizenship training had 'succeeded', and for others, that the 'most dramatically successful case' of planned political culture change had taken place.[13] The changes were partly behavioural. Elections, for instance, began to draw in larger and larger numbers of voters, from 20–30 per cent in the 1920s to 80–90 per cent by the mid-1930s. Fewer people went to church, or expressed a religious belief. And there were substantial increases in socio-political activity. Some of the earliest studies of this kind were conducted by the economist S. G. Strumilin in the 1920s. The average worker, he found, spent about 2.9 hours a month engaged in socio-political activity, and only 3.3 per cent of workers were engaged in activities of this kind. By the late 1960s, when follow-up studies were done, the amount of time devoted to such activities had increased almost seven times, the proportion of workers engaged in them was up to 45 per cent, and a higher proportion of their participation was of an active kind – like running social organisations – rather than simply attending meetings.[14]

The closer relationship between people and regime was in part a result of its programme of socialisation, and in part a result of changes that would have taken place under any form of government as increasing proportions were enrolled in full time schooling, started to read newspapers regularly and moved into managerial and professional positions. But it also reflected the impact of events, and of the Second World War in particular. Substantial numbers of Soviet citizens, in fact, fought on the German side, some under the command of General Vlasov. But there was an overwhelming popular resistance to the German invasion, and an overriding commitment to the wartime leadership – which happened to be communist. The Church signed a concordat with the regime in 1943; soldiers went into battle calling out 'For the motherland! For Stalin'. Communist Party members were expected to be in the front line, and three million of them died – a much heavier loss than among the general population. During these years at least there was some reality in the regime's slogan that the 'party and people were united'.

It had nonetheless become clear, at least by the 1970s, that this elaborate programme of mass re-education was yielding diminishing returns. Political lectures were being attended unwillingly, they were doing little to increase levels of political knowledge, and they were attracting those who were already the best informed and most committed – 'informing the informed and agitating the agitated', as a party journal put it.[15] Relatively few, it emerged, gave any attention to the posters that lined Soviet streets. In the press, it was foreign rather than domestic news that received most attention. Where they could, for instance in the Baltic, Soviet viewers turned to foreign rather than domestic stations. And there was little sign, in daily life, that the communist society of the future was in gestation. There were far more religious believers than party members, young people were listening to Western pop music, there was a flourishing black market, and more and more ordinary workers were finding their consolation in the bottle.

There was little sign, at the same time, that the central values of a 'Soviet' system had simply been imposed by the authorities. A large-scale study was conducted in the 1950s, for instance, funded by the US government and based upon the large numbers of Soviet displaced persons that had been left in the West after the Second World War. Its main product was a book called *The Soviet Citizen*, co-authored by Alex Inkeles and Raymond Bauer.[16] Studies of émigrés, clearly, are problematic; but the authors made every effort to correct for conscious and unconscious bias, and their sample was a large and fairly representative one (members of the Communist Party, for instance, were distributed in approximately the same proportions as among the Soviet population itself at this time). And it was reasonable to assume that a group of émigrés were less likely to be positive towards a regime they had chosen to leave than the population that had remained under the control of the Soviet government.

At least two key institutions of the Soviet system were all but universally rejected: the collective farm and the secret police. But many of its other features were strongly supported, even among those who repudiated the system as a whole. Some 86 per cent favoured state ownership of the means of transport and communications; and there was a high level of commitment to 'collectivist' institutions of public welfare, especially in the fields of education and health. The achievements of the regime in eliminating illiteracy and developing educational provision were widely applauded, even by those who were disposed in the most hostile manner towards the regime itself. 'The desire to live in a welfare state', Inkeles and Bauer concluded, 'is rooted in deep values of the Soviet citizen', and the system more generally 'seemed to enjoy the support of popular consensus'.[17]

The interviews that were conducted during the 1970s, most often in Israel, conveyed a similar impression. There was strong support for a greater degree of religious freedom, and for a wider range of civil liberties. But there was also a substantial measure of agreement that (for instance) the Israeli Communist Party should be banned, and that strikes should be banned. 'There is too much criticism here – there things are better', observed a 60-year-old pensioner; for a young engineering student, criticism of the government should simply 'not be allowed'. Even allowing for the extent to which respondents may have had specifically Israeli circumstances in mind, the authoritarian cast of mind of most respondents – in spite of their high levels of education and overall hostility towards the Soviet system – emerges relatively clearly. One immigrant, asked what was the greatest problem in the USSR at this time, provided a perfect illustration. The greatest problem, he was convinced, was 'the lack of democracy'. And what should the Soviet government do about it? 'Issue a directive to all state institutions to introduce democratic procedures immediately.'[18]

More recent émigrés were likely, in a similar way, to believe that the state should exercise supervision and control over a wide area of national life, from the provision of full employment, housing and welfare to the development of sport, the preservation of social unity and the determination of a single and binding set of national priorities. Many were concerned by the failure of the government in Israel to undertake functions of this kind; and even the excesses of the 1930s seemed justified, to some younger respondents, leading as they had done to the development of industry and the survival of the USSR as a state. Not all attributed the excesses of this period to Stalin ('He was advised by fools'); and in any case there had to be a 'master', a 'head of the household'. And prices had been low.[19]

The state was also expected to play a larger role in economic life than was characteristic of the capitalist West – though there were notable differences of tradition here, for example between the laissez-faire nineteenth-century British tradition and the French *colbertiste* one. A substantial proportion of the émigrés of the 1970s, for instance, favoured public guarantees of full employment (though some went on to point out that this had not been achieved in the USSR, declarations notwithstanding); and most also favoured the principle inscribed in the Soviet Constitution of the time, 'He who does not work shall not eat'. It was widely agreed that extremes of inequality should be avoided, and there was overwhelming agreement that the state had the right and duty to limit such inequalities and to secure a basic and satisfactory standard of living for all its citizens. There was overwhelming support for private or at least cooperative agriculture, but also for state ownership of heavy industry, transport and communications, and (for many) of light industry as well.[20]

CHANGE OF REGIME OR CHANGE OF SYSTEM?

After 70 years of Soviet rule the transition, when it came in 1991, was certainly a curious one. Unlike most of Eastern Europe during the 1980s, where a mass politics had ousted communist administrations and placed very different governments in power, the Soviet transition from communism centred around the defence of a predominantly communist parliament led by a former member of the Politburo. Boris Yeltsin was President of the Russian Soviet Federal Socialist Republic at this time; his running mate, who stood beside him outside the White House, was still a party member. So too were more than 80 per cent of the deputies. There was no national and indefinite strike in response to Yeltsin's appeal, and the crowd that defied the curfew outside the White House numbered about 15,000 (a year later many more Muscovites 'remembered' they had been there).[21] Yeltsin's appeal, in any case, was for the Soviet Constitution to be respected and for the Soviet President and General Secretary to be released from his detention in the Crimea. The Communist Party was suspended, and then banned; but it revived again in early 1993 and soon became the largest and best supported, not just at the elections to the State Duma in 1995 but still more so at local elections throughout the country. Not surprisingly, perhaps, most Russians in the summer of 1994 thought that the communists were 'still in power'.[22]

It was certainly the case that former communists were still in most of the positions of authority. Yeltsin himself had been a loyal party member for more than 30 years, and a member of the Politburo and Secretariat. His prime minister, Viktor Chernomyrdin, had been a member of the Central Committee. More broadly, there was substantial evidence that the old communist nomenklatura had lost little of its former influence. Within the early post-communist government all but one of the ministers was a former party member. Within the Yeltsin leadership as a whole, 75 per cent were former nomenklaturists; within the Russian government, 74 per cent; among Russian parliamentarians 60 per cent had a background in the nomenklatura; at the regional level a massive 82 per cent were former nomenklaturists. And their experience was, on average, a reasonably extended one: for the Yeltsin elite as a whole the average period in the nomenklatura had been 12 years, ranging from 10 years among the members of the President's own administration to 15 years among the regional elite.[23] As Gorbachev's press secretary, Andrei Grachev, put it, the end of communist rule was a sort of 'revolution of the "second secretaries"': they had always wanted to take power from the upper levels of the bureaucracy, and having done so went on in Orwellian fashion to call it an exercise in popular democracy.[24]

Were democrats, more generally, in command of the political system by this time? Only 19 per cent thought so, in the summer of 1994; more than half took a different view.[25] And had the defeat of the attempted coup in August 1991 seen the 'end of the communist regime'? A year later, 41 per cent agreed but 41 per cent disagreed; two years later the jury was still out, with 43 per cent in agreement that the collapse of the coup had brought about the end of communist rule but 45 per cent taking the opposite view.[26] Asked to evaluate the political system in the spring of 1995, more than two-thirds rated the former communist regime positively; 15 per cent were unsure, and 18 per cent were hostile. When asked about the 'current system, with free elections and a multiparty system', opinions were more or less reversed: 54 per cent were hostile, 26 per cent positive, and 20 per cent unsure.[27] A greater degree of freedom of speech was still widely valued, as was the closer relationship that had developed with the West; but there were more, in November 1994, who thought multiparty elections had harmed Russia than thought they had been beneficial (33 per cent as against 29 per cent), and the same was true of the right to strike.[28]

What about human rights more specifically? Just 13 per cent, in a *Eurobarometer* survey that appeared in 1996, thought they were broadly respected; more than five times as many (85 per cent) thought they were not. Among all the former communist countries, the former Soviet republics were consistently the most likely to believe that there had been no fundamental improvement in their human rights, with Armenians and Georgians as pessimistic as Russians. All the former Soviet republics, again, were most likely to express dissatisfaction with the development of democracy in their own country, with Russians the most dissatisfied of all: just 6 per cent of Russians were satisfied, with a massive 86 per cent taking the opposite view.

In both respects there was a sharp contrast with Central Europe, and with the Baltic states.[29]

What about more particular freedoms, such as freedom of conscience and freedom of the press? The picture that emerged from the views of ordinary citizens was a very mixed one (see Table 12.1). Of a list of eight freedoms, five or six were thought to be greater in the mid-1990s than they had been under communist rule, with relatively little differentiation across the generations; but there was a wide range of variation, with a much clearer belief that basic civil rights had been secured (such as the freedom to worship) than that a more effective mechanism had been developed by which citizens could control the government that spoke in their name. Indeed there was less belief that government could be influenced, and less that it treated citizens fairly, than had been the case in the years before perestroika – let alone the liberalised USSR of the last years of communist rule.

There had, in fact, been substantial support for the attempted coup in 1991. According to Gorbachev himself, speaking afterwards to journalists, support ran as high as 40 per cent; for *Pravda* editor Afanas'ev it was as high as 70 per cent.[30] Representative or otherwise, up to 70 per cent of the letters that were sent to the Russian Prosecutor about the arrested conspirators were in their support;[31] and sentiments of this kind were certainly apparent in some of the letters that were sent to the Soviet press after the coup had been launched but before it had been defeated. 'May your hands be firm and your hearts pure', wrote a Moscow pensioner. 'Force everyone

Table 12.1 Political freedoms before and after communist rule

	Better	*Worse*	*Same/Don't Know*
Everyone has a right to say what he thinks	67	7	15
One can join any organisation one likes	67	4	29
One can travel or live anywhere one wants	41	28	31
People like me can have an influence on government	6	20	74
One need not be afraid of illegal arrest	23	15	63
Everyone can decide individually whether or not to take an interest in politics	53	4	43
Government treats everyone equally and fairly	7	32	61
Everyone has freedom of choice in religious matters	77	2	21

Source: Adapted from Richard Rose and Christian Haerpfer, *New Russia Barometer III: The Results*, Glasgow, Centre for the Study of Public Policy, 1994, pp. 27–9.

to obey the Constitution, and introduce some public order.' Or as a group of automobile workers wrote to *Izvestiya*, 'We welcome order and discipline, we welcome the new leadership'.[32] And what kind of a victory had there been for democracy after the coup had collapsed? Perhaps in Moscow and St Petersburg, but in Bashkiria, wrote one of their correspondents, the only difference was that prices were rising even faster; as another writer put it, the local 'totalitarian regime' had remained and even 'strengthened itself'.[33]

What about the ending of the USSR, and of Soviet citizenship? An overwhelming majority, in March 1991, had expressed their support for the retention of the USSR as a 'renewed federation': there was a turnout of 80 per cent, of whom 76.4 per cent voted in favour. An equally substantial majority, three years later, regretted the eventual dissolution of the USSR: 68 per cent thought the decision had been ill-advised, and a still more substantial 76 per cent thought it had depressed living standards.[34] Substantial numbers, in fact, still regarded themselves as Soviet citizens: 61 per cent did so in the summer of 1994, with varying degrees of certainty.[35] Indeed, a form of federal union might have continued, even after the end of communist rule, if circumstances had been otherwise: most of the former Soviet republics had agreed, in November 1991, to establish a new Union of Sovereign States, with a single parliament and presidency, but it failed to materialise because of the Ukrainian referendum on 1 December which delivered a large majority in favour of full independence. A reformed USSR would have made little sense without its second most important member; the result was a rather looser Commonwealth of Independent States, although one that has nonetheless gradually restored some of the forms of association – particularly at the economic and military levels – that were a feature of the USSR it had replaced (indeed in March 1996, in a largely symbolic vote, the Russian Duma denounced the agreement between the three Slavic heads of state that had led to the dissolution of the USSR and the formation of the new Commonwealth).

What about much broader and deeper values, as they emerged from studies that were conducted in the early post-communist years? There was certainly little support for a return to communist rule (23 per cent agreed largely or entirely with a reversion to the previous system but 62 per cent were opposed).[36] But in terms of the basic orientations that underpinned such choices, there was a much greater degree of convergence between 'communist' values and those with which ordinary Russians were willing to identify themselves than with what were seen as 'Western' values (see Table 12.2). More generally, there was strong support for freedom, a 'unitary and invisible Russia', Christianity and glasnost; Marxism-Leninism was generally unpopular (15 per cent in favour, 37 per cent against) and so too was socialism (24 per cent in favour, 33 per cent against), but capitalism was hardly a more general preference (25 per cent were positive, 28 per cent against).[37] Most popular of all, in surveys, was the view that Russia should develop 'according to its own traditions': a decisive majority (78 per cent) took this view in the summer of 1994, with just a small minority that thought Russia should develop along the lines of its European neighbours.[38]

And what about the society in which they lived, about public ownership and the market? Some form of market principles had been popular in 1990 and 1991 (more than half of those who were asked favoured a rapid or more gradual transition in that direction). But as the reality of a market became apparent there was a steady withdrawal of support and a corresponding rise in the proportion that favoured planning. For Russians, in 1991, a market economy was the preferred option (42 per cent as compared with 34 per cent), but by 1995 opinion had moved decisively in the other direction, with 65 per cent believing that a market economy was 'wrong for Russia' and only 19 per cent believing it was 'right'.[39] And there was throughout a much higher level of support for a modest but assured income than for a higher but more speculative one, in line with the principles of market entrepreneurialism. In 1994, more than half those who were asked by the All-Russian Centre for the Study of Public Opinion favoured a 'modest but reliable income and certainty in the future' (54 per cent); they were more than twice as numerous as those who preferred to 'work hard and earn well but without any guarantees for the future'.[40]

There had certainly been important changes in the relationship between regime and society over the late communist and post-communist periods. But arguably, the crucial changes had taken place in the late Soviet years,

Table 12.2 Russian value systems, 1994

Personal values	*'Soviet' values*	*'Western' values*
1 Fairness	Atheism	Entrepreneurship
2 Personal dignity	Enthusiasm	Wealth
3 Love of labour	GUARANTEED SOCIAL RIGHTS	Efficiency
4 FEELING OF OBLIGATION	Precedence for state rights over individual rights	Inviolability of private property
5 EDUCATION	Struggle	Profitability of labour
6 HOSPITALITY	FEELING OF OBLIGATION	Free choice of opinions and behaviour
7 *Professionalism*	Patience	*Professionalism*
8 Equality under the law	Labour discipline	Non-interference
9 GUARANTEED SOCIAL RIGHTS	EDUCATION	Labour discipline
10 Unselfishness	HOSPITALITY	Guarantees of political rights

Source: Argumenty i fakty, 1994, 24, p. 2 (based on a March 1994 poll, n = 2,468, characteristics selected from a list of 37). Words in block capitals are in both the Personal and Soviet lists; words in italics are in the Personal and Western lists.

including the consolidation of fundamental freedoms in all-union legislation. There had, for instance, been a scheme for the privatisation of industry, approved by the Soviet Parliament in July 1991 on the basis of a law on property that had been approved the previous year.[41] The Soviet Parliament, in its final session, agreed a 'Declaration of the rights and freedoms of the individual' that guaranteed equality before the law, freedom of speech and assembly and the right to own property and to engage in business.[42] A law on the press of June 1990 abolished censorship and established the right of individuals as well as private and state bodies to publish their views in any form.[43] And there were fundamental changes in freedom of conscience, with a law of October 1990 that affirmed the right of parents to give their children a religious upbringing and of the churches themselves to take a part in public life, to found schools and universities and to issue their own publications.[44] Most fundamental of all was the end of the Communist Party's political monopoly in March 1990 and the enactment of legislation later in the year that allowed the formation of other parties and movements.[45] Russians, at this time, thought they were as 'free' as Americans (and 'freer' than American blacks); and more thought they were 'free' than were inclined to do so in post-communist Russia three years later.[46]

Where did Russians see themselves, in the post-communist world of the mid-1990s? Generally speaking, on their own: and certainly less closely associated with the European Union countries than the other post-Soviet states (though many of these countries' leaders, for instance in Poland and the Czech Republic, are keen to be seen primarily as part of the West). Russians, for instance, were much less likely to have a positive image of the European Union than Eastern Europe as a whole, although their views were generally positive or neutral rather than negative. Russians were also much more likely than other East Europeans to believe that the European Union was the main beneficiary in the relationship. Russians were more likely to believe that their future lay with the other members of the Commonwealth of Independent States, or with the USA, than with the European Union.[47] And did Russians think of themselves as Europeans? Less than a quarter did so 'often' or 'sometimes', in a 1995 survey; far more did so 'rarely' (18 per cent) or 'never' (58 per cent).[48]

CONTINUITIES AND CHANGE

It will be some time before we can begin to draw even preliminary conclusions about the processes of change that swept across communist Europe in the late 1980s. For some it was the end of a dream, even the end of history: 'Communism: World Tour, 1917–1989', as an inventive T-shirt described it. For others it was too soon to draw any conclusion of this kind. Were these, for a start, regimes that had anything to do with a doctrine that had conceived of a more equal society based on the self-emancipation of the working class, or with a movement that had campaigned for the vote for women, for the right to strike, for the defence of elected governments against Francoists in Spain, and for the abolition of apartheid in South Africa? Were the communist regimes of Eastern Europe not more adequately described as 'bastard socialism', by analogy with the 'bastard feudalism' of late medieval Europe: regimes that used the vocabulary of classical Marxism but were more decisively influenced by Lenin and an authoritarian, 'Asian' political tradition?

And as post-communist parties sought to join the Socialist International they had once despised, was this not, more than anything, a judgement on the attempt to impose centralised forms of organisation upon the workers' movements in other countries, from the '21 conditions' for affiliation to the Communist International in 1920 to the financial subventions that had sustained a small but loyal pro-Moscow following up to the 1980s? In this sense, it was less the 'end of history' than the resumption of a pattern of development that had been suspended but not extinguished in the years after 1917.

For the student of comparative political culture there are certainly several lessons to be learned from the transition. The first is to acknowledge that there was not a single 'transition' but a complex series of changes or indeed non-changes. Some of the communist governments of the late 1980s had been overthrown by force (as in Czechoslovakia and Romania); in other countries the regime itself initiated the process of change, and it took place through consultation (as in Hungary and Poland). In some a right-wing government took power and retained it (the Czech Republic); in others the former communists largely survived (in Romania, Serbia and Slovakia). In others still the former communists were re-elected (as in Hungary, Poland, Lithuania and Bulgaria). Three states collapsed (the USSR, Yugoslavia and Czechoslovakia); one disappeared altogether (the former GDR); but the others survived. And there was little sign, in the mid-1990s, that the remaining communist governments were about to fall: in Cuba, China, Vietnam, North Korea and Laos. It was clear, at least, that liberal capitalism was not the universal destination of all of these countries; and that this variety of outcomes had a lot to do with the variety of political cultures that underpinned them.

The process of change had in any case to be located in a longer time perspective and with a greater willingness to disaggregate the processes that were involved. In virtually all the communist-ruled nations the transfer of power took place over a lengthy period: there were contested elections from the late 1950s (in Poland), the parliaments themselves became more assertive, and courts became more independent. Within the ruling parties a pattern of personalist leadership was gradually replaced by the rule of a group of oligarchs; the single ruling party lost its unity and, by the late 1980s, had become a framework for the expression and (sometimes) resolution of divergent interests, and itself one among a number of legal parties and movements. All of these regimes were 'communist' up to the end of the

1980s, but it was a label that had lost most of its explanatory value as it extended across a variety of regimes from Ceauşescu's dictatorship and the bloodshed of Tiananmen Square to the flourishing alternative societies of Hungary and Poland. In just the same way the 'transition' was a varied one: not only across countries, but across the political and social system, as programmes of privatisation were launched and then suspended, as former communists returned to power, and as regional groupings like Visegrad emerged in place of the uniformity of the Warsaw Pact.

The end of communist rule was something less than a wholesale change of the political cultures of earlier years, and it had its own special characteristics (it was not, in particular, a recapitulation of the Mediterranean or the Latin American experience). Nor was it even clear that it could be called a 'transition', in the sense of a rapid and complete change of system. Rather, just as the Soviet system had a number of defining characteristics, the post-communist cultures had their own particular features: they included weak parties, strong executives, powerful and often criminal business elites, mass publics with very limited rights, a low sense of efficacy and a preference for economic rather than procedural forms of democracy, and a general lack of the civil society of public self-regulation that sustained liberal democracy in the capitalist West.

This was the end, at least in Europe, of the monopolistic rule of Marxist-Leninist parties; but for the societies concerned it was the beginning and not the end of a new form of history, the history of post-communism, a history that would be shaped by their political cultures as well as by the particular circumstances of their change of government. It was easy enough to replace the government, or the ruling party, or later the constitution (after the parliament, in Russia, had been bombed into submission). It was much less easy to develop a form of politics based upon the active involvement of ordinary citizens, one that respected their diversity of views and allowed them a continuing influence upon the decisions that shaped their lives: a change in the culture, and not simply in the regime. To Russians themselves, and to many outside observers, a change of this more fundamental kind was still some distance in the future.

And this was true even though Russians, from the late 1980s, were voting in elections that for the first time allowed them to choose their own parliament and, later, their own president. Russians were certainly willing to vote, and nearly 70 per cent did so in the presidential elections in June 1996. But a changing political culture involved more than an occasional choice of rulers: it required a change in the relationship between rulers and their societies. And it meant an electoral process with organised political parties, and some opportunity to consider their merits through an independent press. This was difficult to reconcile with a strongly presidentialist constitution, and with a government that was not formally accountable to elected representatives. And it was also difficult to reconcile with the strong support that was given to communist and extreme nationalist candidates in December 1995 and

June 1996, and with the heavy bias of the official media at this time which (for many) was reminiscent of the USSR – or even North Korea.[49] A change in political institutions, the Russian experience made clear, was relatively easy to accomplish; a change in the political culture would take much longer if it was going to take place at all.

NOTES

1 *Russian Review*, 1979, 38, pp. 184, 192, 195.
2 'Soviet Politics: From the Future to the Past?', in P. Cocks, R. V. Daniels and N. W. Heer (eds), *The Dynamics of Soviet Politics*, Cambridge, Mass., Harvard University Press, 1976, pp. 337, 340.
3 P. Dukes, *October and the World: Perspectives on the Russian Revolution*, London, Macmillan, 1979, pp. 6–12.
4 A. I. Solzhenitsyn, *The Mortal Danger*, London, Bodley Head, 1980, p. 8.
5 Erzsebet Szalai as quoted by Bill Lomax in G. Wightman (ed.), *Party Formation in East-Central Europe*, Aldershot, Elgar, 1995, p. 179.
6 P. N. Milyukov, *Russia Today and Tomorrow*, New York, Macmillan, 1922, p. 6.
7 S. White, *Political Culture and Soviet Politics*, London, Macmillan, 1979, p. 29. This is the fullest available account of Soviet political culture; see also A. Brown and J. Gray (eds), *Political Culture and Political Change in Communist States*, second edn, London, Macmillan, 1979; A. Brown (ed.), *Political Culture and Communist Studies*, London, Macmillan, 1985; and S. Welch, *The Concept of Political Culture*, London, Macmillan, 1993. The bearing of more recent survey research upon this older literature is considered in Frederic J. Fleron Jnr, 'Post-Soviet Political Culture in Russia: An Assessment of Recent Empirical Investigations', *Europe-Asia Studies*, 1996, 48.
8 P. Avrich, *Russian Rebels*, London, Allen Lane, 1973, pp. 257, 269–70.
9 A. Levin, *The Third Duma: Election and Profile*, Hamden, Conn., Archon Books, 1973, pp. 89–90.
10 For a good overview see J. Blum, *Lord and Peasant in Russia*, Princeton, Princeton University Press, 1961.
11 V. I. Lenin, *Polnoe sobranie sochinenii*, 55 vols, Moscow, Izdatel'stvo politicheskoi literatury, 1958–65, vol. 9, p. 357.
12 *Kommunisticheskaya partiya Sovetskogo Soyuza v rezolyutsiyakh i resheniyakh s"ezdov, konferentsii i plenumov TsK*, eighth edn, vol. 8, Moscow, Izdatel'stvo politicheskoi literatury, 1972, p. 242.
13 Alfred Meyer and Samuel Huntington respectively as quoted in White, *op. cit.*, p. 114.
14 S. G. Strumilin, *Byudzhet vremeni russkogo rabochego i krest'yanina*, Moscow–Leningrad, Voprosy truda, 1924, pp. 24–6; G. E. Zborovsky and G. P. Orlov, *Dosug: deistvitel'nost i illyuzii*, Sverdlovsk, Sredne-Ural'skoe knizhnoe izdatel'stvo, 1970, p. 220.
15 *Kommunist*, 1977, 4, p. 33.
16 A. Inkeles and R. A. Bauer, *The Soviet Citizen: Daily Life in a Totalitarian Society*, Cambridge, Mass., Harvard University Press, 1959.
17 *Ibid.*, pp. 236–42, 246–54, 397.
18 Z. Gitelman, *Soviet Immigrants in Israel*, New York, Institute for Jewish Policy Planning and Research, 1972, p. 30.
19 S. White, 'Continuity and Change in Soviet Political Culture: An Émigré Study', *Comparative Political Studies*, 1978, 11, pp. 384–7.
20 *Ibid.*, pp. 386–7.

21 *Izvestiya*, 17 August 1992, p. 3.
22 *Argumenty i fakty*, 1994, 23, p. 2.
23 *Obshchestvennye nauki i sovremennost'*, 1995, 1, pp. 64–5.
24 A. Grachev, *Dal'she bez menya. . . . Ukhod Prezidenta*, Moscow, Progress-Kul'tura, 1994, p. 9.
25 *Argumenty i fakty*, 1994, 29, p. 2.
26 *Izvestiya*, 20 August 1993, p. 4.
27 R. Rose, *New Russia Barometer IV: Survey Results*, Glasgow, Centre for the Study of Public Policy, 1995, pp. 42–3.
28 *Ekonomicheskie i sotsial'nye peremeny: monitoring obshchestvennogo mneniya*, 1995, 1, p. 10.
29 *Central and Eastern Eurobarometer*, 6, March 1996, Annex Figures 7 and 6.
30 *Izvestiya*, 20 September 1991, p. 3; V. G. Afanas'ev, *4-ya vlast' i 4 Genseka*, Moscow, Kedr, 1994, p. 99.
31 *Pravda*, 26 October 1991, p. 3.
32 *Izvestiya*, 31 August 1991, p. 3.
33 *Ibid.*, 21 October 1991, p. 3.
34 R. Rose and C. Haerpfer, *New Russia Barometer III: The Results*, Glasgow, Centre for the Study of Public Policy, 1994, p. 41.
35 *Moskovskaya pravda*, 20 July 1994, p. 3.
36 Rose and Haerpfer, *New Russia Barometer III*, p. 29.
37 I. Boeva and V. Shironin, *Russians between State and Market: The Generations Compared*, Glasgow, Centre for the Study of Public Policy, 1992, pp. 30–1.
38 Rose and Haerpfer, *New Russia Barometer III*, p. 23.
39 *Central and Eastern Eurobarometer*, 5, Annex Figure 4.
40 *Ekonomicheskie i sotsial'nye peremeny*, 1995, 1, p. 9.
41 *Vedomosti S'ezda narodnykh deputatov SSSR i Verkhovnogo Soveta SSSR*, 1991, 32, art. 904; and 1990, 11, art. 164.
42 *Ibid.*, 1991, 37, art. 1083.
43 *Ibid.*, 1990, 26, art. 492.
44 *Ibid.*, 1990, 41, art. 813.
45 *Ibid.*, 1990, 42, art. 840.
46 See J. L. Gibson, 'Perceived Political Freedom in the Soviet Union', *Journal of Politics*, 1993, 55; *Ekonomicheskie i sotsial'nye peremeny*, 1995, 1, p. 15.
47 *Central and Eastern Eurobarometer*, 5, Annex Figures 13, 14, 8.
48 Rose, *New Russia Barometer IV*, p. 67.
49 The comparison with North Korea is made by *Moskovskii komsomolets* journalist Alexander Minkin in the *Guardian*, 1 July 1996, section 2, p. 15.

13 Scandinavia

Stein Ugelvik Larsen and Ingrid Louise Ugelvik

INTRODUCTION

Four small, but highly affluent, countries (Denmark, Finland, Norway, and Sweden) comprise Scandinavia ('Norden').[1] With the exception of the Eastern borders connected to Russia (Finland and a small strip of Norway), only a part of Denmark (South Jutland) is geographically joined to the Continent. Scandinavia's small size coupled with its peripheral position has contributed to internal national unity and homogeneity, though at times it has also encouraged a temptation for inter-Scandinavian, dynastic expansionism and different phases of national 'greatness' extending beyond Scandinavia. However, in the longer run, a precarious 'balance of nations' seems to have prevented merger into larger units.

In this chapter we shall not discuss particular aspects of the development of Scandinavian culture and identity by focusing in detail on national historical and institutional traits. Today there is such a widely shared everyday culture within the Scandinavian countries, that emphasis on national differences often boils down to trivialities. Instead we shall outline the process leading towards what is called the 'Nordic Model' – a system which many, especially on the moderate left, have seen as a highly desirable model of cultural and political arrangements,[2] though there are now growing doubts about its future viability.

STAGES OF STATE AND NATION BUILDING

The Vikings dominated parts of northern France, England/Scotland and Ireland from early ninth century AD until the Norman invasion. After the Viking period, the Norwegian expansion westward included the more remote islands in the Atlantic. At the same time, Danish interests turned eastwards along the German coast; although the conquests did not last long, Denmark gained prominence when dynastic intermarriages resulted in a three-state union with Norway and Sweden in 1389. Although Sweden later broke away, the Danes dominated the Norwegian union, which lasted from 1520 until 1814. Sweden's 'greatness' came after the Reformation and the installation of absolutism, which gave the king an exceptional new economic power and legitimacy for expansionism. This was also the period of the great religious and dynastic wars in Europe, which helped Swedish expansionism. But as other powers, including Russia, consolidated their forces, the Swedish realm crumbled rapidly. The last period of Swedish 'greatness' came in 1814–1905, after Norway was handed over as compensation for Sweden's participating in the final victories against Napoleon.

By 1920 the internal and external borders of Scandinavia were 'frozen', as were most of the institutional and political structures. Some small territorial changes came as the result of conflicts after the world wars on the borders of Finland and Denmark, but in general the Scandinavian states covered much of the same core territories as they comprised in the Middle Ages. Why did this happen? And why did not the Baltic and Hanseatic territories become parts of Scandinavia, when they at times were greatly interwoven into the commercial and strategic dynamics of the north?

These questions can to some extent be answered by the stages of development theory, especially its important revision by Stein Rokkan.[3] In an early phase of known history, the Scandinavian countries were 'penetrated' and 'standardised' (strong institutions and centralisation of rule) and experienced eras of 'greatness'. This early state building was also decisive for keeping alive traditions of identity when some of the countries experienced centuries of domination through political unions. This also proved to be a crucial force behind the internal 'balance' between them.[4] But why did they achieve such an early identity as states and nations, a question which is not resolved by the stage model?

Before any nation-building process can take place, there must exist some *idea* of which territory and what people constitute its basic core. In the Scandinavian countries the concepts of 'core peoples and territory' can be traced back to the beginning of written history. These demonstrate the early and explicit awareness of ethnic nationality, even though cultural distinctions were not great, not least because the Scandinavian languages were very similar at that time. Important presuppositions for this identity were the natural geographical borders or barriers. Even if the northern and eastern borders were originally very diffuse, geography in general presented hindrances to the creation of wider geopolitical entities.[5]

State- and nation-building theory often see the stage of 'standardisation' as the phase in which unifying cultural standards are imposed from above on the subjects by the political centre (frequently stressing the crucial role of the rise of capitalism in demanding a standardised culture).[6] However, at the turn of the nineteenth century the Scandinavian countries – perhaps with the exception of Denmark – were largely 'underdeveloped' rural societies. Moreover, the Scandinavian Romantic nationalism which began at the turn of the century was not created from above by the monarchies and elites, with the intent of reinforcing their power. It came more from below – from intellectuals tracing their 'national' roots.[7] In Scandinavia they found it in the great deeds of the early state-building period. Instead of becoming a vehicle for inter-Scandinavian integration, it reinforced the ideas of separateness (though the idea of 'Scandinavism' grew in strength at times, particularly when the Prussians and the Russians gained strength and forced the last absolutist kings to abandon their claims of territory outside their 'traditional' cores).[8]

Norway

Nationalism in the nineteenth century was very much characterised by its emancipation from Swedish influence.[9] The effort of cultural liberation from the Danish language, by reconstructing and 'normalising' a separate Norwegian language, was also taken up as a particularly important task. Politically, Norway's 1814 Constitution was exceptionally liberal and democratic. Norwegian nationalism was thus filled with anti-themes (anti-Danish and anti-Swedish) and progressive themes of 'recovery' and liberalisation. With the peaceful dissolution of the union with Sweden in 1905 and the consolidation of the new state, Norwegian nationalism had 'fulfilled its destiny'.[10] Subsequently, nationalism did not become the major theme in fighting communism and radical socialism in the inter-war years, which it did in some European countries – in part a reflection of the moderation of the growing force of Norwegian social democracy. It was therefore difficult for a Norwegian brand of fascism or Nazism to graft itself onto indigenous nationalist roots.

Denmark

Here nationalism in the nineteenth century was very much related to conflicts over the German-dominated provinces of Holstein and Schleswig. Before 1814 Denmark was an important power in Europe (with minor colonies in West Indies, India and West Africa). The loss of Norway was an indisputable fact, and therefore the control of the northern German territories became a vital issue in Danish politics. Together with nationalist feelings against the Germans, a form of Danish liberalism arose which stressed local autonomy and individual freedom.[11] The National-Liberal Party enacted a new anti-absolutist Constitution in 1849, and was also behind the policy of extending full Danish political control over Schleswig whilst abandoning Holstein. But following two wars (1848–50 and 1863–4) and hectic international diplomacy, Denmark lost Schleswig (South Jutland) to the emerging German Reich – a loss which for a time weakened the liberal-democratic movement. After the German surrender in the First World War, a plebiscite returned the northern part, and it was here that the DNSAP (Danish National Socialist Workers' Party) had its greatest support in the 1930s, though this reflected local economic hardship more than a radically different sub-culture.[12]

Finland

In 1809 Finland was created as a grand duchy within the Russian Empire, though it retained the relatively liberal Constitution inherited from the former union with Sweden and initially had considerable political autonomy. Risto Alapuro has characterised the specific content of Finnish nationalism (*Fennomani*) as 'state nationalism, or a territorial-civic conception of a nation'.[13] The upper classes of Finland, who were of Swedish-speaking origin, adapted the Finnish language, but instead of creating a liberal democratic movement, they confined themselves to a paternalistic nationalism in order to create a solid, integrated defence against the 'Russification' which gathered force in the 1890s. In particular, they did not seek to encourage true participation among the peasant population, though they could use a populist language of mobilisation. When major class and democratic issues came to the surface, especially after the breakdown of the Russian Empire in 1917, the nationalist elite over-reacted and a bloody civil war and period of terror ensued.[14] However, Finnish nationalism did serve to underline the importance of a break with both Sweden and Russia, and the desire to possess the Karelian lands, which were central to nineteenth-century mythology.[15] In the inter-war era, pan-Finnish sentiments aiming for a 'Greater Finland' incorporating significant eastern territories grew rapidly: the right wing and nationalistic Academic Karelia Society became perhaps its most typical exponent.[16] However, at the end of the Second World War, border revision and flight meant that over 400,000 Finns moved from the Soviet side: thus Finland even today has 'unfulfilled' nationalist aspirations on its eastern border (a poll in the 1990s disclosed that 60 per cent of the Finnish population believed that the government should take up the question of the territories ceded after 1944).

Sweden

After the 'decline of greatness', finally culminating in the loss of Finland in 1809, the national project emerged especially in what Bo Stråth has called a romantic 'program for the revitalisation of the reduced nation'.[17] The Swedes did not, however, engage in a movement of revenge or irredentism towards Russia. Neither did the wars and rivalry with Denmark cause any post-1814 form of antagonism. The conservatives in Sweden did hope to strengthen control over Norway, but the growing numbers of liberals and the left were inclined to leave Norway autonomous. Thus when the union broke up on Norwegian initiative in 1905, it was hard to find support for an anti-Norway campaign outside the conservative camp.[18] Whereas in Finland nationalism developed a strong populism directed at an outside enemy, in Sweden it was more focused on the theme of the *folkhemmet* ('home for the people') – initially a conservative concept which in the twentieth century was taken over by the Social Democrats and developed into an all-encompassing notion of unity of class and people. *Folkhemmet's* roots lay in the myths surrounding the freeholder peasants in Swedish history. This was also the case in the other Scandinavian countries, but in Sweden the link between the 'free farmer' and the royal protector served to prevent real democratic liberalism evolving. Thus Swedish nationalism did not produce the alliance between the liberal, urban elites and broad-based organisations in the country, as examples demonstrate happened in Denmark in the 1840s and in Norway after the 1860s.

Summing up this overview of nationalism, we may simplify it in the following way:

Nationalism from above, with weak liberalism

Finland   with emphasis on national unity as defence of the state against outside (Russian) pressure.

Sweden   with emphasis on national unity as a powerful link between ruler and the ruled for an organic evolution for the future.

Nationalism from below, allied with liberalism

Denmark   with emphasis on constitutional liberties and local autonomy, and as defence against an outside enemy (Germany).

Norway   with emphasis on the extensions of political liberties enacted in the 1814 Constitution, and with a broad mobilisation against an outside enemy (Sweden, though later Germany loomed large and reinforced tensions with Sweden after 1939, when Norway was occupied and Sweden remained neutral).[19]

The fate of liberalism in the twentieth century was thus tied to the way nationalism played its role in the Scandinavian states in the nineteenth century.

Finland   Here liberalism lost a role when paternalistic policies united the Fennomani movement, and was left very little room in the polarised politics after the Civil War in 1918.

Sweden   Here liberalism got its chance when the decaying conservative regime came under general pressure for reforms in the late nineteenth century, and liberalism more than social democracy was successful in making Sweden a democracy in the first decades after 1900.

Denmark After defeat in the war over the southern borders, liberalism experienced several decades of decay before it again gained strength when full democratisation was on the international agenda. Then it was in the forefront and was ahead of the Social Democratic breakthrough.

Norway Here liberalism was the leading force in the introduction of the democratic system and the victorious fight for independence. It continued to play the role of mediator in the political system when social democracy became the main new actor in politics.

The growth and distinctiveness of the different forms of Scandinavian nationalism explains to a large extent the political landscape of today's culture and identity.[20] However, so far we have focused on the thousand-year-old uniqueness of the concept of the state and the development of the Nordic 'nationalistic mentalities' in the nineteenth century. But what about the converging trends which help explain why Scandinavia is now often referred to as comprising one single model?

SCANDINAVIAN UNIQUENESS AND THE 'NORDIC MODEL'

The 'Nordic' or 'Scandinavian model' (also commonly referred to as the 'middle way')[21] is presented as an economically well-developed democracy, with a low temperature of conflicts, with sound integration of interests, with uniform standards of welfare and a high degree of socio-economic equality.[22] When emphasis is laid on explaining the long rule of Social Democratic parties, the Nordic countries are also described as a total integration of state, nation and class.

Talk of a 'model' is actually rather loose. In fact, there seem to be two ways of talking about a 'Nordic model'. The most simplistic approach is to make a 'comparative table' where one lists similarities and differences between the Scandinavian and other countries on a selected list of items.[23] The other way is to try to explain the coincidence of how some factors contributed to the Scandinavian convergence.

This 'list model' covers all the Scandinavian countries, though with some variations in timing and provision.[24] For instance, the 'lead' was taken by Sweden which, in 1945, had not suffered wartime destruction and was located close to the European post-war market with its immense demand for consumption and reconstruction, stimulated by Marshall Aid. And Finland has lagged farthest behind, partly because of heavy repair payments and economic constraints after 1945. The most typical 'list model' reads as follows: the Scandinavian states are small, characterised by high-growth and open economies, low unemployment, and are run by strong (in terms of competence, in relative proportion of GNP spent, and in numbers of staff) centralised states controlled by Social Democratic parties. The main political issues are solved in corporatist negotiations between the main interest organisations and the government, and are rarely contested by parliament and society. The social security system is based on universalistic principles giving high standards of living to everyone, including the less able members of society. The political and economic elites have thus accepted high levels of taxation and discriminatory rules of redistribution regionally and according to individual needs. The overall cultural backing of this Scandinavian model is laid down in moral principles of fairness, equality and solidarity.

But this 'list model' does not fully explain why the Nordic countries took a route different from their European neighbours. Let us try to give a very brief presentation of the combined development of economy and politics during the last centuries in the development of the 'Nordic model' outlined above with regard to: (a) how the historical roots determined the solutions of the great economic, political and social confrontations in the inter-war years; and (b) how these solutions determined the construction of the contemporary Nordic welfare states.

The main explanation for the transformation of medieval European societies into modern capitalist economies has focused on the transformation of farming from the stage of feudal dependency. In his classic work, Barrington Moore has particularly stressed the need to 'destroy' the peasantry, both as an economic and a political force, as a necessary pre-condition for the democratic path. But this was not the case in Scandinavia.[25] The large literature on the transformation of Scandinavian farming emphasises the following characteristics compared to the Continent, and particularly compared to Eastern Europe (and the Latin world). The farms were small and scattered, and the conditions for large interconnected land-holdings were absent. Thus feudalism was weak (outside Jutland and Southern Sweden), though the majority of the farmers were dependent leaseholders. During the Reformation (1520–35) the king turned Church property into royal property, but later the Nordic kings sold land to peasants in order to finance the absolutist state. As part of the process of power concentration the monarchy ended the former rights of the nobility (hereditary rights, tax exemption, etc.) thus weakening their economic position, which forced or at least tempted many of them to sell their property to their tenants.

There was some variation in the timing and nature of these developments, but the outcome was broadly similar.[26] The farming communities were broken up into scattered, individualised units which changed from partial subsistence farming to commercialised farming dependent on the market. This process mainly produced small farmers living in more or less equal economic and social conditions. This left these small farmers open to market forces; favourable in upward cycles, but difficult in downward ones. At the same time, the growth in population during the nineteenth century did not mean breaking up farms into ever-smaller units: some of the new population went into cities, helping industrial growth, or was attracted to the USA.[27] The basic point is that the Scandinavian societies were thus 'opened' for economic and political mobilisation on a more egalitarian and democratic basis than elsewhere in Europe when industrialisation took off. The Scandinavian countries were underdeveloped in the structural economic sense, as predominantly rural economies, but strongly mentally prepared after the great freeholder movement and through the trust they had in their own national 'destinies'.

Industrialisation came late (Sweden in 1900 still was less industrialised than Britain 100 years earlier).[28] But it happened rapidly, and largely within a milieu of 'rural traditions'.[29] The new industrial workers were 'close' to their background in the sense of not having been born in class-based, densely populated industrial societies, as in some urban areas of the United Kingdom. In Scandinavia, early industrialisation was mostly based on small urban enterprises, particularly in Denmark. In the other countries, industrialisation often grew up outside the urban areas: close to mines, saw mills, pulp industries, dairies, fish-drying plants, etc. Thus both the workers and the entrepreneurs were living in milieus which did not produce the extreme form of class antagonism and rural–urban cleavages often found in other industrialising countries. However, the delayed but rapid industrialisation produced a strong sense of radicalisation within the working class. This politicisation came as a result both of the tensions between owners and workers, and from the former stimulus of farmers' feelings of individual freedom. Thus the political parties founded by the workers' organisations formulated radical principles of social revolution in the early years of this century. The Russian Revolution in 1917 also had a radical impact on both the trade unions and the workers' political parties.

Thus a strong 'participatory movement' was created with serious 'redistributive claims'. Initially, it was not clear whether the state and civil society would be able to channel the pressures into stable and workable solutions, or whether the farming freeholder spirits would encourage polarisation. But gradually the political interests of the farmers and the workers were institutionalised in the party system, and their economic interests were institutionalised in large-scale formal and informal agreements on conflict management. These mechanisms, developed during the inter-war years and fully implemented after the Second World War, had unique Scandinavian origins and features.

The Scandinavian countries were among the first European states to introduce a wide extension of the suffrage and liberal rules for the political game. Thus liberal, parliamentary rule preceded, or was introduced simultaneously with, large-scale industrialisation. It was widely supported by the independent peasantry, the liberal sections of the urban bourgeoisie and the emerging working class. When universal suffrage was introduced, all the Scandinavian countries adopted the system of proportional representation as a broad compromise preventing the effects of 'the winner takes all'. Thus the rapidly declining agricultural population, the weakened conservative and liberal forces, and the fast-growing industrial working class, got their 'fair share' of political influence.

Around 1920, the typical 'Nordic five-party model' appeared and was 'frozen' as a distinctive feature. In the entire period from 1920 until the 1980s this 'model' persisted, even though there were major shifts in occupational structure and increasing 'floating votes' between the parties. The system of two working-class parties, the Communist Party and the Social Democrats, one distinct farmers' party and two of the non-socialist groupings, the Conservatives and the Liberals, was to dominate the political arena for a very long period of time.[30] The most exceptional aspect of this 'frozen position' is perhaps the strength of the Scandinavian farmers' parties. By the 1990s, the percentage of farmers in all the Scandinavian countries had dropped to 2 to 3 per cent of the workforce, but the farmers' parties still get between 7 and 25 per cent of the vote. This stability may be seen as a reflection of the historical 'visions' of the role of the farmers, but the 'frozen stability' may also serve some function in guaranteeing that the traditional interests of all classes will be taken care of. After the Second World War the Norwegian and the Swedish farmers' parties changed their names to 'centre parties'. (It is only the Finnish farmers' party, the Agrarian Party, which has kept its 'occupational' name. The Danish party is still called 'Venstre', which means 'left', i.e. Liberal.)

This party division has both prevented a pure middle-class politics (the large farmers' parties took care of the producers as well as the consumers of agricultural products), and has helped to build bridges between the 'socialist' and the 'non-socialist' camps. However, such 'class compromises' were prevalent even before the farmers' parties gained parliamentary strength. In Sweden and in Denmark, the Liberal parties went into government coalitions with the Social Democrats at a very early stage, especially when the Social Democrats started to make their great electoral gains after the First World War. Moderation and compromise were therefore around before the Great Depression of 1929 – a point which has been stressed insufficiently by most commentators.[31] On the other hand, in Finland and Norway, the last industrialisers, there was a much stronger atmosphere of antagonism. The Finnish Social Democratic Party was not regarded as 'clean' after the Civil War until 1938, and the Norwegian Social Democratic Party has never gone into a government coalition with other parties, left or right.

In all four Scandinavian countries, however, Green–Red (farmer–socialist) compromise agreements were reached in the crisis years of the 1930s. The unique Scandinavian commitment to using Keynesian demand stimulus through public budgets was accepted in principle by concrete contracts between the leaders of the farmers' and the Social Democratic parties. The great symbolic value of these agreements had lasting effects also for the post-war years and diffused to the other parties outside the communist circle. It was an expression of the acceptance of the role of the state as an active participant in the capitalist market, not only as a guardian of the system, or as a promoter of industrial projects or public infrastructures.

The inter-war years saw other compromises of even greater importance. In negotiations between representatives of workers, employers and the state, and gradually accepted by the parliaments, several law-binding enactments were reached where the state took on responsibility for accident insurance, organising public employment offices, adapting provisions for old age pensions, etc. The role of the state thus increased both as an effect of the 'regulative necessity' of the First World War and of the economic fluctuations in the period before the Second World War. State monopolies were founded and comprehensive trade regulation laws in the fishing economy, in the dairy industry, in banking, etc., were enacted by non-socialist governments. Perhaps most notably, in Norway in 1935 the 'Constitution on negotiations for tariffs' between the national leaders of labour unions and business organisations was signed, and indicated that perhaps the most important non-public binding regulation for wage policies ever had been agreed upon.[32] Thus a vital institutional means for compromise was created where 'negotiation' in concert could replace 'open conflict' between the main actors in the labour market. Thus when Hitler started the Second World War, the foundations were already laid for the basic features of the 'Scandinavian model'.

THE SECOND WORLD WAR AND ITS EFFECTS ON POLITICAL INTEGRATION

Finland

The war came first to Finland when the Soviet Union in 1939 demanded territorial control over strategic military positions and an extension of its boundaries. The Finns refused, and waged a brave but hopeless resistance. After the Nazi invasion of the USSR, the Finns re-opened hostilities. They hoped that the Allies would see this as simply an effort to regain lost territories rather than a willing alliance with Germany. However, in September 1944 Finland accepted a treaty of capitulation with the Soviet Union. The results of the 1939–40 war were re-confirmed, the Finns were asked to help rid the USSR of Germans, and were required to pay economic compensation. The result of these wars was 60,000 men lost and 50,000 disabled; there were also 400,000 displaced Karelian Finns, who were forced from their homes by the new frontiers. These wars had an enormous impact on Finnish politics and society. Through a treaty in 1948 Finland escaped the fate of the Central and Eastern states, which were forced into communist dictatorships. But it was cut off from Western influence and for long dominated by Soviet influence. The hardships of war, the losses and the degradation through defeat 'melted' the polarised Finnish society into a more coherent one, different from the polarised culture after the Civil War. The combined efforts at recovery after 1944 also contributed to more internal solidarity; questions of nationalism were left out of politics and a corporative welfare agenda rose to the head of the political agenda.

Norway

This was the other country which suffered badly due to Hitler's war. Allied military expeditions failed and the Norwegians could not stand up against the Blitzkrieg of the Germans in 1940. The notorious Vidkun Quisling carried out a coup d'état on the day of the German invasion, but was initially forced to withdraw. He was later entrusted with control of a National Socialist Government, and ruled Norway until 8 May 1945 under German tutelage and bayonets. As well as losses through death and disablement, Norway suffered badly through the harsh living conditions, by being cut off from normal trade, by feeding the huge German army, and through Gestapo and general control. However, out of the resistance and the powerful mass mobilisations of opinion against the regime, there grew a widespread feeling of cooperation and solidarity. The war, therefore, meant an enormous spiritual, emotional aspiration which had long-term effect in many directions: it stimulated true national identity against the perversion of Quisling's excessive version, and focused on the German occupants. A widespread resentment against a 'strong' Germany in Europe became engrained in Norwegian minds. It also fostered a deep understanding of the value of cooperation and 'staying togetherness' which produced a deep and lasting consensus in the post-war years.

Denmark

Denmark was overrun in one day and almost without military resistance. The government and the king had no opportunity to flee (as they did in Norway) and Denmark experienced more or less 'normal conditions' during the first three years of the war. However, although political relationships with the Germans were cordial (the Danish government was at times extraordinarily cooperative towards German interests), the situation deteriorated and in 1943 the Germans declared a state of emergency which lasted until the liberation in 1945. This action was provoked by widespread demonstrations. The Danes had become tired of the 'giving in policy' (*Eftergivenhets-politikken*), and the tide of the war had firmly turned against Hitler. The Danish resistance during 1943 was also organised under one united leadership, in contact with the Allies in London. These events brought the Danes together across class lines and political barriers, and the experiences of war and resistance had the same 'welding effects' as in

Norway – though the prior compromises of the Danish political class left wounds which threatened this unity.

Sweden

Although 'neutral', Sweden let German troops and goods pass through her territory; indeed, up to 1943 Germany was her most important export country. But Sweden did allow Allied intelligence to operate more or less freely, and after 1943 Sweden also gave the Norwegian refugees opportunity and resources to set up police battalions which by the end of the war had almost full military capability as infantry troops. Pressures both from the outside by the Allies and from within the Swedish opposition circles gradually forced the government (and the king) to reverse concessions given to the Germans. However, this delicate balance reflected Sweden's traditional position of neutrality towards the great powers in international politics, and more opportunistic aims. Certainly Sweden experienced prosperous economic conditions during the war, held normal elections in 1940 and in 1944, and was ready to enter the post-war period with far fewer restrictions and handicaps than were imposed on the other three Scandinavian countries.

For all four countries, no other period of the twentieth century made so much impact as the five years of the Second World War. It shaped their 'mental' destiny and it laid the foundations for the enormous economic growth processes which, after a brief period of reconstruction, soon were to flower at an impressive speed. Before we return to analyse how the 'Scandinavian model' came out of these years of growth, we shall give a condensed view of some ideas of the foundations of Scandinavian economic development from an agriculture-based economy to a full scale industrial, or post-industrial economy under a system of a so called 'mixed economy'. This is an essential aspect in understanding the political culture of today.

THE SCANDINAVIAN WAY OF ECONOMIC MODERNISATION AND ITS POLITICAL IMPLICATIONS

The historical development of norms does not in itself explain the high level of economic growth necessary to be able to fulfil expectations of redistribution and individual welfare. Indeed, there is a strong tendency for discussion of the 'Nordic model' to be based on the 'output' side rather than the 'input' side (how the wealth is produced).

The birth of modern capitalism happened in the core nations of Protestant, north-western Europe in the fifteenth–sixteenth centuries, at a time when the Scandinavian economies were underdeveloped rural economies, with some merchant capitalist groups located in the towns. The rank order of states from 'core nations' to 'economic peripheries' in the world capitalist system seems to be so definite that only very few of the underdeveloped economies ever seem to be able to climb up the ladder. However, the Scandinavian states moved during the nineteenth century through the 'periphery position', entered the 'semi-periphery' and are today part of the 'core'. Why did this happen?

In an overview of the history of the Scandinavian economies, Lars Mjøset has offered an explanation of how the small and open Scandinavian economies in the middle of the nineteenth century were able in the course of their development to avoid the 'trap' of persistent underdevelopment.[33] He refers to the important point that trade had gone on for more than a thousand years, with its basis in the export of raw materials like timber, and primary products from farming, such as meat, wool, fish and butter. Even if there was a concentration of ownership dominating parts of this trade, it was never totally controlled either by foreign capitalists like the Hansa (or later the Dutch and the British), or by the Scandinavian gentry, the Catholic Church or the Crown. When the freeholders' movement took off, the production of export goods from farming was spread among many small units. The economies of Scandinavian countries, therefore, were characterised by this precarious balance: small states, small and scattered towns, many small producers and production and export of goods that gradually came to be in high demand, and which had easy access to the central core of the European industrialising countries, particularly Britain.

The structure of ownership and the fortunate location are, therefore, vital to understanding the growth potential. But the type of goods produced and the internal opening of exchange markets also helped prevent the stagnation typical of Third World dependent economies today. Timber exports illustrate the point well. There were 'forward linkages', namely the farmers (and individual non-farming entrepreneurs) who constructed saw mills and converted raw timber into processed boards and logs, etc., when the state tried by law to prevent the export of raw timber. There were also 'backward linkages', namely expertise in sawing, so that the production of saw mill machinery was developed, bringing a 'spill-over' effect to people other than the farmers cutting and transporting timber. Similar 'linkages' can be found elsewhere, for example where Danish food exports became 'linked forward' in processing better and alternative dairy products or meat products through strong local organisations, which also provided the foundation for 'backward linkages' in terms of stimulating innovations and production of new tools and forms of cultivation.

During the last decades of the nineteenth and the first decades of the twentieth century, industrialisation created much the same difficulties as elsewhere in the Western industrialised world: overproduction, economic misery among poorly paid labourers, etc. But industrialisation also produced labour and industrial organisations, political parties, together with public agencies, providing rules of regulation and initiatives, meeting the challenges created by new circumstances. Earlier we briefly mentioned how the 'rural linkage' was important in easing off some of the contradictions arising from the clash between labour and capital. But it was not automatic that these conditions would have lasting effects when new generations of workers entered the factories and new entrepreneurs came on the scene from within Scandinavia or from outside. The role of the state in industrial relations, and the setting of the political agenda during the inter-war years was of special importance for our understanding of how the Scandinavian countries found their own special route. Now the industrial conditions were 'mature'; the Scandinavian economies were firmly integrated within international capitalism and many of the genuine 'take-off' conditions were absent.

It is in this crucial period of Scandinavian history – the inter-war crises – that the foundations for the economic prosperity of the post-1945 growth were laid and the large-scale institutionalisation of the 'Scandinavian model' was framed. In addition to the economic and industrial conditions, it rested on two pillars already mentioned: class cooperation and political alliances. In most of Europe, class conflicts were severe and violent and few bridges were built across class lines. They were instead often made stiffer in forms of *lagers* (camps) as in Austria, as vertical pillars (*verzuilung*) as in the Netherlands, and with antagonistic fractionalism among the communist and socialist working class all over Continental Europe, making many of them extremely vulnerable to fascism. Thus, whereas the crises of the inter-war period widened the splits in the Continental societies, they stimulated cooperation and furthered consensus in the Scandinavian societies.[34]

Affluence came soon after the first few years of 'controlled' economy following 1945; there seemed to be no end to growth.[35] This provided a genuine opportunity for introducing the Nordic welfare state model. In an accelerating tempo, schemes of public spending were introduced and voted through by parliaments – with the Social Democratic Party often in the lead. Starting with Sweden, the richest country, the messages diffused quickly through the Scandinavian policy arenas and the so-called 'universalistic principles' of welfare were gradually passed as laws making heavy demands on public budgets.[36] There was enough income through taxes and duties to drop qualifications of need, so everybody would get the same support independent of wealth and income. It was a wonderful period and it received full agreement from almost all political groupings. Even if the Conservative (and later the Progressive) parties did resist in the beginning, they were persuaded to support most measures, fearing that they might be punished in the next election.

The Scandinavian welfare model was not simply a question of wealth: other richer countries, like the USA or Switzerland, had very different systems. Political culture was crucial to its development. But without doubt (and usually not explicitly mentioned) a basic foundation for the model was wealth. This has caused increasing problems since the 1970s, as growth has slowed to the point of stagnation at times. A failure to appreciate the economic foundation of welfare states is a major reason why some Scandinavians today cannot 'understand' or accept that there are limits to welfare spending, and why jobs are not given to the unemployed. Others have questioned whether Scandinavia's high taxation should be continued. Indeed, during the 1970s, a populist Progress Party grew up in both Denmark and Norway, with the former initially attracting a notable minority following under the leadership of Mogens Glistrup (it won 16 per cent in 1973, and 9 per cent in 1988). During 1991 these parties found a notable sibling in Sweden when New Democracy broke into parliament. In general, these parties have not made a major or lasting parliamentary break-through, but they have shown a notable potential for a new type of party. In particular, they have sought to combine anti-big-government economics, a form of nationalist, even racist, politics, and charismatic leadership. Immigration has not been as serious an issue as in some European countries, like France and Germany, but these parties have shown an ominous ability to tap an increasingly dealigned electorate (in 1988, 50 per cent of Danish Progress Party voters came from the working class – virtually the same proportion as for the Social Democrats).[37]

More generally, there have been growing doubts about whether the Scandinavian model can persist in a world of apparently increasing economic and cultural globalisation. Many now ponder what will happen to the 'Nordic model' in the face of the rise of the new supra-national system of the European Union. The 'Nordic model' was designed as an instrument to carry originally underdeveloped Scandinavian countries through the challenges of becoming fully modernised industrialised nations in the world economy. It proved efficient for that purpose, but how will it meet the challenges for the future?

THE INCORPORATION OF SCANDINAVIA INTO EUROPE? HISTORICAL-CULTURAL CLEAVAGES AND THEIR PERSISTENCE IN THE 1990s

Nordic cooperation has been a popular topic in Scandinavia since the break up of the Norwegian–Swedish union in 1905. Confronted with the great international crises early in the twentieth century, particularly the First World War, the Scandinavian countries formulated their basic principles of 'neutrality' – i.e. to stay 'outside' the great power conflicts while trading with them and trying to give none of them particular favours. As it turned out, this was an extremely delicate position. On the one hand, they put their trust after 1919 in the League of Nations (but were unwilling to fulfil completely the rules of sanctions formulated by the League) and searched for 'bilateral treaties' with the great powers and multilateral treaties with the smaller states. On the other hand, they started to cooperate more closely among themselves in several arenas as Scandinavian partners, minimising minor differences and looking for a coordination of interests when serious issues of international conflicts threatened Europe and the world. But 'neutrality' meant that they did not sign any security alliances whereby attack on one

Scandinavian country would automatically involve the others. Thus the attack on Finland in 1939 produced no Scandinavian military involvement against the Soviet Union, and both Sweden and Finland remained passive when Germany occupied Denmark and Norway in 1940.

After the Second World War, there was much talk about forming a greater Nordic Union, an economic union (NORDØK), a military alliance, and various proposals for some sort of political confederation. These resulted only in the setting up of the Nordic Council (1953) and the Nordic Council of Ministers, which is a very loose and low-competence organisation, serving mainly as a forum for debate and exchange of views among politicians, with different administrative agencies. One reason for not being able to establish more binding cooperation on broad issues has to do with the alliance systems: Sweden retained its 'neutral' status, whereas Denmark and Norway after 1949 became very committed members of the NATO alliance, and Finland after 1948 was bound to listen to Moscow on important international issues through the imposed treaty of 'Friendship and Negotiation'. However, Denmark, Norway and Sweden agreed to join EFTA after 1960 as a first step to a more binding economic multilateral organisation, transcending national boundaries and competence.

The next main development in this area came when France accepted widening the membership base of the EEC outside the six founding states. Sweden decided to remain 'neutral' but Denmark and Norway started their negotiations to become members. The issue was taken to the people in referenda during 1972, but whereas Denmark voted in favour (63.7 to 36.3 per cent), Norway voted against (53.5 to 46.5 per cent). Thus Scandinavia was really split, with commitments in different directions. This included divisions within and among the major parties on the issue.

Since 1989 much has changed in Europe, at least in terms of perspectives for the future. The EU has become more ambitious: its goal is a greater Europe, both geographically and in terms of increased economic and political integration. Thus all the three Scandinavian non-members (excluding Iceland) negotiated for membership, since Finland had by then achieved complete autonomy in her foreign policy. In referenda held during 1994, Finland and Sweden voted in favour (56.9 to 43.1 and 52.3 to 47.7 per cent respectively), but Norwegian voters again refused to 'sell out national sovereignty' (52.2 to 48.8 per cent). Before these referenda Denmark had demonstrated doubts as regards the effects and commitments with regards to the Maastricht Treaty (1992). In a referendum during 1992 the voters said 'No' to the ratification of the treaty (50.7 to 49.3 per cent). However, the mainstream politicians managed to win the Danes over – and a new referendum in 1993 gave a positive result, confirming that the 'non-loyal' Danes still wanted to stay within the European Union (56.7 to 43.3 per cent).[38]

The results of these referenda demonstrate the negative attitudes among Norwegian voters towards integration into the European Union, and the reluctance of the Danes to accept the regulations imposed, or proposed, in the rules for the future European political and economic union. There was also no strong majority for the EU in Sweden. And whilst the Finns were more enthusiastic about 'joining Europe', elections to the European Parliament in late 1996 showed notable support for the opponents of closer European integration, especially the opposition Centre Party which is critical of the government's pro-EMU stance with unemployment standing at 17 per cent. It is perhaps therefore fair to conclude that there was no real push from the north (except in the first referendum, in 1972 in Denmark, which came shortly after Denmark experienced its most heavy economic recession after the Second World War) to give up national autonomy.

In the voting on Europe, two tendencies were typical. First, in all four countries the main arguments among those voting in favour concerned economic issues: more jobs and higher income, while among those voting against the emphasis was on democracy and self-rule; interestingly, those who voted 'Yes' tended to be those who were already better off. Second, in all the countries – with the notable exception of Denmark – the non-urban areas voted 'No', while the main urban centres voted 'Yes'.[39] It was thus the non-urban areas who kept up the traditions rooted in the identity politics of the nineteenth century. The urban areas are to an extent more integrated in the international, capitalist economy and more susceptible to accepting the spread of 'international' culture. The EU campaign and the results show that even if the outcome of the referenda, with their small margins, gave different results, the Scandinavian countries still have a very similar profile.[40] The special case is Denmark, where the heavy 'Yes' vote came from the rich export and agricultural areas of Jutland, while the 'No' vote reached one of its highest proportions in the capital, Copenhagen, which in all the four referenda since 1972 had a clear 'No' majority.

We shall not go into details over the individual voting results. However, there are several features which will be mentioned briefly because they may illustrate a trend. First, in general the national elites in bureaucracies, within the media, among the party leaders, within the governments and parliaments, and in big business, used their resources heavily in favour of a 'Yes' vote. In some instances, in Sweden in November 1994 and in Denmark in 1993, strategically planned elite tactics, in the last hours before the referenda, gave perhaps the last few percentages needed among the 'don't knows' to tip the balance in favour of full membership. This may indicate that there has been and will develop a split between an elite culture and a culture for the 'common voter'. The survey results also indicate a split between the private and the public sector, where the private sector employers/owners and employees see their future best secured in an even more open economy with a full-scale market society, while public employees and people in farming and fishing favour greater control by the small national state when confronted by multinational firms and the ups and downs of international capitalism.

All in all, the EU issue broke the consensus of the typical Scandinavian cultures into two very distinct camps, which fought each other very bitterly – and the issue still has strong latent potential. Particularly in Norway where the EU issue today has split society from top to bottom, it crops up everywhere in social gatherings and adds considerable heat to discussions (you don't readily identify yourself before you know the position of the others!). It has also made the overall situation within the parliament very difficult since two of the main opposition parties (the Conservatives and the Progress Party) supported the 'Yes' vote, together with the Social Democratic minority government. Moreover, the new 1996 Jagland government included only the pro-EU wing of a party which had nearly split over the issue in 1994: this could create problems in the future.

CONTINUITIES AND CHANGE

In emphasising the histories of the Scandinavian states we started out by criticising and supplementing traditional state- and nation-building theory. The firm conceptualisation of nationhood among the Scandinavian peoples was an extremely important precondition for the early state-building process which laid the foundations of today's Scandinavia. Both the conceptualisation and the process were already strongly imprinted when the 'age of nationalism' in the nineteenth century fired people's imaginations in the aftermath of the great French Revolution, and this prevented the amalgamation of the Scandinavian states into one union ('Scandinavism'), though such an impulse produced large states elsewhere in Europe. The final autonomy and the precarious 'Nordic balance' was achieved in the twentieth century when the Norwegian–Swedish union (1905), the Finnish–Russian incorporation (1917) and the Danish–Icelandic union broke up (1944).

But the four distinct nation-states of Scandinavia (plus Iceland) did not develop in opposite directions. Bound as they were in similar socio-economic configurations they developed similar internal economic structures on the eve of the industrial revolution and modernisation, based on freeholding farmers, a weak urban bourgeoisie and few, small and scattered industrial enterprises. Differences among them were obvious, but compared to the Continental states and the United Kingdom, the basic paradigm was Scandinavian/Nordic and nothing else. The developments of the twentieth century, when the real tests of world politics forced reality on the neutral, Scandinavian north, also caused a particular type of converging development. The differences between the richest country (Sweden) and the fifth ranked (Finland) decreased and models of policy institutions were diffused freely among them.

We have argued that the 'Scandinavian model' was very much based on the affluence of the Scandinavian economies. During the 1970s, strong setbacks were experienced, but it was the 1980s and 1990s which marked the end of growth, with unemployment rates comparable to the 1930s, a heavy toll of bankruptcies and increasing public debt. Denmark had become used to a low growth rate since the 1970s, but when Sweden got into severe economic troubles, belief in 'the Scandinavian model' was less enthusiastic.

It was during the early years of the recession that the great Nordic identity debate took off among historians and other academics.[41] This intellectual awakening also inspired many among the intelligentsia because of the 'threats' from the European Union's growing claims to 'supra-nationality', as well as from the influx of new national entrants, new awareness of traditional ethnic minorities and multimedia influence from outside Scandinavia which penetrated the former single-channelled, centralised media dominance. The publication of new historical textbooks and the organisation of research projects on 'national identity' are parts of this movement (the most 'nationalistic' among the school texts offered in high schools in Scandinavia were the Norwegian books. Perhaps we may find here one of the many roots of the Norwegians' 'No' vote to the EU! Sweden was found to have had most difficulty in 'defining its national identity' in school books, since nationalism had never been really 'stimulated' by any event, such as a threat of war, since 1809). This process is still going on today. Besides a tendency to criticise most earlier historical writings for being too 'nationalistic', it is too early to see the effects of the construction of foundations for new forms of identity. The identity discussion in Scandinavia arose also against the background of 'the second end of ideology' debate, when the hegemony of the neo-Marxist left and the populist left-wing ideologies reached their climax and lost ground after the 1970s.

The real issue when analysing Scandinavian culture and identity today is connected to the enduring governmental rule of the Social Democratic parties, alone or in coalitions.[42] After their electoral breakthrough following the First World War they came to represent 'the people' in a very peculiar way. With their emphasis on the integrative function within 'the working class', and by building tight organisational structures covering all aspects of social life, as well as establishing important links between rural and urban areas, they succeeded in establishing themselves as the incarnation of *folkhemmet* (the people's home) as expressed in Sweden, or in Norway as *the* party which can bring *hele folket i arbeid* (jobs for the entire population). Throughout modern history, the Social Democratic parties of Scandinavia have dropped the ideological baggage containing class war and revolution, the destruction of private property, capitalism and the introduction of socialism, the avoidance of military armament and military alliances with capitalist superpowers, their anti-nationalism in favour of international socialism, etc. Instead, they have introduced and succeeded in implementing broad schemes of state control and rapid public expansion along with extensive redistribution strategies. These tactics have been so successful that today people may describe the Scandinavian democracies as 'Social Democracies'. This confusing interchange of concepts has also resulted in calling the parties '*Socialdemokratiet*' ('*the* Social Democracy') instead of 'the Social

Democratic Party' – as if they were 'democracies for everything social' in the real sense and not just one form of political party among others.[43]

The success of the Social Democratic parties (originally called 'workers' parties') in obtaining such an extraordinary position can be explained from different angles. First, they were in governmental control when the period of reconstruction after 1945 took off, and were given credit for the unbelievable economic growth in the 'golden years', as well as credit for distribution policies which were very much based on consensus among all parties. Second, they were able to crush and completely control the communist challenge, thus providing a sort of 'guarantee' against communist aggression during the years of the Cold War, with the hostile Soviet Union on the opposite side of the Iron Curtain. Third, they profited greatly from the much praised institutional system of proportional representation in Scandinavia, which kept alive a system of opposition parties unable to cooperate efficiently for a sufficient period of time to challenge the much larger Social Democratic parties. And fourth, they profited from ruling in small countries which needed a stronger centralisation of state control and private corporative control to sustain pressure from outside in order to protect essential structures of labour, business, culture and vital resources. They made the Scandinavian people believe that they were irreplaceable, that no other alternatives could be put in their place. How long this belief will remain important is another matter. Certainly there seems to be a notable potential for radical party change, including the rise of new and currently fringe parties.

NOTES

1 This chapter does not specifically discuss Iceland.
2 E. Allardt (ed.), *Nordic Democracy*, Copenhagen, Det Danske Selskab, 1981; O. Petersson, *The Government and Politics of the Nordic Countries*, Stockholm, Fritzes, 1994.
3 L. Binder, J. S. Coleman, J. LaPalombara, L. W. Pye, S. Verba and M. Weiner (eds), *Crises and Sequences in Political Development*, Princeton, Princeton University Press, 1971; S. Rokkan, 'Nation-Building: A Review of Models and Approaches', *Current Sociology*, 1971, 19. NB: there is not space in this chapter to set out the original model, and all Rokkan's revisions.
4 For Rokkan's tentative use of this model on Scandinavia see his 'The Growth and Structuring of Mass Politics' in Allardt, *op. cit.*
5 S. Bagge, 'Fantes det en norsk nasjonal identitet i middelalderen?' in M.-B. Ohman Nielsen (ed.), *Nasjonal Identitet og Nasjonalisme*, Oslo, Den Norske Historiske Forening, 1994; P. Sawyer, *När Sverige blev Sverige*, Alingsås, Victoria, 1991.
6 On nationalism from above see E. Hobsbawm, *Nations and Nationalism since 1780*, Cambridge, Cambridge University Press, 1990; E. Gellner, *Nations and Nationalism*, Oxford, Blackwell, 1983; and *Encounters with Nationalism*, Oxford, Blackwell, 1994.
7 The 'below' tradition is best illustrated by A. D. Smith, *Theories of Nationalism*, Oxford, Blackwell, 1971; *The Ethnic Origins of Nations*, Oxford, Blackwell, 1986; and *National Identity*, London, Penguin, 1991.

8   H. Becker-Christensen, *Skandinaviske drømme og politiske realiteter 1830–50*, Århus, Arusia, 1981; D. Thorkildsen, 'Skandinavisme – en historisk oversikt' in Ø. Sørensen (ed.), *Nasjonal identitet – et kunstprodukt?*, Oslo, Norges Forskningsråd, 1994.

9   Ø. Sørensen, 'The Development of a Norwegian National Identity During the Nineteenth Century' in Ø. Sørensen (ed.), *Nordic Paths to National Identity in the Nineteenth Century*, Oslo, Norges Forskningsråd, 1994. Cf. J. Nærbøvik, 'Den norske kulturnasjonalismen' in Sørensen, *Nasjonal identitet*, 1994.

10   Sørensen, *Nordic Paths*, 1994, concludes with the importance of 'historical luck' in successful nation building, though he does not specify what 'luck' means.

11   U. Østergård, 'Nation-Building Danish Style' in Sørensen, *Nordic Paths*, 1994, stresses both the Norse past and the new belief in the people as crucial aspects in Danish identity. See also his 'Findes der en "dansk" politisk kultur?' in A. Holmen and N. Jørgensen (eds), *Enhedskultur – Helhedskultur. Artikler om dansk kulturel selvforståelse*, Copenhagen, Danmarks Larerhøjskole, 1989.

12   M. Djursaa, *DNSAP. Danske Nazister 1930–1945*, 2 vols, Copenhagen, Gyldenhal, 1981.

13   R. Alapuro, 'Nineteenth-Century Nationalism in Finland. Comparative Remarks' in Sørensen, *Nordic Paths*, 1994. See also his 'The Intelligentsia, the State and the Nation' in M. Engman and D. Kirby (eds), *Finland. People – Nation – State*, London, Hurst, 1989.

14   Alapuro, 'The Intelligentsia'.

15   'Karelia: Battlefield, Bridge, Myth' in Engman and Kirby, *op. cit.*

16   R. Alapuro, *Akateeminen Karjala-Seura*, Helsinki, 1973. See also R. Alapuro, 'Students and National Politics: A Comparative Study of the Finnish Student Movement in the Interwar Period', *Scandinavian Political Studies*, 1973, 8.

17   B. Stråth, 'The Swedish Path to National Identity in the Nineteenth Century' in Sørensen, *Nordic Paths*, 1994

. 18   G. Værnøe (ed.), *Dialog Norge – Sverige. Fra arvefiende til samboer*, Stockholm, Wennergen-Cappelen, 1990.

19   Værnøe, *op. cit.*; S. Ekman and O. K. Gimes (eds), *Broderfolk I ufredstid. Norsk-svenske forbindseler under annen verdenskrig*, Oslo, Universitetsfarlaget, 1991.

20   E. Allardt, 'Ethnic Minorities' in Allardt, *op. cit.* See also I. B. Neumann, *Hva skjedde med Norden? Fra selvbevissthet til rådvillhet*, Oslo, Cappelen, 1992, which includes a discussion of Miroslav Hroch's 'stages' for nation building (*Social Preconditions of National Revival in Europe*, Cambridge, Cambridge University Press, 1985).

21   The classic reference is M. Childs, *Sweden: The Middle Way*, New Haven, Yale University Press, 1936.

22   For instance, N. Elder, A. H. Thomas and D. Arter, *The Consensual Democracies? The Government and Politics of the Scandinavian States*, Oxford, 1988. Perhaps the first foreign author to emphasise and theorise about the absence of conflict was H. Eckstein, *Division and Cohesion in a Democracy. The Case of Norway*, Princeton, Princeton University Press, 1965.

23   A typical example is O. Petersson, *The Government and Politics of the Nordic Countries*, Stockholm, Fritzes, 1994.

24   There is a voluminous literature on Scandinavian welfare states. E. Allardt, *Att Ha, Att Älska, Att Vara. Om välfärd i Norden*, Lund, Argos, 1975, was the first comprehensive project. See also R. Erikson, E. J. Hansen, S. Ringen and H. Uusitalo, *The Scandinavian Model. Welfare States and Welfare Research*, Armonk, NY, Sharpe, 1987; and E. J. Hansen, *Welfare Trends in the Scandinavian Countries*, Armonk, NY, Sharpe, 1993.

25 B. Moore Jnr, *Social Origins of Dictatorship and Democracy*, Boston, Beacon Press, 1966. Cf. F. G. Castles, *The Social Democratic Image of Society: A Study of the Achievements and Origins of Scandinavian Social Democracy in Comparative Perspective*, London, Routledge and Kegan Paul, 1978. See also T. A. Tilton, 'The Social Origin of Liberal Democracy: The Swedish Case', *The American Political Science Review*, 1974, 68, where he also comments on P. Anderson, *Lineages of the Absolutist State*, London, New Left Books, 1974.

26 Ø. Østerud, *Agrarian Structure and Peasant Politics in Scandinavia. A Comparative Study of Rural Response to Economic Change*, Oslo, Universitetsforlaget, 1978.

27 S. Pövtinen, *Patterns of Social Mobility in the Scandinavian Countries*, Helsinki, Vön, 1976; S. Pövtinen, *Social Mobility and Social Structure. A Comparison of Scandinavian Countries*, Helsinki, Vön, 1983; and S. Kuhnle, 'Emigration, Democratization and the Rise of the European Welfare States' in P. Torsvik, *Mobilization, Center-Periphery Structures and Nation-Building*, Bergen, Universitetsfarlaget, 1981.

28 R. Scase, *Social Democracy in Capitalist Society*, London, Croom Helm, 1977, pp. 17–18.

29 See R. Alapuro, 'Origins of Agrarian Socialism in Finland' in Torsvik, *op. cit.*; and G. Esping-Andersen, *Social Class, Social Democracy and State Policy*, Copenhagen, Nyt fra Samfundsvitenskaperne, 1980.

30 S. Berglund, P. Pesonen and G. P. Gislason, 'Political Party Systems' in Allardt, *Nordic Democracy*, 1981. Cf. J.-E. Lane *et al.*, 'Scandinavian Exceptionalism Reconsidered', *Journal of Theoretical Politics*, 1993, 5.

31 B. Rothstein, 'Social Classes and Political Institutions: The Roots of Swedish Corporatism' in L. Karvonen and J. Sundberg (eds), *Social Democracy in Transition. Northern, Southern and Eastern Europe*, Aldershot, Gower, 1991; B. Rothstein, 'State Structure and Variations in Corporatism: The Swedish Case', *Scandinavian Political Studies*, 1991, 14.

32 J. Seim, *Hvordan Hovedavtalen av 1935 ble til. Staten, organisasjonen og arbeidsfreden 1930–35*, Oslo, Tiden, 1972.

33 Mjøset's idea is that the Scandinavian countries fit well within the concepts of 'autozentrierte Entwicklung' ('self-centred development') and the idea of 'dualistic structure' in terms of balance between the domestic and the international market. See *Tidsskrift for Samfunnsforskning*, Oslo, Universitetsforlaget, 1983, pp. 565–76. See also Mjøset's book *Norden dagen derpå. De nordiske økonomiske-politiske modellene og deres problemer på 70- og 80-tallet*, Oslo, Universitetsforlaget, 1986, pp. 29–40.

34 S. A. Nilsson, K.-G. Hildebrand and B. Öhgren (eds), *Kriser og krisepolitikk i Norden under mellankrigstiden. Nordiska historikermötet i Uppsala 1974*, Uppsala, 1974.

35 For a broad discussion of the development of the 'political economy' in Scandinavia see Mjøset, *op. cit.*, 1986. See also his 'Norwegian Political Economy' in A. C. Kiel (ed.), *Continuity and Change. Aspects of Contemporary Norway*, Oslo, Scandinavian University Press, 1993; and his 'The Nordic Model Never Existed, but Does it Have a Future?', *Scandinavian Studies*, 1992, 64.

36 See L. Karvonen, '*Med vårt västra granneland som förebild.' En undersökning av policydiffusjon från Sverige til Finland*, Åbo, Åbo Akademi, 1981.

37 J. G. Andersen, 'Denmark: the Progress Party – Populist Neo-Liberalism and Welfare State Chauvinism' in P. Hainsworth (ed.), *The Extreme Right in Europe and the USA*, London, Pinter, 1993, p. 202.

38 K. Siune and S. Palle, 'The Danes and the Maastricht Treaty. The Danish EC Referendum of June 1992', *Electoral Studies*, 1993, 12; and P. Svensson, 'The

Danish Yes to Maastricht and Edinburgh. The EC Referendum of May 1993', *Scandinavian Political Studies*, 1994, 17.

39 U. Lindström, 'Scandinavia and the European Union: The Referenda in Denmark, Finland, Norway and Sweden 1992–1994', Mimeo, Department of Comparative Politics, University of Bergen, 1995, esp. Chapter 8.

40 See H. J. Nielsen, *EF på valg*, Copenhagen, Danmarks Larerhøjskole, 1993; O. Hellevik and P. G. Nils, *Kampen om EF*, Oslo, Pax, 1994; H. Valen and O. Aagedal, *Brüssel midt i mot*, Oslo, 1996; P. Pertti (ed.), *Suomen EU-kansanäänestys 1994*, Helsinki, 1994. One of the many publications in English discussing Scandinavia's new prospects in the EU-era is T. Tiilikainen and I. D. Petersen (eds), *The Nordic Countries and the EC*, Copenhagen, Copenhagen Political Studies Press, 1993.

41 For a broad overview with extensive references (and with a very short English summary) see S. Tønneson, 'Norden Speiler seg: Identitetsbatten 1986–93', *Historisk Tidsskrift*, Oslo, Universitetsforlaget, 1994.

42 The best history-book on the Social Democratic parties in Scandinavia – though in retrospect somewhat optimistic as to the future – is G. Esping-Andersen, *Politics against Markets. The Social Democratic Road to Power*, Princeton, Princeton University Press, 1985. See also L. Karvonen, 'A Nation of Workers and Peasants. Ideology and Compromise in the Interwar Years' in Karvonen and Sundberg, *op. cit.*

43 See T. Nordby, ' "Velferdsstaten" og "Den sosialdemokratiske stat": norske myter i historisk lys', *LOS-report*, 1990; W. Lafferty, 'Den sosialdemokratiske stat', *Nytt Nordisk Tidsskrift*, Oslo, Universitetsforlaget, 1986.

14 Conclusion: part one

Europe of the 'nation-states'? Concepts and theories

Roger Eatwell

INTRODUCTION

The primary point of the preceding twelve chapters has been to analyse the historic and contemporary characteristics of a broad cross section of European 'national' political cultures. However, these chapters' *longue durée*, macro approach raises a series of sweeping concluding questions. In particular, what are the likely long-term political developments that will result from the growing breakdown of traditional macro and meso influences, like mainstream ideologies, religion, social class and family – especially given Europe's continuing relative economic decline, and associated problems like rising unemployment?

In the short run, some dealigned voters are 'floating' between the mainstream parties, while others have drifted into social isolation (note the general decline of turnout in elections). But these trends could be laying the foundations for a new wave of radical nationalism, which seeks to reforge the community. Does the rise of parties like the AN in Italy, the Front National in France, the FPÖ in Austria, the Vlaams Blok in Belgium, and Zhirinovsky in Russia (parties with charismatic leaders, who tend to appeal to dealigned electorates) herald a dramatic long-term trend? Or does a better guide to the future lie in other developments, notably growing regionalism, which seem to point to the possibility of forging a wider European identity (supporters of the Scottish National Party sometimes refer to their lapel badges, made up of the crossed flags of the EU and St Andrew, as 'the Westminster by-pass'). The European Union is committed by the Maastricht Treaty to the creation of 'an ever closer union of European peoples'. But does a strong sense of affective identity exist between its peoples; if not, can a common set of values be delineated which could serve as a basis for such identity? Or is the EU now encouraging new manifestations of nationalism, even serving as a blockage to a wider universal identity?

These last questions can partly be answered by reference to the preceding chapters, and to other recent empirical work on European values, like the European Science Foundation-sponsored series of works.[1] The latter paints a distinctly more optimistic picture than the one which emerges from many of the preceding chapters. In particular, the series holds that there is still widespread legitimacy in Western Europe (and growing support in parts of Eastern Europe, like Poland, though less so in Russia) for *democratic political systems*, some form of *market-oriented economic systems*, and relatively *extensive welfare systems*. Certainly the preceding chapters point to the fact that these three features should be seen as constituting the core trinity of modern 'European' systemic values. However, stress on the fundamental stability of European politics seems at odds with the more pessimistic parts of the European Science Foundation's works – most notably, where they highlight the decline of the old mainstream party ideologies and the rise of single-issue and populist politics in some countries, or the way they note that young people seem to be characterised increasingly by a concern with unemployment and insecurity rather than the post-material values predicted by Inglehart and others.[2] Part of the explanation for the series' basic optimism stems from the fact that much of its material relates to the 1980s, a period which in general failed to produce the major changes in party support and the rise of unconventional politics which some had predicted.

The preceding chapters of this book should have made clear that it is possible to discern notably different attitudes and trends in terms of the movement towards European union, both within and between countries, over the last 20 years. In general, support for further union comes from the more educated, business and professional classes, with the less skilled and the old tending to be opposed – trends which were especially clear in the Scandinavian entry referenda. There seem to be some notably Eurosceptic states, like Britain, but in most countries, support for further European union has been relatively high. Or it might be more accurate to say that support 'was' high, for opinion polls in many countries now reveal growing doubts, especially over EMU, as economic recession looms. In Germany, for instance, Chancellor Kohl may have strongly backed monetary union, but most Germans remain wedded to the Deutschmark, a potent post-war symbol of prosperity and stability; the Dutch too seem to be reassessing their former strong support, not least as old antipathies to German domination are growing.

However, in analysing these more sweeping concluding issues, it is vital to move beyond opinion poll evidence of micro attitudes. This is not simply because attitudes may be changing. Nor is the problem the more fundamental one that some poll evidence may be misleading. For instance, 'support' for the EU can encompass a notable diversity of views about political and cultural forms: thus in Ireland during the 1970s, or Portugal in 1980s, 'Europe' could mean little more than a desire for modernisation or democracy, whereas today 'Europe' is more commonly understood in terms of support for federalism, or specific policies like EMU. Conversely, apparently nationalist attitudes which are picked up by opinion polls, may essentially reflect a protest against elites. Certainly what seems to be opposition to the EU may reflect a passing phase of alienation from national leadership, a marked phenomenon in the 1992 French Maastricht referendum.

In order to avoid the scatter of short-run data, it is necessary to move on to a more conceptual and theoretical level of analysis, so that crucial questions about the future development of nationalism and Europe can be posed more precisely. There is widespread ignorance – even among students of politics – of a political vocabulary and a set of arguments necessary to understand these issues.

Consider the contemporary discussion of the crisis of the 'nation-state'. Is there really a major 'national' crisis? Some would answer 'yes', like followers of the Frankfurt School who argue that the culture industry (advertising, consumerism and entertainment) provides totalising forces which transcend old ideologies and nation-states. It is interesting in this context to note that in the 1990s Daimler-Benz has abandoned the 'Made in Germany' label for 'Made by Mercedes Benz': the product has become more important than its home. But others would argue that nations and nationalism seem alive and kicking. In Germany – where nationalism has been virtually taboo since 1945 – there has been a burgeoning discussion among intellectuals about national identity. This seems to be having a growing resonance at the popular level: for instance before the final of the 1996 European football championship, the German popular media portrayed their national team as invincible heroes against the old Czech enemy (who had ethnically expelled three million German-speakers in 1945).

Some commentators, like the leading British political philosopher John Dunn, have argued that it is the state rather than the nation which is in crisis. Following the leading American political sociologist Daniel Bell, the argument holds that the state now tends to be too large for some issues (like the democratic management of our local communities, especially if the word 'democracy' has a strong participatory connotation), and too small for others (such as controlling multinational companies and finance, or enforcing global pollution controls).[3] In the economic context, it is only necessary to think of George Soros and other financiers at the time of 'Black Wednesday' in 1992, when Britain was forced out of the European Exchange Rate Mechanism. Their power was greater than that of the Bank of England, and should serve as a warning for those who glibly call for a defence of national sovereignty. This power of the markets also threatens the post-Second World War European Keynesian welfare state system, in which the weak and the poor were offered a life raft. Globalisation seems to imply that the state must be rolled back if Europe is to compete with the new Asian tiger economies.[4] Or does it? Such trends could strengthen long-standing doubts about the normative legitimacy of capitalism, and strengthen a sense of nation (or locality) – perhaps even create a new form of 'national socialist' state?

CONCEPTS

There is a large number of concepts which could be considered relevant to understanding these points about future European identity and politics, including 'democracy', 'markets' and 'welfare'. However, the discussion which follows focuses essentially on the core and related concepts which are necessary to understand the subsequent discussion of theories of nationalism and trans-national integration. In practice, it can be difficult to separate concept from theory, but this form of presentation has heuristic uses, especially in terms of helping to underline a sense of chronological development.

Identity

Probably since the beginning of time, people have come together and adopted some form of identity, a cultural and changing process which is not inconsistent with people having different identities (the tribe, women, the elderly, and so on).[5] Anthropologists claim that identity has tended to be created around three main poles: a common language which facilitates group communication; a shared religion which gives a more affective sense of belonging or purpose; and finally a sense of the Other – the tendency to demonise the outsider, to define oneself partly by what one is not. Certainly all three can be found in ancient Athens, which is often seen as the starting point of European civilisation (not least in the tendency to develop conceptions of self-identity through sets of polar contrasts with others – which led to systematic exclusion or exploitation of non-members of the community).[6] Social geographers would add to this list the importance of a sense of place.[7] Certainly much early legend, for example Norse sagas, has a strong sense of the relationship between people and the landscape. The trend continues to this day, for instance aspects of Europe's West Indian immigrant musical culture or crucial aspects of Irish identity. Identity is usually a multifaceted phenomenon, with no one item necessarily required. For instance, it is possible to imagine a Pole who is not Catholic. Even language is not vital: people who identify as Swiss can have four. Identity is frequently related to ethnicity, a term which has Greek roots, coming from the word *ethnos*, meaning a tribe. Ethnic groups can be considered to exist by virtue of long-standing associations across generations which are based on a common culture. It serves as a form of boundary creation, but it is not necessarily territorial. For example, Jews can be considered to be an ethnic group on account of their shared religion and sense of history, but Jewishness has not always been associated with the claim to their own state (Zionism grew up among Europe's Jews mainly in the late nineteenth and early twentieth centuries as a response to persecution, especially in Eastern Europe).

Nation

The term 'nation' initially derived from the Latin *natio*; it referred to the place of birth and when first coined had blood ties, but later the term became more confused. Typically in the early Middle Ages, it did not refer to a specific territorial political community (the reference was more to different parts of the Church), but from the twelfth century on – earlier in some cases – there were growing signs of national historiographies in countries such as England, France, Spain, Poland and Denmark.[8] This trend had two aspects. The first was the emergence of national identity, especially in reference to an elite linked by culture and a sense of political mission for a particular country. The second strand involved a growing identification between the nation as a set of people and the need for their own government to which they owed a special loyalty, which helps explain why nations were typically identified when there was a clear sense of state continuity or historical mission.[9] Certainly there was a growing sense of national identity among elites in England and the Netherlands, especially from the sixteenth century on, and a tendency to use a language and especially the symbolism of nation to manipulate the masses, most notably to secure economic growth and to fight wars.[10] Elites sought to encourage patriotism (from the Latin *patria*), namely a respect and love – and ultimately a willingness to die for – a state and its political institutions and laws. Thus although in some ways a confused word from the outset, nation can be differentiated from ethnicity by its linking of cultural and political state forms and its sense of mission.

State

The primary modern usage of the term 'state' emerges after the disentanglement of England from France at the end of the Hundred Years' War (1337–1453), and the rise of ethnically-based states like the Netherlands, Sweden, Poland and Portugal by the seventeenth century (which broke the unity of Christendom even before the Wars of Religion and the Counter-Reformation).[11] For political theorists, like Machiavelli and Hobbes, the state came to be seen as the body which organises legitimate coercion and control within a given territory, in particular in a centralised legal-bureaucratic way. This can be considered the state function in terms of internal sovereignty. It is also important to consider it in terms of external sovereignty. Since the Westphalian Settlement (1648), there has been a principle in European international law that states not only have jurisdiction over their own peoples and territory, but the right to non-interference from outside bodies. Initially, the concept of the state had no particular connotation with size, though by the late eighteenth century there was a growing tendency to see the need for relatively large states, or to be involved in some form of federal or confederal grouping – especially to defend external sovereignty.[12] A state could thus include different ethnic groups – and nations.

Nationalism

During the late eighteenth, and especially during the nineteenth century, a new form of ideology began to emerge, closely related to the universalism of the Enlightenment.[13] This linked 'nation' to more radical political ideas, in particular the French revolutionary cry of 'sovereignty of the people'. Previously ultimate political authority had resided with the monarch, acting with the authority of God; the people were viewed as subjects. If the people were to be sovereign, it became necessary to define who they were – who made up the nation? For the French revolutionaries, the people were essentially defined by their being citizens who shared – or adopted – French culture: it was a community of choice rather than a community of birth. It was also a community of activism and civic virtue, for this form of nationalism was closely associated with new democratic ideas. This doctrine had a further external dimension. The world was divided into nations, which in order to be truly free, needed their own states – a doctrine which posed a major threat to the European multinational empires of Russia and Austro-Hungary.

This civic nationalism was very different from another form, which emerged in the late nineteenth century – though it has much longer continuities, especially in Central and Eastern Europe: namely, ethnic nationalism. This closed rather than open form is best epitomised in its early days by Herder, one of the great German Romantic critics of the Enlightenment, who believed that each people had a spirit (*Volksgeist*), uniquely embodied in culture and landscape, which required its own form of government. During the late nineteenth century this type of nationalism began to take on a more widespread form, partly because it became associated with the rise of racial ideology. The word 'race', in the sense of common stock, had been in use from the sixteenth century, but in the late nineteenth century, racist ideology began to emerge, a development which was closely associated with Social Darwinism and the division of the world into hierarchical races.[14] Whereas ethnicity is not necessarily territorial, ethnic nationalism is. And in its racist form, it does not hold that all people have a right to their own state. Ethnic nationalism has been associated historically more with dictatorship than liberal democracy; it has also frequently been associated with 'ethnic cleansing' and the coercion of minority groups into the dominant culture (for instance in Greece, as well as the commonly cited examples of Nazi Germany and the former Yugoslavia). However, the relationship is a complex one and some forms of ethnic nationalism have been democratic. In this sense, a more clear-cut distinction exists between what could be termed liberal nationalism and authoritarian nationalism.

It is important to distinguish nationalism in its various ideological forms from national consciousness in the mass sense. As the French revolutionary armies moved outside France's borders, they often met notable opposition. But it is far from clear whether this was based on local national conscious-ness – though French expansionism unquestionably encouraged intellectual consciousness of nation, albeit not always in its French form. Resistance in Russia and Spain was based more on hostility to the foreign invader, and the defence of the ruling dynasty, or religion. Even in France itself, the font of modern nationalist politics, it is far from clear how strong a sense of national consciousness existed as late as the mid-nineteenth century. In Eugen Weber's famous phrase, it took a combination of a deliberate policy of symbolic politics like the celebration of Bastille Day, combined with the forces of growing popular education, economic development, and the impact of the draft to turn 'peasants into Frenchmen' during the late nine-teenth century. (Behind these trends lay the introduction of manhood suffrage in 1848 and the disastrous impact of defeat at the hands of Prussia in 1870 – events which highlighted the need to integrate the masses.)[15]

Regionalism

Even Britain, frequently seen as the 'first nation', has been characterised by notable internal divisions – especially ones based on class and region. It is also important to remember that in some ways Britain is a multinational state, encompassing Wales, Scotland and Northern Ireland (and all of Ireland between 1801 and 1921). Recently, both regionalism[16] and especially ethno-regionalism have been gathering force within Britain, and several other European countries, for instance Belgium and Spain. These especially elusive concepts seek varying degrees of formal autonomy within the existing state – such as their own parliament and ability to raise local taxes – unlike nationalists who seek their own state. However, the dividing line can be narrow: certainly many regionalists support a federal or confederal Europe as a means of boosting the status of their own tier of government, and often espouse the argument that globalisation means that the age of the nation-state is dead (though not necessarily a cultural sense of the nation, which is perfectly consistent with both greater regionalism and univer-salism). They see the future as lying in the development of a stronger relationship between regional and trans-national government, which, far from losing sovereignty, will actually regain powers currently lost by national governments to international business and other forces.

THEORIES OF NATIONALISM

In order to understand these concepts more fully, it is necessary to turn more specifically to theories of why the nations and states discussed in the preceding chapters (and other European ones) emerged and grew – and in some cases withered. Four are highlighted here on the basis of their selection of the primary driving force behind nationalism, though it is important to stress at the outset that there are variations within these broad approaches and some overlaps. Moreover, although generally referred to as theories of 'nationalism', part of the explanation of their varying foci is that they are seeking to answer different questions. In particular, some are primarily interested in the rise of national identity among an elite, others in the emergence of different bodies of nationalist ideology, whereas yet others seek more to explain the onset of mass national consciousness.

The primordialists

The first broad set of approaches can be termed the primordialist. One recent work in this vein has argued that

> None [of the main works on nationalism] has dealt adequately, if at all, with the fundamental importance of the territorial factor, or the physical facts and perceptions of the 'homeland' which, celebrated in song and poetry, are often 'primordial' in the sentiments of the communities who inhabit them.[17]

This type of argument is often used to help explain the break-up of Yugoslavia, which is viewed as a polyglot state encompassing groups with notably different ethno-histories and strong traditional rivalries. This argument can be extended to claim that the bloody collapse of this tragic country reflects not so much the failure of nationalism as of the multi-ethnic state situated on multiple historic demarcation lines (especially between Eastern Orthodox and Western Christianity, and between Christian Europe and Muslim Asia).

The primordialist approach holds that nations reflect deeply-rooted cultural traits, and that there is a sense in which 'nations' have existed virtually since the beginning of time. The argument is sometimes based on anthropological studies which show the powerful bonds, including deeply-rooted myths, which have held groups together. It is also commonly associated with the psychological claim that people need to belong and tend to reject outsiders. In its strongest form, the primordialist argument borrows from socio-biology, seeing nationalism as an extension of kinship selection.[18] This accepts that there is no such thing as race in the old sense, but argues that ethnicity cannot be created out of nothing and states that it is a clear fact there are large differences in the frequencies of genotypical and phenotypical traits. For 50 years there has been a strong tendency to discount genetic arguments in politics, partly a legacy of memories of Nazi racial 'science'. Whilst there are signs that this is changing, it remains a highly controversial area, and nationalism cannot essentially be explained in such terms. But what could be termed the 'weak' primordialist approach offers many insights. The key figure here is Anthony Smith, who argues that a strong sense of ethnic identity is important for successful nation creation –

and that the prior nature of ethnicity ('ethnies' in his term) affects the process of nation building.[19] Hence the historic success of nation building in countries like England or France, which can trace ethnic roots back to Anglo-Saxon or Frankish times.

The modernists

One of the great exponents of the modernist approach is Ernest Gellner. Gellner admits that nationalism uses pre-existing, historically inherited cultural texture, but argues that 'the cultural shreds and patches used by nationalism are often arbitrary historical inventions. Any old shred and patch would have served as well.'[20] According to this influential – though much-contested – view the origins of nations are to be sought not in the mists of time, but in the process by which capitalism grew out of feudal and more localised society: hence the early emergence of nationalism in England, the 'first industrial nation'. Capitalism required high levels of mobility in geographical and class terms; it required the creation of a new culture to underpin the new system. This culture – including the standardisation of language – would allow people to communicate and be integrated into new structures which could no longer rely on feudal or religious authority. The new technology of printing, and new social institutions such as the spread of education, helped diffuse a sense of belonging among the masses. Out of this process allegedly grew nationalism – the desire to protect the culture. And from this nationalism emerged greater economic wealth, which helped legitimise the system – though this was an erratic and uneven process.

The second main modernist approach focuses on the rise of anomie. Sometimes this is seen as an inevitable process, but in other accounts the stress is more on social rootlessness caused by specific developments, most notably religious decline – an interpretation which sees nationalism as a form of secular millenarianism.[21] The approach has reached its most sophisticated form in 'mass society' theory, which was developed particularly to explain the rise of fascism in Germany and Italy. This holds that 'atomised' man, disoriented by rapid social change (including the disastrous impact of war), is attracted by new collectivist mass movements, especially ones which cleverly use language and symbols, exploiting the new means of mass propaganda. The isolated individual is reborn in a new community. The interpretation has fertile insights, but does not fully explain the economic and idealistic appeal of fascism. Moreover, anomie approaches generally struggle to account for nationalism's strong appeal in highly religious, historically 'backward', countries – like Ireland and Poland.

The third of the main modernist approaches relates more to the structural problem of uneven development, both within and between states. The argument can be seen clearly in relation to nineteenth-century Italy.[22] At the time of unification, parts of the north were adopting modern capitalist structures in both industry and agriculture, but much of the centre and south had changed little since feudal times. Nationalism was a device used by northern elites, and a small section of the southern elite, in an attempt to forge social unity. Italy's relatively weak international position also encouraged a sense of being a 'proletarian nation', a desire to unify society in order to foster economic growth and achieve foreign conquests. One obvious problem with such approaches is that they do not explain the rise of early nationalism in hegemonic states like England and France. Nevertheless, similar arguments have shown considerable staying power in explaining post-1945 nationalism within developing countries, or the rise of nationalism in relatively underdeveloped areas such as Scotland. However, once again, this approach fails to explain major phenomena, like the recent rise of Umberto Bossi's separatist Northern League in the wealthiest part of Italy.

The statists

The third broad set of approaches can be called statist. There is a large literature surrounding the origins and nature of modern state forms, a body of writing which often clearly overlaps modernisation theory. One of the most influential accounts has come from the American social scientist, Barrington Moore Jnr. He identifies three trajectories of state development: the first was the bourgeois-capitalist-democratic path of countries such as Britain and France; the second, typified by Germany, saw a weaker middle class and the coercive or corporatist state being used for modernisation; in the third, typified by Russia, the peasantry was large and the state autocratic.[23] Such approaches offer fertile insights (though not always correct ones: for instance the German *Sonderweg* thesis has been much over-stated) into the relationship of nationalism to democracy and dictatorship, but three other more truly statist approaches offer better insights into the rise of nationalism per se.

The first concerns the growth of the inter-state system, and the rise of great powers (Europe in 1500 included some 500 or so more or less independent units; the Europe of 1900 had approximately 25). This argument sees socio-economic developments as less crucial than the relationship between states – though the arguments are not exclusive.[24] The military struggle for power in Europe during and after the sixteenth century gave a considerable impetus towards bureaucratic organisation. The modern large state could extract more from its population to fight wars; small – and often economically successful – units like the Hanseatic League or the Italian city-states could not hope to compete militarily. The composite modern state also had to think more carefully about the bonds that linked the people to the state in order to avoid harsh discipline to ensure internal order, especially on the peripheries. This – together with the primitive sense of hostility to the enemy – is seen as the beginning of modern nationalism. On this view, Henry VIII of

England, Louis XIV of France, Gustavus Adolphus of Sweden or Frederick the Great of Prussia are seen as the makers of modern nation-states.

However, wars at this time were still essentially fought by professional armies and it seems vital to add another dimension to the process of state building – the Reformation. Here the approach of Stein Rokkan, among others, is crucial. Rokkan developed a conceptual map of European development with both a north–south and an east–west axis.[25] These lines of division have both socio-economic and geographical aspects (for example, the thriving city-states of core Europe from Italy to the Baltic are seen as militating against large state formation). But the crucial point is the way in which the north–south axis reflects a religious division. Rokkan sees the Reformation as a first crucial step on the road to nation building because of its challenge to the universal pretensions of the Catholic Church. Thus the formation of nation-states in northern Europe was intimately bound up with the fact that these were Protestant states.

A final major form of statist approaches can be called the manipulative. This can be seen in its clearest form in the work of the British Marxist historian Eric Hobsbawm, who together with Terence Ranger has popularised the idea of the 'invention of tradition'.[26] The main focus is on a later period of development, especially the era of the rise of the masses, the demand for the vote, and the growth of socialism. National consciousness is seen as a sentiment manufactured by elites to manage dangerous challenges to the power of the bourgeoisie; and crucial to forming such consciousness is the manufacture of a strong sense of cultural continuity. According to Hobsbawm, three major innovations were vital to the invention of tradition: first was the growth of primary education; second was the introduction of public ceremonies and symbols so that the nation could celebrate its existence; and third, traditions needed to be reinforced by the mass production of public monuments such as statues and public buildings. Although Hobsbawm's main focus is on the past, the approach can be used to explain contemporary developments. Thus Bossi seeks to legitimise his proposed state of Padania by harking back to the loose federation of cities formed to keep at bay the power of the Holy Roman Empire (the federation's forces defeated the imperial troops in 1176 at Padania). To reinforce this mythology, the Northern League has developed a host of ceremonies and uniforms harking back to this mythical past.

The political mythologists

The fourth broad set of theorists of the rise of 'nationalism' can be termed the political mythologists. The focus here is more on the power of ideas and symbols and those who disseminate them, especially intellectuals. Although the argument has similarities with the 'invention of tradition' statist approach, it differs by not assuming any necessary connection between nationalism and state or class interests. Ideas and propaganda are seen as having an autonomous power. It is also important to stress that the term 'myth' is not being used in its popular sense to mean something which is false. Political myths are more forms of argument which are capable of simple formulation and which are designed to influence behaviour (though they can be demobilising as well as mobilising).

The approach can be seen in an extreme case in Conor Cruise O'Brien's claim that nationalism emerged as a collective emotional force with the Hebrew Bible – which linked deity to a specific land and chosen people.[27] It seems more helpful to note that Old Testament thought subsequently had a notable effect on Protestants at the time of the Reformation, especially the identification of the English as the chosen people (there were similar sentiments in the Netherlands, which for a time eclipsed English power). In the same period, it is also worth underlining the new theory of sovereignty, and especially its implication that successful states had to homogenise their populations in all those aspects which affected their ability to remain united enough to maintain their citizens' survival.[28] Later, alienated intellectuals, often living in territorially peripheral areas, played a major part in developing and disseminating nationalist doctrine – for example, in Poland (it is also interesting to note that many Nazi leaders were born outside the Reich, including Hitler and the leading theorist of blood nationalism, Alfred Rosenberg).

One of the main political myth approaches has come from Elie Kedourie.[29] He has argued that the chronology of European nationalism does not fit Gellner's theory: for instance, nationalism was articulated in German-speaking lands well before they had seen industrialisation. (The same key point has been made by others who have not necessarily adopted a mythical approach, for example in analysing the rise of nationalism in pre-industrial Scandinavia.)[30] Kedourie's basic approach is that of the historian of ideas. He sees nationalism as a body of doctrine arising from a variety of intellectual developments associated with the Enlightenment. Of particular importance was the Kantian conception of human beings as autonomous, which led to politics replacing religion as the key to salvation. It is important to stress that Kedourie did not see nationalist doctrine as being of high intellectual quality (a view he shares with virtually all the other theorists of 'nationalism', though recently nationalist theory has begun to be taken more seriously by a handful of philosophers, for example in the way it highlights the need to build social trust and create a sense of community which permits uncoerced redistribution).[31] The crucial point is more its affective and motivating power. This seems to help solve a problem which Gellner admits in his theory: namely, its inability to explain why some nationalisms, such as Hitler's, have become so virulent and destructive. Kedourie's approach points to the specific nature of the ideas, and their quasi-religious force. Moreover, although Kedourie's theory is in many ways associated with the Enlightenment, it does not necessarily predict the decline of nationalism in a contemporary world which seems to have lost faith in many of the other great ideologies, notably socialism.

Another major mythical approach has come from Benedict Anderson, who has popularised the idea that the nation is an 'imagined community' in a way that family and local communities are not.[32] Anderson clearly sees the beginnings of nationalism in the process of modernisation and the rise of the modern state, but he argues that rather than thinking of the nation as fabricated, it is more important to understand it in terms of its style of imagination and the institutions which make it possible. Pre-eminent among the latter are print capitalism, and the growth of the new genres of newspapers and the novel, which portrayed the nation as a sociological community. The argument can be seen more clearly by taking a specific example: in their desire to show that religion was dead, the French revolutionaries turned the Pantheon, built as a church, into a hall of fame for the heroes of the Revolution, and devised a new calendar which started at Year Zero rather than with the death of Christ. Put another way, Anderson argues that the imagined community is not a simple historical-ethnic construction but an elaborate façade which needs studying as such. Anderson under-states the importance of a texture of existing myths and he ignores the more serious side to nationalist ideology, but his approach points to the fact that as the nation is in a sense imagined, the community need not be restricted in a territorially limited sense – it is possible to 'imagine' more universal social groupings, like 'Europe'.

THEORIES OF EUROPEAN INTEGRATION

Some of the approaches to nationalism have clear implications for contemporary European unity. Smith, for instance, does not believe that there is a sufficient sense of ethnicity to build a common European identity, transcending its nations. The existence of deeply entrenched cultural nationalism is thus seen as inconsistent with building a united Europe. Gellner, on the other hand, has argued that it is now possible among the developed Western nations – and he was clearly thinking in particular of Europe – to move beyond the nation to a higher state form, more capable of handling issues like trans-national business or environmental protection.

Although there is a large academic literature on the European Union, very little of it is theoretical: most consists largely of journalistic accounts of recent developments, descriptions of institutions, histories – or even propagandist tracts. Given the erratic path which the EU has followed in recent years, it is perhaps not surprising that the main approaches to integration were developed during the more optimistic 1950s and 1960s. Arguably the most influential recent contribution to the debate has come from supporters of the realist school of international relations (which stresses the primacy of national self-interest in explaining behaviour). They argue that countries like France and West Germany accepted the movement towards unity, and some limitations on sovereignty, because it led to great gains elsewhere. For instance, West Germany's economy required trade liberalisation, and the removal of Allied controls came more quickly through Germany becoming associated with a wider community.[33]

Among integration theories, four stand out – interpretations which, like theories of nationalism, focus essentially on primacy.[34] There is a further parallel in that part of the explanation for the alternative foci is that they are seeking to answer different questions. Some concentrate on the immediate forces of integration, whereas others look more at deep underlying commonalities, and yet others concentrate on the state form which a united Europe allegedly should take.

The culturalists

The emphasis in what I call the culturalist approach (usually referred to as the transactionalist or interactionist approach) is on the broad variety of links which have existed between European countries before 1945. There has been a high level of shared culture, epitomised by Britain's use of the opening bars of the 'German' Beethoven's Fifth Symphony as its victory theme during the Second World War. At the level of popular culture, the post-1945 period has witnessed a considerable increase in inter-European tourism, school exchanges and town-twinning programmes. These forces reinforce strong historic economic and trade links within a Europe characterised from an early date by a high level of internal communications, for instance along major waterways like the Rhine or Danube. Moreover, there has also been a long tradition of inter-European diplomacy, bringing elites together to further doctrines such as the balance of power. In its most sophisticated form, as developed by Karl Deutsch during the 1950s, the culturalist argument holds that increasing communicative interaction at popular and especially elite levels strengthens a sense of community, which drives integration: the result is a 'security community', where people accept the necessity of peaceful change and the ability to bargain incrementally over disputes.[35] By pointing to such factors, Deutsch highlights the problems which would afflict any political organisation which was not based on a high level of political trust, and acceptance of general rules of distribution or economic activity within a society. In particular, without such sentiments, it is difficult to see how legitimacy could ever be transferred from the nation-state.

However, the culturalist approach glosses over differences between European cultures. It is also weak at explaining the stops and starts in European integration – except perhaps the leap forward in the period immediately after 1945, when there was clearly a desire on the part of elites (particularly in the Western countries which had suffered defeat) to stress a new understanding among Europe's peoples. Certainly there was a desire in France, still haunted by the First World War and defeat in 1940, and (West)

Germany to forge a reconciliation in order to avoid further conflict. Such sentiments, combined with a strong dose of national self-interest, helped to forge an elite Franco-German understanding which would dominate the movement towards European unity. They also helped to overcome more popular memories of atrocities, like German troops murdering virtually everyone in Oradour-sur-Glane in 1944: the French village has been preserved as a memorial, though its universal brother/sisterhood implications are underlined by the familiar form of the warning at the entrance – '*Souviens-Toi*'.

The functionalists

During the Second World War, an academic school began to emerge, initially associated with David Mitrany, which believed that increasing world interdependence would come through economic links.[36] This functionalist, primacy of economics, argument has been applied to moves towards European unity in the immediate post-war era. For instance, the Organisation for European Economic Cooperation clearly had a specific economic function: its initial task was to help distribute American Marshall Aid to the war-ravaged economies of Germany and elsewhere in the Western orbit.

But sweeping economic arguments have a variety of problems. In the specific context of the movement towards European unity immediately after 1945, the approach seriously underestimates other factors, like shared culture, the desire to prevent future wars, and the anti-communist aspect of American policy. The early functionalists also envisioned the gradual emergence of supranational government above the nation-state, placing little or no emphasis on political problems such as the need to broker deals, to allocate resources to different social groups – or to contend with public opinion, which might remain wedded to nationalism. Certainly in Europe today there is considerable opposition to proposals to cut government expenditure, especially in sensitive areas like welfare, in order to bring Europe 'into line' with the low taxation 'tiger economies' of South East Asia. A good case could be made that these pressures are more likely to lead to the creation of Fortress Europe than a truly global economy – yet alone world political order.

The neo-functionalists

These problems in functionalist theory encouraged the emergence of a group of revisionists, like E. B. Haas, who agree that economics is a primary motor, but do not see the process as entirely automatic.[37] The neo-functionalists believe that politicians, pressure groups, bureaucrats and others have pushed forward the movement at crucial times. Their central concept is 'spill-over', the way in which discussion of specific issues spills over to wider ones – though the neo-functionalist focus is regional integration rather than the world orbit of the original functional theorists. The way in which discussions about the European Coal and Steel Community, formed in 1951, spilled over into wider issues under the influence of French Europeanists like Jean Monnet, or politicians from the recently-formed Benelux Union, is a common example of this process.

This approach is preferable to the simple functionalist one, as there have clearly been times when 'politics' mattered. Certainly, neo-functionalism has been the most influential approach among academics. However, the initial theory implied that there was no going back. So the subsequent pattern of stops and starts has led to notable modifications, in particular the idea of 'spill-back', where elites – for example, the French at the time of the 1973 oil crisis – departed from common policies and openly pursued the national interest. There have also been problems with the neo-functionalist theory in relation to public opinion. The approach usually assumed that growing economic success and linkages would initially produce an instrumental support which would then turn into a more effective one: public opinion was thus essentially seen as reactive (though in later neo-functionalist writings there was a growing awareness that such opinion helped set the policy agenda).[38] The evidence for the growth of diffuse support for the EU is at best weak; indeed, support may be declining in the late 1990s as economic doubts mount and politicians in general are less inspired by grand European visions.

The federalists

This is the most political model in that it stresses the role of federal ideals, pushed by European visionaries like Monnet (though there has been a split among federalists about means, with some holding that a popularly elected assembly could produce a new constitution, whereas more recent federalists usually accept the need to work inter-governmentally).[39] Federalism was fostered by the Second World War, especially in the moderate resistance movements, and helped lead to the creation of the Council of Europe in 1949. However, this body never fulfilled the federalists' dreams, though its attached Court of Human Rights achieved a growing reputation and role. The anti-federalist states, like Britain, sidelined the Council. Perhaps the best opportunity to found a more truly federal organisation, the European Defence Community, foundered during 1954 in the French Chamber of Deputies on an unholy alliance of nationalist Gaullists and pro-Soviet communists (the two largest parties in a system characterised by a polarised political culture and a form of proportional representation which could help radical parties).

Federalism is perhaps most useful as an approach for comparing what the EU has achieved, and for discussing ways in which it could develop. There is no question at present that the EU has developed anything like the federal political structure of the USA, though it is wrong to see it as simply a grand customs union. In areas like the Common Agricultural Policy, it has developed a notable body of supranational law, and whilst the Maastricht Treaty is in many ways ambiguous, it is hard not to read it as a commitment towards growing political union. Some argue that a better parallel would be the relationship between the different American states at the birth of their nation in the eighteenth century. But is there any real basis of comparison? America was not created by trying to integrate existing sovereign states. It did not have to overcome the forces of particularist nationalism – in the way in which a federal Europe would have to. Nor are European precedents more promising. The Swiss federation, for instance, was built over a long period of time and initially reflected strong forces, such as a perceived external enemy, which do not currently apply to the EU. Moreover, there are usually notable ambiguities in the federalists' view of Europe's future, especially about the exact workings of different tiers of government. A federation would need common policies in many areas, such as defence, but federalists normally try to deflect centralising 'Big Brother' charges by claiming that they really support a devolution of power and 'subsidiarity'. Thus the great political myth of the federalists – of a Europe leading the way to a world of peace – has tended to be pushed from centre stage. Even more problematically, the federalists today are too obsessed with the technocratic planning of new institutions, when the crucial need is to forge a wider cultural unity.

NOTES

1 Vol. 1: H.-D. Klingemann and D. Fuchs (eds), *Citizens and the State*; Vol. 2: O. Niedermayer and R. Sinnott (eds), *Public Opinion and Internationalized Governance*; Vol. 3: O. Borre and E. Scarbrough (eds), *The Scope of Government*; Vol. 4: J. W. Van Deth and E. Scarbrough (eds), *The Impact of Values*; Vol. 5: M. Kaase and K. Newton, *Beliefs in Government*, Oxford, Oxford University Press, 1995.

2 R. Inglehart, *The Silent Revolution*, Princeton, Princeton University Press, 1977; R. Inglehart, *Culture Shift*, Princeton, Princeton University Press, 1990.

3 J. Dunn (ed.), 'Contemporary Crisis of the Nation States?', special issue, *Political Studies*, 1994, 42. See also D. Bell, ' "American Exceptionalism" Revisited: The Role of Civil Society', *The Public Interest*, 1989, 95; and his classic 1960s work *The Coming of Post-Industrial Society*, London, Penguin, 1976.

4 R. Robertson, *Globalisation*, London, Sage, 1992.

5 Inevitably it is impossible to deal with all concepts and theories in their full complexities – including the many differences of opinion on key issues. The following two sections should, therefore, be supported by various introductory/text sources, such as J. Hutchison and A. D. Smith (eds), *Nationalism*, Oxford, Oxford University Press, 1994.

6 See, for example, P. Cartledge, *The Greeks. A Portrait of Self and Others*, Oxford, Oxford University Press, 1993.

7 See, for example, D. Hooson (ed.), *Geography and National Identity*, Oxford, Blackwell, 1994.

8 E. Kamenka, 'Nationalism: Ambiguous Legacies and Contingent Futures', *Political Studies*, 1993, 27.

9 S. J. Woolf (ed.), *Nationalism in Europe: 1815 to the Present*, London, Routledge, 1996, p. 9.

10 For the claim that England was the first modern nation see L. Greenfeld, *Nationalism. Five Roads to Modernity*, Cambridge, Mass., Harvard University Press, 1992. See also L. Colley, *Britons: Forging the Nation, 1707–1837*, New Haven, Yale University Press, 1992.

11 See K. Dyson, *The State Tradition in Western Europe*, Oxford, Martin Robertson, 1980; and C. Tilly (ed.), *The Formation of National States in Western Europe*, Princeton, Princeton University Press, 1975.

12 See M. Forsyth, *Federalism and Nationalism*, Leicester, Leicester University Press, 1989.

13 On nationalism as ideology, see E. Kedourie, *Nationalism*, London, Hutchinson, 1963; and D. Miller, *On Nationality*, Oxford, Clarendon Press, 1995.

14 G. L. Mosse, *Toward the Final Solution*, New York, Howard Fertig, 1978.

15 E. Weber, *Peasants into Frenchmen*, Stanford, Stanford University Press, 1976.

16 See M. Keating, *The Politics of Modern Europe*, Aldershot, Elgar, 1993.

17 Hooson, *op. cit.*, p. 370.

18 P. van den Berghe, *The Ethnic Phenomenon*, New York, Elsevier, 1981; and P. L. van den Berghe, *Race and Ethnicity*, New York, Basic Books, 1970.

19 Among his main publications are *The Ethnic Origin of Nations*, Oxford, Blackwell, 1986; *National Identity*, London, Penguin, 1991; *Nations and Nationalism in a Global Era*, Cambridge, Polity, 1995.

20 E. Gellner, *Nations and Nationalism*, Oxford, Blackwell, 1983, p. 56. See also his *Encounters with Nationalism*, Oxford, Blackwell, 1994.

21 See W. Kornhauser, *The Politics of Mass Society*, Glencoe, Free Press, 1959; and H. Arendt, *The Origins of Totalitarianism*, London, Deutsch, 1986. See also C. C. O'Brien, *God Land*, Cambridge, Mass., Harvard University Press, 1988.

22 See, for example, R. Zariski, *Italy: The Politics of Uneven Development*, Hinsdale, Dryden Press, 1972; T. Nairn, *The Break-up of Britain*, London, New Left Books, 1977. See also I. Wallerstein, *Geopolitics and Geoculture*, Cambridge, Cambridge University Press, 1991.

23 B. Moore Jnr, *The Social Origins of Democracy and Totalitarianism*, Harmondsworth, Penguin, 1967; see also C. Tilly, *Coercion, Capital and European States*, Cambridge, Mass., Blackwell, 1990.

24 On the general argument of the importance of the state see J. Breuilly, *Nationalism and the State*, Manchester, Manchester University Press, 1982; note his review of Gellner and Anderson (see notes 20 and 32) 'Reflections on Nationalism' in Woolf, *op. cit.* See also Dyson, *op. cit.* and H. Spruyt, *The Sovereign State and its Competitors*, Princeton, Princeton University Press, 1995.

25 S. Rokkan, 'Cities, States and Nations: A Dimensional Model for the Study of Contrasts in Development' in S. N. Eisenstadt and S. Rokkan (eds), *Building States and Nations*, London, Sage, 1973.

26 E. J. Hobsbawm, *Nations and Nationalism since 1780*, Cambridge, Cambridge University Press, 1993; E. Hobsbawm and T. Ranger (eds), *The Invention of Tradition*, Cambridge, Cambridge University Press, 1983.

27 O'Brien, *op. cit.*

28 I. Hont, 'The Permanent Crisis of a Divided Mankind: "Contemporary Crisis of the Nation State" in Historical Perspective', *Political Studies*, 1994, 42, esp. p. 217.

29 See especially Kedourie, *op. cit.*

30 For instance, S. Tägil (ed.), *Ethnicity and Nation Building in the Nordic World*, London, Hurst, 1995.

31 For example, Miller, *op. cit.* See also C. Taylor, *Reconciling the Solitudes*, Montreal and Kingston, McGill-Queen's University Press, 1993.
32 B. Anderson, *Imagined Communities*, London, Verso, 1983.
33 See especially A. S. Milward, *The European Rescue of the Nation State*, London, Routledge, 1993. Note too the emphasis on the nation-state in S. Hoffman, 'Obstinate or Obsolete? The Fate of the Nation State and the Case of Western Europe', *Daedalus*, 1966, 95.
34 For an introduction to a more theoretical literature on European integration see M. O'Neil (ed.), *The Politics of European Integration*, London, Routledge, 1996; and J. Michelmann and P. Soldatos (eds), *European Integration: Theories and Approaches*, Lanham, University Press of America, 1994. See also Niedermayer and Sinnott, *op. cit.*, especially R. Sinnott, 'Bringing Public Opinion Back In'.
35 On the importance of communicative interaction see K. Deutsch, *Nation-Building*, London, Atherton Press, 1963.
36 D. Mitrany, *A Working Peace System*, London, RIIA, 1943.
37 E. B. Haas, *The Uniting of Europe*, Stanford, Stanford University Press, 1958.
38 For example, P. C. Schmitter, 'A Revised Theory of Regional Integration' in L. N. Lindberg and S. A. Scheingold (eds), *Regional Integration: Theory and Research*, Cambridge, Mass., Harvard University Press, 1971.
39 A good example is E. Wistrich, *Europe after 1992*, London, Routledge, 1991.

15 Conclusion: part two

Reflections on nationalism and the future of Europe

Roger Eatwell

INTRODUCTION

The causes of the rise of nationalism in Europe were multiple. Even within specific countries different forces operated, which changed in importance through time. For example, nineteenth-century Greek nationalism exhibited a division between the intelligentsia and merchants, who tended to support a rational movement, and the clergy and peasants, who were characterised more by a yearning for an ethno-religious revival of the Orthodox Byzantine Empire. In the Germanic states at the turn of the nineteenth century, Romantic intellectuals helped to define German nationalist ideology. But later, an authoritarian state led by a dynamic chancellor was responsible for creating the new Reich through a series of successful wars. Later still, various elite groups strove – following the terminology of George Mosse – to 'nationalize the masses'.[1] Although Germany in the early twentieth century is normally considered to be a leading example of nationalism, it is far from clear whether widespread national consciousness existed at this time. It is interesting to note in this context that Gregor Strasser, one of the leading figures on the early Nazi 'left', was deeply affected during the First World War when one of the men under his command asked what was the meaning of 'Fatherland': neither he nor his father had any land, and they had often gone hungry.

So is it impossible to generalise usefully about the causes of nationalism in the past? And are there no insights offered by theories of nationalism into the possibilities of creating a more truly united Europe in the future – points which could reinforce one of the theories of integration?

EUROPEAN NATIONALISM

The Greek and German examples outlined above highlight the dangers of four of the most common generalisations which are typically made about the character and process of European nationalism. One concerns the distinction between Eastern and Western European nationalisms.[2] The latter are seen as liberal and civic, whereas the former are viewed as ethnic and authoritarian. Certainly the potential for strife is much greater in the East today, and disputes seem to be less amenable to the incremental processes of modern political bargaining.[3] There is a high level of xenophobia, including low trust in neighbouring countries and in Jews. But the Greek example shows that liberal strands have existed in the East, and similar elements can be found elsewhere, for instance among a section of the pre-1917 Russian elite.[4] More commonly, there have been notable forms of ethnic nationalism in the West, including Nazism. Other non-liberal forms can be discerned within the IRA, which was founded on a 'moral elitism' involving the belief that a virtuous minority earned the right to rule through blood sacrifice.[5] It is even possible to question the liberality of the French tradition: certainly there has been a taste for Bonapartist leaders and the strong state which does not conform to Anglo-American visions of liberalism.

A second common generalisation concerns the very distinction between East and West. Many have argued that it is important to add a third area, namely Central Europe. The case usually centres on the charge that the Russian tradition is not truly European.[6] Historically, Russia has been cut off from mainstream European development by factors such as the Mongol conquest, lengthy tsarist despotism, the persistence of serfdom well into the nineteenth century, and the Bolshevik Revolution. Another notable influence has been the Orthodox Church, which has tended to glorify obedience and to celebrate suffering. Predictably, individual freedom is hardly central to Russian thinking and civil society is weak, though there is a strong sense of solidarity. But some of Russia's problems have parallels in Central Europe – for instance, the Catholic Church in Poland has historically argued for the need to serve the Polish nation no matter what particular regime is in power (though it played a part in the ultimate downfall of communism, aided by a Polish Pope and American conniving).[7] There is also the question of what is included in Central Europe? Does it embrace the Balkans and South East European ex-communist states, which have a more fragmented and anarchical culture than Russia? And where is Greece – often seen as the font of Western values and the only South East European country not to fall under communist control – to be fitted in? Turning westwards, where does Germany belong? Since 1945, Germany has normally been considered Western, but at the beginning of the century there were some who saw it both culturally and geopolitically as part of '*Mitteleuropa*'. Although Germany's boundaries then extended much further to the east, there has been a recent revival of the debate within Germany.[8] The discussion could become even more crucial as the European Union shifts its borders eastwards, and the old generation of leaders pass away (it is hard to imagine a future German premier emotionally holding hands with a French president at the First World War shrine of Verdun as Helmut Kohl did with François Mitterrand in the 1980s).

A third common generalisation about European development concerns the distinction between state-led and society-led nationalisms.[9] On this approach, in countries like France the creation of the state preceded any clear conception of national identity, yet alone national consciousness. But in other cases, for instance in the Balkans, ideologised intellectuals and elites helped create the state. Again, there are some insights in this argument, but not all old nations were created by the state. In England, national identity was forged partly by key groups, like the clergy, the new middle class and part of the aristocracy. It is also far from clear that all the new nations were entirely manufactured from above. Czech national identity had its roots in farmers who saw themselves as the nation, and who developed a linguistic sense of belonging which largely by-passed the gentry: they saw the Enlightenment as meaning centralisation and Germanisation (though later intellectuals added significantly to the cause, not least by inventing a past).

A fourth common generalisation concerns the belief that extensive mass national consciousness existed by 1914. Where this has been challenged,[10] the main force of the argument has been to set a later date for the nationalisation of the masses. Thus it has been argued that the working class in France was not truly integrated into the national community until after the reforms, including votes for women, which followed the Liberation in 1944.[11] But it is also useful to deconstruct national consciousness, to take a cross-sectional rather than chronological view. Before the First World War, there had been considerable talk in left-wing circles of mass resistance to a 'capitalist' conflagration; there were also pockets of non-socialist pacifism. Yet when war came, only a handful of conscientious objectors could be found among the main combatant nations. So why did people flock to the colours, where they died in large numbers? In Russia especially there was an element of coercion from the outset. Brutal discipline undoubtedly helped keep other armies together as the losses mounted (even so, there were problems, like the mutiny of French forces after the disastrous Nivelle offensive in 1917). Within Britain, there seems little doubt that large numbers felt a strong affective identity: they fought because they were part of a nation. But others fought for different principles. It is doubtful if a Marxist South Wales miner felt any strong loyalty to a Britain characterised by monarchy and tradition, though he could fight in a war for freedom against German militarism and authoritarianism – a sentiment encouraged by the most vicious British propaganda (the evil 'Hun' was accused of all kinds of dastardly deeds, including raping nuns and eating babies).[12] Some British workers may even have fought for their jobs: the term 'Made in Germany' was first coined in the 1890s, and there had been hard times before the war, not least in industries facing increasing German competition.

These last points highlight the central point made in Chapter 1: namely the need to explain micro (individual) behaviour. Nationalism's powerful attraction to individuals stems from the fact that it has the potential to appeal to the three major dimensions of human behaviour in modern society. First, nationalism has an affective side: it fulfils the desire to be part of a community, to feel a sense of belonging. Second, it usually has an economic side: it promises members of the community that they will prosper, or at least benefit in some way, under nationalism. Third – and perhaps least appreciated – it has a more serious idealistic side: the language of nationalism has frequently been that of liberty, equality, fraternity and progress (even the Nazis talked much of freedom, though this was clearly not liberal freedom).[13] At a functional level, nationalism helps provide the sense of trust which is vital for the working of society, for instance by encouraging people to believe that equitable treatment will be accorded to all members of the nation. In an important sense, nationalism is highly rational rather than irrational.

The dangers of sweeping generalisations about nationalism have already been noted, but viewed within this individual spotlight, it is possible to highlight crucial aspects of the theories which were discussed in the previous section. The first concerns the affective dimension. It seems clear that it is easiest to build a sense of community when there is a strong existing texture of ethnicity and myth. The ability to demonise the 'Other' helps to crystallise this sentiment. The second concerns the economic dimension. The rise of nationalism is clearly linked to the arrival of modern society in the sense that economic issues become central, in a way that they were not in older, religious societies.[14] But nationalism is not necessarily linked to the victims of uneven development, or depression; it is possible to defend the nation as a means of preserving and enhancing relative wealth (though in the latter case there usually needs to be some form of real or imagined threat to fire nationalism). Finally, the idealism of nationalism is linked to a new post-Enlightenment vocabulary, particularly the ability of intellectuals and elites to refine and target this language – to make it appear legitimate and relevant.

These last points clearly underline that individuals do not live isolated from broader norms and trends. In order to understand the rise and staying power of nationalism in a socio-economic context, it is necessary to highlight crucial meso and macro factors. Taking the rise of national identity in the early period first, there seems little doubt that modernisation theory has not placed sufficient emphasis on the role of war and religion in the rise of the nation. Religion is especially important, for it was central to the daily lives of people in a way that war usually was not – though war (or the constant threat of it) could reinforce a lingering sense of the 'Other', and as states began to raise large armies the military itself became a unit of socialisation. Turning more to the rise of national consciousness, there seems little doubt that the state, elites and nationalist intellectuals have all played a crucial role in creating an imagined community, though this has often worked best when they could gain the support of, or penetrate existing organisations, like churches. This point can be seen in a dramatic form by considering the breakdown of the 'nation' in the former Yugoslavia in the 1990s. There was nothing spontaneous about ethnic cleansing and genocide, and it certainly did not stem simply from primordial-ethnic differences (though there had been atrocities in the past, including mass killings in the Second World War by Croats and Serbs). During the 1980s, hatred was developed from above by politicians in Serbia, aided and abetted by others – notably a group of scholars who developed a warped anthropology purporting to show the Bosnian Muslims as non-European sub-humans, and by a section of the Serbian Orthodox Church which helped create an almost hysterical hatred of non-Serbs.[15]

Academics have frequently mocked politicians who create a pastiche past. For example, in 1996 the leader of the French National Front, Jean-Marie Le Pen, turned up at a major rally accompanied by a new effigy to stand beside Joan of Arc (historic symbol of unifying the French and expelling the foreigner). The iconographic novelty was Clovis, a Frankish king who had been crowned in Rheims cathedral around AD 496, and a man whom some see as the father of the modern French nation. But he was garbed like the cartoon character Asterix the Gaul, though this was a different tribe and the Gauls had in the past been a source of a counter-founding myth of French identity (Clovis' Germanic, possibly Belgian, background had not appealed to some, who sought to discover purer French roots). Perhaps Le Pen is ignorant of French historiography, but it seems more likely that he is a master of propaganda – a man who realises the need for symbolism to be familiar, and the fact that the power of political myths cannot be understood simply in terms of their truth value.[16]

TOWARDS A UNITED EUROPE?

This stress on mythology has obvious implications for the European Union and its quest to achieve an 'ever closer union' of the European peoples. Anthony Smith has doubted whether a true European 'Community' can be formed, arguing that

> There is no European analogue to Bastille or Armistice Day, no European ceremony for the fallen in battle, no European shrine of kings or saints. When it comes to the ritual and ceremony of collective identification, there is no European equivalent of national or religious community.[17]

In some ways, the recent revival of nationalism is making the situation worse. Germany, increasingly the main power within the European Union, may not in the past have celebrated Armistice Day per se, but it has seen 1945 as a turning point in the universal triumph of democracy and the rule of law. Now, a controversial new generation of nationalist intellectuals portray the end of the war as a *German* tragedy (with the implication that the Russians, Poles and others were responsible), and search for *German* political roots – a quest which is often linked to dreams of returning to *Mitteleuropa* and a distaste for the individualist materialism of Western liberal democracy. The Clovis affair in France reveals a similar quest for identity in the past, though it is more true to say that intellectuals, who were once so important in interpreting the past for the French masses, have recently found themselves losing faith in grand causes, including those of the left – the traditional affiliation of the French intelligentsia.[18]

But is Europe so devoid of common traditions? There have certainly been attempts to create mythological linkages, dating back at least as far as the Middle Ages when Europe was united in religious terms (it would perhaps be more accurate to say relatively united, as there were always different sects, some of which helped define early local and national identity). A common focus of such myths has been the Frankish king, Charlemagne, who died in AD 814 after consolidating a vast empire which comprised most of Europe west of the Elbe and north of the Pyrenees. Early texts can be found which refer to him as '*rex, pater Europae*', though the term does not seem to have had great social or political significance. Indeed, Charlemagne more commonly appears in nationalist mythology (he is *Karl der Grosse* to the Germans, who have a better claim to being his successors than the French).

Historically, conceptions of 'Europe' have been protean, and took on various facets before the French Revolution, when the term came into common usage.[19] The word had first emerged in Ancient Greek times as a geographical reference, though not one covering the boundaries of contemporary Europe: until around the sixteenth century, the Alps constituted a major natural frontier and 'Europe' was at times used as a synonym for the non-Asian and African Mediterranean area. Later, the term became associated with ideas such as freedom, dating back to Ancient Greece; with Christendom; and with civilisation. Sometimes there was a teleological attempt to relate these traditions. For example, the Renaissance's conception of beauty owed much to Classical art; and the fall of Athens could be portrayed as stemming from a combination of internal division and the rise of less civilised, but more martial, external enemies.

Some of these linkages are at best highly debatable in academic terms. Athens is commonly seen as the font of modern democracy, but political rights applied solely to freeborn males, excluding both women and slaves (slavery was actually defended by Aristotle in thinly veiled racial terms).[20] Moreover, Athens was only for a brief time a democracy, a form of government which subsequently largely disappeared until after the eighteenth century.[21] Even then, it has not been the most common form of government within Europe (North America has a better claim to being the embodiment of 'European' values in this sense). Similarly, the Renaissance may have seen a great flowering of the arts and learning in Europe, but this came after other societies had built their own great civilisations. Many Europeans lived in animal skins at the time of the first great Chinese or Egyptian dynasties. Moreover, the rise of European 'civilisation' did not prevent the periodic occurrence of wars, including bloody colonial ones where non-European peoples were often treated appallingly. It is interesting to note in this context that the Turks, often demonised in modern European thought as the historic epitome of fanatical Islam, were frequently more tolerant in areas they governed than their Christian contemporaries.

In 'European' myth-making terms, these are not necessarily damning problems. The French academic, Ernest Renan, taught long ago that in nation building it is more important to forget – even deliberately to get history wrong – than to remember. What is problematic within the usual mythical European historiography is its implied conception of identity: namely, the celebration of a male, white, Christian culture – onto which is grafted somewhat uneasily the Classical legacy, via the theme of democracy and civilisation. Even more dangerously, this version of the European tradition tends to depict those with dark skin as inferior or menacing, a trend which for centuries has been reinforced by Western memories of the Crusades and Western artistic conceptions of beauty and the connotations of superiority linked to them. This mythology has major implications for current and future politics. Internally, it makes the task of creating a multicultural Europe, which includes those of dark skin and the Muslim faith, more difficult. Externally, it encourages a sense of threat, a tendency to view television pictures of 'smart' weapons 'clinically' striking Iraqi or other targets as a legitimate use of violence against the old enemy (though this is not to deny that there are potential real enemies).[22]

A further dimension of European identity has concerned its relationship to modernity and progress in the socio-economic sense: Europe as the home of the Industrial Revolution; Europe as the birthplace of the extensive welfare state. The apparently relentless onset of globalisation now seems to threaten Europe's economic future. Some countries, like the Netherlands, have become heavily post-industrial societies, with three-quarters of their labour force working in the tertiary economy. But in the foreseeable future, Europe still needs to employ many people in industry if there is not to be extensive unemployment. Moreover, many tertiary sector jobs are low paid and often insecure, such as video-rental shop assistants – hardly an appealing prospect, especially to men who have worked previously in long-term well-paid sectors, like the car-making industry. Extensive welfare too now seems to be a luxury many countries cannot afford. This is resulting in countries like Germany trying to enforce some cuts in order to reduce company social security bills and government expenditure – though the power of worker resistance and the desire to defend welfare provisions is illustrated by the successful French lorry drivers' strike in 1996, which involved the state in a private sector dispute.

These developments have important implications for the process of European integration, and relations with external states. Although it is important not to ignore the idealistic side to the movement, there has unquestionably been a strongly instrumental attitude to EU membership. This is not simply true of late joiners, like Britain and Denmark, where an important section of opinion saw membership primarily in terms of the economic benefits it would bring. Even within the states which have been most idealistic about creating a new federal Europe which would lead to both peace and prosperity, this tendency is growing. For instance, in the Netherlands, Frits Bolkenstein, the leader of the Conservative-Liberals, has reintroduced the term 'national interest' into politics. Recent opinion polls in Belgium show that, whilst most Belgian voters support monetary union, they oppose the related budget cuts which are likely to trim their generous welfare system. Belgium, which had previously been a major net beneficiary of the EU budget, is beginning to perceive union in a different light. Indeed, across the EU as a whole there is a growing reassessment of both the economic implications of further unity and the viability of generous welfare provision in a world of competition with countries which have little or no welfare – though different conclusions are being drawn.[23] Growing fears about EMU tend to work against further unity: the initial entry criteria are (supposedly) strict and expenditure cuts to make the targets could push countries further into recession. Moreover, once locked into a single currency, a country will not be able to pursue policies such as exchange rate modification to boost its economy. Fears about welfare, on the other hand, tend to point more towards a united Fortress Europe, where most foreign goods are kept out. Behind this wall, old practices could stay largely unchanged, or be altered in the long run with minimal electoral harm to the current mainstream parties.

But Fortress Europe is fraught with its own dangers. Economic ones include Europe's dependency on key external resources, such as energy. Protection could also encourage inefficiency and a long-term drop in living standards. Politically, there are also dangers. The current socio-economic situation, especially high unemployment in many European countries, encourages the rise of extreme nationalist/Eurosceptic parties. However, mainstream elites will have great difficulty defusing this appeal by adopting a Fortress Europe policy. Certainly a past lesson from the rise of leaders like Le Pen or Fini in Italy is that they benefit from similarities with mainstream rhetoric (and especially any form of association with mainstream parties, or support in the media, which give them legitimacy).[24] Fortress Europe could both destabilise internal politics and exacerbate external relations – not least with the USA, which might retreat into isolation, or retaliate economically and trigger a major downturn in world trade.

It therefore seems more sensible to imagine Europe in terms of an open identity which is willing to learn from others, and which is linked to the creation of an economic programme which avoids the worst scenarios of globalisation or Fortress Europe. It is true that since the eighteenth century European identity has been characterised by a sense of superiority (though this has not prevented hierarchical ethnic divisions among groups: for instance, British jokes about the lazy and stupid Irish often prove equally amusing for many French people if you substitute the Belgians, or Germans if you substitute the Poles). However, the relationship between European culture and the outside world has not been entirely a one way process.

Modern Scandinavian and German Bauhaus design are important parts of twentieth-century European artistic culture, but they owed much to the impact in artistic circles during the nineteenth century of much older Japanese design. Nietzsche and Heidegger are widely recognised (especially outside Britain) as great thinkers, but they were intrigued by the stress on communal life embodied in Oriental thought and a key theme in their writings was the need to import aspects of this culture. In economic terms, Europe has borrowed from America (Ford Model T production lines) and most recently Japan (the identity between workers and management within the factory).[25]

Placing stress on the need to learn from abroad does not mean engaging either in a form of politically correct, or a New Right, demonisation of the European tradition, whilst ignoring faults in others. Free market America is characterised by poverty and racism: if anything, these facets are becoming worse, and general social inequality is growing too in an apparently irreversible way, with a small overclass becoming relatively ever richer. Non-European cultures frequently repress women, have overly strict family relationships and suppress dissent, often brutally: again, the trend seems to be in a worrying direction (though it is more difficult to generalise on such a broad canvas). Even the most democratic emerging states, like Malaysia, are ambivalent about opposition and tend to impose cultural conformity (*vide* its paranoia about the Internet). It is also important not to be carried away by utopian universalism. The leading British political theorist, David Held, has recently argued that the Westphalian model of world order based on sovereign states is giving way to cosmopolitan democracy, where the basic building blocks are groups and associations produced by a global order.[26] We undoubtedly live in an age of growing trans-national organisations, like Greenpeace as well as Exxon; of trans-national problems, such as pollution as well as poverty; and of trans-national communities, like Internet users as well as Islam. It is also true that ideas shape politics, and utopian academics could be the New Age priesthood.

But utopian internationalist views play down the 'democratic deficit' which afflicts the EU, the major current example of trans-national government. This is in part a problem which could be solved by institutional change within the EU. For instance, the Parliament could be given added powers, and a second chamber introduced representing the regions. These changes should increase interest in this body's workings (currently, knowledge of its powers and operation is almost non-existent, though most people realise that the EU is essentially run by elites).[27] Parties contesting European elections could also be required to run a minimum percentage of candidates in more than one country, and to be accorded representation only if they received a minimum of, say, 5 per cent wherever they ran. This would encourage trans-national party cooperation and the writing of programmes that faced wider issues, and would help foster a common European identity.[28]

However, there are more fundamental problems to the democratic deficit. Liberal democracy was intimately linked to the rise of nations and a relatively cohesive sense of identity. Some commentators have argued that the EU does not need to develop any strong sense of loyalty, because it faces no serious external threat: the Eurosceptic taunt 'Who would die for Brussels?' is, therefore, misguided.[29] All that is required is trust and a basic framework of law. But as well as discounting future dangers, this argument ignores crucial issues relating to democracy. Some critics have argued that the EU can only usurp two democratic dimensions: the 'contract' function (whereby the state protects its citizens' rights in exchange for their support) and the 'control of power' function (whereby the citizen can replace one governing elite by another). On this analysis, a third democratic dimension, the 'representational' function, should remain with the nation-state, whilst a fourth, the 'participatory' function, is increasingly best served at a more local or regional level, where people feel the greatest sense of concern and identity.[30]

This argument usually does not make clear how the control of power function could move to the trans-national level. Moreover, a strong sense of identification with regions or nations is not necessarily inconsistent with a move towards further European unity. Loyalty towards, say, Bavaria or Yorkshire was not broken in the process of founding the British and German states, and to this day remains strong. Yet unless a wider sense of European identity can also be achieved, there will be a series of problems which afflict the EU, a point which the culturalist theory of integration highlights. This is not simply a question of abstract issues relating to democracy. There are more everyday problems of policy and institutional organisation. In terms of policy, redistributive policies in particular require some form of affective or idealistic identity; they highlight that trust alone is not enough. In institutional terms, a strong sense of local political identity which is not tied to a wider one could mean that a future United States of Europe is persistently troubled by 'Quebecs' seeking to secede, or exercising the threat in order to gain concessions. This could dominate the agenda, and cause resentment in other regions/nations. Indeed, whilst a dimension of local participation is democratically important, there are major problems in multi-tier government, including proliferating bureaucracy and lack of clear responsibilities, as well as the institutionalisation of particularist disputes.

There is a need to create an identity which, in the short run at least, is less universal than the one implied by Held – though one which is essentially open rather than exclusionist. Instead of conceiving potential membership in terms of a rigid set of countries, the EU should be open to others who accept core values, such as human rights. On this score, some past applicants for membership – notably Turkey – struggle to qualify in the late 1990s. But they should not be rejected simply on geographical grounds, yet alone on the colour of their skins or the nature of their religions (there are liberal readings of Islam, for instance in its relationship to women). Similarly, Russia in the past failed to comply with core values. But it should be welcomed now if

it seeks to join – and not as an area ripe for 'colonisation' by individualistic
and capitalist values. Although economic problems seem paramount in
people's minds, there has been a demand for democratic freedoms; moreover, there is an important sense in which Russia's more communal and
egalitarian values have much to teach others. In this context it is worth
noticing that one of the European countries which has recently seen one of
the lowest levels of unemployment, combined with very high levels of affluence, is the Netherlands – where executive salaries are comparatively low
and a sense of social solidarity is still fairly strong in spite of the breakdown
of the old social 'pillars' on which its consociational democracy was based.

Frequently, the Soviet Union (like the Austro-Hungarian Empire before
it) is used to illustrate the futility of the EU seeking to create a new multinational state. Certainly the USSR spectacularly broke up into 15 sovereign
states, and Russia continues to be plagued by further secessionist pressures
including significant ethnic violence. But it is misleading to see the collapse
of the USSR as the result of the power of primordial nationalisms.[31] In its
early days, communism did much to encourage nationalism: the languages
of the main nationalities were declared the official languages of the Soviet
Republics, which had their own symbols, such as flags. The later
Russification programme, on the other hand, encouraged a hostile response.
This was fanned after the 1970s by the Americans, the Catholic Church,
émigré groups, and others who deliberately fostered a nationalist revival in
Eastern Europe. Whilst relative economic failure was undoubtedly an
important catalyst, the re-emergence of nationalism in this area owed much
to propaganda and a re-imagining of the community.

The task of creating a more truly European identity is undoubtedly problematic, not least as value change is difficult in any normal circumstance.
Where new political cultures have been created relatively quickly, for
example in West Germany after 1945, very specific factors were at work –
such as the stigma of Nazism, the Allied re-education programme, and the
1950s economic miracle which meant that West Germany had Western
Europe's largest GDP by 1961. In other cases where there has been apparent
rapid change, for example in Portugal and Spain after the fall of the Salazar
and Franco dictatorships in 1974–5, it is important to note that there was a
significant wave of economic modernisation before the collapse of the dictatorships. Besides, some of the state elite were already preparing for the
transition to democracy as a prelude to entering 'Europe'.

These features have been much less true in post-1989 Eastern Europe,
where countries have experienced serious difficulties in promoting individualistic and market values – particularly Russia, where communist
socialisation went deepest. Egalitarian social solidarity in these areas
remains strong, and whilst there was a sense of self-interest under communism, this was usually linked to party nepotism rather than Western
concepts of entrepreneurship, risk and the importance of legally enforceable
contract. Moreover, old groups, like the military and secret service, appear

to remain powerful, or fester ominously, behind the scenes. There remain unanswered questions about the sources of money which financed Zhirinovsky's surprisingly successful Russian nationalist election campaign in 1991. In Belarus, President Lukashenko's links with the old guard seem even clearer, and his 1996 presidential election was notably manipulated. Lukashenko's rhetoric at times also has an ominously old, Cold War tinge to it – though his favourable references to Hitler's ideas are a new ideological twist for a man who seems to have aspirations to be president of a revived greater Russia. This anti-Western rhetoric clearly poses a major potential problem, both in terms of a possible new military threat, and in terms of integrating parts of Eastern Europe into a new 'Europe'. These problems are made even greater by the desire of countries like Poland to draw the boundary of 'Europe' along their eastern frontiers, and to enter NATO and the EU as quickly as possible. This inevitably causes further fears and tensions in the East.

This last point again highlights the crucial need to define a European identity which is not dangerously exclusionary. Although Jean Monnet remarked near the end of his life that if he could have started again he would have begun with culture, there has been a notable lack of serious attention paid to the issue of common European identity. There have been some signs since the 1970s that the EU Commission has begun to recognise this lacuna, and the Maastricht Treaty referenda in Denmark and France during 1992 seem to have come as a particular shock (they not only revealed the extent of opposition to further integration but also major social splits between the young, more educated and business-oriented groups, and the old, more rural and less skilled).[32] However, the beginnings of the campaign during 1995–6 to launch EMU demonstrated a remarkable continued commitment to a neo-functionalist framework. Although it is important to note that the early stages of the EMU 'information programme' were aimed more at elite than mass opinion, it is clear that most in the Commission did not see identity as a crucial problem. It is an organisation run by technocrats rather than myth-makers, a reflection of its essentially bureaucratic nature; even the former politicians at its head are usually characterised by a background of consensual politics and behind the scenes deals rather than evangelical zeal.

There have been some signs recently of more perceptive academics reviving the idea of European unity as having prevented war – and as being crucial to prevent further Yugoslavias. This view is often linked to support for a common foreign and security policy, including the use of European troops in 'policing' actions.[33] Although the absence of war in most of Europe since 1945 was a result of the existence of NATO rather than the EU, these myths and policies have considerable potential for fostering unity, for the fear of major war is potentially a powerful one. However, most academics have largely adopted a kind of 1930s fellow-travelling with communism view of the EU, seeing it as part of an inevitable movement towards progress and necessarily led by a Platonic Guardian class. Whilst there has been some growth of interest in the issue of identity recently, this is typically linked to a desire to use citizenship as the great civic symbol which will unite the peoples.[34] There is no doubt that the post-war West German experience has shown that what Jürgen Habermas and others call 'constitutional patriotism' can appeal to sections of opinion, especially educated left-liberal opinion. Moreover, in large political units which pose problems in terms of democratic control and participation, clearly defined rights (and duties) are unquestionably important. But it is not clear how strong a sense of affective community can be built around such symbols; and they completely ignore the economic dimension of behaviour.

Whether it is possible to delineate an attractive European identity, or to disseminate it without provoking a nationalist backlash, is a vast topic beyond the scope of this book. But there are some pointers which offer hope. A recent major study of West European values sponsored by the European Science Foundation has shown that there are some notable political trends which could be interpreted as preparing the way for such an identity. The first concerns the decline of religion, though a sense of religiosity remains strong and people seem to be seeking something new to believe in.[35] Another trend concerns the growth of post-material values and the decline in the quest for ever greater personal wealth, regardless of social consequences – though the post-material argument, especially the emphasis on generational change towards new values, has frequently been over-stated: many young people are increasingly concerned about jobs and security. More widely, people are still strongly committed to old values in other ways, in particular the defence of welfare (over 90 per cent of West Europeans support extensive welfare provision in fields like health, education, housing and provision for the old). However, it is important not to confuse values, such as support for welfare, with a necessary defence of old forms. There is far more suspicion of big government than there was 50 years ago. This is linked to a greater awareness of the strengths of markets.

These arguments point to the possibility of reviving the idea that in modern times Europe has been characterised by a Third Way (a theme which was especially strong within both Social Democratic and Christian Democratic circles after 1945). In the immediate post-war context, the synthesis which many sought was between American capitalist democracy and Soviet communism. Today the need is more to draw lessons from the business success and social solidarity of the rising new states in South East Asia, without losing sight of their failures, and to combine these lessons with a view of the strengths and weaknesses of American democracy and business. In particular, it is important not to confuse the growing acceptance of Hayekian-type arguments in defence of markets with the values of capitalism, or a total rejection of the state. In Japan, for example, the state has unquestionably been important through its links with business, especially during the post-war take-off years (subsequently large companies have often had the funds and confidence to invest for the future: the Japan Victor Corporation spent $3 billion to develop the domestic video recorder). Moreover, it is possible to have markets where people are not governed by neo-classical economic principles of rational individual short-run maximisation.[36] Various proposals for new cooperatives, or forms of stake holding, are linked to the creation of a different economic culture, more concerned with community and the long run. In Singapore, which in 30 years has transformed itself into one of the most dynamic economies in the world with a per capita GDP well above that of its former colonial master, Britain, *wa* or harmony among groups, including the government, is the order of the day. The call for a Third Way, therefore, must be linked to an up-dated conception, and much less tied to old ideas of the large state and corporatism. It must be willing to look to new ideas, including private provision, to help fund welfare, which in some non-core areas (like health spa treatment in Germany) will have to be trimmed. Essentially, the Third Way must be a cultural more than an institutional goal in the short run – though new banking institutions to finance new ventures with the hope of long-run success may well be called for.[37] It is especially important to tread warily in terms of creating new EU economic or political structures, which could harm business performance, or alienate voters yet more from a broader conception of 'Europe'.

It must be stressed that this is not an argument for tearing down the EU, which would mainly give succour to extreme or particularist nationalism, or for letting it languish as a primarily economic grouping. For all its faults, the long-term goal should be to reform the EU rather than to consign it to the dustbin of history: in particular, its institutional structure, including the relationship to lower tiers of government, needs defining more carefully – and democratically. The point is more that the immediate focus needs to be on values, and on expanding the EU to encompass the still fragile new democracies of Eastern Europe. It is especially important not to lose sight of this last dimension, or to see it in limited terms of admitting only the most 'suitable' richer and more Westernised countries, like the Czech Republic and Poland – which appears to be the emerging EU Commission view. To adopt the words of Mikhail Gorbachev, Russia too needs to be admitted into the common European home. It is an apposite time, for Europe is returning to itself after half a millennium of outward expansion, a change which implies the need for a new vision of itself. Moreover, the rapid collapse of communism in Russia has destroyed or weakened important macro and meso forces which helped give individuals a sense of belonging. The Russian authoritarian tradition has been over-stated, but there is no doubt that it has a political culture which poses problems for the establishment of democracy. There also seems little doubt that there is a potential for radical nationalist politics, especially if the economic situation fails to improve rapidly. Given that Russia still possesses a major military capacity, this is an ominous prospect. It is, therefore, vital that 'Europe' helps to provide a new sense of affective community – though the process will need an economic dimension as well, for the OECD estimates that Russia may have lost approaching half its GDP during 1990–3. In order to sell such aid to Western Europeans, leaders will need to emerge on the European scene who are capable of using the language and myths of idealism – including the fear of war – effectively. The success of post-1945 Marshall Aid, which benefited its donor, America, as well as Europe, offers fertile ground here. A new 'Monnet Aid' programme for the East is vastly more important than the highly risky introduction of EMU in the very near future.

Within the existing EU, there are undoubtedly developments within meso and macro structures which could help further a stronger European identity. Groups like trades unions now look increasingly to the European Union to protect their rights and workers, especially as corporatist structures within states continue to weaken. The same is true of many other voluntary groups, such as environmental and anti-racist ones. Schools and universities have widespread programmes of exchange, in the latter case often funded by the EU. The rise of regionalism and small-scale nationalisms, which are often specifically linked to creating a wider understanding at the European level, will help shape values in the future too. At a more diffuse level, people travel much more within Europe than they did even 30 years ago: whilst on occasion this can reinforce old stereotypes (Germans grabbing all the beach chairs), in general the process promotes communication and understanding. More fundamentally, many of the old structures, like social class or religion – even family – have been dramatically weakened and the scope exists for significant political change. Major national symbols and traditions are also under threat: in 1996 a majority of British people told opinion pollsters that they believed that the monarchy would cease to exist in the not too distant future. Perhaps even more surprisingly, an October 1996 MORI poll found that 57 per cent of British people would support closer cooperation between the countries of the EU, though a majority opposed EMU: even the most Eurosceptic of states sees the need for many forms of closer links and understanding. There are dangers of over-stating the European rather than specific national nature of many changes. In particular, the threat to dominant parties from radical new ones seems much greater in some countries than others.[38] But taking a general view it is hard not to see evidence that the pattern of politics, which in many ways has shown remarkably little change since 1945, is on the verge of a major shift.

Whether the new forces which emerge will be those of extremist or particularist nationalism, or those which seek a more universal and consensual form of problem solving, will be the great European question for the future. The answer to this conundrum may well lie in the hands of political elites – and other groups capable of setting the agenda, like the media – for there is strong evidence that opinion flows from top to bottom.[39] The problem here is that, whilst there is general support for further union among most countries' political mainstreams, cracks are beginning to emerge, and the idea of

national self-interest is re-emerging. Moreover, deepening European unification is beginning to face the problem of internal politicisation. There was a
relatively high degree of consensus on key issues like tariff reduction among
the six members of the EEC during the 1950s and 1960s. But as the terms of
reference have broadened and economic problems grown, at least one party
within each state – sometimes from within the mainstream, sometimes a
radical new entrant – is tending to oppose further European unification and
to pander to anti-'European' sentiments in a populist way (though there are
notable exceptions, like Portugal and Luxembourg, both of which combine
high levels of Euro-enthusiasm with a strong sense of national identity). The
introduction of EMU could cause further political problems in the sense
that it will be tempting to blame expenditure cuts, especially on popular
items like welfare, on 'Europe'. Last but by no means least, the expansion of
NATO to Russia's frontiers could fire a new wave of nationalism in this
unstable, but still highly armed, country.

Against a background of the collapse of old social structures and
symbols, continuing economic problems, the politicisation of 'Europe', and
the breakdown of mainstream ideologies, there is clearly much to do if
Europe is not to enter a new Dark Age.

NOTES

1 G. L. Mosse, *The Nationalization of the Masses*, New York, New American
   Library, 1977.
2 For example, H. Kohn, *The Idea of Nationalism*, New York, Macmillan, 1944.
3 C. A. Kupchan (ed.), *Nationalism and Nationalities in the New Europe*, Ithaca,
   Cornell University Press, 1995, especially the chapter by G. Schöpflin,
   'Nationalism and Ethnicity in Europe, East and West'.
4 D. Lieven, *The Aristocracy in Europe, 1815–1914*, Basingstoke, Macmillan,
   1992. For a rare example of the claim that there was an emerging democratic
   culture before the Bolshevik Revolution see J. Walkin, *The Rise of Democracy in
   Pre-Revolutionary Russia*, New York, Praeger, 1983.
5 T. Garvin, *1922: The Birth of Irish Democracy*, Dublin, Gill and Macmillan,
   1996. Cf. T. P. Coogan, *The IRA*, London, HarperCollins, 1995.
6 For example, M. Kundera, 'The Tragedy of Central Europe', *New York Review
   of Books*, 26 April 1984; D. Rancour-Laferriere, *The Slave Soul of Russia*, New
   York, New York University Press, 1995; T. Garton Ash, *The Magic Lantern*,
   New York, Vintage, 1993; and G. Schöpflin, 'Central Europe: Definitions Old
   and New' in G. Schöpflin and N. Woods (eds), *In Search of Central Europe*,
   Cambridge, Polity, 1989.
7 On this example of the under-studied role of the covert operation in politics see
   C. Bernstein, *His Holiness: John Paul II and the Hidden History of Our Time*,
   New York, Doubleday, 1996.
8 On the growing new German nationalism see J. Ely, 'Forum: The *Frankfurter
   Allgemeine Zeitung* and Contemporary National-Conservatism', *German
   Politics and Society*, 1995, 13; see also G. Langguth, *In Search of Security: A
   Social-Psychological Portrait of Today's Germany*, Westport, Praeger, 1996.
9 See the section on theories of nationalism in Chapter 14.
10 For example, W. Connor, 'When Is a Nation?', *Ethnic and Racial Studies*,
   1990, 13.

11 B. Jenkins and N. Copsey, 'Nation, Nationalism and National Identity in France' in B. Jenkins and A. A. Sofos (eds), *Nation and Identity in Contemporary Europe*, London, Routledge, 1996, p. 103.

12 On the varied aspects of British First World War propaganda see K. Haste, *Keep the Home Fires Burning*, London, Allen Lane, 1977; and G. S. Messinger, *British Propaganda and the State in the First World War*, Manchester, Manchester University Press, 1992.

13 For the argument that Nazism was a serious ideology see R. Eatwell, 'Towards a New Model of Generic Fascism', *Journal of Theoretical Politics*, 1992, 4; and 'How to Define the "Fascist Minimum": the Centrality of Ideology', *Journal of Political Ideologies*, 1996, 1. See also R. Griffin (ed.), *Fascism*, Oxford, Oxford University Press, 1995. On the economic appeal of Nazism see W. Brustein, *The Logic of Evil*, New Haven, Yale University Press, 1996.

14 K. Polanyi, *The Great Transformation*, Boston, Beacon Press, 1971; L. Dumont, *From Mandeville to Marx*, Chicago, University of Chicago Press, 1977.

15 See N. Cigar, *Genocide in Bosnia*, College Station, Texas A & M University Press, 1995. Cf. M. Glenny, *The Fall of Yugoslavia*, New York, Penguin Books, 1996.

16 On Le Pen and the rise of his party, see J. Marcus, *The National Front and French Politics*, Basingstoke, Macmillan, 1995; and H. G. Simmons, *The French National Front*, Boulder, Westview, 1996.

17 A. Smith, *National Identity*, London, Penguin, 1991, pp. 73–4.

18 A. Hazareesingh, *Political Traditions in Modern France*, Oxford, Oxford University Press, 1994.

19 For an introduction to the European idea see K. Wilson and J. van der Dussen (eds), *The History of the Idea of Europe*, London, Routledge, 1995. Note also more specialised works like R. Bartlett, *The Making of Europe: Conquest, Colonisation and Cultural Change 950–1350*, London, Penguin, 1993; and S. J. Woolf, 'The Construction of European World-view in the Revolutionary Napoleonic Years', *Past and Present*, 1992, 137. See also N. Davies, *Europe: A History*, Oxford, Oxford University Press, 1996.

20 P. Springborg, *Western Republicanism and the Oriental Prince*, Cambridge, Polity, 1992, p. 2.

21 On the development and different forms of democracy see J. Dunn (ed.), *Democracy: The Unfinished Journey*, Oxford, Oxford University Press, 1993; and D. Held, *Models of Democracy*, Cambridge, Polity, 1987.

22 Note S. Huntington, 'The Clash of Civilizations?', *Foreign Affairs*, 1993, 4, which depicts a world divided between antagonistic cultures.

23 See O. Niedermayer and R. Sinnott, *Public Opinion and Internationalized Governance*, Oxford, Oxford University Press, 1995. See also K. Reif and R. Inglehart (eds), *Eurobarometer: The Dynamics of European Public Opinion*, Basingstoke, Macmillan, 1991.

24 R. Eatwell, *Fascism: A History*, London, Vintage, 1996.

25 On the latter, and change in micro policy more generally, see M. Regini, *Uncertain Boundaries: The Social and Political Construction of European Economies*, Cambridge, Cambridge University Press, 1995.

26 D. Held, *Democracy and the Global Order*, Oxford, Polity, 1995.

27 Niedermayer and Sinnott, *op. cit.*, p. 446.

28 For this proposal see A. Weale, 'From Little England to Democratic Europe?', *New Community*, 1995, 21, pp. 223–4. See also M. Newman, *Democracy, Sovereignty and the European Union*, London, Hurst, 1996.

29 B. Boxhorn, 'European Identity and the Process of European Unification: Compatible Notions?', in M. Wintle (ed.), *Culture and Identity in Europe*, Aldershot, Avebury, 1995, p. 142.

30   O. Waever (ed.), *Identity, Migration and the New Security Agenda in Europe*, London, Pinter, 1993.

31   R. G. Suny, *The Revenge of the Past: Nationalism, Revolution and the Collapse of the Soviet Union*, Stanford, Stanford University Press, 1993.

32   C. Shore, 'Inventing the "People's Europe": Critical Approaches to European Community "Cultural Policy" ', *Man*, 1993, 28. On continuing Commission elitism see G. Ross, *Jacques Delors and European Integration*, Cambridge, Polity, 1995.

33   For instance, J. Howorth and A. Menon (eds), *The European Union and National Defence Policy*, London, Routledge, 1997.

34   For example, D. Delanty, *Inventing Europe*, Basingstoke, Macmillan, 1995. See also E. Meehan, *Citizenship and the European Community*, London, Sage, 1993.

35   J. W. van Deth and E. Scarbrough, *The Impact of Values*, Oxford, Oxford University Press, 1995, pp. 531f. See also R. Inglehart, *Culture Shift*, Princeton, Princeton University Press, 1990.

36   For a socialist version of the last argument see D. Miller, *Market, State and Community*, Oxford, Clarendon Press, 1989.

37   See W. Hutton, *The State We're In*, London, Viking, 1996.

38   This point is also made by H. Schmitt and S. Holmberg, 'Political Parties in Decline' in H.-D. Klingemann and D. Fuchs (eds), *Citizens and the State*, Oxford, Oxford University Press, 1995.

39   Niedermayer and Sinnott, *op. cit.*, p. 439.

Index